Assessment of Parenting

As the incidence of reported child maltreatment continues to rise, there is an urgent need for guidance on how to determine the risk of future abuse and the likelihood of successful rehabilitation. Professionals are required by the Children Act to base their opinions on detailed assessments. This book considers the principles and practice involved in making such assessments and examines how they influence the decisions taken in court. A theme shared by the chapters is an interactional approach to parenting breakdown in order to serve the best interests of the child and at the same time take account of the parent's potential to improve his or her caretaking skills.

Experienced psychiatrists and clinical psychologists suggest a number of frameworks for parenting assessments, especially with a view to deciding whether a child has suffered 'significant harm'. Their contributions are divided into two main parts: 'Components of parenting assessment' and 'Specific circumstances'. Topics covered include how to assess family functioning, the effects on the child of the parenting they have received, emotional abuse, a parent's capacity to protect their child from future abuse, a parent's potential to benefit from treatment and influences of race and culture. Drawing on a wide range of related literature and case material, contributors advise on sensitive issues, including the impact on children of parents who have psychiatric problems, abuse drugs or alcohol, have a learning disability or are gay or lesbian.

Assessment of Parenting: Psychiatric and Psychological Contributions is designed as a guide for experienced mental health practitioners undertaking complex child care assessments for the courts. Aiming to promote greater integration between various professional assessments, the book will also be a valuable source of reference for paediatricians, social workers, lawyers, magistrates, judges and senior trainees in all of these fields.

Peter Reder is Consultant Child and Adolescent Psychiatrist at the Child and Family Consultation Centre, and Director of the Centre for Relationship Studies, Riverside Mental Health Trust, London. **Clare Lucey** is Consultant Child and Family Psychiatrist with the Children and Families Consultation Service, West London Healthcare NHS Trust.

Assessment of Parenting

Psychiatric and psychological contributions

Edited by Peter Reder and Clare Lucey

Routledge
Taylor & Francis Group

LONDON AND NEW YORK

First published 1995
by Routledge
27 Church Road, Hove, East Sussex BN3 2FA

Simultaneously published in the USA and Canada
by Routledge
711 Third Avenue, Milton Park, Abingdon, Oxon OX14 4RN

Routledge is an imprint of the Taylor & Francis Group, an Informa business

Typeset in Times by
Ponting–Green Publishing Services, Chesham, Bucks

British Library Cataloguing in Publication Data
A catalogue record for this book is available from the
British Library

Library of Congress Cataloging in Publication Data
A catalog record for this book is available from the Library
of Congress

ISBN 978–0–415–11454–7 (pbk)

To

Mannie and Beattie, Michael and Mary,
who laid the foundations of our own parenting capacity;
Nicky, James and Clara,
who evoked it;
and Geraldine and Shay,
who shared the discovery.

Contents

Illustrations

FIGURES

TABLE

Contributors

Tony Baker, Consultant in Child and Family Psychiatry, Baker and Duncan Child Care Consultants, Ashwood Centre, Woking, Surrey.

Dora Black, Consultant Child and Adolescent Psychiatrist; Director, Children and Families Programme, Traumatic Stress Clinic, Camden and Islington Community NHS Trust; Honorary Senior Lecturer, Royal Free Hospital, London; Honorary Consultant Psychiatrist and Honorary Senior Lecturer, Great Ormond Street Hospital for Children, London.

Kevin Browne, Chartered Psychologist and Chartered Biologist; Senior Lecturer in Clinical Criminology, School of Psychology, University of Birmingham.

Diana Cassell, Consultant Child and Adolescent Psychiatrist, Child, Adolescent and Family Centre, Surbiton, Surrey.

Rosalyn Coleman, Consultant Psychiatrist, Shrodells Hospital, Watford, Hertfordshire.

Sylvia Duncan, Consultant Clinical Psychologist, Baker and Duncan Child Care Consultants, Ashwood Centre, Woking, Surrey.

Geraldine Fitzpatrick, Consultant Child and Adolescent Psychiatrist and Clinical Director, Pathfinder Mental Health Trust, St George's Hospital, London; Honorary Senior Lecturer, St George's Hospital Medical School; Psychoanalyst.

Ann Gath, Consultant Developmental Psychiatrist, Child Health Centre, Bury St Edmunds, Suffolk.

Danya Glaser, Consultant Child and Adolescent Psychiatrist, Great Ormond Street Hospital for Sick Children, London.

Helga Hanks, Consultant Clinical Psychologist (Chartered) in Psychotherapy and Family Therapy, St James's University Hospital, Leeds; Honorary Lecturer, Psychology Department, University of Leeds; Clinical Director, Leeds Family Therapy and Research Centre, Psychology Department, University of Leeds.

Sue Jenner, Freelance Consultant Clinical Psychologist.

Michael B. King, Reader and Honorary Consultant, University Department of Psychiatry, Royal Free Hospital School of Medicine, London; Honorary Senior Lecturer, Institute of Psychiatry, London.

Caroline Lindsey, Consultant Child and Adolescent Psychiatrist, Family Systems Therapist and Chair, Child and Family Department, Tavistock Clinic, London; Honorary Senior Lecturer, Royal Free Hospital, London.

Clare Lucey, Consultant Child and Family Psychiatrist, Children and Families Consultation Service, West London Healthcare NHS Trust, Ealing, London.

Gerard McCarthy, Clinical Psychologist, MRC Child Psychiatry Unit, Institute of Psychiatry, London.

Begum Maitra, Consultant Child and Adolescent Psychiatrist, Wolverton Gardens Child and Family Consultation Centre, Riverside Mental Health Trust, London.

Peter Reder, Consultant Child and Adolescent Psychiatrist, Wolverton Gardens Child and Family Consultation Centre; Director, Centre for Relationship Studies, Riverside Mental Health Trust, London; Honorary Senior Lecturer, Charing Cross and Westminster Medical School; Family Therapist.

Gerrilyn Smith, Freelance Consultant Clinical Psychologist; Family Therapist.

Peter Stratton, Senior Lecturer in Developmental Psychology and Director, Leeds Family Therapy and Research Centre, Psychology Department, University of Leeds.

Preface

The seeds of this book were sown in 1989 when we worked together in the Charing Cross Hospital's Child and Family Psychiatry Department (now known as the Wolverton Gardens Child and Family Consultation Centre). Members of that Department were regularly involved in assessing and treating abused children and their families and providing court reports in child care proceedings. We realised that the literature on assessment of parenting was relatively sparse and so we devoted a number of our clinical workshops to identifying the factors that we commonly addressed in these assessments. Our conclusions were brought together in a brief paper for the house journal of the Royal College of Psychiatrists (Reder and Lucey 1991).

Meanwhile, the 1989 Children Act had become law and was implemented in November 1991. The Royal College of Psychiatrists was among the many professional bodies to organise study days to anticipate, and later review, the workings of the Act. It was during the College's review conference in early 1993 that we realised that mental health professionals still had few guidelines upon which to base their assessments, and we decided to plan this book.

We approached the task primarily as practising clinicians and asked ourselves, 'what information, if coherently collated, would enable our assessments to be more solidly based in theory and research?' A number of areas immediately suggested themselves, such as: 'is there any evidence that parenting capacity is impaired by psychiatric disorder, by drug or alcohol abuse, or by learning disability?'; 'is there any research available on the outcome for children brought up by a homosexual couple?'; 'what constitutes emotional abuse?'; and 'what criteria could be used for recommending reasonable contact between a parent and child?' Having confirmed that these and other questions were shared by colleagues, we set out to encourage practitioners with acknowledged experience in the topics to contribute chapters. They were invited to make their chapters a balance between academic and clinical material, so that clinical discussions would be under-pinned by literature reviews and theoretical formulations.

The book therefore developed into one about specialist assessment, with contributions from psychiatrists and psychologists who provide expert opinions to courts in child care cases. We made an early decision to focus on mental health professionals' opinions, rather than attempt to include social workers' assessments of risk in acute crises or their 'comprehensive assessments' based upon the so-called 'Orange Book' (Department of Health 1988), which have different aims and take place within different contexts. For example, social workers' assessments immediately following allegations of child abuse seek to establish the level of risk and whether the child is safe. Child protection teams who are gathering evidence for possible criminal prosecution must follow the guidelines laid down by the 1991 Criminal Justice Act (Home Office and Department of Health 1992). Reports by mental health professionals, on the other hand, are based on different types of assessments, follow on from initial investigations by social workers or child protection teams, occur within a different time frame and are for family court proceedings. Nonetheless, because specialist assessments must complement those of social workers and other 'frontline' practitioners, we believe the book will be as relevant and interesting to them as to mental health professionals.

In the introductory section, we consider the professional, social and ethical contexts within which parenting assessments take place and propose a structure to guide practitioners undertaking them.

The second section contains chapters about the various components of parenting assessments that contribute to an overall picture. Peter Stratton and Helga Hanks first summarise techniques for assessing dysfunctional family interactional patterns and Peter Reder and Sylvia Duncan then argue that consideration of the psychological meaning of the child to the parent(s) should be included in all assessments. We have joined Geraldine Fitzpatrick to consider the effects on children's development of the parenting they have received, after which Danya Glaser presents a framework for assessing the 'elusive' problem of psychological abuse. Gerrilyn Smith goes on to report her experiences of evaluating non-abusing parents' capacity to protect their sexually abused children from future abuse. Geraldine Fitzpatrick then discusses the factors that indicate whether parents are able to benefit from psychotherapeutic help and this is followed by Kevin Browne's review of factors which might guide prediction of child maltreatment. Sue Jenner and Gerard McCarthy review the quantifiable measures of parenting that are available and Begum Maitra focuses on the benefit to the assessment process of cultural and racial awareness.

The third section covers specific parenting circumstances that expert witnesses may be asked to comment upon. Diana Cassell and Rosalyn Coleman consider parents with psychiatric problems and parents who misuse drugs or alcohol. Ann Gath addresses issues concerning parents with learning disability, while Michael King reviews current knowledge about children brought up by gay or lesbian parents. Dora Black then reports her experience of working with families where one parent has killed the other. Caroline

Lindsey discusses the placement of children with alternative caretakers and Tony Baker considers the factors that guide recommendations about contact between separated parents and children.

Finally, we summarise the main messages from these chapters, suggest how assessments can be integrated into balanced opinions, present a framework for writing court reports and highlight some of the skills necessary for giving expert evidence.

The two figures in Chapter 3 are reproduced from Reder *et al.* (1993) and the figure in Chapter 6 is reproduced from Smith (1994). Both books were published by Routledge.

Begum Maitra has asked us to record her gratitude to Mr Lennox Thomas and Ms Aisha McKenzie Mavinga for useful preliminary discussions when preparing her chapter and to Dr Roland Littlewood, Dr Ajita Chakraborty, Dr Sushrut Jadhav, Dr John Eade, Dr Suman Fernando and Ms Meenakshi Krishna for their invaluable comments on her early drafts.

Many people have added to our understanding of parenting breakdown and child maltreatment over the years and their influence runs through our own contributions to the book. We are most especially grateful to Arnon Bentovim, John Bowlby, Ron Britton, Dinora Pines, George Stroh and Harry Zeitlin, whose knowledge, experience, wisdom and guidance inspired us during our respective trainings. More recently, we have both had the privilege of working with Sylvia Duncan, whose deep interest and commitment, thoughtfulness and creativity helped transform our work.

We would also like to express our appreciation to our contributors for the time and effort they put into researching and writing about their selected topics. With multi-authored books, there is a need to achieve a balance between chapters and this often calls for the editors to ask for omissions from, or even refocusing of, early drafts. Sometimes, this means that cherished ideas have to be sacrificed for the benefit of the overall work. We are very grateful to the authors for agreeing to our editorial requests and not only redrafting their chapters but endeavouring to get their manuscripts back to us on time, despite heavy schedules of other clinical or academic work.

It is our intention that, by bringing together the ideas, knowledge and experience of the various authors, the book will guide and help professionals undertaking the complex assessments required in cases of parenting breakdown. As a result, we hope that it will make a difference to the lives of children who are maltreated by their caretakers and to parents who have not yet been able to find a path away from abusive or neglectful behaviour.

REFERENCES

Department of Health (1988) *Protecting Children: A Guide to Social Workers Undertaking a Comprehensive Assessment*, London: HMSO.
Home Office and Department of Health (1992) *Memorandum of Good Practice: On*

Video Recorded Interviews with Child Witnesses for Criminal Proceedings, London: HMSO.

Reder, P., Duncan, S. and Gray, M. (1993) *Beyond Blame: Child Abuse Tragedies Revisited*, London: Routledge.

Reder, P. and Lucey, C. (1991) 'Assessment of parenting: some interactional considerations', *Psychiatric Bulletin*, **15**, 347–8.

Smith, G. (1994) 'Parent, partner, protector: conflicting role demands for mothers of sexually abused children', in T. Morrison, M. Erooga and R. Beckett (eds) *Sexual Offending Against Children: Assessment and Treatment of Male Abusers*, London: Routledge.

Peter Reder and Clare Lucey
London, December 1994

Part I

Introduction

Chapter 1

Significant issues in the assessment of parenting

Peter Reder and Clare Lucey

INTRODUCTION

The parenting children receive is a cornerstone for the development of their emotional, interpersonal and social well-being. The quality of relationships they form with others, including their own children when they become parents, will be shaped by their caretaking experiences. Therefore, as Bowlby (1988) put it 'engaging in parenthood is playing for high stakes'. Perhaps not surprisingly, discussions about parenting problems tend to evoke very personal feelings and passionately held beliefs – about family, gender, society and so on. It is essential that professionals trying to help children and their families in crisis are not driven by personal bias, but are guided by up-to-date knowledge and experience. The purpose of this book is to add to that knowledge base through the contributions of mental health professionals experienced in the area of parenting assessment. More particularly, this book is about the expert evidence of psychiatrists and psychologists in court proceedings about children's welfare.

These mental health professionals become involved in child care hearings for a number of reasons. Children depend on others to recognise their distress, to act to remedy it and to speak for them. Courts making decisions that permanently affect their lives have to weigh up complex issues and such difficult judgements rightly should be guided by informed opinion. Psychiatrists and psychologists lean heavily on research evidence, academic argument and clinical experience in their professional practice and have access to an accumulated body of knowledge about child development and family relationships. Their academic trainings also instil in them an ability to gather information in an unbiased manner, to generate and explore hypotheses and to arrive at balanced opinions. In particular, they are able to consider whether change is possible and what interventions, if available, might be helpful. They are skilled at talking with children and parents and making sense of their communications and observable behaviour. Finally, their independent professional role enables them to act as unbiased representatives of children's views and needs.

In this first chapter we shall discuss the legal and social context for this work and comment on some of the ethical issues it raises. We shall suggest a theoretical framework for understanding problems of parenting and present a structure which has guided us through parenting assessments.

THE LEGAL CONTEXT

Parenting assessments principally take place within the context of the 1989 Children Act. The Act is a radical piece of legislation which has already been analysed widely (e.g. White *et al.* 1990; Eekelaar and Dingwall 1990; Lindsey 1991). Core philosophies are that children's welfare is paramount and that children are generally best looked after within their natural families. Professionals are required to work in partnership with parents and to ascertain children's views about their future. Courts should not make orders unless it is clearly better for the children to do so and one guide is whether the child has suffered, or is likely to suffer, 'significant harm'.

The definition of significant harm continues to exercise psychiatrists and psychologists (e.g. Adcock *et al.* 1991; Bentovim 1991). It is our view that the concept is essentially a legal one, introduced by the Children Act and one that sits more comfortably within the legal than the clinical domain. The legal process tends to dichotomise issues into 'true' or 'false' and such absolute distinctions are intolerant of the ambiguities faced by mental health professionals. We believe that clinicians should not allow themselves to be constrained by the limits imposed from another domain and must defend their areas of expertise. Mental health professionals *are* able to describe children's developmental lines (i.e. physical, emotional, social, educational, relationship and behavioural), the interplay between them and how they may be adversely affected by experiences of care. Although prediction is difficult, we can hypothesise about the possible consequences of any particular events and whether they might harm the child's development. Whether this constitutes *significant* harm is essentially a matter for legal debate.

Implementation of the Children Act has required mental health professionals to modify some aspects of their assessments. As well as discovering the children's wishes about their future, assessors must consider whether the children have sufficient understanding about any proposed interventions and are capable of giving, or withholding, informed consent (Devereux *et al.* 1993). The assessment must also take account of families' cultural and racial characteristics. New orders defining those with whom children can have contact or reside, together with revised criteria of parental responsibility, lead assessors to widen the net of family members interviewed. The intended difficulty in obtaining care orders has been particularly influential in compelling assessors to ascertain parents' strengths as well as their limitations and consider whether treatment might help them meet their children's needs. In addition, reports need to show that the likely effects of changing children's circumstances have been addressed.

While mental health professionals are able to make valuable contributions to child care cases under the Children Act, it is not practical for them to be involved in all instances. In England, the names of 24,700 children were entered on child protection registers during the year up to 31 March 1993; in England and Wales, during the year ending 30 September 1993, applications were made for 5,628 care orders (3,000 of which were granted), 1,054 supervision orders, 2,508 emergency protection orders, 94 child assessment orders and 1,326 Section 8 (i.e. residence, contact, prohibited steps and specific issues) orders (Secretaries of State for Health and for Wales 1994). Decisions to refer for specialist assessment are as much determined by the resources available as considerations of need, but a reasonable guide is to seek an additional opinion when there are outstanding questions about the case.

A THEORETICAL FRAMEWORK

Professional assessments need to be grounded in a valid theoretical framework. This is evident from the Department of Health (1988) guidance to social workers on their assessment of families at risk, which contains an extensive list of recommended questions but provides no theoretical framework to help them make sense of the answers.

The model to which we subscribe for understanding parenting behaviour is interactional. It derives from Winnicott's (1960) observation that 'there is no such thing as an infant'; in other words, that children and parents exist in relationship to each other. The feelings and behaviour of one affects the feelings and behaviour of the other in a circular manner and the feedback between them modifies each person's participation in their relationship. As an example, an infant's cry draws a parent nearer and evokes a comforting response. Eventually, the infant stops crying and gradually tolerates greater distance between them. However, if a second adult is present who resents the attention paid to the child, the first parent might react by withdrawing, resulting in renewed crying. These interactional sequences occur moment to moment and, over time, give rise to recurrent relationship cycles. Environmental factors will, in turn, influence family relational patterns. For example, a poor single mother living at the top of a high-rise block with two ill children is likely to have a lower frustration threshold when she realises that her social security book is missing, and so she more readily lashes out in anger.

Everyone has an innate biological ability to parent, which a child evokes, but the detailed form that this takes hinges on individual experiences (Bowlby 1988). Becoming a parent involves a fundamental change in identity from that of child (to one's parents) into parent (to one's child). The transition is liable to reawaken unresolved conflicts with one's family of origin (Pines

1993) and these issues may need to be reworked before the new parent–child relationship can flourish. Resolution of such conflicts is also likely to facilitate development of the parental couple's relationship. Other psychological conflicts will arise if the reality of the baby, its needs and development contrast with the parents' expectations and fantasies about the child they wished for.

The parental role is, in essence, to facilitate the child's developmental lines within a safe environment. Parents must respond to the child's early helplessness and dependency, but also encourage the child to differentiate and acquire a separate identity. Balances need to be struck between the child's need for socialisation and exploratory learning versus the need for protection and limit setting. The way a parent approaches these tasks will be influenced by the model of care that they experienced as a child and whether they continue to be troubled by conflicts around self-esteem, identity, self-control and so on.

Development of the attachment dynamic (Bowlby 1969; 1973; 1980) is particularly significant, in which the provision of a secure emotional base in early life facilitates the development of self-esteem, a capacity for autonomous functioning and empathy for others (Steele 1980). Interference with normal attachment processes, on the other hand, may lead to unresolved dependency conflicts which are carried into adult life and relationships, including the parent–child relationship.

Parenting breakdown, therefore, is also understandable in relationship terms. Severe child maltreatment has generated the greatest amount of research and clinical experience (e.g. Spinetta and Rigler 1972; Friedrich and Boriskin 1976; Steele 1980; Belsky 1984; Wolfe 1987; Dale *et al*. 1986; Greenland 1987; Roberts 1988; Quinton and Rutter 1988; Bentovim 1992; Reder *et al*. 1993) which has contributed to the model. There is now general consensus that child maltreatment is the end-result of interplay between predisposed caretakers who are caught in conflictual relationship patterns, vulnerable children, and external stressors, with no single factor 'causing' the abusive behaviour. Parents, or other primary caretakers, carry into adult life unresolved residues of adverse childhood experiences which may intrude into their relationships with partners and with their own children and can be exaggerated by social stress. Some children trigger the residues of these emotional conflicts, or can be the focus of the parents' frustration in the face of acute external stress.

Contributory factors

Maltreating parents usually have experienced psychological deprivation and/ or maltreatment as children and suffer persisting conflicts about care and control. In adult life, they form relationships in which these conflicts are re-enacted through excessive, but often ambivalent, dependency on others and undue sensitivity to loss, whether actual or threatened. They often look to their children for emotional comfort (sometimes referred to as role reversal) giving priority to their own needs instead of their children's. Children who fail to meet the parents' expectations are either punished violently or regarded as worthless and become neglected. Demands for caretaking from adults or infants readily provoke the parent's anxiety, frustration and angry responses. Conflicts with control might appear as excessively aggressive behaviour, attempts to dominate others and intolerance of people (mis)perceived as controlling them. These parents tend to be rigid and inflexible, especially in child care activities, and have inappropriate expectations of their children. Low self-esteem, lack of empathy for, and mistrust of, others and conflicts about intimacy may follow from earlier experiences of insecure attachments and lead to brittle and unstable adult relationships and unresponsiveness to the child's attachment needs.

Children are emotionally and practically dependent on their parents and therefore very young children are the most at risk from abuse and neglect. Children born prematurely, with physical or intellectual defects, who are poor feeders, suffer illnesses or experience early separations also make extra stressful, emotional demands on their parents.

Although child maltreatment occurs across the social strata, there is no doubt that adverse social circumstances, such as poverty, poor housing and ill-health, intensify the risk. In addition, maltreating parents are commonly socially isolated, having lost contact with their family-of-origin through geographical mobility, or make little use of social support networks. Suspicion of others, especially representatives of 'authority', and low self-esteem probably contribute to this picture.

This model proposes that parents can move into and out of abusive interactional patterns depending on circumstances. However, Steele (1980) has described 5–10 per cent of abusing parents who repeatedly and cruelly injure children. They attack indiscriminately and without remorse, irrespective of the circumstances, and their lack of empathy towards children reflects shallow, exploitative and violent interpersonal relationships generally. The label 'sociopath' or 'psychopath' has been applied to such people. We would suggest that the use of such labels in parenting assessment is generally unhelpful, since it can organise clinicians' thinking into narrow dichotomies – this person is, or is not, a sociopath – rather than help them describe the nature, vicissitudes and origins of the parent's interpersonal relationships.

A FRAMEWORK FOR ASSESSMENT

The framework that we use for the assessment of parenting is presented here as a number of themes grouped together under various headings. The framework is not meant as an interview schedule, but to direct the assessor towards significant areas when reviewing the case history and interviewing family members. The themes are equally relevant to all varieties of family structure and to parents from different classes or cultures. The themes come together to provide an overall picture, but some will be more important than others in particular cases.

The framework is our own synthesis of a number of previous descriptions of the tasks of parenting (Kellmer Pringle 1978; Pugh and De'Ath 1985) and accounts of how the adequacy of parenting can be assessed clinically (Steinhauer 1983; Adcock and White 1985; Wasserman and Rosenfeld 1986; Adcock *et al.* 1991; Kennedy 1991; Reder and Lucey 1991; Sturge 1992; Bentovim 1992; Glaser 1993). It also borrows from research tools (e.g. Polanski *et al.* 1981; Quinton and Rutter 1988), although it is not intended to be used in a structured or quantifying way.

The themes are grouped under the following headings: (1) the parent's relationship to the role of parenting; (2) the parent's relationship to the child; (3) family influences; (4) the parent's interaction with the external world; and (5) the potential for change.

1 The parent's relationship to the role of parenting

Does the parent provide basic essential physical care?

A number of facets of physical care are essential for children's healthy survival. These are provision for: feeding, warmth, health, safety and cleanliness (which are usually first assessed by the social worker). Parents must anticipate children's physical requirements in order to provide them, starting with antenatal preparation. Physical care also describes the nature of parents' physical contact with their children and whether it is deemed overpunitive or abusive.

Does the parent provide age-appropriate emotional care?

Parents must help reinforce their children's self-esteem and be sensitive to cues during spontaneous interaction between them, as well as when they are distressed. Children require opportunities to explore new situations safely and to learn through formal and informal education. Parents also provide role models for problem solving and facilitate socialisation by encouraging interaction with others and imposing appropriate behavioural limits.

Does the parent encourage development of the attachment dynamic?

Parents should promote secure attachment for young infants; gradually allowing them greater autonomy over the years, by being consistently available physically and emotionally and handling separations sensitively.

What attitude does the parent have to the tasks of parenting?

Parents acquire most of their views about the parenting role from their childhood experiences of care and the formative models provided by their own parents. If the parents can also recognise this link they are less likely to repeat blindly any of their own adverse experiences. Particularly relevant are the parents' current attitudes to discipline and limit setting and developmental expectations of their children.

Does the parent accept responsibility for their parenting behaviour?

If child maltreatment has occurred, an important indicator for successful rehabilitation between parents and children is that the parents accept responsibility for their role in the abuse (Dale *et al.* 1986; Bentovim *et al.* 1988; Bentovim 1992). Some parents attribute responsibility to someone else, such as their partner, social services or the housing department. A related issue is whether the parents have a sense of personal agency in what has happened in their lives, or instead attribute all responsibility to others. Accepting appropriate responsibility for their behaviour and for their relationships enables parents to plan for their children's future protection.

Is the child expected to be responsible for his/her own protection?

Parental responsibility includes monitoring whether children are protected from exposure to dangerous people or circumstances. Some parents do not consider this to be one of their tasks and instead leave children to be responsible for their own safety. An important factor is whether the parents are able to anticipate their children's needs, especially for protection from harm, and plan adequate safety measures. This might include preventing contact with suspected or known abusers.

If there are problems, does the parent acknowledge them?

Some parents cannot accept that child care problems exist and believe that, if they were left alone, everything would be all right. They do not acknowledge that change is needed, especially in their parenting behaviour, or that therapeutic intervention might be helpful. At best, they believe that concrete help, such as rehousing, is required, even though others emphasise concerns about their relationship with their children.

2 The parent's relationship with the child

What feelings does the parent have towards the child?

Parents will experience a range of emotions towards their children at different times, but some relationships are dominated by a persistent feeling. Extreme affection or excessive hatred are both ultimately damaging, but the degree to which the parents enact anger, blaming, belittling or rejection is particularly relevant, as is the basis for those feelings.

Does the parent empathise with the child?

A capacity for empathy shows in a variety of ways. The parents will demonstrate concern for, and interest in, their children's general well-being and particular experiences. It also allows parents to put themselves in their children's place, appreciating experiences from their perspective, and to acknowledge how the children must have felt when subjected to adverse caretaking.

Is the child viewed as a separate person?

Empathy for children also entails recognising that each one is a separate person with feelings, ideas and an identity that is different from the parent. If sufficient differentiation exists, the child's needs and experiences are recognised and addressed and overintrusiveness avoided. Also, the child must be allowed to develop psychological autonomy over the years and eventually to separate from the parent(s) into a chosen life.

Are the child's essential needs given primacy over the parent's desires?

Empathy for a child and recognition of the child as a separate being are the prerequisites for parents' putting their children first whenever necessary. For example, a particular parent may have to resolve the dilemma over whether to sacrifice loyalty to an abusing partner in order to ensure greater protection of their child.

3 Family influences

What awareness and attitude does the parent have regarding their own parenting experiences?

It has been shown that mothers are more sensitive to their infants if they have retained vivid memories of their own parents and the responses they wished they had received from them when they were distressed. If they manage to become reflective about adverse experiences, they are able to break free of any tendency to re-enact unsupportive parenting (Grossman *et al.* 1988; Emde 1988). Furthermore, an ability to recall some good relationships in childhood is a good indicator that abusing parents can benefit from treatment (Healy *et al.* 1991).

Is the parent able to sustain a supportive relationship with a partner?

There is impressive evidence that a warm and supportive relationship with a partner is a significant protective factor against intergenerational repetition of abuse (e.g. Quinton and Rutter 1988; Egeland *et al.* 1988). Clearly, 'supportive' needs to be differentiated from 'overdependent' and the capacity to sustain such a relationship is crucial. When it comes to rehabilitation, Dale *et al.* (1986) are of the view that if there is continuing conflict between the parental partners so that the family is not viable, then the child should not return home.

Is the child overinvolved in the family's discordant relationships?

A child may become entangled in dysfunctional family relationships, such as being drawn into loyalty conflicts between warring parents, to the detriment of their development. Parental couples need to achieve sufficient cooperative agreement around decisions which affect the child (Minuchin 1974). Children may be at risk of abuse when they become the focus of their parents' unresolved care or control conflicts – for example, whenever one parent threatens to leave the other or during an episode of excessive drinking. Carroll (1994) summarises the literature on children who witness violence between their parents, or from one parent to another, and argues that their emotional well-being is significantly harmed.

How sensitive is the family to relationship stresses?

All families experience episodes of tension, but some are either brittle or inflexible and react adversely to stress. They feel that they have few internal resources to overcome problems, a limited repertoire of solutions, and experience all stress as a crisis.

What is the meaning of the child to the parent?

Some parents have particular attitudes to a child which are determined by unresolved conflicts from their own past. For example, the child's birth may have coincided with a major life crisis, following which the child becomes an unwanted reminder of the associated feelings. The child may be blamed for problems in the parent's life or expected to help resolve them.

What is the child's contribution to the parenting relationship?

It must be recognised that some children are more difficult to care for than others, being temperamentally demanding or extrovert, for example. Some more readily show their feelings towards their caretakers, such as a step-child

who rejects a step-parent, while others have physical or behavioural characteristics that upset the parent, such as clumsiness. Such children place extra
demands for tolerance and flexibility on their parents. However, it is also
clear that children possess varying degrees of resilience and capacity to
recover from adverse circumstances and will respond differently to life events
(Crittenden 1985; Rutter 1985).

What attitude does the child have to his/her caretakers?

Children are usually able to give coherent accounts of the way they have been
looked after, what it has been like living with respective caretaking figures
and whether they trust and feel secure with them.

4 Interaction with the external world

What support networks are available?

Families have varying sensitivity to internal and environmental stress and
their repertoire of coping mechanisms might need to be complemented by
support from outside. Research shows consistently that socially isolated
parents are more prone to neglect and abuse their children (e.g. Seagull 1987).

What is the pattern of the parent's relationships with professional workers?

Clearly, it is not easy for parents to maintain a benign relationship with
professionals who are threatening to remove their child. However, some
people evolve characteristic attitudes to all professionals whatever the
circumstances, such as defensive hostility or dependency (e.g. Hardwick
1991). The history of previous family–professional contacts is an important
basis for understanding current relationships with professionals and hypo-
thesising how they might develop in the future. For example, a history of
hostile avoidance of child protection workers would weigh against the parents
being willing to put aside personal feelings for the sake of the child.

5 The potential for change

What is the potential to benefit from therapeutic help?

Change may occur spontaneously, be negotiated amongst the family members
themselves, or facilitated by therapeutic help. Many of the themes discussed
above have relevance to the family's potential to be helped. These include:
acknowledgement that there is a problem; concern about it; acceptance of
responsibility for their contribution to it; recognition of the need for outside

help; a wish for things to be different; and ability to view others as potentially helpful.

What responses have there been to previous attempts to help?

The pattern of previous responses to interventions is a further guide to the viability of therapy. Some people develop as characteristic a relationship to the idea of 'being helped' (Reder and Duncan 1990) as they do to helping professionals, including asking repeatedly for a therapy but failing to turn up to the sessions, or moving from therapist to therapist before the previous ones have had a chance to be effective. On the other hand, previous benefit from an intervention might suggest that further similar help could be valuable again.

THE ASSESSMENT

We have emphasised that parenting is not a quality that someone does, or does not, possess, but is a relationship that responds to fluctuations in other relationships. The assessor needs to consider all such influences. As an example, by the time cases reach psychiatrists and psychologists, a considerable number of other professionals is usually already involved – from social workers and their legal department, to health visitors, counsellors, probation officers, police, solicitors, guardians *ad litem*, even the Official Solicitor. It can be a huge network of professionals, each of whom may represent a different opinion about the family. Such multi-agency networks develop their own dynamics (Reder 1985) and the family may be 'lost' in the middle. An independent assessor needs to form an opinion about the adequacy of previous assessments and the appropriateness of previous interventions, together with the effect on different family members of previous professional decisions – in other words, obtain an overview of the case as a whole.

In cases with local authority involvement, we believe it is advisable first to meet the allocated social worker in order to collate the case history and discuss social services' plans. At that meeting, we construct a family genogram and review the chronology of events in order to clarify the history of (1) the family, (2) the problems they have shown, (3) professional involvement and (4) interventions and their effects. We ask the agency requesting the assessment to send copies of all previous documents and reports, including the child's school report and, if major gaps still remain, we might consider calling a network meeting or attending a case conference. Interviews will then be necessary with all relevant adults and all children, separately and in various combinations. Each case calls for a different constellation of meetings depending on the issues, but typically this calls for between five and ten separate appointments.

We use an unstructured style, but guide the conversations towards the themes relevant to our framework. We do not use a checklist approach because we are more concerned with interactional behaviour and less with the *individual* attributes so commonly itemised in high-risk checklists, such as Greenland's (1987). Thus, parental youth as an alleged risk factor is only meaningful if the parents show immaturity in their relationships with others. As interviewers, we tend to be somewhat more active and direct than when conducting therapy, perhaps even occasionally confrontive. For example, we might need to emphasise to parents that their willingness to attend for appointments forms part of our assessment and in cases of suspected sexual abuse we are less tentative than usual about asking the parent's sexual history. While we might rely on our countertransference to help us understand the person's way of relating, we are careful not to confuse the context with therapy and do not offer direct interpretations. However, we might offer one or two comments that test whether therapy can be utilised.

ETHICAL CONSIDERATIONS

The following chapters will illustrate in greater detail specific aspects of the assessment process and how coherent opinions are achieved from the observations and information obtained. First, though, it is necessary to recognise that assessment of parenting by mental health and other profes-sionals raises important ethical issues.

There is the question whether standards of caretaking expected from parents exist in any clear form. A number of authors (Freeman 1983; Taylor 1989; Reder *et al*. 1993) have argued that the phenomenon of 'child abuse' is not an objective condition but a social construction, the meaning of which arises from ever-changing social values. Standards of acceptable and un-acceptable child care have evolved over time in response to new knowledge about children's needs and development and changing attitudes in society towards children and families. However, the distinctions remain blurred. Extremes of child maltreatment can be recognised unequivocally, but when does neglect become critical, or psychological tormenting too severe? And when does a parent's caretaking stop being 'good enough'? Psychiatrists and psychologists will continue to influence this debate by identifying the effects of different parenting experiences on children. However, despite the scientific bases of these disciplines, observer subjectiveness and the potential for personal bias must be acknowledged. Therefore, professionals engaged in this critical work have a responsibility to monitor regularly whatever assumptions and beliefs they hold which would colour their opinions.

Clearly, this topic does fall prey to political agendas and in recent years the United Kingdom has witnessed major government initiatives on various aspects of 'the family'. In particular, a political philosophy has been expounded about the value of two-parent families and the importance of both maternal and paternal responsibilities. Whether these initiatives are primarily driven by economic constraints, beliefs about the nature of society, or genuine concern for children's welfare remains open to question. Even so, they do create the context within which child care cases and professional assessments are heard by courts.

Perhaps not surprisingly, then, some colleagues express reservations about whether parenting assessment is relevant to their role, arguing that their main task is to provide treatment and not to take part in a social and political exercise. They also have an abhorrence of the court process, in which concerns about children appear to become submerged by the thrust and counterthrust of the courtroom drama. It seems to us that such crucial decisions about children's lives should be informed by mental health professionals' knowledge and skills, if only because children are ill equipped to represent themselves.

There is a legitimate concern whether the artificial circumstances of the specialist assessment provide valid information and observations about the parent–child relationship. Parents are sent, often unwillingly, to be interviewed and it is unlikely that any parent could have a relaxed and enjoyable interaction with their child while being watched by a psychologist or psychiatrist. The problem of observer subjectiveness is compounded by the effect that the observer has on what is being observed. We believe that the power imbalance between parent and professional should not be denied: courts do have authority and do request advice from professionals. However, open and sympathetic acknowledgement of this during an interview can go some way towards helping parents make the most of the situation and accept that the resulting opinion will be independent and balanced. Therefore, a useful question to a parent during interviews is: 'how is it different at home?' It is important to comment in a court report on such a constraining atmosphere to the interview and the limits it may have imposed on the assessment.

Finally, the very fact that courts invite professionals to comment on parents' abilities raises a philosophical issue about the relationship between the individual and the state. This is an ongoing debate to which many have contributed, including Freeman (1983), Donzelot (1980) and Parton (1985). In our view, there must be an acknowledgement that the state does intervene in many aspects of people's lives, through public health regulations, mental health legislation, education laws, and so on. Indeed, an acceptance that representatives of the state may need to act to protect children is a reflection of society's regard for children's welfare. Without doubt, however, the responsibilities placed on courts to change children's and parents' lives are awesome and this must be a reason for humility by those advising them.

REFERENCES

Adcock, M. and White, R. (eds) (1985) *Good-Enough Parenting: A Framework for Assessment*, London: British Association for Adoption and Fostering.

Adcock, M., White, R. and Hollows, A. (1991) *Significant Harm: Its Management and Outcome*, Croydon: Significant Publications.

Belsky, J. (1984) 'The determinants of parenting: a process model', *Child Development*, **55**, 83–96.

Bentovim, A. (1991) 'What is significant harm? – a clinical viewpoint', in *Proceedings of the Children Act Course 7/8 May 1991*, London: Royal College of Psychiatrists.

Bentovim, A. (1992) *Trauma Organised Systems: Physical and Sexual Abuse in Families*, London: Karnac.

Bentovim, A., Elton, A., Hildebrand, J., Tranter, M. and Vizard, E. (1988) *Child Sexual Abuse within the Family: Assessment and Treatment*, London: Wright.

Bowlby, J. (1969) *Attachment and Loss. Vol. 1: Attachment*, London: Hogarth.

Bowlby, J. (1973) *Attachment and Loss. Vol. 2: Separation: Anxiety and Anger*, London: Hogarth.

Bowlby. J. (1980) *Attachment and Loss. Vol. 3: Sadness and Depression*, London: Hogarth.

Bowlby, J. (1988) *A Secure Base: Clinical Applications of Attachment Theory*, London: Routledge.

Carroll, J. (1994) 'The protection of children exposed to marital violence', *Child Abuse Review*, **3**, 6–14.

Crittenden, P. (1985) 'Maltreated infants: vulnerability and resilience', *Journal of Child Psychology and Psychiatry*, **26**, 85–96.

Dale, P., Davies, M., Morrison, T. and Walters, J. (1986) *Dangerous Families*, London: Tavistock.

Department of Health (1988) *Protecting Children: A Guide to Social Workers Undertaking a Comprehensive Assessment*, London: HMSO.

Devereux, J.A., Jones, D.P.H. and Dickenson, D.L. (1993) 'Can children withhold consent to treatment?', *British Medical Journal*, **306**, 1459–61.

Donzelot, J. (1980) *The Policing of Families: Welfare Versus the State*, London: Hutchinson.

Eekelaar, J. and Dingwall, R. (1990) *The Reform of Child Care Law: A Practical Guide to the Children Act 1989*, London: Routledge.

Egeland, B., Jacobvitz, D. and Sroufe, L.A. (1988) 'Breaking the cycle of abuse', *Child Development*, **59**, 1080–8.

Emde, R. (1988) 'The effect of relationships on relationships: a developmental approach to clinical intervention', in R.A.Hinde and J.Stevenson-Hinde (eds) *Relationships within Families: Mutual Influences*, Oxford: Oxford University Press.

Freeman, M.D.A. (1983) 'Freedom and the welfare state: child-rearing, parental autonomy and state intervention', *Journal of Social Welfare Law*, March, 70–91.

Friedrich, W.N. and Boriskin, J.A. (1976) 'The role of the child in abuse: a review of the literature', *American Journal of Orthopsychiatry*, **46**, 580–90.

Glaser, D. (1993) 'Emotional abuse', in C.J.Hobbs and J.M.Wynne (eds) *Clinical Paediatrics: International Practice and Research. Vol. 1, No. 1: Child Abuse*, London: Baillière Tindall.

Greenland, C. (1987) *Preventing CAN Deaths: An International Study of Deaths Due to Child Abuse and Neglect*, London: Tavistock.

Grossman, K., Fremmer-Bombik, E., Rudolph, J. and Grossman, K.E. (1988) 'Maternal attachment representations as related to patterns of infant–mother attachment and maternal care during the first year', in R.A.Hinde and J.Stevenson-Hinde (eds) *Relationships within Families: Mutual Influences*, Oxford: Oxford University Press.

Hardwick, P.J. (1991) 'Families and the professional network: an attempted classification of professional network actions which can hinder change', *Journal of Family Therapy*, **13**, 187–205.

Healy, K., Kennedy, R. and Sinclair, J. (1991) 'Child physical abuse observed:

comparison of families with and without history of child abuse treated in an in-patient family unit', *British Journal of Psychiatry*, **158**, 234–7.

Kellmer Pringle, M. (1978) 'The needs of children', in S.M.Smith (ed.) *The Maltreatment of Children*, Lancaster: MTP Press.

Kennedy, R. (1991) 'Parental responsibility', *Psychiatric Bulletin*, **15**, 129–32.

Lindsey, C. (ed.) (1991) *Proceedings of the Children Act 1989 Course 7/8 May 1991*, London: Royal College of Psychiatrists.

Minuchin, S. (1974) *Families and Family Therapy*, London: Tavistock.

Parton, N. (1985) *The Politics of Child Abuse*, Basingstoke: Macmillan.

Pines, D. (1993) *A Woman's Use of her Body: A Psychoanalytic Perspective*, London: Virago.

Polanski, N.A., Chalmers, M.A., Williams, D.P. and Buttenwieser, E.W. (1981) *Damaged Parents: An Anatomy of Child Neglect*, Chicago: University of Chicago Press.

Pugh, G. and De'Ath, E. (1985) 'Parenting in the 80s', in *The Needs of Parents*, Basingstoke: Macmillan Education.

Quinton, D. and Rutter, M. (1988) *Parenting Breakdown*, Aldershot: Gower.

Reder, P. (1985) 'Multi-agency family systems', *Journal of Family Therapy*, **8**, 139–52.

Reder, P. and Duncan, S. (1990) 'On meeting systems', *Human Systems*, **1**, 153–62.

Reder, P. and Lucey, C. (1991) 'The assessment of parenting: some interactional considerations', *Psychiatric Bulletin*, **15**, 347–8.

Reder, P., Duncan, S. and Gray, M. (1993) *Beyond Blame: Child Abuse Tragedies Revisited*, London: Routledge.

Roberts, J. (1988) 'Why are some families more vulnerable to child abuse?', in K. Browne, C. Davies and P. Stratton (eds) *Early Prediction and Prevention of Child Abuse*, Chichester: Wiley.

Rutter, M. (1985) 'Resilience in the face of adversity: protective factors and resistance to psychiatric disorder', *British Journal of Psychiatry*, **147**, 598–611.

Seagull, E.A.W. (1987) 'Social support and child maltreatment: a review of the evidence', *Child Abuse and Neglect*, **11**, 41–52.

Secretaries of State for Health and for Wales (1994) *Children Act Report 1993*, London: HMSO.

Spinetta, J.J. and Rigler, D. (1972) 'The child-abusing parent: a psychological review', *Psychological Bulletin*, **77**, 296–304.

Steele, B. (1980) 'Psychodynamic factors in child abuse', in C.H.Kempe and R.E.Helfer (eds) *The Battered Child*, 3rd edn, Chicago: University of Chicago Press.

Steinhauer, P.D. (1983) 'Assessing for parenting capacity', *American Journal of Orthopsychiatry*, **53**, 468–81.

Sturge, C. (1992) 'Dealing with courts and parenting breakdown', *Archives of Disease of Childhood*, **67**, 745–50.

Taylor, S. (1989) 'How prevalent is it?', in W.S.Rogers, D. Hevey and A. Ash (eds) *Child Abuse and Neglect: Facing the Challenge*, London: Batsford and the Open University.

Wasserman, S. and Rosenfeld, A. (1986) 'Decision-making in child abuse and neglect', *Child Welfare*, **65**, 515–29.

White, R., Carr, P. and Lowe, N. (1990) *A Guide to the Children Act*, London: Butterworths.

Winnicott, D. W. (1960) 'The theory of the parent–infant relationship', *International Journal of Psycho-Analysis*, **41**, 585–95.

Wolfe, D.A. (1987) *Child Abuse: Implications for Child Development and Psychopathology*, Newbury Park CA: Sage.

Part II

Components of parenting assessments

Chapter 2

Assessing family functioning in parenting breakdown
Peter Stratton and Helga Hanks

The position taken in this chapter is that an assessment of the family is essential in any assessment of parenting. The behaviour of individuals within the family is framed, influenced and given meaning by the various dynamics of that family. We would argue that the behaviour and characteristics of subsystems of the family such as the parents, or the mother–infant dyad, are usefully understood within the context of the whole family. Our own approach is mainly based on therapeutic work with families in which family breakdown is threatened or has occurred.

This chapter therefore has two objectives: to review major concepts which are necessary for understanding families, and show how these can be used within an assessment of parenting breakdown. Second, to review briefly the range of standardised family assessments that are now available and discuss their application in such cases. We have made a wide interpretation of parenting breakdown, to include not only problems of child maltreatment, but also cases in which the young person is considered to be beyond parental control or oscillates between home and local authority care.

Family assessment is likely to employ a combination of interview and observation, backed up by the records. These sources will generate a very substantial amount of information which needs to be organised around a framework. We therefore start by describing such a framework (see also Walsh 1982; Burnham 1985; Jones 1992; Stratton *et al*. 1990).

A BASIC FRAMEWORK FOR FAMILY FUNCTIONING

Almost all approaches now accept the need to see the family as an interactive system. We take a specific approach to this related to the concept, from developmental psychology, of transactions (Sameroff and Fiese 1990; Stratton 1992). The transactional perspective emphasises the way that people within a family are involved in a continuing series of negotiations in which the response of one person to an initiative of another will in turn influence that other person.

Zoe's parents needed and expected an unrealistically high standard from her in terms of her behaviour, her learning, and the responsibility she was expected to take for her own actions. Whatever she achieved was a disappointment and she learned that she was always failing her parents. Zoe then started to avoid any situation in which she might be judged and, for example, concealed her school results from her parents. They then concluded that she was devious and a complete failure (why else would she be hiding her reports?). Zoe started to give up any attempt to do well and expressed her unhappiness in various ways. Her parents found this behaviour so threatening that they got into a cycle of severely punishing her.

Recognition of such transactional processes allows one to see patterns of family behaviour not as styles imposed by a dominant person, but as the outcome of a progression in which each person influences the other. The transactional framework gives a basis for conceptualising mutual influences without denying differences in power and without the need to apportion blame.

An essential component of this view is that children within a family are responding to their situation with a series of *adaptations*. A person will adapt to any situation in terms of their needs and motivations. Children (and also adults under stress) are especially likely to adapt in ways that are the best they can manage in the short term, but which do not include thinking of longer term consequences. We have argued (Stratton 1992) that good parenting consists of eliciting adaptations from children which equip them to function well in the future, and in other contexts outside the family.

We regard this perspective as crucial because it shows that a family assessment is not a question of judging fixed attributes of individuals. The task is not to decide whether Zoe's low achievement and alternation between sullen withdrawal and angry outbursts should be described in terms of a personality deficiency or a stage of adolescence. And it is not to decide whether the intolerant and punitive behaviour of her parents means that they are inadequate, wicked or aggressive. The task of an assessment is to understand how the family came to this pattern of interaction so that we can judge whether this is an irretrievable breakdown or whether, given professional involvement, and with whatever new resources may realistically be forthcoming, the family may be able to function less destructively towards themselves in future.

Successful parenting must first avoid producing damaging adaptations and secondly must produce adaptations which develop the child's competencies. An example of the first kind of failure is the sexually abused child who adapts by responding to sexual demands of adults, and so is at risk of adopting this pattern of behaviour in other contexts. This kind of case assessment is directed to judging whether the child's adaptations put him/her at risk within the family and/or whether remaining in the family will increase the adaptations which put the child at risk outside. We are suggesting this as a general framework from which to consider all of the issues and case examples described in this chapter.

The second requirement of fostering competencies is a basic task of the family, and all children depend on an appropriate range of competencies for their safety. For children in a potentially abusing environment it may be necessary to foster adaptations which enable the child to be more than averagely responsible for their own protection. While even young children need to learn to become responsible, e.g. for not touching hot things, for learning to feed themselves, dress themselves, etc., in an abusing environment children are often responsible for things which are way beyond their age and competence. Leaving the garden gate open when a 2 year old is playing in the garden is a risk for the child; having no fireguard is a risk; making an 8 year old responsible for younger siblings while parents leave the house is too much to ask. Finding that a child does not play, has poor language and is focused on adult needs should lead to considering what is going on in the family to make this pattern necessary. But until it is certain that the child will be removed from the family or a care order put in place, treating the child to modify the adaptation may simply put them at greater risk.

Thinking in terms of adaptation therefore leads in three directions: it helps take us back to an understanding of the conditions in the family that produced that adaptation; it makes us think forwards to the near future where it must be decided whether the family will be able to care adequately for the child who has adapted in this way; and it makes clear that inadequate parenting must be judged by looking further into the future to decide whether the adaptations that the family is requiring from the child will leave her/him seriously incapacitated later in development.

We can now use this basic position to review those concepts of family functioning which are central to the operation of an assessment interview.

INTERVIEWING

The interview is the basis on which most families are assessed and judgements made about their functioning. The interview may be carefully planned, or allowed to take its course; it may be highly structured and leading to defined measures, as with the Darlington Family Assessment System (Wilkinson 1993) discussed below, or one of the diagnostic interviews (Wiens 1991). It is important to recognise that the way the interview is conducted will convey a message to the family, and so will influence their responses. Less structured approaches risk a well-rehearsed presentation with the parents 'telling the assessor what she wants to hear'. The interviewer will have objectives and a framework of understanding that is not shared with the family, but has to use the interview to obtain a clear idea of how the family works. In general, a non-judgemental stance, with an emphasis on the need for the family to explain so that the interviewer can understand, has the best chance of success.

Interviewing will remain the core of family assessment, but it is essential to recognise that it can be influenced by the motivations and social functioning of both the interviewer and the family. Working out in advance what will count as evidence for any particular conclusion, and negotiating with the family a shared objective for the conversation is important. Therefore the wider and stronger the assessor's basis of understanding, the better founded their judgements will be. Furthermore, having the essential aspects clearly spelt out and articulated enables the practitioner to present judgements and conclusions in a form that will be convincing and readily comprehensible by the court. This chapter therefore aims to provide the material for understanding and describing families.

The family life cycle

The family has its own life cycle (Carter and McGoldrick 1989) and events must be interpreted in terms of the family's current stage. As a very simple example, a failure to control a child's diet, or a child running away from home, will have different meanings depending on whether the child is 5 or 15. The life cycle approach draws attention to two essential aspects of families: the transgenerational and the developmental momentum.

The transgenerational

Families often are aware of three, and sometimes even four, generations of influence. For most families the mix of generations is an extra resource but for dysfunctional families a problem which persists across generations may be especially resistant. When a parent is sexually abusing one of their children, it is not uncommon to discover that they (the parents) were abused by one of their parents, and that this grandparent also abuses his/her grandchild. Talking about the family and its structure can be used to formulate a genogram which in turn can give clues to patterns and expectations in the family arising from their understanding of their earlier history.

A mother brought her daughter (Kim, aged 11 years) to the clinic because the child had recurrent urinary tract infections and had recently said to her mother that her father had sexually abused her. The mother had discussed this with the father's sister who had told her that she had to believe her daughter. The sister-in-law thought the story was credible because she had also been sexually abused by her father. The mother told us that the sister-in-law was in the waiting room and if we did not believe her she could come in and explain. We agreed and then talked about the disclosure using the phrase 'what *if* the father and the paternal grandfather where in the room and heard us talk. What would they say?' Kim, having listened to the conversation with great concentration, butted in and said that both her father and her paternal grandfather would say it was not true. Kim felt that none of them would be believed. Dad had said to her that he would simply tell people that she was lying and everybody would believe him, not her. He had also told her that such sexual behaviour was quite normal and that the paternal grandfather had also done it to him. Father said he had learnt a lot from his father and was passing the knowledge on to Kim. Both mother and sister-in-law were astonished and upset to hear Kim speak so clearly and decisively.

Intergenerational patterns are very common in many spheres of life, with the positive aspects of family mores passing from generation to generation. However, the dysfunctional aspects are also passed on unless considerable effort is made to break the cycle. What needs to be recognised is that the functional as well as dysfunctional rules are known to the family, but are not always so clear to outsiders. Using such phrasing as 'what would happen if . . .?' leaves the field open for the family and individuals within it to state what they think. This can lead to a better understanding and is not only used as a therapeutic tool but is particularly relevant in assessment interviews which need to elicit the family's underlying beliefs.

Once the family's beliefs about intergenerational patterns have been understood, the task is to judge whether they will be able to break free from destructive expectations, and whether they will need specific forms of help in order to do so. Note that we would not present the existence of parenting breakdown in previous generations as evidence that the present generation will be unable to cope. There may be a statistical link but this does not predict what will happen for a specific family. As in the case example of Kim (above) it is the beliefs, understandings and expectations within the family which determine what will happen. In that case it had been necessary to unravel what was believed by different family members about the behaviour of the paternal grandfather and how this connected to the behaviour of the father.

The 'Kim' case illustrates a further point: that the assessment interview may bring into the open facts and beliefs of which some family members were previously unaware. The situation is then changed, and the family may be better able to cope in future. Or a risk situation may have been intensified because the information has come into the open. Assessment must be of the level of risk in the family with this new understanding and in this new situation.

The developmental momentum

Carter and McGoldrick (1989) and Wilkinson (1993) talk of the family as a system moving through time which must adapt to changes. But as their writing indicates, this does not in any way imply that stasis is normal. Every member of a family is continuously becoming older, and there are continuous developmental changes and comings and goings from the family. A family might wish to stay unaltered through these developments, but only be able to do so with considerable effort and determination. The virtual impossibility of staying the same is one of the most powerful factors working to help a therapist; but when attempting to predict to a court how a family will function in future, it poses difficulties. The case quoted below came to light because neighbours had complained that the boy was being left unattended and neglected while his mother left the house. A parenting assessment was requested because the mother was resistant to changing her behaviour.

> Mrs K arrived with her 4 year old son, who was very obese, in a pushchair complaining that he did not want to walk. She said she knew he probably had something wrong with his muscles, but she needed help to know how to cope with the child. Extensive hospital investigations had not shown up any physical illness or disability in the child, though there had been some concern in the past that the child had been admitted with factitious illnesses including a very severe skin infection. She described how he was still in nappies, needed spoon feeding, had hardly any language, and he needed to be carried everywhere. The mother stated 'I want him to walk, he is too heavy for me now.' She also stated clearly that she did not want him to feed himself, speak, come out of nappies, play with other children, etc. Mrs K. indicated that the sole purpose in her life was to look after her son.

In terms of an assessment, this case shows how parenting breakdown can at times be quite difficult to detect. This child was kept in a state of 'underdevelopment' which would keep him dependent and without skills which he needed to lead an ordinary, age-appropriate life. He was kept in this state in order to fulfil the mother's unmet needs. An approach to assessment for Munchausen by proxy was important to indicate that significant harm was at issue in this case and that interventions could not be achieved without a care order because mother would be unlikely to comply. Once the parenting breakdown was detected, the mother needed help in accepting the developmental changes which had to occur in her son and at the same time teach the child to walk, talk, play, etc.

The life cycle perspective is especially useful in conceptualising processes around family dissolution and reconstitution. It provides essential reminders in family assessment that change is inevitable, but it also offers an understanding of which changes are to be expected.

The use of these ideas about transgenerational patterns and the developmental momentum depends on having methods to acquire a clear understanding of how they work and are understood within the family. The main tool for achieving this is the genogram, so we will describe this technique before moving on to attachment.

The genogram

For either assessment or therapy, a starting point is to construct a genogram of the family. Apart from being a convenient reference, essential when the family has a complex structure, a genogram brings out and makes visible the intergenerational and life cycle issues. Genograms are powerfully visual accounts of a family and its history. Repeated patterns, characteristics, illnesses and talents as well as single and multiple tragedies can be detected. If a child in the current generation attempts suicide, then it may be well to explore who she/he is most like in the family's perception and construction of their genogram. Byng-Hall's (1988) idea of a family script would be relevant here. Such connections can alert the professional to potential difficulties and also strengths.

Oliver and Graham (1985) published an extensive study about families in Wiltshire and chronicled these families' intergenerational patterns. A genogram can begin to elicit such patterns. McGoldrick and Gerson (1989) give detailed instructions, and a standard nomenclature, for constructing genograms. In our experience, when constructing genograms it is useful to:

- use a standard set of symbols so that genograms can be shared among workers;
- use colours freely to show the relationships especially across generations;
- date all events in real time and by ages so that repetitive patterns can be identified;
- indicate where any members of the family are unaware of the genogram information;
- put the youngest child at the bottom, not in the middle, of your sheet of paper when starting to draw the genogram;
- once the genogram is drafted, redraw it in the clearest way you can;
- develop the genogram on your own first. Later you may wish to share it with the family, but we have found this to be a powerful process that needs to be handled very carefully.

Attachments

Attachment theory (Bowlby 1969; 1988) was initially directed to the relationship between mother (or permanent mother substitute) and the infant from 6 months to 3 years. The three patterns of attachment that Ainsworth *et al.* (1978) identified have become the major focus of research in this age group. The most common form – secure attachment has come to be seen as the ideal, with ambivalent, insecure or resistant attachment – being attributed to over-intrusive mothering and avoidant attachment occurring when the mother is hostile or distant. Bentovim (1991) considers relevant in assessments that 'there can be a major disruption of attachment if, for example the parents are unable to maintain consistency, predictability and a physical presence.'

The foundation of a baby's secure attachment usually takes place between the age of 6 and 12 months. Even at that age, a child can attach to a number of caretakers close to the child. The presence of an attachment figure reduces anxiety in stressful situations and in a climate of secure attachment(s) provides the child with confidence in new and unknown situations. Importantly, it also provides the foundation and security to make lasting relationships.

The early attachment patterns lay the foundations for later development. Attachment can change over time and should not be seen as a static process but as a dynamic one which is closely linked to the child's experience. It is an important process which shapes the development of the self through internal representational models. These internalised attachment figures are later used as models for parenting when the children become parents themselves. It is in this way that important parenting skills are transmitted from generation to generation (Ricks 1985). For parents to behave in a consistent, loving and nurturing way, they themselves need to have experienced good-enough attachment in their own childhood. If they have not, they will need both extra emotional support and practical guidance about parenting skills.

> At a first appointment Kerry and her 13 month old child entered the room. The mother within the first 2 minutes left the room without explanation. The 13 month old child stayed, as if without concern, playing with the toy he had picked up. Only at close observation of the child was it possible to detect his frozenness and inability to react to the mother's leaving. Children who are securely attached would be expected to show considerable disturbance, and protest, at the separation from a primary figure in strange situations. The child did not respond in any way to the mother when she came back into the room and exhibited an 'insecure' attachment pattern. When the child was examined by a paediatrician many bruises were found on the child's body and a cigarette burn on the back of his hand. Further investigation into the case revealed that mother, who was 17 years of age, had herself experienced a difficult childhood. Her own mother was 18 when she had Kerry who was taken into care on and off throughout her childhood. An intergenerational pattern with poor attachment between mother and child gave rise to considerable concern. The observation of a poor attachment pattern, the child unable to react to the separation, indicated that an assessment with regard to parenting breakdown was necessary.

The assessment of attachment patterns includes observations about how the child copes in strange situations, and with unfamiliar people present and how the child reacts when the caretaker/mother leaves and returns. (For a detailed description of the 'strange situation' the reader is referred to Ainsworth *et al.* 1978; Crittenden 1988; Bowlby 1988).

It is sometimes believed that because children are observed to run and greet the abuser with some enthusiasm, therefore this person cannot be abusing the child. Such behaviour should not automatically be seen as a good attachment pattern. The child may well be having to work to maintain the attachment. Alternatively, if the child stays close or clings to the maltreating adult it may erroneously be interpreted as good attachment. Close observation of the responses from both the attachment figure and the child is essential to gain an informed view. Summit (1983) drew our attention to what he called the 'accommodation syndrome' and pointed out that such behaviour observed in children who are sexually abused is common but nevertheless dysfunctional and damaging to the child. Once the issues around the 'accommodation syndrome' are understood by the assessor and then assessed, the consequences for the child can be seen more clearly.

Crittenden (1988), in her study of abusive families, noted that children in physically abusive families can become compliant to reduce the risk of physical abuse. She describes an assessment procedure for families with abusing patterns and distinguishes between 'abusing families', 'neglecting families' and 'abusing and neglecting families' with striking differences which identify the different family groups. In this study she looked at the skills, family structure, childhood experience of parents, expectations, network support, parental coping strategies and the index children.

The children in the 'abusing family' group were described as difficult and acting-out or wary, compliant and inhibited. The children in the 'neglecting' families were described as very passive in infancy, sometimes very active when older, having a limited ability to attend to others and 'significant developmental delay'. The third group, the 'abusing and neglecting families' children, were described as: 'out of control, cannot learn to manage their parents as abused children can, cannot safely ignore their parents as neglected children can' and they have 'numerous intellectual, physical, and behavioural anomalies'.

Bentovim (1991) states that 'Significant harm may be defined as the state of a child which is attributable to ill treatment or failure to provide adequate care'. Both the cases quoted above fall into that category and show that it can be difficult to assess such cases but that it is also very important from the child's point of view that the assessment is done. Definitions and criteria of significant harm are provided in Adcock et al. (1991) and the Children Act of 1989.

Beliefs and perceptions

In any attempt to understand a family it is essential to recognise that they may have a very different perception of events. When working with families it rapidly becomes obvious that you can never assume that they see things the way that you do, and it is necessary to check out their understanding at every point. There are many different 'stories' to be told about any event, each with their own value, but each being only a partial description (Gergen 1992). The stories a family tells are partly derived from the culture within which it is located (Stratton 1988), so making false assumptions about what a family believes is especially likely when the observer is from a different culture, whether professionally or ethnically (Lau 1991).

A number of concepts have been derived from family therapy to understand the unique forms of belief system that families create. For example the idea that families develop 'myths' (Bagarozzi and Anderson 1989) which are complex belief systems, frequently with a transgenerational flavour, about the family. It is quite common to find that these myths have never been fully expressed and yet they are shared and believed by all family members. If they can be identified, they offer an important route to understanding how the family is likely to function.

Causal attributions

One approach to family belief systems is to record the causal beliefs or attributions made by family members to explain their own and each other's behaviour. Stratton *et al.* (1986) have developed a system for identifying and analysing causal beliefs as they are expressed in any kind of interview. The attributions of abusive parents about their child's behaviour have been found to differ consistently from those of other parents (Bugental *et al.* 1989; Silvester and Stratton 1991). The major pattern to look out for is when parents account for bad events in terms of important characteristics of the child, or of their partner, while good events are attributed to luck or trivial causes. Stratton and Swaffer (1988) have shown that this kind of pattern is a consistent feature of abusive mothers while Silvester and Stratton have shown that abusive parents tend to believe their child has more control over bad events than they do themselves.

These tendencies are quite easy to detect during an interview by paying particular attention to the explanations offered for bad events including the maltreatment itself. How much responsibility do the parents take? Are most explanations in terms of inherent characteristics of the child ('because he is nasty'), or of choices by the child such as 'just to be difficult'? And is the child given credit for any positive achievements? Of course all parents sometimes (and justifiably) say negative things about their children. What is striking and reportable about dysfunctional families is the consistency – the remorseless blaming of the child for everything that goes wrong.

Levels of meaning

A useful idea when assessing families is that of different contextual levels influencing the meaning attributed to events. These are described by Pearce and Cronen (1980) in their theory of the Coordinated Management of Meaning

(CMM). The basic idea in CMM is that people and families operate with a hierarchy of levels and that the level taking priority (the 'highest context marker') may change in different circumstances. Clinically this theory helps to make sense of families which have presented in certain ways and seemed incomprehensible. Parents may recognise that safety of the child is a priority for a social worker and talk in these terms. But if for them maintaining their (violent) marital relationship is an overriding consideration, an observer may be seriously mislead. So one function of an assessment interview is to explore with family members why they behaved in certain ways and be sufficiently clear and specific to allow the identification of the parents' priorities.

Putting these ideas together allows a *summary overview* which we think is helpful in assessing a family from what it says about itself, and what it does. A family will have a set of stories about itself. These stories are not usually spelled out, but are implicit in the explanations it gives and the ways its members react to events. The stories are strongly influenced by the history of the wider family as understood and transmitted by the parents. Different stories will be salient in different circumstances because different levels of influence will be operating and present in the thinking of the family. The care provided for children is influenced by these stories and particularly by how they relate to the way the family construes the current stage of its life cycle.

The particular contribution of a family interview to the assessment of parenting is that it gives direct access, within the context of a family interaction, to both the accounts of family members, and to the ways the family members behave in relation to each other. It is true that parents will attempt to present themselves in the best possible light during such an interview, but our experience is that families cannot operate outside their habitual patterns, even if they are emphasising the better aspects of those patterns.

STANDARD ASSESSMENTS

A number of attempts have been made to formulate detailed procedures for assessing families. There are three reasons why it is important for the practitioner to be informed about them: (1) they can be a source of ideas and techniques even if not used in their full form; (2) they are used by other practitioners who may be representing a different position in a case; and (3) they may become more routinely used in the future.

We have given brief descriptions here, to indicate what is available from the well-established methods. In order to use any of the methods in practice it will be necessary to obtain a more detailed description. A number of texts offer excellent accounts, including Holman (1983), Fredman and Sherman (1987), Grotevant and Carlson (1989), Touliatos *et al.* (1990) and L'Abate and Bagarozzi (1993). The standardised measures reviewed below are described in detail and evaluated in these texts. Wilkinson (1993) and

L'Abate (1994) review current methods and then proceed to develop their own general approaches.

We start with the attempts that have been made to give a formal structure to interviews, of which the most detailed is the Darlington Family Assessment System.

The Darlington Family Assessment System (DFAS)

A recent innovation in family assessment is the DFAS (Wilkinson 1993). This method differs from other standard procedures by being partly based on a structured interview which was constructed to be a basis for training clinicians in assessment of families. The interview works through four systemic levels:

- the child's perspective;
- the parental perspective;
- the parent–child perspective (parenting style);
- the whole family perspective.

Each perspective is examined through a standard set of topics, working through the major issues at that level. The 'Problem Dimensions' examined at the level of the family are:

1 closeness and distance;
2 power hierarchies;
3 emotional atmosphere and rules;
4 family development.

Wilkinson (1993) argues that family assessment cannot depend on a single approach or a single method. He has therefore developed a package based on the idea of 'multisystem multimethod (MSMM) assessment' (Cromwell and Peterson 1983; Walker et al. 1984). The structured interview is accompanied by a checklist which follows the same dimensions, and generates a rating scale through observation of the interview. The material can then be supplemented by questionnaires and family tasks.

The DFAS has much to offer as a model for how to go about a reasonably comprehensive evaluation. Among its strengths are that it was developed as a combined assessment and training tool, so it not only comes with a clear system of training in how to use the method for evaluation, but it functions as a general training in family interviewing. By following the instructions a coherent picture of family functioning at different levels is achieved.

The Circumplex Model

This model is based on a study of over 1,000 functional families (Olson et al. 1983). The authors are responsible for a number of family assessment measures, all based on self-report by family members filling in question-naires.

The core of the model is the idea that families can be measured on two separate dimensions of *adaptation* and *cohesion*. The significance of calling these aspects 'dimensions' is that they are presumed to be independent of each other, and so a two-dimensional space can be set up. A questionnaire is used to rate the family on each of the dimensions, so that they become placed within one quadrant of the two-dimensional space. They are then placed at one of three levels of functioning: *balanced*, *mid-range* or *extreme*. This allows each quadrant to be divided into four, with adaptability ranged through:

rigid, structured, flexible and chaotic;

and cohesion through:

disengaged, separated, connected and enmeshed.

In each case the middle two categories are regarded as healthy. For example, the quadrant defined by high cohesion and low adaptability has:

- balanced families being structurally connected;
- mid-range families as either rigidly connected or structurally enmeshed;
- extreme families as rigidly enmeshed.

The questionnaires have gone through progressive development, with the addition of a third dimension of *family communication* which is believed to be facilitating because it allows the family to move on the cohesion and adaptability dimensions. They are currently known as FACES III (Family Adaptation and Cohesion Scale, Version 3, Olson *et al.* 1989).

Other statistical analyses of self-report questionnaires have produced quite different sets of dimensions (see below). However, Olson *et al.*'s work has produced a range of questionnaires which may be useful in their own right, and which can be related to each other through the circumplex model. Practitioners may find any of the following useful additions to a family interview:

- ENRICH: Enriching and Nurturing Relationship Issues, Communication and Happiness;
- FILE: Family Inventory of Life Events and Changes;
- F-COPES for family coping strategies;
- Quality of Life measures.

Some of their questionnaires are specially adapted for use with adolescents. All of the scales are printed in Olson *et al.* (1983) and also reproduced in texts such as Touliatos *et al.* (1990). It is worth knowing about the existence of such scales in case a specific issue to which they apply arises. If, for example, you know that you need to report on the level of positive relationships within the family, or the forms of their coping strategies, then these tests may be very useful. And because they are standardised measures allowing comparison with other families, they will have credibility in court.

However, any questionnaire approach has limitations: the first is that there is a limited choice available for families. So for a given assessment requirement, there may simply be no questionnaire available to do the job. Second, questionnaires are language based, and even if presented verbally, assume certain levels of comprehension. Family assessment is especially likely to be dealing with groups for whom this is a problem: for example, young children, families with minimal verbal skills and minority cultural groups perhaps with a different first language. Chronic psychological disturbance or current crisis may also influence ability to concentrate on the kinds of question asked by the questionnaire. Also, people will vary in their willingness to provide the information in this form, especially if they suspect that the assessment may work to their disadvantage. All of these concerns apply equally to interviews. Furthermore, it is usually quite easy for the respondent to judge the interpretation that will be made of answers to questionnaires, and because they rely on self-report, it is not difficult for respondents to create false impressions. In general questionnaires should only be used when the person doing the assessment and the people being assessed have compatible goals.

The Family Environment Scale (FES)

One of the most widely used measures is the FES created by Moos and Moos (1976). This scale was derived by similar techniques to those of Olson *et al.* (above), and generated the three dimensions of:

- relationships;
- personal growth;
- system maintenance.

Each has subscales, giving ten scales in all. The test contains ninety items, (nine for each scale) and the scores of different family members can be compared to discover how many items, and of what kind, they disagree on. With this kind of measure it can be assumed that agreement between family members on a negative item, *and* disagreement about a positive item, are both indicative of problems. The advantages and limitations of questionnaire-based methods discussed above apply equally to the FES.

The McMaster Family Assessment Device (MFAD)

The McMaster Model of Family Functioning (MMFF, Epstein and Bishop 1981) was developed over many years to provide an evaluation of those dimensions of functioning which have most impact on the family. The procedures are geared towards specifying the treatment needs of the family but can be used for assessment. This is a systemic approach which assumes that the functioning of a family cannot be reduced to summing the behaviours of individuals. Early work by the group defined three kinds of task that the family must deal with effectively:

- basic tasks, such as providing food and shelter;
- developmental tasks, based on life cycle concepts;
- hazardous tasks, or the handling of crises that arise through illness, loss of job, etc.

A systemic analysis of these tasks, geared towards specifying an appropriate behavioural treatment, distinguished six major components of functioning:

- problem solving;
- communication;
- roles;
- affective responsiveness;
- affective involvement;
- behavioural control.

There is also a global measure called 'general functioning'. For the McMaster Model of Family Functioning judgements on these dimensions are made by trained observers which means that the system is less easily used than the questionnaire measures. The MFAD was produced by Epstein *et al.* (1983) as a standard questionnaire derived from the MMFF.

Epstein *et al.* (1982) compare the McMaster Model with other assessments, including some reviewed here, and conclude that all of the others make untested assumptions, and are more restricted in what they measure than the MMFF. While this last claim is true, there is a direct cost in terms of complexity. All of the systems have been developed by researchers (and sometimes, as with the McMaster Model, clinicians) with substantial background knowledge of families, and all of them have had detailed justification offered for their choice of variables. So far none has emerged as clearly more effective in providing definitive answers of the kind needed when assessing families for parenting breakdown.

Other measures

A number of other measures of family functioning are available, though less widely used.

Dunst *et al.* (1988) constructed a series of scales to assess needs and social support, which are designed to specify the form and extent of intervention needed.

Reiss and Oliveri (1980) developed a system of assessment by asking families to undertake tasks, while their interactions were recorded. They were rated on two dimensions of 'coordination' and 'configuration' with the assumption that a healthy family would score highly on both dimensions.

Kinston and Loader (1988) took up this approach and have now developed a standard system of family tasks, which are presented in a fixed form (a tape-recording of the instructions may be used to ensure consistency). Families are asked to engage in a series of activities such as planning an outing, and their responses are scored by observers. There is a standardised set of seven family tasks in the 'Family Task Interview' which can be used to generate clinically relevant behaviour. At present this is regarded as a research instrument rather than a standard method of assessment, but the idea of a well-researched set of tasks on which families can be compared seems worth pursuing.

Finally, L'Abate (1994), in attempting to get below the surface of the family's self-presentation, claims that there are two primary abilities necessary for smooth family functioning: the *ability to love* and the *ability to negotiate*. He goes on to claim that most dysfunctional families are defective in both of these abilities. At present these strong claims depend on L'Abate's credibility rather than on empirical evidence. However, if we could evaluate such processes, we would certainly be making major progress in family assessment. L'Abate (1994) provides ideas about how the two abilities could be evaluated which may eventually be turned into a practicable assessment instrument.

CONCLUSION

In this chapter we have described some of the most important aspects of family functioning and, where available, ways of measuring these aspects. All have been developed in an attempt to come closer to understanding how families work and how it may be possible to predict the capacity of a family to care for its children. Any of the measures, techniques or single indicators might be incorporated into an assessment, depending on the objectives. But equally, an assessment of a parent, a child, or any other family combination, can be enriched through being cast in a family perspective using the concepts described in this chapter.

REFERENCES

Adcock, M., White, R. and Hollows, A. (1991) *Significant Harm*, Croydon: Significant Publications.

Ainsworth, M., Blehar, M., Waters, E. and Wall, S. (1978) *Patterns of Attachment: A Psychological Study of the Strange Situation*, Hillsdale NJ: Erlbaum.

Bagarozzi, D.A. and Anderson, S.A. (1989) *Personal, Marital and Family Myths: Theoretical Formulations and Clinical Strategies*, New York: Norton.

Bentovim, A. (1991) 'Significant harm in context', in M. Adcock, R. White and A. Hollows (eds) *Significant Harm*, Croydon: Significant Publications.

Bowlby, J. (1969) *Attachment and Loss. Vol. 1: Attachment*, New York: Basic Books.

Bowlby, J. (1988) *A Secure Base: Parent-Child Attachment and Health Human Development*, New York: Basic Books.

Bugental, D.B., Mantyla, S.M. and Lewis, J. (1989) 'Parental attributions as moderators of affective communication to "abuse-eliciting" children', in D. Cicchetti and V. Carlson (eds) *Child Maltreatment*, New York: Cambridge University Press.

Burnham, J. (1985) *Family Therapy*, London: Tavistock.

Byng-Hall, J. (1988) 'Scripts and legends in families and family therapy', *Family Process*, **27**, 167–79.

Carter, B. and McGoldrick, M. (1989) *The Changing Family Life Cycle*, Needham Heights MA: Allyn and Bacon.

Crittenden, P. (1988) 'Family and dyadic patterns of functioning in maltreating families', in K. Browne, C. Davies and P. Stratton (eds) *Early Prediction and Prevention of Child Abuse*, Chichester: Wiley.

Cromwell, R.E. and Peterson, G.W. (1983) 'Multisystem-multimethod family assessment in clinical contexts', *Family Process*, **22**, 147–63.

Dunst, C., Trivet, C. and Deal, A. (1988) *Enabling and Empowering Families: Principles and Guidelines for Practice*, Cambridge MA: Brookline.

Epstein, N.B. and Bishop, D.S. (1981) 'Problem-centred systems therapy of the family', in A. Gurman and D. Kniskern (eds) *Handbook of Family Therapy*, New York: Brunner/Mazel.

Epstein, N.B., Bishop, D.S. and Baldwin, L.M. (1982) 'McMaster Model of Family Functioning: a view of the normal family', in F. Walsh (ed.) *Normal Family Processes*, New York: Guilford.

Epstein, N.B., Baldwin, L.M. and Bishop, D.S. (1983) 'The McMaster Family Assessment Device', *Journal of Marital and Family Therapy*, **9**, 171–80.

Fredman, N. and Sherman, R. (1987) *Handbook of Measurements for Marriage and Family Therapy*, New York: Brunner/Mazel.

Gergen, K. (1992) 'Social constructionism in question', *Human Systems*, **2**, 163–82.

Grotevant, H.D. and Carlson, C. (1989) *Family Assessment: A Guide to Methods and Measures*, New York: Guilford.

Holman, A.M. (1983) *Family Assessment*, Beverley Hills CA: Sage.

Jones, E. (1992) *Family Systems Therapy*, Chichester: Wiley.

Kinston, W. and Loader, P. (1988) 'The family task interview: a tool for clinical research in family interaction', *Journal of Marital and Family Therapy*, **14**, 67–87.

L'Abate, L. (1994) *Family Evaluation*, Thousand Oaks CA: Sage.

L'Abate, L. and Bagarozzi, D.A. (1993) *Sourcebook for Marriage and Family Evaluation*, New York: Brunner/Mazel.

Lau, A. (1991) 'Cultural and ethnic perspectives on significant harm: its assessment and treatment', in M. Adcock, R White and A. Hollows (eds) *Significant Harm*, Croydon: Significant Publications.

McGoldrick, M. and Gerson, R. (1985) *Genograms in Family Assessment*, New York: Norton.

Moos, R. and Moos, B. (1976) 'A typology of family environments', *Family Process*, **15**, 357–71.

Oliver, J.E. and Graham, W.J. (1985) 'Generations of Maltreated Children in North-East Wiltshire', report from Unit of Clinical Epidemiology, Oxford University.

Olson, D.H., Russell, C.S. and Sprenkle, D.H. (eds) (1989) *Circumplex Model: Systemic Assessment and Treatment of Families*, New York: Haworth.

Pearce, B. and Cronen, V. (1980) *Communication, Action and Meaning: The Creation of Social Realities*, New York: Praeger.

Reiss, D. and Oliveri, M. (1980) 'Family paradigm and family coping', *Family Relations*, **29**, 431–44.

Ricks, M. (1985) 'The social transmission of parental behaviour: attachment across generations', in I. Bretherton and E. Waters (eds) *Growing Points of Attachment*

Theory and Research, monographs of the Society for Research in Child Development. Chicago: University of Chicago Press.

Sameroff, A.J. and Fiese, B.H. (1990) 'Transactional regulation and early intervention', in S.J. Meisels and J.P. Shonkoff (eds) *Handbook of Early Childhood Intervention*, New York: Cambridge University Press.

Silvester, J. and Stratton, P. (1991) 'Attributional discrepancy in abusive families', *Human Systems*, **2**, 279–95.

Stratton, P. (1988) 'Parents' conceptualization of children as the organizer of culturally structured environments', in J. Valsiner (ed.) *Child Development within Culturally Structured Environments*, Norwood NJ: Ablex.

Stratton, P. (1992) 'Integration of developmental concepts with systemic techniques for intervention with families', *Educational and Child Psychology*, **9**, 28–41.

Stratton, P. and Swaffer, R. (1988) 'Maternal causal beliefs for abused and handicapped children', *Journal of Reproductive and Infant Psychology*, **6**, 201–16.

Stratton, P.M., Heard, D.H., Hanks, H.G., Munton, A.G., Brewin, C.R. and Davidson, C. (1986) 'Coding causal beliefs in natural discourse', *British Journal of Social Psychology*, **25**, 299–313.

Stratton, P., Preston-Shoot, M. and Hanks H.G.I. (1990) *Family Therapy: Training and Practice*, Birmingham: Venture Press.

Summit, R. (1983) 'The child sexual abuse accommodation syndrome', *Child Abuse and Neglect*, **7**, 177–93.

Touliatos, J., Perlmutter, B.F. and Straus, M.A. (eds) (1990) *Handbook of Family Measurement Techniques*, Newbury Park CA: Sage.

Walker, L., Thompson, N. and Lindsay, W. (1984) 'Assessing family relationships: a multi-method, multi-situational approach', *British Journal of Psychiatry*, **144**, 387–94.

Walsh, F. (1982) *Normal Family Processes*, New York: Guilford.

Wiens, A.N. (1991) 'Diagnostic interviewing', in M. Hersen, A.E. Kadzin and A.S. Bellack (eds) *The Clinical Psychology Handbook*, New York: Pergamon.

Wilkinson, I.M. (1993) *Family Assessment*, New York: Gardner Press.

Chapter 3

The meaning of the child
Peter Reder and Sylvia Duncan

'I'm sure I didn't mean – Alice was beginning, but the Red Queen
interrupted her impatiently.
'That's just what I complain of! You *should* have meant! What do you
suppose is the use of a child without any meaning?'

(Lewis Carroll, *Through the Looking Glass*: Chapter IX)

We introduced the notion of 'the meaning of the child' in our book *Beyond
Blame* (Reder *et al.* 1993), which reported a reanalysis of thirty-five fatal
child abuse cases that had been the subject of public inquiries. One question
we had asked ourselves was: 'is it possible to conjecture why particular
children were abused more severely than others so that they died?' By
analysing each family history and the chronology of events in each case, we
were able to infer that some children had a special significance to their
parent(s) and, as a result, were at greater risk of harm than other children in
the household. This led us to recognise the importance of understanding the
psychological meaning of children to their parents as part of all assessments
of parenting.

In this chapter we shall review a number of psychological concepts and
integrate them together to show how one person develops meaning for
another. We shall indicate that such processes form part of all relationships
and that it is normal for children to acquire psychological meaning to their
parents. However, in some families the parent–child relationship becomes
adversely affected by these influences and the child's welfare is compromised. We focus on families in which child maltreatment is suspected or
confirmed and shall illustrate through case material how assessing the
meaning of the child can usefully be woven into an overall evaluation of
parenting.

THE MEANING OF ONE PERSON TO ANOTHER

'Meaning' is central to the theory and practice of a wide range of psychological therapies, all of which aim to elucidate and revise the constructions

put on behaviour and relationships. However, the word is surprisingly absent from the index of most standard psychotherapy texts or dictionaries. Our use of the term is based upon concepts primarily utilised by psychoanalysts and family therapists, although we acknowledge the parallel contributions of cognitive psychologists.

In psychoanalysis, the idea that one person has an unconscious meaning for another is implicit in the concept of 'transference' (see, for example, Sandler *et al.* 1973), which describes how patients recreate in the relationship with the analyst crucial aspects of formative relationships with parents. Sandler *et al.* (1979) extend this notion beyond the therapeutic encounter, arguing that people base many relationships in their everyday lives on aspects of their early parental relationships and they call this the 'transference of habitual modes of relating'. In other words, new relationships come to incorporate aspects of psychological meaning belonging to significant figures in the past.

'Projection' refers to the process by which unresolved conflicts are disowned and unacceptable personal tendencies ascribed instead to others. These people are then related to as though they embody the attributes.

For example, Winnicott (1965) records an interview with the mother of a boy born with congenital webbing of his fingers and toes. The mother had had the same deformity and expected every child she bore to inherit it. Each time a baby was born without such a defect, she experienced enormous relief but, when the boy was born, her first involuntary thought was that this was punishment for her free sex life. When she first saw the baby she hated him and felt she could never see him again. This was quickly replaced by an idea that she would leave no stone unturned to find surgeons to repair the boy's deformity and from then on she found herself loving him even more than her other children and driven to obtain orthopaedic surgery for him.

The family systems approach to therapy grew out of psychoanalysis but extended the focus to multi-person interaction and the influence of past and present interactional patterns. The importance of history was no longer confined to formative relationships with parents but also included inter-generational patterns that appeared to be unwritten rules governing people's behaviour from the past. Ferreira (1963), Stierlin (1973) and Byng-Hall (1973; 1985) write about family myths and secrets that are handed down the generations and distort perceptions that current family members have of each other, seeming to coerce them into following a script. Lieberman (1979), McGoldrick and Gerson (1985) and Reder (1989) show how analysis of family trees (genograms) can reveal hitherto hidden patterns in family relationships over the generations and explain the meaning of individuals and their behaviour in the present.

Family therapists conceptualise family systems developing through time and facing a series of life cycle transitions, such as births, deaths, inclusions of new members, departures and natural changes such as puberty. External events, such as illness or unemployment, also impinge on family life. These transitions affect all members of the family system because everyone must adapt to them and the role and meaning that each person has for each other must be modified and their relationships renegotiated (e.g. Hoffman 1982). Some families find particular adjustments especially difficult and seem to become stuck in old, dysfunctional relationship patterns. An example would be an adolescent remaining at home, as though to try and replace a lost grandparent, because of an unspoken belief that the parents would not cope with their grief (Haley 1980). Such unresolved adjustments may leave a family member carrying an emotional meaning for others that is difficult to shed.

Bowen's (1978) concept of 'family projection process' proposes that parents' problems about 'differentiation of the self' (i.e. personal autonomy) may be projected on to a vulnerable child in a family. It is equivalent to Stierlin's (1974) 'delegation', in which one member appears to be allocated a mission on behalf of the family. Furniss (1984) takes up this idea in describing typologies of families in which sexual abuse occurs. He proposes that in 'conflict-avoiding' families, a daughter is delegated to take over the mother's sexual role to avoid family breakup.

In terms of current interactional patterns, Minuchin (1974) describes 'triangulation', in which one person becomes drawn into the role of defusing anxiety between two others. In particular, a child can become a 'marital distance regulator' (Byng-Hall 1980), an emotional intermediary between parents who oscillate in their degree of closeness. Too much intimacy and they fear being emotionally overwhelmed, too much detachment and they fear being left alone. Different behaviours of the child may unwittingly bring distant parents closer together, such as sharing concern for an upset child, or give them a reason for pushing each other apart, such as arguing about how to set limits for a disobedient child.

The Great Ormond Street Hospital group (e.g. Kinston and Bentovim 1981; Glaser et al. 1984) are one of the few to use the word 'meaning' when discussing family relationships. They consider that families' behaviour on the surface ('surface action') covers a deeper meaning to their relationships ('depth structure'). Family members also tend to share 'common meanings', which include beliefs, attitudes, guiding principles, fears or expectations about the world and other people. 'Intersubjective meanings' are more deep-rooted self-definitions about the family as a whole. Both types of meaning act as if there were coercive rules governing the way others should be related to. Bentovim (1992) goes on to discuss the patterns of meaning in a number of families in which abuse occurred.

In one example, the mother had herself been a much wanted adopted baby who was regarded as perfect by her adoptive mother. When her own daughter was born, the mother believed that she, too, would be perfect.

However, the baby failed to live up to this expectation when she developed colic at the age of 3 months. The mother could not cope with her crying and from then on the child was neglected and physically abused.

An early family study of child abuse by Terr (1970) comes closest to encapsulating our ideas about meaning. The parents interviewed were found to hold specific fantasies about the abused children, which were derived from their own distant past and had to do with fears of the child or disappointment that the child was not fulfilling a wish.

One mother considered her baby as punishment for a violent argument she had had with her husband 3 days prior to her premature birth, after which the father had left home. The baby continued to remind her mother of these events. Another mother set out to become pregnant to escape an unhappy home life and saw the infant as a saviour and a release from all her miseries. A step-mother, who feared rivals for her husband's love, insisted that he permanently give up each of his six children, one by one.

We intend 'meaning', then, to describe a facet of interpersonal relationships in which one person has a particular significance for the other, such as carrying certain expectations of role or behaviour, representing unresolved conflicts and influences from the past or has part of a web of wider interactional patterns in the present. As a result of these influences, children may acquire an undeclared script or blue-print for their life that is consistent with the family themes but submerges each child's personal identity and character-istics. The children become, in the words of Ron Britton (personal com-munication), 'actors in someone else's play'. Hence, the meaning of the child includes overt and covert motivations for wanting and having a child, as well as conscious and unconscious determinants of the parent's attitudes, feelings and relationship with the particular child.

THE MEANING OF THE CHILD IN PARENTING BREAKDOWN

We believe that all children have a psychological meaning to their parents which, if made overt, helps make sense of the relationship between them. Exploration of this meaning is especially relevant when there has been breakdown in the parent–child relationship resulting in rejection, neglect or abuse. Our study of fatal child abuse cases (Reder et al. 1993) highlights that consideration of the meaning of the child could have added significantly to the overall assessments and guided placement decisions.

This can be illustrated through the Maria Colwell case (Inquiry Report 1974), which proved a watershed in the practice of child protection in the United Kingdom. Maria is usually remembered as the 6 year old child who was killed after she was removed from a foster home, where she was thriving, and forced to live with her natural mother and step-father because of the importance given to the so-called 'blood-tie'. However, carefully piecing together the family history suggests that the meaning of Maria to her mother was probably an important contribution to the decision to return Maria to her.

Pauline Kepple's first child was from an unmarried liaison and she placed her with the maternal grandmother from birth (see Figure 3.1). The father of Pauline's next five children was Raymond Colwell and Maria was the youngest of that family. Raymond left the household 1 month after Maria's birth and he died 3 months later. Pauline quickly became depressed and neglected all her children. However, she treated Maria differently from the others and just a few weeks after Raymond's death she decided to take Maria to Raymond's sister's family (the Coopers), who agreed to look after her. Eventually, the remaining children were taken into care because of neglect and two were also placed with their maternal grandmother. However, Maria was the only one of the children with whom Pauline kept in contact and the only one of her absent children whom she insisted remain Roman Catholic, like herself. Over the next 6 years, Pauline made a number of requests for Maria to return to her, always at times of transition in her own life. These attempts to be reunited with Maria occurred when Pauline was planning to settle down with, and then marry, William Kepple and again when she became pregnant by him. She made yet another request to have Maria back when her youngest baby was 3 months old, the age Maria had been when she gave her up. Maria was eventually returned when she was 6 years old and she was neglected, assaulted and rejected over the next year until dying from violent abuse by William Kepple.

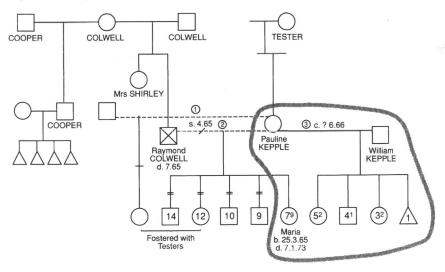

Figure 3.1 Genogram of Maria Colwell's family
Source: Reder *et al.* 1993

This story suggested to us that Maria had a special meaning to her mother because her birth was associated with the loss of Raymond Colwell. Pauline was then unable to let Maria go as she had done the other children, clinging on to the memory of the 3 month old baby and wanting to be reunited with her as a way of dealing with her unresolved feelings about the loss of Raymond. However, Maria's actual identity when she did return must have contrasted dramatically with the fantasised meaning that predominated in her mother's mind. She was not the baby who might help her mother resolve the loss of the father, but a 6 year old who was upset and regressed after being displaced from her foster home and who continued to reject her new caretakers in preference for her old ones. Unfortunately, the inquiry report contained insufficient information about William Kepple to enable us to consider the meaning that Maria might have had for him.

Concerns about the psychological meaning of children to parents who abuse them is also raised by the Doreen Aston case (Inquiry Report 1989).

Doreen's mother, Christine Mason, experienced abuse as a child, including sexual abuse by her father, and three of her siblings died in infancy, with the death of one, named Karl, reported as 'suspicious circumstances' (see Figure 3.2). She became pregnant with her first child at the age of 17, whilst she was still in care and placed at home with her divorced father, and named the child Karl. Anticipating the baby's birth, Christine said that if it were a boy she would strangle him and after he died, aged 10 weeks, Christine admitted to her social worker that she had smothered him, but she also kept

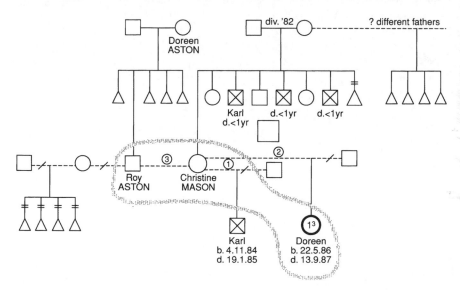

Figure 3.2 Genogram of Doreen Aston's family
Source: Reder *et al.* 1993

his ashes in her flat and carried them around with her. Eight months after Karl's death, Christine became pregnant with Doreen, openly stating that she wanted another boy and even buying clothes for a baby boy. Once Doreen was born, Christine neglected her and seemed intolerant of her dependency and needs and when Doreen was 2 months old Christine expressed disappointment that a pregnancy test had proved negative. Over the next year, Christine twice requested that Doreen be taken into care and once threatened her with a knife. Doreen eventually died aged 15 months from a blow to the head.

We wondered what unresolved conflicts about her brother's death Christine carried with her from her childhood and led her to name her first child after him, as though to replace him. Did Christine hope that this first baby might give her the love she had missed previously and provide a means of escape from sexual abuse by her father? However, because he was male, did Christine also associate him with her negative feelings towards her abusing father? Despite these strongly ambivalent feelings towards Karl it seems possible that Doreen hoped that her second baby could replace Karl and the special connotations that he had for her. Doreen was probably rejected, neglected and abused because she failed to fulfil these expectations.

UNDERSTANDING THE MEANING OF THE CHILD

It is evident that children's psychological meaning is determined by factors at different contextual levels of family life. These may be at the broadest sociopolitical level down to specific individual characteristics and behaviours. Hence, an assessor needs to consider the possible contribution of cultural beliefs, patterns in the family's history, parents' unresolved conflicts, current interactional patterns, the child's personal history and the child's characteristics.

We have separated out these levels in order to describe them more easily but they are clearly interrelated. As an example, a parent's unresolved conflicts need to be understood both at a personal level and within the context of the family history. In addition, a child's meaning may be influenced simultaneously by a number of different contextual levels.

Cultural beliefs

Although sweeping generalisations should not be made, some trends can be recognised about the way children are viewed within social groupings. For instance, many cultures hold the male child, particularly the eldest, in the highest regard (e.g. Messent 1992). This sometimes leads to the abortion of female foetuses or murder of newborn girls, while those who survive may suffer rejection and neglect.

In other examples, Wieselberg (1992) points out that the birth of a handicapped child tends to be perceived by orthodox Jews as a divine punishment for a previous misdeed of the mother, while Lau (1984) recalls the traditional Chinese moral imperative that responsibility to care for one's parents transcends responsibilities to one's children.

A cultural influence of a different order can be observed in those immigrant or indigenous families who place extraordinarily high importance on their children's education, which they believe will enable the family to break free of previous experiences of deprivation and missed opportunity. This sometimes leads to extreme pressure on the children to succeed scholastically and to sacrifice the usual pleasures of childhood. Other groups of parents expect their children to maintain a family tradition and follow them through the same school, even if this means that they leave home at a young age to spend their formative years living in an institution. Later, they may be encouraged to pursue particular careers in order to remain loyal to a family tradition, irrespective of their own interests and abilities.

Family history

One form of historical influence on families is a child who becomes associated with the emotional impact of another significant event in their family's past because it coincided with their conception, birth or early years. This is illustrated by the Maria Colwell case, summarised above, in which her birth coincided with the father's departure from the family and his death.

> Again, Lewis (1979) discusses a mother who had murdered her 8 year old daughter. The pregnancy had coincided with her husband's sudden death and the baby kept reminding her of her loss, which she had failed to mourn through the remaining months of the pregnancy. It was as though the child had been a reflection of the mother's own hurt self that she wanted to destroy.

The 'replacement' child refers to a baby conceived shortly after the death of a previous child who has not been adequately mourned and is cast in the role of substitute for the lost sibling (Poznanski 1972; Lewis 1979). It is also useful to include children born after a number of miscarriages or stillbirths (Bourne and Lewis 1984). The replacement child usually inherits a legend of expectations generated by the dead child. However, it is impossible to compete with the idealised image that the parents retain of the unmourned dead child and the replacement child suffers problems of identity and self-esteem. Similarly, an adopted child is usually intended to replace the baby who could not be conceived but, for a number of adoptive parents, this 'lost' child remains unmourned.

Sometimes, children are conceived as a way for their parent to leave home and escape conflicts in their family of origin. The children are then expected to continue to be the solution to the parents' problems and inevitably fail.

Other children are singled out as having similar personalities to another member of the family, for example being 'just like his father'. Such children could be favoured while the parents are close but acquire a negative meaning if their relationship deteriorates. Indeed, children who become linked in their parents' minds with the breakdown of the couple's relationship are liable to be blamed for it and for their remaining parent's loneliness.

Parents' unresolved conflicts

Those who have had their caring and dependency needs unmet in childhood tend to form relationships in adult life which are an attempt to fulfil dependency wishes, or else are a compulsive attempt to ward off dependency on others. For example, some people rely excessively on support from partners or professionals, while others leave home precipitously and move repeatedly from partner to partner. Overwhelming demands for care from their children can reawaken these conflicts, resulting in frustration and outbursts of aggression to them. The children take on the meaning of persecutors who deliberately frustrate and provoke the parent.

Emotionally deprived parents may conceive babies in the hope that they will provide the affection that they never received and still long for (Steele 1980; Pines 1993). Some are then punished for failing to do so or, once they show signs of autonomy, are discarded in preference for another baby (Deutsch 1945).

In our study of fatal child abuse inquiry reports, a number of parents revealed their emotional deprivation by requesting to have their children returned home from alternative care after someone else had expressed a strong interest in looking after them. This desire did not appear to be for the children in their own right but more as pieces of property that would otherwise be lost and threaten their sense of intactness. The children's return home in these circumstances precipitated a crisis of abuse because their reality contrasted with the fantasy that they could fulfil their parents' needs.

Alternatively, children might reawaken other dormant conflicts of their parents that originated in their childhood.

For example, Pines (1993) presents the psychoanalytic treatment of a woman who was referred during her third pregnancy. When the woman had been 10 years old, her mother had borne an unplanned son and she had developed intense jealousy of this younger brother. In adult life, the woman's first child was a girl to whom she was able to relate well, since the daughter became the representation of the pretty girl that she had been and she loved her as an extension of herself. However, her second child was a demanding and clinging boy whom she compulsively rejected. She punished him excessively and felt unable to give him physical affection, as though he represented her unwelcome and hated brother.

Current interaction

Children who become caught up in their parents' relationship difficulties often acquire a significance to them that results in their own needs being overlooked. This is illustrated in the case of Karen Spencer (Inquiry Report 1978), another of those we reviewed in our study of fatal child abuse inquiries.

> The marriage of Karen Spencer's parents was stormy from the outset and they separated and reunited on a number of occasions. After Karen was born, she seems to have become caught up in the oscillating phases of their relationship, much like a marital distance regulator. While Karen was living with her parents, they argued; when Karen was abused and removed to a place of safety, their fighting subsided and they came closer together again; they then asked for Karen to return to live with them and the visiting professionals agreed because their relationship appeared to have improved. However, once Karen was back, her father increasingly accused her mother of incompetent care and their rows increased again. Karen was killed 2 weeks after her return home from care and, with hindsight, we inferred that her parents' renewed closeness was only possible because Karen was not there; as soon as there was a chance that they might become too intimate, they needed her back to help increase their emotional distance.

Children's triangulation may also be manifest by competing demands for loyalty from both parents. In custody disputes, the child then becomes the vehicle through which the parents continue their battles and is wanted by each one in order to wound and deprive the other (Goldstein *et al.* 1973).

The child's history

Lynch (1975) found child abuse significantly associated with an abnormal pregnancy, labour or delivery and with neonatal separation and, clearly, children can acquire a special meaning as a result of factors associated with their conception, the pregnancy, their birth, or early life.

Motivation to conceive a child can reflect unresolved parental conflicts or be an attempted solution to family transitions. Thus, there may be a strong desire for 'a son and heir', or the hope of repairing a failing marriage or a wish to confirm a reconstituted family as a new family.

On the other hand, pregnancies can be the unplanned and unwanted consequences of rape or incest or, alternatively, of sexual contacts that were intended to satisfy the wish for physical affection (Pines 1993). Many of the mothers in the inquiry reports we studied considered termination of the pregnancy or adoption, had minimal antenatal care, or discharged themselves prematurely from the postnatal ward. This is consistent with the report of Holman and Kanwar (1975) that over one-third of abusing mothers admitted resenting the pregnancy and that the child was unwanted.

Bonnet (1993) reports interviews with mothers for whom the fact of being pregnant was an intolerable life cycle crisis, since the presence of the foetus triggered re-emergence of traumatic childhood memories, including sexual abuse. Fearing their violent fantasies towards the unborn baby, the mothers had denied that they were pregnant and the babies were born without preparation and were killed, abandoned or rejected.

In addition, it is well recognised that memories of a traumatic birth or postnatal period can colour a parent's feelings for the child thereafter.

The child's characteristics

Many authors have reported that babies who are born prematurely or have feeding problems are more at risk of abuse (e.g. Greenland 1987; Browne and Saqi 1988), possibly because of their increased dependency and demands on their parents. Handicapped or ill children are also reported to be more at risk, perhaps for similar reasons of increased dependency as well as parental disappointment or guilt.

Other children are experienced as difficult to parent because they scream for no apparent reason, are temperamentally unresponsive or provocative, or have physical characteristics similar to someone else (such as a violent father). The parents might then interpret the children's behaviour as rejecting of them or else confirming that they are failures as parents.

Alternatively, parents may focus on aspects of their children's behaviour and ascribe meaning to it that originates in their own unresolved conflicts or family background. They may generalise from their own experiences and believe that their children's behaviour is typical of a hated/feared group, such as 'all men'.

> A mother seen by one of the authors had suffered sexual abuse from her father when she was a child and ascribed sexual intent to her 8 month old son as he crawled around the room and approached another woman.

In these ways, some children are perceived as 'bad' from an early age by their parents and treated accordingly.

Although much has been written about risk factors associated with children's sexual abuse (e.g. Finkelhor *et al.* 1986; Bentovim *et al.* 1988), little has been said about the reasons for a particular child becoming the victim of such abuse. De Young (1982) suggests the vulnerability of the eldest daughter and hypothesises that a daughter who looks like her mother is more especially at risk. La Fontaine (1990) also considers that eldest daughters are most at risk, as are step-daughters.

ASSESSING THE MEANING OF THE CHILD

Setting out to assess the meaning of the child does not necessarily imply that a child's psychological significance constitutes a problem. We do believe, however, that the meaning of the child is an important dimension of the parent–child relationship and should be included in assessments of child care or risk of maltreatment. Some children will be more endangered if they are failing to fulfil the expected meaning allotted to them, while others will be more at risk as a direct result of the meaning attributed to them.

It is important to bear in mind that the meaning of the child is not a self-evident truth about a family, or something which the parents can be expected to volunteer spontaneously. It is essentially an hypothesis, a construction built up by the assessor as information becomes available before and during the interviews, which the parents may either acknowledge or refute.

We have discussed elsewhere the value of using an interactional framework when assessing parenting (Reder and Lucey 1991), since it allows parental attitudes to the child and their origins to emerge as part of the overall assessment. In undertaking such assessments, it is first necessary to collate information already known about the case, including the family's composition and history and the nature of their problems over the years. Constructing the family genogram (see Reder *et al.* 1993) is an essential step and helps identify gaps in knowledge that must be filled. Patterns may then become apparent; for example that abuse of a child escalated each time the parents separated, or that the child was conceived immediately after an important loss.

Face-to-face interviews with the parents and the family as a whole allow the meaning of the child to be understood further, alongside other aspects of the parenting relationship. We use an interview style based on the systemic approach to work with families (e.g. Boscolo *et al.* 1987; Tomm 1987) which includes exploring the connections between people and events through questions of fact, circular questioning and hypothetical questions. Both sides of the family history are built up by drawing the genogram with each respective parent wherever possible. We attempt to reconstruct their life story, asking about the relationships in their family of origin and the impact of significant transitions as they grew up and eventually became parents in their own right.

Some of the parents' beliefs about their children are generally observable in family meetings, during which the children might be seen to behave in ways that confirm their parents' attitudes towards them. For instance, unwanted and rejected children may act as though they are unlovable. In subsequent individual meetings, the children are also able to convey through play or words the beliefs they hold about themselves and their place in the family.

It would be inappropriate to recommend further the form that interviews should take or suggest a list of questions that should be asked, since the assessor must be responsive to the content of the unfolding story and the accompanying emotions. However, the following excerpts from an assessment interview with a parent serve to illustrate our approach.

Ms Smith, aged 21, was referred for assessment within a few months of the birth of her son, Michael, who had been placed with foster parents on an interim care order. Staff on the postnatal ward and in a mother and baby unit had expressed considerable concern about her handling of him, which had not improved despite intensive support and advice. They felt that Ms Smith ignored Michael's everyday needs, including leaving him crying in his cot, remaining asleep herself when his feeding time was due and letting others care for him. She was described as seeming more concerned about having her own needs satisfied.

Ms Smith's had a mild physical handicap following a birth injury. She had never known her father and her mother had abandoned her to the care of her lesbian partner when she was aged 7, where she was physically and sexually abused. Ms Smith had left home in the north of England at the age of 18 and come down to London, living rough on the streets until falling pregnant with Michael from a casual liaison. She only attended for antenatal care late in the pregnancy, when encouraged to do so by a social worker.

Assessment included two individual meetings with Ms Smith and a conjoint one with the 8 month old Michael. The interviews with Ms Smith explored her personal history and its impact on her life, including these extracts:

Interviewer: What difference did it make becoming pregnant?
Ms Smith: I didn't know for a long time that I was pregnant
Interviewer: Were you pleased when you knew?
Ms Smith: Yes – when it started moving. I knew it would be a boy.
Interviewer: Were you wanting a boy or a girl?
Ms Smith: I didn't mind a boy or a girl – just so long as it was healthy.
Interviewer: How did you feel when Michael was born?
Ms Smith: Do you want to see a photograph of him – he's different now.
   I was just pleased I could have a healthy baby that was alive.
Interviewer: What did you imagine he would be like?
Ms Smith: I knew he'd be fine.
Interviewer: What made the staff on the ward worry about the way you
   were looking after Michael?
Ms Smith: I don't know what they were going on about – it was OK. They
   don't think I'm capable, just because of cerebral palsy doesn't mean I
   can't look after a child.

Later in the interview, Ms Smith was asked to anticipate her life in 5 years' time. She denied any possibility of having a permanent partner or another child.

Interviewer: What makes you say that?

Ms Smith: They'd take that one away as well. And, in any case, if I had another, Michael would then have a half-brother because I won't have another with his father. I don't want Michael having a half-brother – he'd have to have a whole brother and would have to be with his father.

Interviewer: What is Michael's father like?

Ms Smith: He's amazing . . . He's not a human being, he's an angel. I could write so many things about him. I want Michael to live with him.

Interviewer: How come?

Ms Smith: I know they won't let me have him [Michael] back. I don't want Michael to think that anyone else is his father. He's got to know who his dad is.

It appeared that the meaning of Michael to his mother operated concurrently at a number of different levels and the following constructions were developed. Ms Smith feared being a damaging mother in the same way that she experienced women having damaged her. This contrasted with an idealised fantasy about her father, which she projected on to her son and the casual partner who fathered him. She was convinced that Michael's real father would provide all he needed but this was based on a fantasy about her own absent father. Ms Smith was unable to value herself and Michael's birth was experienced as proof that she had the capacity to create something good from within her. She also wanted the child to be a boy so that he could love her as she imagined her father would have loved her. However, in reality, Michael could neither prove that she was undamaged nor love her as she wanted. Instead, she re-enacted her own history of deprivation and abandoned Michael psychologically in the same way that her parents had abandoned her.

The report to the court condensed these various ideas into an opinion that Ms Smith had an idealised image of Michael and a selective view of his emotional needs. Taken together with many other aspects of the assessment, this suggested a poor prognosis for rehabilitation.

Professionals should begin their assessments with an open mind and be prepared to consider the range of possible meanings of a child. However, in practice, it usually becomes apparent which factors are most relevant. Ms Smith, for example, offered a number of clues which linked her own sense of damage with her idealisation of Michael and his father. Sensitive interviewing enables emotional disclosures or casual comments to be used as pointers to areas which merit further exploration.

One mother commented about her 8 month old son that 'he's growing up too fast' and 'only babies accept you for what you are'. When the interviewer asked her to explain what she meant, it became evident that the mother expected young infants to be able to redress her childhood experiences of deprivation and abuse.

Finally, assessing the meaning of the child provides an opportunity to consider the potential for change and whether a parent is able to view the child differently, free from a particular meaning, and thereby reduce the risk of future maltreatment.

> The Martin couple was referred for assessment after the father had fractured his 3 month old son's femur. Mr Martin had been married before, but had no previous children, and had felt betrayed by his first wife when she had an adulterous affair. Mrs Martin was previously married to a violent man and had a 5 year old son by him. This child had transformed from a nervous and insecure boy into a happy and confident one as a result of Mr Martin's support. At assessment, it was established that both parents had wanted a child together and the pregnancy was much celebrated. His birth was felt to cement their relationship and confirm their status as a new family. Later in the interview, Mr Martin's early history was reviewed. His father had died when he was 8 years old, following a long illness. His mother had remarried soon afterwards and he had always considered his step-father as his father because the man had accepted him totally and assumed responsibility for him.
>
> During discussion about his natural father, Mr Martin cried profuse, silent tears, much to his astonishment that he would cry about someone whom he had not thought about over the years and believed he did not miss. He had presumed that his confidence as a step-father, which was based on the step-relationship he had known as a child, would be repeated with his own son. Instead, it seemed that the son's birth had awoken in him unresolved early feelings of loss and vulnerability associated with the death of his father. On the day of the son's injuries, a number of other stress factors had come together to compound this meaning, including worries about his job security, a painful back injury and anxiety about his marriage following an argument. When his son had made extra demands for care on him that he found hard to satisfy, he increasingly lost control of his feelings. Mr Martin was surprised, but interested, at the link made during the assessment interview and readily agreed to return for further psychotherapeutic work after the criminal proceedings.

CONCLUSIONS

A number of authors have touched upon the psychological meaning of children to their parents, but without fully exploring its significance. Thus, Anna Freud observes, almost as an aside, that:

> We all know from the analyses of adults how many different conscious and unconscious meanings parenthood may have to them, the infant which they have produced representing for them a continuation of their own personality, confirmation of their sexual identity, fulfilment of ideals, reincarna-

tion of loved or hated figures of the past, either a welcome or an unwelcome addition to the family, a burden, etc.

(Freud 1982: 22)

We have argued that the meaning of the child is a dynamic in all families, but some children carry a powerful meaning to their parents, which dominates their relationship and contributes to parenting breakdown. Attempts to understand this meaning should be included in all assessments of parenting.

REFERENCES

Bentovim, A. (1992) *Trauma Organised Systems: Physical and Sexual Abuse in Families*, London: Karnac.

Bentovim, A., Elton, A., Hildebrand, J., Tranter, M. and Vizard, E. (eds) (1988) *Child Sexual Abuse within the Family: Assessment and Treatment*, London: Wright.

Bonnet, C. (1993) 'Adoption at birth: prevention against abandonment or neonaticide', *Child Abuse and Neglect*, 17, 501–13.

Boscolo, L., Cecchin, G., Hoffman, L. and Penn, P. (1987) *Milan Systemic Family Therapy: Conversations in Theory and Practice*, New York: Basic Books.

Bourne, S. and Lewis, E. (1984) 'Pregnancy after stillbirth or neonatal death: psychological risks and management', *Lancet*, 2, 31–3.

Bowen, M. (1978) *Family Therapy in Clinical Practice*, New York: Jason Aronson.

Browne, K. and Saqi, S. (1988) 'Approaches to screening for child abuse and neglect', in K. Browne, C. Davies and P. Stratton (eds) *Early Prediction and Prevention of Child Abuse*, Chichester: Wiley.

Byng-Hall, J. (1973) 'Family myths used as a defence in conjoint family therapy', *British Journal of Medical Psychology*, 46, 239–50.

Byng-Hall, J. (1980) 'Symptom-bearer as marital-distance regulator: clinical implications', *Family Process*, 19, 355–66.

Byng-Hall, J. (1985) 'The family script: a useful bridge between theory and practice', *Journal of Family Therapy*, 7, 301–5.

Deutsch, H. (1945) *The Psychology of Women. Vol. 2: Motherhood*, New York: Grune and Stratton.

De Young, M. (1982) *Sexual Victimization of Children*, Jefferson NC: McFarland.

Ferreira, A. J. (1963) 'Family myth and homeostasis', *Archives of General Psychiatry*, 9, 457–63.

Finkelhor, D. *et al.* (1986) *A Sourcebook on Child Sexual Abuse*, Beverley Hills CA: Sage.

Freud, A. (1982) 'The widening scope of psychoanalytic child psychology, normal and abnormal', in *Psychoanalytic Psychology of Normal Development*, London: Hogarth.

Furniss, T. (1984) 'Conflict-avoiding and conflict-regulating patterns in incest and child sexual abuse', *Acta Paediatrica Scandinavica*, 50, 299–313.

Glaser, D., Furniss, T. and Bingley, L. (1984) 'Focal family therapy – the assessment stage', *Journal of Family Therapy*, 6, 265–74.

Goldstein, J., Freud, A. and Solnit, A.J. (1973) *Beyond the Best Interests of the Child*, New York: The Free Press.

Greenland, C. (1987) *Preventing CAN Deaths: An International Study of Deaths due to Child Abuse and Neglect*, London: Tavistock.

Haley, J. (1980) *Leaving Home: The Therapy of Disturbed Young People*, New York: McGraw-Hill.

Hoffman, L. (1982) 'A co-evolutionary framework for systemic family therapy', *Australian Journal of Family Therapy*, **4**, 9–21.

Holman, R.R. and Kanwar, S. (1975) 'Early life of the "battered child"', *Archives of Disease of Childhood*, **50**, 78–80.

Inquiry Report (1974) *Report of the Committee of Inquiry into the Care and Supervision in Relation to Maria Colwell*, London: HMSO.

Inquiry Report (1978) *Report by Professor J.D. McClean concerning Karen Spencer to the Derbyshire County Council and Derbyshire Area Health Authority.*

Inquiry Report (1989) *The Doreen Aston Report*, London: Lewisham Social Services Department.

Kinston, W. and Bentovim, A. (1981) 'Creating a focus for brief marital or family therapy', in S.H. Budman (ed.) *Forms of Brief Therapy*, New York: Guilford.

La Fontaine, J. (1990) *Child Sexual Abuse*, Cambridge: Polity Press.

Lau, A. (1984) 'Transcultural issues in family therapy', *Journal of Family Therapy*, **6**, 91–112.

Lewis, E. (1979) 'Inhibition of mourning by pregnancy: psychopathology and management', *British Medical Journal*, **2**, 27–8.

Lieberman, S. (1979) *Transgenerational Family Therapy*, London: Croom Helm.

Lynch, M. (1975) 'Ill-health and child abuse', *Lancet*, 16 August, 317–19.

McGoldrick, M. and Gerson, R. (1985) *Genograms in Family Assessment*, New York: Norton.

Messent, P. (1992) 'Working with Bangladeshi families in the East End of London', *Journal of Family Therapy*, **14**, 287–304.

Minuchin, S. (1974) *Families and Family Therapy*, London: Tavistock.

Pines, D. (1993) *A Woman's Unconscious Use of her Body: A Psychoanalytic Perspective*, London: Virago.

Poznanski, E.O. (1972) 'The "replacement child": a saga of unresolved parental grief', *Journal of Paediatrics*, **81**, 1190–3.

Reder, P. (1989) 'Freud's family', *British Journal of Psychiatry*, **154**, 93–8.

Reder, P. and Lucey, C. (1991) 'The assessment of parenting: some interactional considerations', *Psychiatric Bulletin*, **15**, 347–8.

Reder, P., Duncan, S. and Gray, M. (1993) *Beyond Blame: Child Abuse Tragedies Revisited*, London: Routledge.

Sandler, J., Dare, C. and Holder, A. (1973) *The Patient and the Analyst: The Basis of the Psychoanalytic Process*, London: George Allen and Unwin.

Sandler, J., Kennedy, H. and Tyson, R.L. (1979) 'Discussions on transference: the treatment situation and technique in child psychoanalysis', *The Psychoanalytic Study of the Child*, **30**, 409–41.

Steele, B. (1980) 'Psychodynamic factors in child abuse', in C.H. Kempe and R.E. Helfer (eds) *The Battered Child*, 3rd edn, Chicago: University of Chicago Press.

Stierlin, H. (1973) 'Group fantasies and family myths – some theoretical and practical aspects', *Family Process*, **12**, 111–25.

Stierlin, H. (1974) *Separating Parents and Adolescents*, New York: Quadrangle.

Terr, L.C. (1970) 'A family study of child abuse', *American Journal of Psychiatry*, **127**, 125–31.

Tomm, K. (1987) 'Interventive interviewing: Part II. Reflexive questioning as a means to enable self healing', *Family Process*, **26**, 167–83.

Weiselberg, H. (1992) 'Family therapy and ultra-orthodox Jewish families: a structural approach', *Journal of Family Therapy*, **14**, 305–29.

Winnicott, D. (1965) *Therapeutic Consultations in Child Psychiatry*, London: Hogarth.

Chapter 4

The child's perspective

Geraldine Fitzpatrick, Peter Reder and Clare Lucey

Assessments of parenting would be incomplete without a contribution from the child's perspective. It is essential that the children's views about their caretakers are fully represented and integrated with evaluations of the effects on their development and personality of the parenting they have received. A focus on the child also allows consideration of the child's contribution to the parenting relationship and how easy or difficult they may be to be looked after.

The importance of the child's perspective is embodied in the Children Act, which requires that, before a court grants an order on a child, it must be satisfied that 'threshold criteria' have been demonstrated and that a 'welfare check list' has been considered (Eekelaar and Dingwall 1990; White 1991). The threshold criteria first pose questions about the child. Is the child suffering, or likely to suffer, harm through ill-treatment, impairment of health, or impairment of development? Is it different from what could reasonably be expected of a similar child? If so, is the harm significant? The criteria go on to pose questions about the parents. Is the child's significant harm attributable to the care being, or likely to be, given? Is the child beyond parental control? Is the care different from what it would be reasonable to expect a parent to give? The welfare checklist includes a requirement to ascertain the wishes and feelings of the child and consider them in the light of the child's age and understanding; to consider the child's physical, emotional and educational needs; the age, sex, background and relevant characteristics of the child; and the likely effect of any changes in the child's circumstances. Many of these factors can be addressed in that part of the parenting assessment which focuses on the child.

This chapter considers how interviews with children can complement other components of the assessment and help guide opinions about their future. We shall describe a developmental framework for assessing children and illustrate how it translates into clinical practice and then comment on specific factors which need to be considered in assessments for courts. We shall confine our discussion to planned assessments of children's welfare. Initial interviews with children to investigate allegation of sexual abuse, which may become evidence in criminal proceedings, have their own specific demands and much has already been written about them (e.g. Sgroi *et al.* 1982; MacFarlane and Krebs 1986; Bentovim *et al.* 1988; Jones and McQuiston 1988; Furniss 1991; Heiman 1992). We shall refer to this literature when considering the principles of assessing children that are common to the different contexts.

At the outset, we wish to dispel a number of myths that have grown up about assessing children, which have originated from rather inflexible adherence to particular clinical models. They include beliefs that: children below the age of 7 years should not be seen individually; sessions with children should only last a few minutes to avoid them becoming anxious; a single meeting with a child is adequate for assessment; the best indicator of significant harm is a diagnosable psychiatric disorder; young children cannot be talked with; children should not be asked direct questions; and professionals' interpretations about children's play material are truths. We do not consider any of those beliefs to be valid.

A DEVELOPMENTAL FRAMEWORK

In court cases under the Children Act, mental health professionals need to base their assessments on the child's emotional and relationship development. The model that we use is our own adaptation of the concept of 'developmental lines' introduced by Anna Freud which became elaborated into the Hampstead Diagnostic Profile (Freud 1966; 1976; Eissler *et al.* 1977). This model identifies a number of pathways along which children develop physically and psychologically and allows the child's attainments to be compared with other children of a similar age and culture. The model recognises the interdependence of innate characteristics (i.e. nature) and environmental provision (i.e. nurture) and has the advantage of integrating consideration of the child's inner and outer world and the impact of real events in the child's life.

Anna Freud describes how disturbance along a particular pathway can be the result of an arrest in development, a deviation from the normal pathway, or a regression from a previously attained stage.

As each pathway is summarised, it will be apparent that there is considerable interplay between them, so that development in one area may reinforce or inhibit development in another.

Developmental pathways

Physical development

This includes the child's general physical growth and acquisition of motor skills. Stepping stones on this developmental path include the motor milestones such as the ability to walk or to manipulate objects, as well as the physical and physiological transitions that accompany adolescence. For an infant, an increasing ability to move around and explore physical space is accompanied by a psychological development of curiosity, while the sense of motor mastery is accompanied by the acquisition of body image and a sense of bodily and self-confidence.

Hence, running parallel with physical and motor development are many emotional and psychological changes. As an example, the bodily transformations and hormonal changes of adolescence are accompanied by a new sexual body image, a range of fantasies and a drive towards different relationships with others of the same and opposite sex.

As with all the other developmental lines, the fate of the pathway of physical development depends on the individual's innate biological processes and the way that the environment reinforces or discourages the natural drives.

Attachment

The pioneering work of John Bowlby emphasised that infants are social beings from birth with an innate drive to seek relationships with others. Initially the infant is emotionally, as well as physically, reliant on the parental figures and gradually is able to tolerate greater distance from them and develop towards independence. The pathway from dependence to relative independence is accompanied by increasing ability at self-care and interest in relating to others.

Good-enough experiences of attachment during the first sensitive years encourage a healthy self-esteem and sense of confidence and the ability to negotiate later separations from important figures. They also facilitate development of empathy for others and a desire for mutual give and take in relationships with them.

Socialisation

Initially, the infant exists almost in a private world with its mother, but this close dyadic relationship gradually opens up to include other family members and then those in the outside world. Motor mobility and the psychological move towards independence encourage the child's interest in, and capacity for, social interactions. Early peer group relationships are egocentric, but these become more mutual as the capacity for empathy develops. The balance of the child's relationships gradually changes from being centred in the family to greater involvement with the peer group and with adults other than the parents, such as the extended family and teachers.

Other developmental processes which affect the pathway of socialisation are the child's capacity to contain their impulses and their ability to reality test.

Moral sense

The development of morality both affects and is affected by the child's socialising behaviour. From birth, children discriminate between pleasurable and unpleasurable experiences, which later develops into preoccupations about good and bad, right and wrong. On to this primitive morality are superimposed the values of their family, culture and society and they gradually become familiar with what others consider to be right or wrong. They develop awareness of the difference between truth and falsehood, are able to experience a sense of conscience and, through monitoring their own actions and its impact on others, acquire a sense of guilt.

Awareness of an inner emotional life

Initially, the infant is mainly aware of bodily experiences and gradually becomes aware of an inner psychic world of thoughts, feelings, memories and fantasies. The child's relationship with this inner world depends on development of symbolic thought and, eventually, language. The capacity to experience and name a range of feelings increases with age. The content of fantasy life also changes with age and is influenced by inner developmental processes and by the child's external experiences. The content of this inner world appears in their drawings and imaginative play, as well as in their verbal communications.

Hence, integral with this awareness of an inner emotional life is development of the capacity to distinguish fantasy from reality and to reality test, so that behaviour is appropriate to a given situation. Children also learn to moderate their behaviour so that impulses and feelings are not immediately discharged into action.

Alongside becoming aware of their inner psychic life, children need to develop tolerance of their feelings and appropriate defences against anxiety, which, in turn, become integrated into their emerging personalities and social relationships.

Language

The development of symbolic thought and language enables children to make sense of their inner psychic processes and attribute meaning to their world. As they develop the ability to put these into words, they become able to communicate with, and understand, others and be understood by them. Symbolic thought is also an important intermediary between impulse and action, so that deviations along this pathway will affect behaviour and social interactions.

Learning

The process of learning is dependent on children's innate cognitive abilities, their curiosity and motivation to explore and encounter experiences, their concentration and emotional states and the degree to which people in their environment provide facilitation, feedback and models. The early stages include the infant's exploration of its own and its mother's body, followed by curiosity about the surrounding physical world. Tolerance of inner experiences also allows learning to take place, since the child must psychically 'take in' and 'digest' stimuli in order to discover their meaning.

Children must receive age-appropriate input from their environment and their capacity to learn from parents and teachers will depend on their relationship with them. Acquisition of a sense of morality and of a secure self-esteem and the development of social skills are examples of the other developmental pathways which run parallel with the process of learning and interrelate with it. For instance, people in the child's environment will contribute to the learning process by shaping behaviour, being models whom the child can imitate and figures with whom the child can identify.

In practice, it is possible to condense these various pathways into a number of facets of a child's functioning which can be assessed and described in a report. These are:

1 the child's appearance (e.g. size, cleanliness);
2 the child's behaviour (e.g. motor skills, concentration, containment of impulses, rapport);
3 the child's cognitive capacities (e.g. scholastic attainments, level of understanding);
4 the child's emotional life (e.g. affective state, worries, self-esteem, fantasy life, empathy, sexuality, aggression, defences);
5 the child's relationships (with self, family, peers and significant others).

The effects of adverse parenting on development

Wolfe (1987), Lynch (1988) and Corby (1993) usefully summarise the relevant literature on the consequences of adverse parenting on children's development. A number of emotional and relationship problems are commonly described and this knowledge can help guide the assessment.

A consistent finding with physically abused children is that it is the emotional quality of the parenting, rather than the actual physical abuse, that is so psychologically damaging. The inconsistent care, rejection and neglect that they also suffer leaves them with many of the following features. They may develop compulsively self-reliant and pseudo-mature behaviour, or else are clinging and anxiously attached (Bowlby 1977). Some are overactive, aggressive and provocative, while others appear excessively compliant and eager to please, which in extreme cases appears as frozen watchfulness

(Ounsted 1972). An impoverished self-esteem is common, together with a tendency for self-blame, and relationships with peers are often characterised by isolation, lack of trust and aggressiveness, perhaps coupled with indifference to the distress of others. They underachieve at school and show generally depressive affect and joylessness. Growth failure is not uncommon.

Sexually abused children tend to show either anxious and fearful withdrawal or aggressiveness, often have poor self-image and perform inadequately at school. Precocious sexualised behaviour is exhibited by a significant number of sexually abused children. Smith (1992) describes disturbances to children's sense of identity, self-esteem, affective range, communication skills, sense of responsibility, attitudes to power and authority, ability to judge people and situations, capacity to make and sustain relationships and sexual development as a result of sexual abuse.

Anna Freud (1976) points out that there is no one-to-one relationship between adverse parenting and the distortions that might result in the child's personality development. Cruel treatment can produce either an aggressive and violent, or a timid, crushed and passive being; parental seduction can result in either complete inability to control sexual impulses, or in severe sexual inhibition. She adds that: 'The developmental outcome is determined not by the environmental interference per se, but by its interaction with the inborn and acquired resources of the child.'

Resilience

The resilience of some children to poor parenting has been commented on by Mrazek and Mrazek (1987) and Lynch (1988), among others. While reliable predictions are not possible in individual cases, these authors suggest that children are less damaged by adverse care when they are of above average intelligence, have few placement changes and are able to form friendly and trusting relationships with others.

Rutter (1985) proposes that resilience to adverse experiences comes about through a combination of factors. A secure relationship with one parent can substantially mitigate the effects of an insecure relationship with the other. Children are more protected from the adverse effects of separations if they are not anxiously or insecurely attached, have been well prepared for the separation, have had previous happy separations, are below the age of about 6 months (because very young infants lack the capacity for enduring selective attachments), or are of school age (because they have the cognitive skills to appreciate that it is possible to maintain attachment relationships over a period of absence). The meaning attributed to the events is also relevant, especially the degree to which children adjust their self-perceptions towards failure, shame, helplessness or hopelessness about the future. This may be a function of the temperament of the child, the timing of the event, or the availability of support. A capacity to distance themselves emotionally from unalterable bad situations is also protective, as is the ability to find a coping strategy and to act rather than react. Success in one arena of life, such as good experiences at school, lead to enhanced self-esteem and a feeling of self-efficacy and help overcome poor care experiences.

CLINICAL APPROACH

Assessment from the child's perspective can be divided into three phases – organising the history, interviewing the child and observing the child together with the relevant adult(s). This information is then integrated together with assessment of the parental figures and family in order to generate an overall opinion.

The history – 'punctuating around the child'

It is usually possible to review what is known about the history of the family from submitted documentation and by meeting with the involved social worker. As part of this, we draw up a chronology of significant events that were experienced by the child, such as changes of caretakers, separations, lengths of time spent with significant caretakers (and therefore opportunities for attachment), house moves, births, deaths, exposure to family violence or abusing adults. All this is interwoven with information about any problems shown by the child or concerns about maltreatment.

This produces a summary of family events as they would have impinged on the child and allows preliminary ideas to emerge about which aspects of the interview might be particularly important. For example, we would be especially interested in the quality of attachment behaviour when seeing a child who has had many changes of caretaker. The chronology also suggests whether additional information would be helpful to the overall assessment, such as school or medical reports.

Individual interviews

More than one appointment with the child is generally required and it may take three, five or more meetings to gain a child's confidence and adequately understand their functioning and views. Each meeting usually lasts between 45 minutes to an hour, although this is tailored to the length of time that is tolerable for the child. The interviewer should appear as a real, interested, sympathetic person who is allied to the child's ego functioning and observing self – in other words, is concerned to understand with the child their thoughts, feelings and experiences and will facilitate reality testing. For example, it is essential that the interviewer begins by enquiring about the child's understanding of the purpose of the meetings and to confirm or clarify this if necessary. Preferably, the child should be seen alone, but young children may need to be reassured by a trusted adult sitting in the corner of the room or immediately outside the door.

Assessment begins with observation, and even the first meeting in the waiting room is an opportunity for the professional to observe aspects of the child's development and functioning. These include the way that the child behaves, how the child relates to the accompanying parent or adult and how the child separates from them. In the interview room, other important observations are how the child engages with a strange adult and uses the play material and the opportunity to convey to an interested person something about their life. Any specific characteristics, such as a mannerism, will also be noted. The child's physical care is usually reflected in their general appearance, such as cleanliness and size. The child's motor and learning skills can usually be gauged informally during interviews and confirmed by school reports, but, occasionally, arrangements need to be made for more formal psychological assessment. If failure to thrive or neglect is suspected, the child will require a full medical examination.

Ideally, the interviews should be conducted as unstructured 'chats' which enable the child to share their preoccupations, worries and wishes. Sometimes, the process needs guiding by the professional, but the child should not feel unduly pressured to disclose something, because the professional will have no way of *knowing* what there is to be revealed and the pace needs to be one that is comfortable for the child. The child will also be aware that they have the choice of either communicating verbally or through other means, such as play or drawings. Hence, pencils, crayons, paper, doll's house, dolls and other simple toys are put out and available for use. The child should be able to understand the professional's questions because care is taken to use age-appropriate language, concepts and sentence construction (Steward *et al.* 1993).

Occasionally, children who are finding difficulty communicating may be engaged through more structured play. It may be useful to ask the child to draw their family, since they can convey an impression of their relationships and feelings to others through simple line drawings. The Bene–Anthony Family Relations Test (Anthony and Bene 1957) encourages children to report their feelings about family members by 'posting' descriptions about them into different boxes.

By the end of the individual meetings, the interviewer should have some understanding of the child's experiences *from the child's perspective* and the impact of these on the child's development, functioning and feelings towards important people in their lives. The child, too, should have gained a sense that they can be understood and that someone is interested in their welfare.

Observing the child with relevant adults

Observing a meeting between the child and relevant adult (such as father applying for a residence order) helps assessment of the parent's attitude to the child, the child's attitude to the parent and their responses to each other. Even though such meetings have an air of artificiality when they occur in a clinical setting, they do, nonetheless, reveal many aspects of the parent–child relationship.

In particular, it is possible to notice whether a child is comfortable in the parent's presence, wants the parent to be interested in what they are doing and is able to turn to them for comfort. Alternatively, a child may appear apprehensive or fearful of the adult, perhaps turning instead to the interviewer. Children's loyalty conflicts, or anxiety about their parents' hostility to each other, may show in their reluctance to greet the non-custodial parent and withdrawal from him or her, which only thaws as the meeting progresses.

The quality of the attachment can be noted, such as a child who cannot bear any separation from the parent, or a child who appears indifferent and self-reliant. Observing interaction between child and parent may reveal a child desperate to elicit some response from the parent who does not respond. The child might draw greetings cards for the parent and offer them as a present, or climb up on their lap in order to be cuddled. Some parents do not react, perhaps because of lack of interest or else because of a psychiatric disorder that blunts their affective responses. Such sequences can be described from the child's perspective in reports to courts.

SPECIFIC CONSIDERATIONS

There are a number of specific issues which assessors need to be aware of when forming opinions based on interviews with children. It is important to have already considered their relevance during the assessment, since they may be raised during cross-examination in court, and they include issues of children's memory, cognitive ability, communication, suggestibility and the validity of their statements and interpretations made of their drawings. The literature on these topics has tended to focus on assessing allegations of child sexual abuse and the current knowledge and has been well reviewed by Waterman (1986), Jones and McQuiston (1988), Fundudis (1989), Sivan (1991), Perry and Wrightsman (1991) and Steward *et al.* (1993). The principles are clearly applicable to other examples of parenting breakdown and we shall summarise their main conclusions.

Memory

Children's memory of an event, like that of adults, may change, depending on the circumstances under which the event occurred and on the psychological state of the person subsequently. A forgetting curve occurs in both adults and children, but the long-term capacity of children to recall past events appears to be as good as adults. Young children (below the age of about 5) tend to recall fewer details than adults about any particular event, but this improves and becomes comparable to adults by the age of 10–12. Events of central importance to the child are better recalled than peripheral ones and even young children have the capacity to place events in the correct temporal order if they are of central importance to them. After the age of approximately 6 years, children are as accurate as adults at identifying a face from memory.

Young children often need support for their memories through external cues or reminders. The amount and accuracy of events recalled during interviews increases when familiar types of toys are available to help the child play out or demonstrate what happened and there is no evidence that their presence distorts the child's memory.

Children with learning disability have poorer memory ability than children of average intelligence and require more time to respond. They perform much better on recognition memory (for example, 'have you seen the man in this picture before?') than on free recall memory (for example, 'when did the man give you money?').

Cognitive ability and communication

Pre-schoolers have adequate vocabulary for talking about the here and now, but, although they can recount past experiences accurately, they do not have a fully developed concept of time, or use the past tense or recall information sequentially. By their fourth year, children are using past and future tense, but their judgements about time are still tied to associated routines, such as meals or television programmes, and more accurate judgements related to clocks or calendars develop in the school years.

When children begin to use language, they have difficulty separating out exemplars from classes, so that a pre-schooler may use 'daddy' to represent all male adults. Pre-school children are not able to keep two concepts in mind at the same time and most children's accounts of complex events, or of issues with a high level of abstraction, improve when they are broken down into simple, more manageable units. Otherwise, they may only respond to that part of the question they have understood, ignoring other elements that the interviewer might consider crucial. Pre-schoolers also need to have yes/no questions followed up by more open-ended ones. Three year olds begin to understand 'what', 'where' and 'who' questions, but only 5 or 6 year olds can consistently respond to 'why', 'when' and 'how'. Five to ten year olds gradually understand and use longer and more complex sentences and multisyllabic words. Nonetheless, even young children can give quite accurate, logical and well-structured accounts of events that have meaning for their lives.

MacFarlane and Krebs (1986) recommend clarifying with children precisely what objects or persons they are talking about and asking them to demonstrate with drawings, toys or dolls exactly what happened.

Suggestibility

Both adults and children are suggestible, which may distort their memory, but the memories that are most susceptible are of events of less central importance or personal poignancy to them. Children's suggestibility may be particularly vulnerable to the perceived authority of the interviewer. Although persistent leading questions during an interview can produce errors, especially with younger children, events of central importance to the child are more difficult to distort in this way. Furthermore, children will resist agreeing with misleading, abuse-related questions.

Children may be rehearsed by an adult to report abuse that did not happen, although this is said to be rare (MacFarlane 1986). Their verbal accounts are more likely to be valid when: they contain explicit detail, including peripheral information about the context of the events (although under fives are generally not able to relate as much detail as older children); their words and phrases are age appropriate, but the sexual content is not; they are described from the child's perspective; they are accompanied by appropriate affect, including initial hesitancy at relating anxiety-laden material; and they are consistent over time (see also MacFarlane and Krebs 1986; Jones and McGraw 1987; Faller 1988; Heiman 1992). In Jones and McGraw's study, only 2 per cent of children were deemed to have made fictitious allegations of sexual abuse, a figure with which Adshead (1994) would concur from her literature review.

Validity

Children do not generally confuse fact and fantasy and they acquire the capacity to make the distinction from about the age of 2 years. This comes about through development of the ability to distinguish self from others, to name and identify objects, to make simple inferences about cause and effect and to appreciate the concept of permanence of objects. Three year olds clearly recognise the difference between pretend play with material and its real nature. Although young children may have problems distinguishing between what they have actually done and what they thought of doing, only a small percentage recall fantasy in their reports of abuse and they are capable of distinguishing between actual events and what they dreamt of doing.

Hill (1985) summarises a number of studies which show that the accuracy of children's self-reports depends on their developmental capacities, including their ability to understand the question and the interviewer's purpose, but, when their answers are able to be verified by an impartial parent, there is a high degree of consistency. Younger children are more likely to focus on observable aspects of emotions, such as its behavioural manifestations and the setting in which it was experienced, rather than provide a detailed account of their feelings.

Four year olds know the difference between telling the truth and telling lies and that it is considered wrong to lie. In reporting unpleasant bodily experiences, children are more likely to make errors of omission than commission. When allowed to tell a tale in their own words, pre-school children do not create a false picture. They may ignore particular features, but, when prompted, they can add relevant and true details.

With regard to sexual fantasies, Waterman (1986) concludes that pre-schoolers tend to wonder where babies come from and are interested in physical differences between boys and girls. Most children become very aware of sex-role differences when they reach school age. However, concern about sexual intercourse or other forms of adult sexual behaviour is very rare in children who have not been involved in, or exposed to, such behaviour.

There is also good evidence that aggressiveness in children is associated with excessive physical punishment by parents, especially when coupled with coldness and rejection (Shaffer *et al.* 1980; Vissing *et al.* 1991) and it is a widespread clinical impression that children repeat in their play aggression that they have experienced themselves (e.g. Kempe and Kempe 1978).

Denial

Children, like adults, may not acknowledge the existence of current problems because they fear the possible consequences of doing so. Psychological conflict leads them to deny allegations by others that they are being abused, or to retract their own previous disclosure (Summit 1983). Four per cent of the children studied by Jones and McGraw (1987) subsequently recanted their allegations. Furniss (1991) summarises the likely feared consequences of children once they have disclosed sexual abuse. These include: fear of being taken into care; of losing one or both parents; of not being believed; of being punished or the abuser's threats coming true; of being the cause of the abuser's punishment; of being blamed; or adverse reactions from peers. Children can be asked during the interview whether particular fears are affecting what they feel able to say. Loyalty to one of the parents, especially during acrimonious divorce proceedings (MacFarlane 1986; Bresee *et al.* 1986), may produce similar conflicts for children.

Furthermore, we know from clinical work with children that they have different ways of processing adverse experiences. Some can only deal with them internally, without talking to someone else; others may need to recall them just one small element at a time, over a lengthy period (e.g. Alvarez 1992).

MacFarlane and Krebs (1986) note that children may initially deny that they ever experienced abuse, but then acknowledge it in a displaced way – such as suggesting that it occurred while they were asleep, or to another child. Asking a denying child if something 'may have', or 'sometimes' happened can give them an opportunity to begin to acknowledge abusive experiences and go on to describe them in more detail.

Interpretation of children's drawings

Children use drawings as a means of symbolic expression and communication about inner experiences and therapists commonly focus on the meaning of children's drawings, generating hypotheses and exploring them with the child (e.g. Szur 1983; Dale 1992). Burgess and Hartman (1993) review research on children's drawings and conclude that children can divulge unconscious attitudes by altering line quality, disguising shapes and using unusual signs or symbols. For example, Burgess (1988) compared the drawings of abused and non-abused children and showed that abused children more frequently included sexualised body parts or shaded over the body parts and drew sad or expressionless figures.

Moore (1994) concludes that the human figure drawings of abused children offer a valid and reliable measure of self-expression. She reports that children usually represent anxiety through intensity of line pressure, excessive shading, smallness of the figure and rigidity of the drawing process. Graphic representation of genitals on a figure is likely to be associated with a history of sexual abuse. Heavily scratched areas and repeated overworked lines across the body may reflect physical abuse. Arms drawn as though the hands have been torn off are said to be common from children who have been tied up during their abuse. Despite these common associations, Moore adds the important warning that inferences about children's drawings must be correlated with other independent sources of information.

Practical implications

Psychological and clinical research has been important in dispelling many prejudices about the veracity of children's reports. However, research findings do not always accurately translate into everyday experience. For example, while young children are *capable* of distinguishing fact from fantasy, they also occasionally relate stories that their parents know did not happen (albeit, usually about innocuous happenings rather than mistreatment). When clinicians hear a seemingly fantastic story from a young child, they are faced with the difficult task of assessing whether the account is true, exaggerated or made up. Is the child blurring fact and fantasy? Is the child struggling with an intolerable psychological conflict? And if a child denies that any mistreatment occurred, might this be because of repression, or loyalty, or fear of the consequences?

Sometimes, the assessor will never know whether a child's report of specific experiences or denial of any adverse experiences are true or not and they must be prepared to end the assessment still unsure. A child's account of events is very likely to be valid if the events are not within the normal range of experiences for a child of that age and background or within the usual range of such a child's fantasy life (see Waterman 1986). According to Sivan (1991), 'the rich fantasy life of the pre-schooler is over-worked; it is a myth' and it is most likely that the reports of young children about abuse are based on reality and their constructions, whether in words or play, are not likely to be pure fantasy. Bowlby (e.g. Bowly 1940; 1979) had long held that children's material, often dismissed as fantasy by therapists, should be considered as based on actual experience.

It is helpful to distinguish children's reports about events from the more abstract issues of their feelings about other people or opinions about their future. Children can often discuss their wishes about their future, but the assessor must also be prepared for children to change their mind. If the issue concerns which parent the child will live with, changes of mind over time usually reflect mixed feeling, which can be explored over a series of meetings. In addition, children may express a wish to remain with abusing parents for a variety of reasons. They may be unaware that better care is possible, or believe that they do not deserve to receive it. They may have an internalised view of themselves as a powerless victim, or have experienced phases of good-enough parenting between episodes of maltreatment.

CONCLUSIONS

Assessment from the child's perspective enables a picture to emerge of their physical, emotional and relationship development and whether these developmental lines have been harmed by adverse parenting experiences. Therefore, the concept of significant harm introduced in the Children Act is a valuable one. In order to address the significance of any harm, mental health professionals will need to weigh up the relative impact of each developmental disturbance on the child's overall functioning, as well as their cumulative effect. Extremes of disturbance will pose little difficulty, but few adequate guidelines exist to assist the opinion in marginal cases. In our view, the presence or absence of a psychiatric disorder is not an adequate guide to significant harm, since psychiatric diagnoses do not do justice to the complexities of children's emotional and relationship development.

The final opinion to a court will be a balancing out of many issues: the degree of harm suffered by the child along each developmental pathway; the impact of such harm on the child's overall development; an understanding of the child's views in the light of their experiences and conflicts; the likely outcome for the child's development of the present care continuing, or of proposed changes in care; and whether therapeutic help would make a difference to the child's development.

It is essential that detailed assessments of the impact on the child of their experiences are able to be fully considered by courts. However, court hearings sometimes become skewed by an assumption that, if allegations have been made about one form of child abuse, then all that needs to be considered is whether that abuse did, or did not, take place. For example, courts commonly become so preoccupied with the question of whether a child was sexually abused that they ignore the wider question of whether the child has suffered serious neglect or emotional abuse. The component of assessment which focuses on the child should aim to integrate all aspects of the child's experiences and ensure that they are made known to the court.

REFERENCES

Adshead, G. (1994) 'Looking for clues: a review of the literature on false allegations of sexual abuse in childhood', in V. Sinason (ed.) *Treating Survivors of Satanist Abuse*, London: Routledge.

Alvarez, A. (1992) 'Child sexual abuse: the need to remember and the need to forget', in *Live Company: Psychoanalytic Psychotherapy with Autistic, Borderline, Deprived and Abused Children*, London: Routledge.

Anthony, J. and Bene, E. (1957) 'A technique for the objective assessment of the child's family relationships', *Journal of Mental Science*, **103**, 541–55.

Bentovim, A., Elton, A., Hildebrand, J., Tranter, M. and Vizard, E. (eds) (1988) *Child Sexual Abuse within the Family: Assessment and Treatment*, London: Wright.

Bowlby, J. (1940) 'The influence of early environment in the development of neurosis and neurotic character', *International Journal of Psycho-Analysis*, **21**, 154–78.

Bowlby, J. (1977) 'The making and breaking of affectional bonds', *British Journal of Psychiatry*, **130**, 201–10 and 421–31.

Bowlby, J. (1979) 'On knowing what you are not supposed to know and feeling what you are not supposed to feel', *Canadian Journal of Psychiatry*, **24**, 403–8.

Bresee, P., Stearns, G.B., Bess, B.H. and Packer, L.S. (1986) 'Allegations of child sexual abuse in child custody disputes', *American Journal of Orthopsychiatry*, **56**, 560–9.

Burgess, A.W. and Hartman, C.R. (1993) 'Children's drawings', *Child Abuse and Neglect*, **17**, 161–8.

Burgess, E.J. (1988) 'Sexually abused children and their drawings', *Archives of Psychiatric Nursing*, **2**, 65–73.

Corby, B. (1993) 'The consequences of child abuse', in *Child Abuse: Towards a Knowledge Base*, Milton Keynes: Open University Press.

Dale, F. (1992) 'The art of communicating with vulnerable children', in V. Varma (ed.) *The Secret Life of Vulnerable Children*, London: Routledge.

Eekelaar, J. and Dingwall, R. (1990) *The Reform of Child Care Law: A Practical Guide to the Children Act 1989*, London: Routledge.

Eissler, R.S., Freud, A., Kris, M. and Solnit, A.J. (eds) (1977) *Psychoanalytic Assessment: The Diagnostic Profile*, New Haven CT: Yale University Press.

Faller, K.C. (1988) 'Criteria for judging the credibility of children's statements about their sexual abuse', *Child Welfare*, **67**, 389–401.

Freud, A. (1966) *Normality and Pathology in Childhood*, London: Hogarth.

Freud, A. (1976) 'Psychopathology seen against the background of normal development', *British Journal of Psychiatry*, **129**, 401–6.

Fundudis, T. (1989) Annotation: 'Children's memory and the assessment of possible child sexual abuse', *Journal of Child Psychology and Psychiatry*, **30**, 337–46.

Furniss, T. (1991) *The Multi-Professional Handbook of Child Sexual Abuse: Integrated Management, Therapy and Legal Interventions*, London: Routledge.

Heiman, M.L. (1992) Annotation: 'Putting the puzzle together: validating allegations of child sexual abuse', *Journal of Child Psychology and Psychiatry*, **33**, 311–29.

Hill, P. (1985) 'The diagnostic interview with the individual child', in M. Rutter and L. Hersov (eds) *Child and Adolescent Psychiatry: Modern Approaches*, 2nd edn, Oxford: Blackwell.

Jones, D.P.H. and McGraw, J.M. (1987) 'Reliable and fictitious accounts of sexual abuse to children', *Journal of Interpersonal Violence*, **2**, 27–45.

Jones, D.P.H. and McQuiston, M.G. (1988) *Interviewing the Sexually Abused Child*, London: Gaskell.

Kempe, R.S. and Kempe, C.H. (1978) 'The abused child', in *Child Abuse*, London: Open Books.

Lynch, M. (1988) 'The consequences of child abuse', in K. Browne, C. Davies and P. Stratton (eds) *Early Prediction and Prevention of Child Abuse*, Chichester: Wiley.

MacFarlane, K. (1986) 'Child sexual abuse allegations in divorce proceedings', in K. MacFarlane, J. Waterman, S. Conerly, L. Damon, M. Durfee and S. Long (eds) *Sexual Abuse of Young Children*, London: Holt, Rinehart and Winston.

MacFarlane, K. and Krebs, S. (1986) 'Techniques for interviewing and evidence gathering', in K. MacFarlane, J. Waterman, S. Conerly, L. Damon, M. Durfee and S. Long (eds) *Sexual Abuse of Young Children*, London: Holt, Rinehart and Winston.

Moore, M.S. (1994) 'Common characteristics in the drawings of ritually abused children and adults', in V. Sinason (ed.) *Treating Survivors of Satanist Abuse*, London: Routledge.

Mrazek, P. and Mrazek, D. (1987) 'Resilience in child maltreatment victims: a conceptual exploration', *Child Abuse and Neglect*, **11**, 357–66.

Ounsted, C. (1972) 'Biographical science: an essay on developmental medicine', in B. Mandelbrote and M.C. Gelder (eds) *Psychiatric Aspects of Medical Practice*, London: Staples.

Perry, N.S. and Wrightsman, L.S. (1991) *The Child Witness: Legal Issues and Dilemmas*, Newbury Park CA: Sage.

Rutter, M. (1985) 'Resilience in the face of adversity: protective factors and resistance to psychiatric disorder', *British Journal of Psychiatry*, **147**, 598–611.

Sgroi, S.M., Porter, F.S. and Blick, L.C. (1982) 'Validation of child sexual abuse', in S.M. Sgroi (ed.) *Handbook of Clinical Intervention in Child Sexual Abuse*, Lexington MA: Lexington Books.

Shaffer, D., Meyer-Bahlburg, F.L. and Stokman, C.L.J. (1980) 'The development of aggression', in M. Rutter (ed.) *Scientific Foundations of Developmental Psychiatry*, London: Heinemann.

Sivan, A.B. (1991) 'Preschool child development: implications for investigation of child abuse allegations', *Child Abuse and Neglect*, **15**, 485–93.

Smith, G. (1992) 'The unbearable traumatogenic past: child sexual abuse', in V. Varma (ed.) *The Secret Life of Vulnerable Children*, London: Routledge.

Steward, M.S., Bussey, K., Goodman, G.S. and Sayitz, K.J. (1993) 'Implications of developmental research for interviewing children', *Child Abuse and Neglect*, **17**, 25–37.

Summit, R.C. (1983) 'The child sexual abuse accommodation syndrome', *Child Abuse and Neglect*, **7**, 177–93.

Szur, R. (1983) 'Sexuality and aggression as related themes', in M. Boston and R. Szur (eds) *Psychotherapy with Severely Deprived Children*, London: Routledge and Kegan Paul.

Vissing, Y.M., Straus, M.A., Gelles, R.A. and Harrop, J.W. (1991) 'Verbal aggression by parents and psychosocial problems of children', *Child Abuse and Neglect*, **15**, 223–38.

Waterman, J. (1986) 'Developmental considerations', in K. MacFarlane, J. Waterman, S. Conerly, L. Damon, M. Durfee and S. Long (eds) *Sexual Abuse of Young Children*, London: Holt, Rinehart and Winston.

White, R. (1991) 'Examining the threshold criteria', in M. Adcock, R. White and A. Hollows (eds) *Significant Harm*, Croydon: Significant Publications.

Wolfe, D.A. (1987) 'A developmental perspective of the abused child', in *Child Abuse: Implications for Child Development and Psychopathology*, Newbury Park CA: Sage.

Chapter 5

Emotionally abusive experiences
Danya Glaser

INTRODUCTION

In the context of the assessment of parenting, the consideration of emotional abuse is particularly relevant. When professionals become concerned about the welfare of a child for any reason, emotional abuse may well lie at the root of the problems. Due to its pervasive and long-lasting nature, emotional abuse is particulary damaging to the child.

Unlike some forms of child abuse where the abuser and caregiver are not usually one and the same person (for instance in child sexual abuse), in emotional abuse, the abusing (or neglecting) and caregiving functions are expressed by the same person. Attachment Theory assumes innate proximity-seeking behaviour by the child towards his or her caregiver in the underlying quest for physical and emotional comfort and, ultimately, survival (Bowlby 1989). It might be postulated that the cognitions underpinning Attachment Theory contain assumptions by the child about the availability, benevolence, dependability and coherence of the attachment person(s) and their actions. The young child's need to make sense of their experiences, and the child's tendency to self-referential and egocentric explanations, often lead them to attribute to themselves the causes of the cognitive dissonances (between their expectations of the attachment person and their actual experiences). In clinical encounters, children who are considered to have suffered emotional abuse often describe themselves as bad, believe themselves to be worthless and unlovable and feel stupid.

Two issues arise. The first pertains to the question of the actual presence of emotional abuse. The second is the question of the capacity for sufficient change in the parent(s)' relationship to the child. Implicit in the term 'abuse' is the concern that the nature of this parent–child relationship may not continue to serve the child's best interests and needs, unless a change in the relationship is possible. It suggests the need for an assessment whose purpose is to determine whether there are grounds for mandated intervention. Abuse is thus more than socially undesirable interaction and carries with it an implication for professional action.

The physical consequences of the various forms of child abuse and neglect are well recognised and include injury and death, poor growth, infection and pregnancy. Beyond the physical sequelae, it is likely that the meaning of these experiences affect the development and emotional and psychological well-being of the child. However, for their expression and effects on the child, emotional and psychological abuse and neglect do not require any physical contact with, or physical neglect of, the child by the parent. Emotional abuse often coexists with other forms of child maltreatment and neglect, including non-accidental injury (Claussen and Crittenden 1991), neglect, sexual abuse and Munchausen syndrome by proxy. There are thus various circumstances which are associated with emotional abuse or neglect of the child.

DEFINITIONS OF EMOTIONAL ABUSE

The difficulties met in attempting to define emotional abuse have been repeatedly noted. An entire issue of a journal was devoted to this problem (Cicchetti and Nurcombe 1991). The issues raised by the various contributors include the question of whether the definition of emotional abuse requires both the evidence of parental action as well as evidence of damage to the child (Barnett *et al.* 1991). Both are required in the definition of emotional abuse in *Working Together* (Home Office *et al.* 1991). However, evidence of either is accepted as sufficient in the definition of significant harm in the Children Act (1989), while McGee and Wolfe (1991) consider that the definition should be based on parental action alone. The problem with awaiting evidence of damage before intervening, especially with young children, lies in the difficulty of predicting whether, or for how long, a resilient child will continue to be so. There is also the uncertainty of having to depend on other, secondary relationships to be protective for the child. For these reasons, it is preferable to attend to the parental behaviours and attitudes in seeking to recognise emotional abuse. However, it is important to note that, in practice, mandated intervention, as opposed to assessment, is likely to require evidence of harm to the child. The task of assessment of parenting, once initiated, needs to focus equally on the presence or absence of the abuse and on the capacity for change.

As will be discussed, the definition of emotional abuse relies on quantitative as well as qualitative considerations, since aspects of emotionally abusive interactions probably occur sporadically in many parent–child interactions. Qualitatively, emotional abuse may well have at its core the targeting of the child's emotional and psychological well-being and development through acts of omission and commission. The parent(s)' intent may not be actively malevolent and the harm often occurs by the failure to attend to the child's needs and rights. There are several different dimensions along which emotional abuse and neglect may be expressed. Qualitative dimensions facilitate description of, and communication about, the aspects of the otherwise undefined field of emotional abuse. These dimensions may coexist but each one carries qualitatively different implications and meanings for the child. Furthermore, therapeutic intervention, the response to which often becomes part of the assessment, will differ according to the nature of the emotional abuse.

QUALITATIVE DIMENSIONS OF EMOTIONAL ABUSE

Persistent negative or mis-attributions to the child

Parental beliefs about the child determine to a considerable extent the nature of the parent's attitude to, behaviour towards and expectations of the child. This dimension is expressed by repeated or persistent denigration, hostility, belittling or blaming of the child; by holding the child responsible for misfortunes and by threats of, or actual, severe punishment, consonant with the parental belief about what the child deserves. Conditional parenting, in which the child's secure place within the family is made contingent on her or his good behaviour is another consequence of negative attribution to the child.

Parents' attributions to their children are often related to the parents' own childhood experiences or may be based on the perceived similarity between the child and a related family member such as an absent father. Mis-attributions may also arise as an explanation for the child's behaviour. The difficulty with attributions is their implied innateness in the child and the consequent improbability of possible change. For example,

a mother attributed much of the bad behaviour of two of her three children to the Chinese ancestry of their father. She consequently felt unable to prevail over them. They, in turn, regarded themselves as bad and tended to behave accordingly.

A mother of a 4 year old girl believed her daughter to hold power over her. She perceived the child as making her mother do things and blamed her for many of her difficulties.

The mother and step-father of an 8 year old, very able girl found great difficulty controlling her behaviour and in interacting with her in a positive way. The girl and her brother had been in care twice during their early years and the girl had subsequently been beaten by the step-father, who had by now relinquished any responsibility for her. The mother believed that the girl was deliberately persecuting her and was seeking a change in the girl, threatening her with a request for accommodation into care.

A mother of a girl who had been sexually abused by her step-father persisted in blaming her daughter for seducing the abuser and for wilfully failing to alert her mother to the abuse.

Emotional unavailability, unresponsiveness and neglect

Maternal depression, parental alcohol abuse and childhood experiences may leave parents unable to recognise or respond to their children's attachment and emotional needs. For example,

> a mother was observed in a day unit to repeatedly fail to console her young child when the latter was hurt.

> The departure of his children's mother left a father devastated and unable to respond to his two children's emotional needs, including strongly discouraging mention of their mother, even though they wanted to talk about her loss. He was nevertheless able to continue to care for their physical needs.

> The mother of a 2 year old child was diagnosed as suffering from chronic fatigue syndrome, rendering her severely fatigued and unable to respond to her son's emotional needs. His father was more responsive but following the birth of a much wanted girl, turned his attention to her, leaving the boy feeling unwanted.

Failure to recognise or respect the child's individuality and psychological boundary

This is expressed by parental behaviours and attitudes towards the child, or deployment or deprivation of the child who finds himself or herself fulfilling the psychological needs of the parent(s). A parent's poor sense of their own self, an extreme degree of self-centredness and preoccupation with their own emotional needs which may include substance misuse, or a deep sense of identification with the child may all lead to the exploitation of, and detriment to, the child. For example,

> an anxious boy of 10, the only son of divorced parents, was living with his mother. The father, himself a very anxious man, had not forgiven his ex-wife for leaving him. As well as repeatedly denigrating her to the boy, he gave the boy a telephone and would speak to him several times during a day. The boy was encouraged to contact his father whenever he felt worried or in any conflict with his mother, whom he came to abuse verbally.

> A mother was unable to believe the credible allegations of sexual abuse made by her 7 year old daughter against her step-father, even in the presence of compatible physical signs. The mother was also unable to face her own severe childhood sexual abuse and blamed the child for threatening her second marriage.

Inappropriate or inconsistent developmental expectations and considerations

These considerations and expectations differ according to the child's position along the developmental spectrum and are expressed by:

- premature imposition of physical and psychological responsibility on the child;
- inappropriate or inconsistent expectations of a young child in terms of understanding, behaviour and internal controls;
- failure to protect from inappropriate experiences;
- confusing communication and distortions of 'objective truth';
- overprotection and failure to provide age-appropriate opportunities for cognitive and emotional learning experiences.

Some parents lack basic parenting skills to a significant degree. They are unaware of children's developmental needs and capabilities and have inappropriate and unreal expectations of them. They may also be oblivious to the harm which may be caused by inconsistency or the failure to protect children from exposure to some experiences. Others believe that threats or harsh punishment and deprivation of pleasure are effective ways of inculcating and maintaining discipline and control. These beliefs are often based on parents' own childhood experiences. For example,

the parents of a 6 year old girl repeatedly expected her to look after her 2 year old brother around the house. When he hurt himself, they rounded on her.

The parents of a 5 year old boy persisted in telling him that his dead baby brother had been taken by Jesus while asleep in his cot. The boy became fearful of lying down at night and refused to go to church for which his parents disciplined him, despite advice from the health visitor.

The mother of a 4 year old boy was inconsistent in her responses to his active and adventurous behaviour, at times punishing him and at others admiring his independence. Due to her oppressive and punitive upbringing, she would frequently threaten him with extreme punishments, which she was then unable to carry out.

A 9 year old, anxious and able boy, the only child of middle-class older parents, was at the point of exclusion from school due to his very aggressive retaliatory behaviour towards other children. He had suffered from several bouts of major illness in earlier years, and ptosis of one eye. Like his maternal uncle, he was fearful at night and clingy to his parents at home. The parents were extremely reluctant to encourage his independence at home, to allow him to increase his tolerance for frustration and to master his anxieties and accept limits.

Mis-socialisation in context

This is expressed through actively promoting the child's mis-socialisation or failing to promote the child's social adaptation. A parent incapacitated through psychotic or delusional beliefs may involve the child in the expression of, or response to, these beliefs and experiences. For example,

> a mother who suffered from recurrent paranoid states lived in complete isolation with her 4 year old daughter, sharing food on the same plate as well as sleeping in the same bed. The child was unable to play with toys, did not interact with other children when she met them and spoke using adult phrases.

> The uncle of a child whose care had been entrusted to him and his wife by the boy's mother repeatedly involved the 5 year old boy in stealing.

> A 6 year old girl from a non-English-speaking ethnic minority was dressed by her family in shabby and often smelly clothes. She was shunned by her peers and often verbally insulted.

Firmer operational definitions and the detailed applicability of these dimensions in different cultural, social and ethnic groups, await the results of current research. In many ways, these dimensions represent the converse of good-enough parenting. It is important to gain an understanding of the evolution of parents' emotionally abusive interaction with the child, since this points the way towards possible areas of change.

Unlike other forms of child abuse, the expression of emotional abuse is often observable, and it is possible to distinguish observation from inference in proving the presence of emotional abuse.

QUANTITATIVE ASPECTS

In order to qualify for definition as emotional abuse, one or more of these dimensions of parental relationship to the child needs to be sufficiently pervasive to be considered characteristic of the interaction and for there to be serious concern about the child's functioning and emotional state. This is important since the operational definition of abuse requires it to constitute a relationship which calls for (if necessary, mandated) intervention. To fulfil the criteria for the définition, there is also a need for prediction that the child's troubled state is unlikely to improve in the absence of change in the parental relationship to the child. The extent to which an extreme expression of any one dimension would be sufficient to constitute grounds for removing the child in the absence of change, remains to be tested. Unlike other forms of child abuse, the recognition of emotional abuse calls for a trial of intervention or of therapy rather than for immediate protection from further abuse, which is not possible without separating the child from their caregiver.

THE EFFECT OF EMOTIONAL ABUSE ON THE CHILD

The effects on the child of emotionally abusive interactions depend on the qualitative nature of the interaction. It is likely that the child's adaptation will include the development of self-blame by the child (Crittenden and Ainsworth 1989). In the furtherance of his or her attachment needs, and unlike other forms of child abuse, the child who is being emotionally abused may not recognise the damaging nature of the interaction. Furthermore, the child may not be wholly aware of their emotional and psychological discomfort and its source.

Effects of emotional abuse on the child are well recognised. Children whose parents consistently attribute badness or other characteristics to them, incorporate these in their internal working models (Bowlby 1989) and increasingly act on them. The child may behave badly or may harm him- or herself deliberately. Other children feel racked by blame. Insecure attachment which may follow conditional parenting is likely to lead to preoccupation with attachment issues and security at the expense of negotiating other developmental tasks (Crittenden and Ainsworth 1989). In particular, ex-ploration and learning, which require physical and psychological distancing from the attachment figure, may be adversely affected.

Emotional unavailability may leave the child feeling abandoned, sad or worthless. She or he may become withdrawn or be vulnerable to others to whom the child turns in seeking a response.

Children who are unable to fulfil their parents' inappropriate develop-mental expectations, feel themselves to blame for this failure. This is reinforced by the frequent parental condemnation of their failure. They may have considerable difficulties in peer relationships and accepting discipline from teachers. Confusion and untruth leave the child feeling mystified and, at times, stupid. Children who remain overprotected fail to overcome anxieties and are likely to develop a self-view of frailty.

The failure to respect the child's individuality interferes with the develop-ment of a sense of self. The child may be unable to leave the parent or feel too guilty to express her or his own wishes.

Children who experience mis-socialisation may fall foul of the law or will experience considerable unhappiness in their peer relationships.

Children may thus present with a variety of emotional and behavioural difficulties in response to emotional abuse, as a result of the intrapsychic, cognitive and emotional processes which follow.

THE PROCESS OF IDENTIFYING EMOTIONAL ABUSE

In a recently reported study, the possibility of gaining a degree of both professional and lay consensus on the recognition of emotional abuse was demonstrated. Burnett (1993) sought the response of social workers and lay citizens to vignettes purporting to describe respectively, single and typical interactions between parents and a child. There was good agreement about which of these interactions (9/10) were considered as emotionally abusive. These comprised of the following: confining a child to a small space; coercing a child into delinquency; not allowing emotional growth; threatening a child with physical injury or abandonment; cinderella syndrome; severe verbal abuse; denying psychological treatment when it is prescribed by a mental health professional; not providing a loving home atmosphere; and severe public humiliation.

Brassard *et al.* (1993) demonstrated that blind ratings of video-taped interactions between parents and child correlated moderately well with previously defined status of emotional abuse. This study points a way towards identifying emotional abuse by observing interactions. Many of the aspects described as emotional abuse are observable, or may be inferred from reports of parental attitudes and descriptions of interactions. It is, however, unsafe to infer emotional abuse simply on the basis of a child's difficulties without clear observation of the parent–child interaction.

THE CONTEXT OF ASSESSMENT OF PARENTING

Thus, there are now some indications of the possibility of identifying emotional abuse and neglect. However, in the context of the assessment of parenting, the task in relation to emotional abuse is not merely the decision about the existence or otherwise of this form of maltreatment. Further questions require clarification, namely the degree of harm already occasioned by the child, and the parents' capacity for sufficient change. By the time a parenting assessment is requested, there has almost invariably already been considerable concern about the child's well-being and development. The child will have been recognised symptomatically, may have suffered other abuse, may be underachieving educationally, may have difficulties with peer relationships or may be living in a family whose life pattern and interactions in relation to children have already alerted professionals.

The question to be asked is what the likely causes for the child's difficulties are. Emotional abuse is one causal explanation for the observed concerns about the child. In some cases, other explanations for the worrying state of the child may exist alongside, or in the absence of, emotional abuse. These include situations where the child's own innate endowment, or very evident adverse environmental factors are contributing significantly to the child's difficulties. Even then, in the spirit of Winnicott's 'good-enough parents' (Winnicott 1960), questions arise about the reasons for the parents' inability to mediate between the child and the adverse environment, or to deal more optimally with the child's own difficulties. Although these may not amount to emotional abuse, a change in the parents' interaction with the child is likely to be indicated.

It is important to embark on this enquiry without seeking to blame the parents. The distinction between parental responsibility and culpability may, at times, seem illusory and a deal of clinical sensitivity is required in continuing to work with the parents.

In families from ethnic minorities or other well-defined cultural, religious or social groups, questions need to be asked about the contextual appropriateness of the interactions which have given rise to concern. One way is to enquire, especially within the minority group, about the cultural appropriateness and acceptability of the particular interactions which are giving rise to concern. This is a variant of the 'vignette test' reported by Burnett (1993).

Only rarely will active child protection be deemed necessary or appropriate during the assessment stage in this form of abuse which is not a single, or a series of, events but rather a continuing relationship. Protection, which requires the supervision of all contact between the child and the abuser – in this case the parent(s) – would therefore require separation of the child from the parent(s), which is unlikely to be undertaken at this early stage.

THE PROCESS OF ASSESSMENT

Formation of a working relationship with the family

The process of assessment requires at its inception the formation of a working relationship with the parents. This relationship only comes into existence because of the child's difficulties or vulnerable situation. There are occasions in which there is no consensus between parents and professionals even about the justification for concern. The establishment of, and agreement about the need for, an assessment thus forms the first task for the newly formed relationship. At this early stage, it is necessary to define the areas of concern about the child. These may differ between parents and professionals. Reasons for the respective perceptions need to be made explicit and this includes prognostication about likely outcomes for the child in the event of no change for the better. It is sometimes useful, or even necessary, to have the person who holds the main worry present at the initial assessment meeting. The concern about the child's welfare may be based on statutory considerations, on directly observed worrying interactions between the parents and the child or on other information about family life and relationships. The person making the assessment needs to maintain a degree of neutrality (Glaser 1991) and this can more easily be achieved when the assessor receives the respective views of parents and professionals in each other's presence.

Seeking the family's explanations

The next step is to seek the parents' explanations for the child's difficulties. This is a crucial process which will yield important information. Hitherto unrecognised facts and experiences may emerge, which may alter the view of the parents' interactions with the child as abusive. Given that emotional abuse is sometimes recognised relatively late in a child's life, the child's own behaviour may be given as the explanation for the difficulties encountered. An older child may well be in a position to proffer their own explanation. Sadly, children often blame themselves. The nature of the parents' explanations may hint at their attributions to the child, expectations of the child or point to a parent's inability to distinguish between their own and the child's needs. This conversation or 'story' (White and Epston 1990) could well form the basis for later therapeutic trials or, indeed, therapy. The non-verbal expressions towards, and interactions with, the child are also useful indicators of the parents' view of the child.

Based on the parents', and possibly child's, explanations and their agreement about the need for concern, one may gain their views about what requisite changes are needed and how these can be effected.

Gathering information about the family

Having established a working relationship which acknowledges the need for an assessment, it is possible to learn more about the family. The move is towards forming some view about the dimensions of emotional abuse which may be involved. This requires a detailed account of the *family history*. This includes the *parents' own childhood experiences* as well as salient events in the history of the family of procreation, significant separations, departures and arrivals of new members and any migrations. An account is needed of the *child's developmental milestones*, as is information about any significant *ill-health and impairments* which the child might have suffered. As well as direct observations of *family interactions*, further light might be shed from results of the Adult Attachment Interview (Main and Goldwyn 1984) with the parents, which provides a useful indicator of some qualitative aspects of the parent–child interaction. Detailed information is required about the *child's current functioning* in physical, developmental, behavioural and emotional terms. In order to address the developmental dimension, the child's cognitive potential and attainment requires assessment. There is also a need to gain some understanding about the *child's current mental state*. Finally, family life can only be understood within its *social context*, which includes socioeconomic factors, extended family relationships and support and the wider social network. From this information, a view can be formed about the presence and nature of emotional abuse.

Assessing the capacity for change – a trial of intervention or therapy

Different dimensions of emotional abuse may coexist. If it is thought that this form of interaction is contributing significantly to the child's difficulties, considerable skill and sensitivity is required in the way this is conveyed to the parents without alienating or persecuting them. The view is offered as an alternative or additional one to the parents' explanations. Predictably, the difficulty is based on the professional belief that the responsibility and onus for change lies primarily with the parents. The parental response is an important factor. Indeed, the further assessment focuses on the demonstrable capacity for change in the parental interaction with, and attitude towards, the child and on the prediction of the power of protective factors. Change will require various modes of intervention. However, in the context of an assessment, even therapy can only be viewed as a therapeutic trial, which needs to be time limited, in accordance with the child's age and developmental needs.

Engaging parents in the process of therapeutic trials requires the parents' recognition and acceptance of the basis for professionals' concern. This is facilitated considerably by finding a way of helping the parents to reflect upon their interactions with the child. Inviting parents to comment on their behaviour towards the child from the perspective of their next door neighbour is one such way. Video-taping interactions for the parents' observation is another example. Exploring conjoint ways of convincing statutory bodies that there is no further need for concern is a way of actively involving parents in the process of change.

Change may require information about child development. Parents are likely to need direct advice about more appropriate ways of gaining the child's cooperation through effective, benign control of the child. Examples of this include the Parent Child Game (Jenner 1992) and well-developed programmes for dealing with conduct disorder (e.g. Webster-Stratton 1991). Some parents are unaware of the effects on the child of their behaviour towards her or him. It is an essential task of the assessment to test the degree to which the parents respond to understandable and jargon-free explanations. The trial here involves the parents' willingness to participate, as well as the degree to which the parents can adapt their previous patterns. These approaches are primarily cognitive, information based and experiential. They include close attention to, and monitoring of, actual patterns of interaction between parent and child.

Other parents who are believed to abuse their children emotionally, are likely to benefit from personal, individual therapy to overcome their own psychological difficulties and recognise that their emotional needs cannot be reasonably met by their child. The difficulty here is that such therapeutic work may well extend beyond the time limit imposed by the child's needs. Furthermore, some parents only enter into therapy under sufferance or for the sake of the child, without acknowledging their own personal need for this. It would be appropriate to await further improvement, provided the parent is able to show the beginning of a meaningful response to individual therapy, based on the therapist's estimate of the likely rate of change and if there is observable change in the parent–child interaction. It is also sometimes necessary to offer individual psychotherapy to the child. Here, the continuing monitoring of the child's functioning is important. There are, however, situations where the parent is not sufficiently motivated or the rate of parental response is too slow. In these cases, the search for alternative carers for the child is indicated.

Exploration of family myths and attributions as part of family therapy work form another aspect of the therapeutic trial. This is one example of the active involvement of the children in the process. It may also be appropriate to meet with the older child individually, in order to explore their feelings and perceptions. With the child's agreement, these can also be helpfully conveyed to the parents.

Evaluation of the therapeutic trial

Evaluation includes recording actual changes in the parent–child interaction, a tangible evidence of a greater understanding of the child's needs by the parent and the beginnings of insight into the part which the parent's own past experiences have contributed to the current situation. Some diminution in the concerns for the child him- or herself is also to be expected. Data upon which to base this improvement will be available from the initial assessment of the child's functioning.

A trial of intervention is unlikely fully to remove concerns for the child. In order to satisfy criteria for supporting the continuation of this parent–child relationship, there needs to be a degree of certainty about the continuation of intervention, support and therapy where indicated. This requires both a willingness and undertaking by the family to continue in this work and a commitment by those providing the service to continue to do so, as well as to monitor the progress of change. This carries significant resource implications. It is, however, useful to point out that the alternative course will, in the long term, be far more costly in resources and unhappiness.

In reaching a view about the adequacy of observed change, the contribution of protective factors needs to be evaluated (Farber and Egeland 1987). There are some children who, in the face of observable emotional abuse, continue to survive emotionally and who, despite being troubled are able to function and continue to learn and sustain meaningful relationships. Several factors contribute towards this. They include the child's innate resilience, which is often recognisable although may be more difficult to describe. Early secure attachment is another important protective factor. Finally, the availability to the child of other non-abusive, secure and enduring relationships may counterbalance continuing unresolved difficulties.

The difficulty is in deciding whether and to what extent the child will continue to be safe when there is little prospect for significant change in the parental interaction with the child. The younger the child, the more vulnerable she or he is and the more likely to retain the capacity to form meaningful new relationships with alternate carers. Older children, particularly if they are very reluctant to leave their home, are less likely to settle elsewhere. The decision on how to proceed with a resilient, but emotionally abused child will also depend on the position of siblings. If they are less resilient, a decision to find alternative parents may be determined by their needs. If other siblings have not been significantly subjected to emotional abuse, it is preferable to support a resilient child within the family, since removal to a new family is inevitably perceived as a rejection by the parent. Those who make the decision about a child's future are primarily accountable to the child and, whatever the decision made, it must stand up to the test of being honestly and fully explicable to the child, both now and later. A resilient child offers a considerable challenge.

Preparation of a case for court

The case is made on the basis of the initial concerns about the child, which will have been documented and are likely to have been of sufficient severity to initiate the assessment in the first place. The appropriate dimensions of emotional abuse which have been identified in this case can then be described, using observations to illustrate the description. A hypothesised explanation of the evolution of the child's difficulties in the light of the dimensions, based on family history and interactions, as well as on the child's own person, adds coherence to the case. Since the dimensions point to specific forms of intervention which will have been the subject of a trial, the results of this can be reported. The evaluation of the outcome includes the extent of the family's cooperation and observable changes in the child's functioning, as well as in the parent(s)' emotional welfare and interaction with the child. On the basis of this information, a prognosis can be offered about the respective likely outcomes for the child remaining in this family or being permanently cared for in another setting.

CONCLUSIONS

Emotional abuse is easier to recognise than to define. When present, it is likely to contribute adversely and to a significant degree to the concerns about children's welfare. There is a need for the assessment of the parenting received by many of these children. The process of assessment involves the formation of a relationship with the parents and child. The purpose of this is to observe the parent–child interaction and to gain an understanding about the evolution of the concerns about the child. If aspects of emotional abuse are identified, they will point to areas of intervention, allowing for a trial of intervention or therapy to proceed. The aim is for sufficient change which, combined with protective factors, will ensure the child's emotional behavioural welfare and optimal development. Likely indications that this is happening will need to be followed by continuing support and work for the child and the family. Alternatively, where insufficient change is gained, a clearer case for advocating a change of caregivers for the child will emerge.

REFERENCES

Barnett, D., Todd Manly, J. and Cicchetti, D. (1991) 'Continuing toward an operational definition of psychological maltreatment', *Development and Psychopathology*, **3**, 19–29.

Bowlby, J. (1989) *A Secure Base*, London: Tavistock/Routledge.

Brassard, M.R., Hart, S.N. and Hardy, D.B. (1993) 'The psychological maltreatment rating scales', *Child Abuse and Neglect*, **17**, 715–29.

Burnett, B.B. (1993) 'The psychological abuse of latency age children: a survey', *Child Abuse and Neglect*, **17**, 441–54.

Cicchetti, D. and Nurcombe, B. (eds) (1991) *Development and Psychopathology*, **3**, 1–124.

Claussen, A.H. and Crittenden, P.M. (1991) 'Physical and psychological maltreatment: relations among types of maltreatment', *Child Abuse and Neglect*, **15**, 5–18.

Crittenden, P.M. and Ainsworth, M.D.S. (1989) 'Child maltreatment and attachment theory', in D. Cicchetti and V. Carlson (eds) *Child Maltreatment: Theory and Research on the Causes and Consequences of Child Abuse and Neglect*, Cambridge: Cambridge University Press.

Farber, E.A. and Egeland, B. (1987) 'Invulnerability among abused and neglected children', in E.J. Anthony and B. Cohler (eds) *The Invulnerable Child*, New York: Guilford.

Glaser, D. (1991) 'Neutrality and child abuse: a useful juxtaposition?', *Human Systems*, **2**, 149–60.

Home Office, Department of Health, Department of Education and Science and Welsh Office (1991) *Working Together under the Children Act 1989: A Guide to Arrangements for Inter-agency Co-operation for the Protection of Children from Abuse*, London: HMSO.

Jenner, S. (1992) 'The assessment and treatment of parenting skills and deficits: within the framework of child protection', *ACPP Newsletter*, **14**, 228–33.

McGee, R.A. and Wolfe, D.A. (1991) 'Psychological maltreatment: toward an operational definition', *Development and Psychopathology*, **3**, 3–18.

Main, M. and Goldwyn, R. (1984) 'Predicting rejection of her infant from mother's representation of her own experience: implications for the abused–abusing intergenerational cycle', *Child Abuse and Neglect*, **8**, 203–17.

Webster-Stratton, C. (1991) Annotation: 'Strategies for helping families with conduct disordered children', *Journal of Child Psychology and Psychiatry*, **32**, 1047–62.

White, M. and Epston D. (1990) *Narrative Means to Therapeutic Ends*, London: Norton.

Winnicott, D.W. (1960) 'Ego distortion in terms of true and false self', in *The Maturational Processes and the Facilitating Environment*, London: Hogarth, 1982.

Chapter 6

Assessing protectiveness in cases of child sexual abuse

Gerrilyn Smith

This chapter will focus on identifying and assessing the capacity of parents to protect children from future sexual abuse where sexual abuse has been an issue. Relevant research will be reviewed and a framework for assessment of the non-abusing parent's capacity to protect will be provided.

The importance of engaging a child's natural network in protection cannot be overemphasised (Boushel 1994; Wurtele and Miller-Perrin 1992; Smith 1994). It is apparent from surveys of incidence and prevalence that a substantial amount of sexual abuse goes unreported to public child protection agencies – as much as 95 per cent (Kelly *et al.* 1991).

The importance of the response to the child following disclosure has been clearly identified as significant in the child's recovery from the sexual abuse (Conte and Schuerman 1987; Gomes-Schwartz *et al.* 1990). A believing stance and clear messages regarding who is responsible for the sexual abuse are considered positive and helpful parental responses (Hagans and Case 1988; MacFarlane *et al.* 1986). It is evident that parents play a significant role in the recovery process in the majority of child protection cases. Cases that come to the attention of the statutory agencies perhaps reflect that the usual protective responses of the family and community have failed. The reasons for this failure need to be explored, as it may be that, with professional help, the natural network can become activated to offer the protection necessary for the child's continued placement within the family and recovery from the abuse.

In cases that involve statutory child protection agencies, protection should always be sought first from the natural social network surrounding the child and only in extreme circumstances should future protection be delegated to a professional network. The natural network surrounding the child includes not only non-abusing parents but also members of the extended family, neighbours, siblings, friends, as well as those professionals who have regular contact with the child, such as teachers.

THEORETICAL FRAMEWORK

The risk for any child can be represented by the diagram in Figure 6.1. In Circle A, the child is surrounded by a community of adults. Within this community are both possible protectors and possible perpetrators. It can be difficult to know who is a potential perpetrator for any one child unless there is an identified sexual offender already within the child's network, as in the case of a parent with a Schedule 1 offence. In the main, the balance of

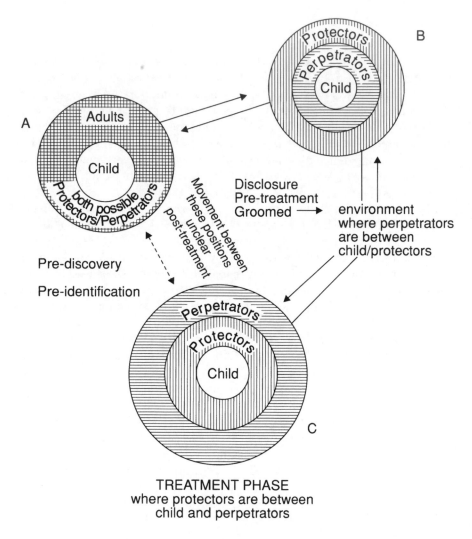

Figure 6.1 Protecting children from the risk of future sexual abuse
Source: Smith 1994

potential protectors to perpetrators should be weighted in favour of protectors. However, there are circumstances where this is not the case, such as in institutional abuse or where all family members are participating in sexually abusive acts with each other. The likelihood of having to remove children from such a community is much higher.

Circle B represents the configuration of adults when sexual abuse may be occurring, with the perpetrator closest to the child and possible protectors at a greater distance. This diagrammatically represents the 'groomed' environment.

Circle C represents the necessary transformation required to help the child begin to recover from sexual abuse. Possible protectors must be helped to be more effective and the distance between the child and the non-abusing parent must be reduced, with the perpetrator removed from their central position in relation to the child and placed at a greater distance.

The framework proposed for assessment of a non-abusing parent's capacity to protect makes two very important assumptions. The first is that the general level of parenting provided in the family is good enough. The framework focuses specifically on protection rather than general parenting skills. In part this is because the framework is intended to guide and suggest interventions in cases where *sexual abuse* is an issue. Hence, it is an assessment tool connected to the presenting problem. Good general parenting skills are not synonymous with good protection skills. Poor general parenting skills may be correlated with an increased risk of sexual abuse, but attempting to improve general parenting skills alone is unlikely to impact on future protection from sexual abuse.

The second assumption made is that there is a non-abusing parent to be assessed. In the vast majority of cases, the non-abusing parent will be the mother. Despite the increasing attention given to female sexual offending, it is still overwhelmingly men and male parents who sexually abuse both boy and girl children. The term non-abusing parent can be applied to both mother and father when the sexual abuse is extra-familial, or where the perpetrator is a juvenile (as in the case of brother–sister incest).

If there is a clear indication that the mother has been directly involved in the sexual abuse by participating, then it is not appropriate to consider her a non-abusing parent. If there is a suspicion that she knew but did not take adequate protective measures, she can be considered a non-abusing parent. Knowledge and concealment of sexual abuse, whilst a poor prognostic indicator for future protectiveness, does not constitute participation for the purposes of this assessment.

PROTECTIVE INTERVENTIONS

This model provides a means not only of assessing protectiveness at any one point in time, but also the ability of the parents to use interventions constructively in moving towards a more protective stance over the period of the assessment.

The following issues represent the minimal amount of work that needs to be implemented to improve the protection for any one child. These issues include identifying the protector, strengthening their capacity to protect, enhancing boundaries, addressing secrecy and alerting the network.

A protecting adult must be identified from within the child's existing network. It is preferable that the child is living with this protecting adult. Ideally, it should be the non-abusing parent, but placement within the extended family may be necessary in the initial crisis phase because the non-abusing parent may not have been identified.

Having identified a protecting adult for the child, they will need help to strengthen their capacity to protect all the children in the family, not just the target child.

It is important that appropriate boundaries are established within the family. This includes the removal of the perpetrator, as represented by Circle C in Figure 6.1. It also involves supporting maternal authority within the family (or adult parental authority if the child is placed outside the nuclear family). Children who have been sexually abused are frequently sensitive to, and disrespectful of, authority (Smith 1992). They will challenge the authority figures who care for them to a greater degree than non-abused peers. This includes not only the authority of the non-abusing parent, but also foster parents, residential care staff and any other adults who function *in loco parentis*.

The secrecy surrounding the sexual abuse has to be addressed. If the child remains within the family of origin, it is important to plan how to tell siblings and extended family members in a way that will minimise the stigmatisation for the target child. It is important for the child to know that it was right for them to disclose, that they are believed and that it was not their fault.

The network surrounding the child must be alerted to the current crisis in a way that is sensitive to issues of confidentiality and privacy. This network needs to know what are the behavioural indicators of distress for this child so that protective and supportive interventions can be activated as and when needed. This network will need to both devise and rehearse the protective plan. For the non-abusing parent, this will need to be done both within the family and with the wider network.

The different treatment modalities of family, group and one-to-one work all lend themselves to different components of this protection plan. Not all modalities may be available or desirable. However, it is essential that protective workers engage non-abusing parents with their families.

ASSESSING PROTECTIVENESS

This framework is based on clinical experience. It attempts to provide guidance by identifying examples of optimum and dismal functioning. It requires professionals to make judgements and to locate their client's current functioning on a continuum. Professionals should view mid-range functioning as the norm and to expect changes in either direction over time. Priority areas of change and minimum criteria for effective protection will be identified for each dimension.

Position regarding the child's disclosure

The non-abusing parent's position regarding the child's disclosure needs to be assessed. Optimum functioning depends on a believing parent. Research suggests that this is most likely to occur if the perpetrator is outside the immediate family, the sexual contact is regarded as minimal or less severe, the non-abusing parent was not in the house when it happened and the child is young (Sirles and Franke 1989). There is little research which looks at the impact of gender of both the target and the perpetrator on the likelihood of belief. Anecdotally, it would seem that boys who have been sexually abused by men are more likely to be believed and less likely to be blamed, as their experience is considered outside the bounds of normal heterosexual conventions. It also seems that boys and girls who disclose sexual abuse by a female perpetrator are often met with disbelief. For girls disclosing sexual abuse by a woman, the supposed homosexual nature of the contact, rather than increasing the likelihood of belief (as in the case of boys sexually abused by men), seems to operate in the reverse, with disbelief and denial as the overwhelming response (Saradjian, personal communication).

It is also clear that belief by a non-abusing parent (usually mothers) is not related to victim characteristics as much as it is by her relationship with the offender (Everson *et al*. 1989; De Jong 1988; Sirles and Franke 1989; Gomes-Schwartz *et al*. 1990).

In assessing the non-abusing parent's position, professionals need to consider whether the parent is minimising the extent of the abuse. This is understandable in the immediate crisis of discovery, but becomes less acceptable over time.

More worrying are parents who disbelieve what the child has disclosed. In part, they may still be leaving open the possibility that, with additional information, they may believe the child's disclosure. This information is usually an admission by the perpetrator, medical evidence corroborating the child's statement and/or a criminal conviction. Parents in this position need to shift the criteria for believing to something more realistic, such as listening to what the child has said or observing the supporting behavioural signs of distress the child is exhibiting.

For parents who deny even the possibility of sexual abuse, the room for therapeutic manoeuvrability is extremely limited. It may be that separating the identity of the perpetrator from the act of sexual abuse will help. The parent can believe their child was sexually abused, but not by the person named by the child. If this level of belief cannot be achieved, leaving the child with this parent constitutes high risk for future episodes of sexual abuse from the identified perpetrator or any others. The capacity to protect from an unimaginable act is very limited.

Consequently, helping a mother believe her child has been sexually abused is extremely important to the child's future protection. It can secure their place within the immediate family and will be the foundation for the child's recovery work.

Role in the disclosing process

The non-abusing parent's role in the disclosing process is crucial. Optimum functioning is where a mother brings the allegation to light and alerts the child protection agencies. However, assessment in this area needs to reflect the research which indicates that only a very small minority of parents would involve statutory child protection workers (Berrick 1988). The majority of parents assessed on this item will function in the mid-range, where they may have been told about the sexual abuse but not relayed this information to statutory agencies.

In many studies, there is clear evidence that mothers do alert statutory agencies (Gordon 1989; Hooper 1993). There is also evidence which suggests that referrals from professional agencies are given more weight than those by private individuals (Milner 1993). This weighting in favour of public sector notification is reflected in policy and procedures which do not view the non-abusing parent as a potential resource and invaluable support to the investigating process. All parents are viewed suspiciously until the extent of their involvement can be ascertained. Unfortunately, such an approach is likely to exacerbate the distance between the child and her potential protector at a time when, therapeutically, one should be bringing them closer together.

There are cases where a non-abusing parent has explicitly concealed sexual abuse. It is important for workers to explore why. If the parent believes the child has been sexually abused, it may still be possible to engage them constructively in recovery work once the perpetrator of the abuse is at a greater distance from both the child and the possible protector.

Feelings towards the child

Supportive and empathic reactions by non-abusing parents to the child following discovery of sexual abuse aid a child's recovery and mitigate against some of the most negative consequences of sexual abuse (Conte and Schuerman 1987; Gomes-Schwartz et al. 1990). The vast majority of non-abusing parents are often confused regarding the feelings they have towards the child.

It is important to recognise that the non-abusing parent is likely to be in shock following the disclosure of sexual abuse and, as such, be less emotionally available to her children. This acute emotional unavailability will be compounded by the more chronic circumstance of distance between possible protector and child that has been promoted by the abuser.

Position regarding responsibility for sexual abuse

The most helpful response for the child's recovery is that the perpetrator is deemed responsible for their actions. This message needs to be given in a developmentally appropriate manner. It seems that it is easier for protectors to understand and convey this message when the target of the sexual abuse is very young (Sirles and Franke 1989).

Many protectors will apportion blame. This is probably connected to several factors, including the child's age and gender and the relationship with the identified perpetrator. If the protector is connected emotionally to the perpetrator, all of the evidence suggests they will find it harder to believe and, by conjecture, will be more likely to apportion blame to the child as a means of rationalising or minimising the offender's actions.

In situations where the child is seen as responsible, the likelihood that the child will be excluded from the family is higher.

Perceived options

In assessing a non-abusing parent's capacity to protect, it is essential that the options available to them for protection are fully explored. This takes into consideration that many protectors (i.e. mothers) are financially dependent on the perpetrators (i.e. partners).

If a range of options are perceived and acted on, this represents optimum functioning. The options may not involve using statutory agencies, but could include use of the extended family, church or religious community, or women's refuge.

If a protector had options available to them and did not use them, or, worse, perceives no options and thinks sexual abuse is an inevitability which requires endurance skills rather than escape mechanisms, the prognosis is poor. However, it is important to recognise that, if the protector believes and is emotionally available to the child, any interventions offered should increase the number of available options rather than persecute the protector for not perceiving those options in the first place (Dale *et al.* 1986).

Cooperation with statutory agencies

A number of protectors will not engage constructively with statutory child protection agencies. The reasons for this will need to be ascertained. The workers may have failed to engage their clients for a number of reasons. For families from minority ethnic communities, engaging statutory help is a complex issue given the history of past inappropriate state interventions. For a family who have previous knowledge and/or experience of this, seeking alternative support may be seen as preferable.

Jones (1991) identified previous failure at engaging in treatment and non-compliance as risk factors in assessing protectiveness. The continued isolation of the protector from a wider community of adults who can assist in the protection of the children is, perhaps, of more importance. Professional child protection workers need to convey to potential protectors that, to reduce the risk of future sexual abuse, the child and protector need an outside referent group that will support the recovery process. If a viable community resource can be found, then cooperation with statutory agencies is less of an issue.

However, in cases where some of the first prerequisites of protection have not been met – including belief in the child's disclosure, appropriate distance between the child and perpetrator and emotional availability of the protector to the child – then it will be necessary for statutory child protection agencies to exercise their authority in the child's best interest.

Openness regarding sexual abuse

If a protector refuses to discuss the issue of sexual abuse with other children in the family, especially if the identified target has had to be removed following disclosure, there is an increased risk for the children who remain at home. The secrecy regarding the sexual abuse is still the organising family mode of communication and may be coupled with promoting alternative explanations as to why the identified target child is no longer living at home. If this is the case, the likelihood of a sanctioned return to the family should be reduced, as the alternative explanations deny the child's reality and are probably indicative of scapegoating.

Because secrecy is such a fundamental part of the process of sexual abuse, it is important that protectors develop a language and an ease in talking about it. In the vast majority of cases, they will need help to do this. The goal is for the non-abusing parent to be able to deal with continuing questions in a developmentally appropriate manner. It also involves discussion with the extended family network and community, in particular the child's school.

Hesitant and tentative discussion is usually the starting point. Many protectors are unsure of what to say to the other children in the family, to the extended family and to the wider community. Indiscriminate discussion can further stigmatise the child.

History of sexual abuse

The finding that many mothers of children who have been sexually abused have themselves also been sexually abused, needs to be viewed against prevalence figures which suggest that 47 per cent of the population report having an unwanted sexually intrusive experience before the age of 18 (Kelly *et al.* 1991). Hooper (1993) suggests that this overrepresentation of mothers who have themselves experienced sexual abuse (and it is questionable whether this is an overrepresentation), may be due to this group of mothers being more likely to seek professional help for their children.

If a protector has a history of sexual abuse themselves, which includes not only a resolution but also a personal protection plan, then this history is unlikely to decrease their effectiveness as a protector. Indeed, it may make them more effective as a protector.

For protectors who have not previously disclosed, it may be that the child's current disclosure triggers the memory of past sexual abuse for them (Courtois and Sprei 1988). Their capacity to protect may be limited in the short term as they deal with *both* disturbing episodes of sexual abuse. If they can find help for themselves, their own healing and recovery process may have positive spin-offs for the child.

The worst scenario, which is probably overrepresented in statutory cases, is where a non-abusing parent is still being sexually abused by their childhood perpetrator. This constitutes a high-risk situation for any children of the current family, as they may also be targeted by the perpetrator.

Other vulnerabilities

In some cases, a non-abusing parent may have other vulnerabilities which increase their dependency on the perpetrator. This can include physical disabilities, mental health problems, limited intellectual capabilities, social isolation, lack of fluency in spoken English, either through a hearing impairment or due to cultural differences. In all of these cases, if the non-abusing parent is connected to a support network that reduces that vulnerability and also has taken on the issue of child protection, then the risk is substantially reduced. However, in the majority of cases, there may be support networks that exist, but they have not yet dealt with the issue of child sexual abuse. Consequently, to raise such an issue in, for instance, the Deaf Club might jeopardise the connection to what can be an individual lifeline and major support network. In fact, the Keep Deaf Children Safe Project has done an excellent job in raising the profile of child protection within the deaf community as a whole, according to Kennedy (quoted in Gault 1989).

PRACTICAL EXAMPLE

The following example from the A. family highlights the use of the framework in practice. Kelly was a 14 year old white girl who had been sexually abused by her Asian step-father, for which he had served a custodial sentence. She had two half-brothers and all three children in the family were on care orders due to a number of concerns regarding the parenting of their mother and the violence of their father/step-father. The three children had been placed in separate residential facilities, where they continued to display high levels of disturbed behaviour, including, for the two older children, absconding to the family home.

Kelly was placed in a specialist unit in a different geographical area from her family and her behaviour improved dramatically. At the same time, her mother and step-father applied to have the care order revoked on all three children and to have them returned home to their full-time care. The maternal grandparents, Mr and Mrs K., also applied for increased contact and the possibility that they be considered as placements for two of their three grandchildren, Kelly and the youngest child, John. The middle child, Andrew, was very much out of control and was showing the greatest amount of challenging behaviour.

Mr A. had had no treatment for his sexual offending behaviour. He was now maintaining that he had not sexually abused his step-daughter. Using Finkelhor's (1984) Four Preconditions Model of Sexual Abuse, it was clear that Factors 1 (motivation to sexually offend) and 2 (internal inhibitors against offending) had not changed since the original episode of sexual abuse.

Using the framework described in this chapter, an assessment was made of the strength of the external inhibitors (Factor 3). In this case, both Mrs A. and possibly Mr and Mrs K. could be considered as external inhibitors.

Position regarding the child's disclosure

Mrs A. still denied that Kelly had been sexually abused. Additionally, she denied the disclosures of her children that she had beaten them on many occasions and frequently left them on their own with no supervision. She had a serious drink problem, which she also denied. Her denial put her in the dismal range of functioning as a protector of her children. She had had a variety of inputs to help her with her children and to deal with the issue of sexual abuse in the family, including a residential placement for her and her three children. Consequently, her continued denial of any difficulties indicated a very pessimistic outcome in relation to her capacities to protect.

In contrast, Mr and Mrs K. had believed Kelly since she first disclosed. Despite familial tensions, they had maintained their belief throughout and had not needed extra resources to sustain it. The belief of the grandparents placed them in the optimum range of functioning as potential protectors.

Feelings towards the child following disclosure

Mrs A. was clearly fond of Kelly and enjoyed the very limited contact that they had. They behaved like sisters when they met and never discussed the sexual abuse or the other allegations of parental failures. Mrs A. showed no understanding of Kelly's feelings and remained preoccupied with her own. At best, she could be rated as confused on this dimension.

Mr and Mrs K. demonstrated a great deal of empathy regarding Kelly's feelings. When Mr K. thought there was something bothering Kelly before she disclosed, he encouraged his wife to follow it up, as he thought Kelly might find it easier to talk to a woman. They understood some of the difficulties for Kelly as a step-child in the family and, on consideration of the court reports, withdrew their wish to offer a placement for both John and Kelly, as they recognised that the needs of both children were incompatible. However, they wished to maintain contact with all grandchildren but to offer a home to Kelly, whom they had previously parented when she was much younger. Their understanding of the emotional issues for each child placed them in the optimum range of functioning on this dimension.

Role in the disclosing process

According to Kelly's disclosure, she had told her mother on a number of occasions about her step-father's behaviour. This suggested that Mrs A. may have concealed the sexual abuse and would probably do so in the future. This placed her in the dismal range of functioning.

Kelly disclosed to her maternal grandmother who, in turn, had informed the statutory child protection agencies. The grandparents were pivotal in the disclosing process and directly involved the statutory agencies. Their behaviour regarding the disclosure placed them in the optimum range of functioning.

Position regarding responsibility

As Mrs A. did not think abuse had taken place, it was difficult to rate her on this dimension. This demonstrates the importance that belief plays in any protective strategies.

Both Mr and Mrs K. clearly felt Mr A. was responsible for the sexual abuse. This is in line with research which suggests it would be easier for them to believe and recognise the adult's full responsibility because Mr A. was not related to them other than through marriage. However, whatever their reasons, their attitude placed them in the optimum range of functioning.

Perceived options

It was likely that Mrs A. had learned to live with sexual abuse and physical violence. This was worrying because professionals would have to consider why she was so much more apathetic than her parents. The possibility that she had been sexually or physically abused in her family of origin had to be considered. The history suggested that, following her mother's death when she was aged 11 years (Mrs K. was Mrs A.'s step-mother, but the only grandmother that Kelly had known), Mrs A. became disconnected from her family and began to rely on her peer group for much of her support. She was involved in drinking and sexual activity in her late teens. She married at 18 and had Kelly very soon after. Her first marriage was violent and, after the birth of Kelly, she separated from her husband and asked her father and her step-mother to look after Kelly until she sorted herself out. She became involved with Mr A. and married him despite familial disapproval. Her drinking increased and violence also erupted in this relationship. Despite offers of help from the extended family, she remained with Mr A. On the dimension being considered, she functioned on the dismal range.

Mr and Mrs K. had demonstrated that they were prepared to use a range of protective options. They functioned in the optimum range.

Cooperation with statutory agencies

Mrs A. was very angry with statutory agencies. She reluctantly came to her appointments for the court proceedings but did not talk in them. At best, she could be assessed as complying with agencies.

Mr and Mrs K. were also very angry with the statutory child protection agencies. They felt that they had been ignored, despite having tried to protect Kelly. Kelly had been placed with them in the crisis period following disclosure, but moved to a residential unit because of uncertainties over their ability to cope with her. Their contact with Kelly was supervised and had to occur within the residential unit. Rather than it being increased gradually, it was being curtailed. Although they had previously alerted and cooperated with statutory agencies, they were now angry and suspicious. However, they were now complying with the statutory agencies, as they had decided to join in the legal proceedings and put their point of view across.

Relationship history

Mrs A. demonstrated a high degree of dependency involving violent and abusive partners. This put her in the dismal range of functioning.

There was no reported violence in Mr and Mrs K.'s relationship. Mrs K. had a large degree of autonomy and undertook many tasks on her own in relation to Kelly where the couple felt Kelly would benefit from having a close relationship with a female figure.

Openness regarding sexual abuse

Mrs A. did not see the importance of letting her sons know why Mr A. was away from the family. When they were admitted to the residential unit as a family group, she promoted an alternative explanation, saying he had returned to his extended family in Asia. The boys' behaviour was such that there was a high probability that they, too, had been sexually abused but had not yet disclosed this. Mrs A. functioned at the dismal range on this dimension.

Mr and Mrs K. functioned at the mid-range. They were unsure how much to say to anyone about what had happened. With help, this area could be explored further as part of some recovery work for the children.

Own history of abuse

Mrs A. did not discuss any aspect of her past. The current violence in her relationship was denied. It was difficult to rate Mrs A. on this dimension.

Neither Mr nor Mrs K. had a history of abuse. They did discuss their childhoods during the assessment, which demonstrated an openness on their part. They could also see how childhood experiences could make it difficult to respond to some of the issues their grandchildren were currently dealing with.

Vulnerabilities

Mrs A. was isolated and disconnected from her extended family network and this isolation increased her dependency on her husband. Additionally, her unacknowledged drink problem also increased her vulnerability. She would be at the dismal range of functioning on this continuum.

Mr and Mrs K. were connected to a support group because Mr K.'s son from his first marriage suffered from a schizophrenic illness. They saw this support group as very important. Mrs K. attended a primary caregivers' group that was run in the residential unit where Kelly was placed and found the opportunity to speak with other women caring for adolescents who had been sexually abused invaluable. The couple operated at the optimum range on this dimension.

Overall recommendation

This brief summary of the assessment of two potential protectors demonstrates the effectiveness of the framework. It was clear that Mrs A. was not able to be an effective protector for her children. Consequently, to return the children to her care would have been a high-risk situation, with the statutory agencies dependent on the children's ability to protect themselves from any future episode of abuse. This was considered an unacceptable level of risk.

However, the assessment of protectiveness made the social services department re-evaluate their assessment of the grandparents as possible protectors for their grandchildren. They were functioning in the optimum range on a number of important dimensions. With help, they could aid the recovery work of all the children. As an alternative placement for their granddaughter, it was clear they should be considered. They had previously demonstrated that they felt able to stand in opposition to their daughter and were able to put the children's need for protection above her needs.

SUMMARY AND CONCLUSIONS

This framework allows for movement over time and should help professionals shape their interventions as new information comes to light or progress is made in key areas.

Recognising the gendered experience of parenting is important in assessing a non-abusing parent's capacity to protect. It is important that both mothers and fathers are involved in the assessment if the perpetrator is outside the immediate family. This reinforces the idea that protection is not the sole responsibility of the female parent.

If the suspected perpetrator is the male parent, then it is vital that an attempt is made to see both parents separately. This ensures that the female parent is provided with the choice of allying herself with protection workers or continuing to ally herself with her partner. Research clearly indicates that this group of non-abusing parents are likely to experience high levels of conflict over the incompatible role demands of being a good mother and a good partner when confronted by a disclosure of sexual abuse involving both their child and their partner.

Involving parents as partners in protection evokes the spirit of the 1989 Children Act. Focusing on protection and recovery from sexual abuse provides a constructive approach to the task. It moves away from persecutory interventions, 'anxious surveillance' (Dale *et al.* 1986) of what is essentially a secret act unlikely to be witnessed and the often overriding preoccupation about identifying *who* did it.

The assessment helps to identify the key factors that help a non-abusing parent become a protective one. It maintains sexual abuse as its focus but pushes potential protectors to recognise the crucial role they play in the child's recovery. Although it has been devised to be used with parents, it is equally relevant for professional protectors (foster parents, residential workers, family workers) employed by local authorities to take over when families of origin cannot manage to protect. The optimum functioning identifies a set of conditions and a frame of mind that can be worked towards by all adults who view the protection of children from sexual abuse as one of the primary tasks of a responsible and civilised society.

REFERENCES

Berrick, J. (1988) 'Parental involvement in child abuse prevention training: what do they learn?', *Child Abuse and Neglect*, **12**, 543–53.
Boushel, M. (1994) 'Keeping safe: strengthening the protective environment of children in foster care', *Adoption and Fostering*, **18**, 33–9.

Conte, J.R. and Schuerman, J.R. (1987) 'Factors associated with an increased impact of child sexual abuse', *Child Abuse and Neglect*, **11**, 201–11.

Courtois, C.A. and Sprei, J.E. (1988) 'Retrospective incest therapy for women', in E. Walker (ed.) *Handbook on Sexual Abuse of Children*, New York: Springer.

Dale, P., Davies, M., Morrison, T. and Waters, J. (1986) *Dangerous Families: Assessment and Treatment*, London: Tavistock.

De Jong, A.R. (1988) 'Maternal responses to the sexual abuse of their children', *Paediatrics*, **81**, 14–21.

Everson, M.D., Hunter, W.M., Runyon, D.K., Edelsohn, G.A. and Coulter, M.L. (1989) 'Maternal support following disclosure of incest', *American Journal of Orthopsychiatry*, **59**, 197–207.

Finkelhor, D. (1984) *Child Sexual Abuse: New Theory and Research*, New York: The Free Press.

Gault, T. (1989) 'The silent nightmare – recognising sexual abuse of deaf children', *Soundbarrier*, **22**, 9–12.

Gomes-Schwartz, B., Horowitz, J.M. and Cardarelli, A.P. (1990) *Child Sexual Abuse: The Initial Effects*, Newbury Park CA: Sage.

Gordon, M. (1989) 'The family environment of sexual abuse: a comparison of natal and stepfather abuse', *Child Abuse and Neglect*, **13**, 121–30.

Hagans, K.B. and Case, J. (1988) *When Your Child Has Been Molested. A Parent's Guide to Healing and Recovery*, Lexington MA: Lexington Books.

Hooper, C. (1993) *Mothers Surviving Sexual Abuse*, London: Routledge.

Jones, D.P.H. (1991) 'The effectiveness of intervention', in M. Adcock, R. White and A. Hollows (eds) *Significant Harm*, Croydon: Significant Publications.

Kelly, L., Regan, L. and Burton, S. (1991) *An Exploratory Study of Sexual Abuse in a Sample of 1244 Young People*, London: Child Abuse Studies Unit.

MacFarlane, K., Waterman, J., Conerly, S., Damon, L., Durfee, M. and Long, S. (eds) (1986) *Sexual Abuse of Young Children*, New York: Guilford.

Milner, J. (1993) 'A disappearing act; the differing career paths of fathers and mothers in child protection investigations', *Critical Social Policy*, **10**, 48–63.

Sirles, E.A. and Franke, P.J. (1989) 'Factors influencing mothers' reactions to intrafamily sexual abuse', *Child Abuse and Neglect*, **13**, 131–9.

Smith, G. (1992) 'The unbearable traumatogenic past', in V.P. Varma (ed.) *The Secret Lives of Vulnerable Children*, London: Routledge.

Smith, G. (1994) 'Parent, partner, protector: conflicting role demands for mothers of sexually abused children', in T. Morrison, M. Erooga and R. Beckett (eds) *Sexual Offending Against Children: Assessment and Treatment of Male Abusers*, London: Routledge.

Wurtele, S.K. and Miller-Perrin, C.L. (1992) *Preventing Child Sexual Abuse: Sharing the Responsibility*, Lincoln NE: University of Nebraska Press.

Chapter 7

Assessing treatability
Geraldine Fitzpatrick

INTRODUCTION

A core principle of the 1989 Children Act is that children should be cared for within their natural families if at all possible. Courts will only grant orders if they are satisfied that it would be better for the child than not doing so. Therefore, assessments of parenting must not only address whether children have been significantly harmed as a result of the parenting they have received, but also the degree to which change is possible. Reports to courts need to include opinions about parents' capacity to benefit from treatment and whether therapy could help achieve improvements in parenting, or rehabilitation of parents and children who have been separated.

A wide range of treatments have been described, based on psychodynamic (Steele 1980), systemic (Trepper and Barrett 1989) or behavioural (Wolfe *et al.* 1981) principles; taking place in the home (Nicol 1988), out-patients (Elton 1988), family centre (Dale *et al.* 1986), day unit (Asen *et al.* 1989) or in-patient (Kennedy 1988) settings; for problems of physical (Lynch and Roberts 1982), sexual (Furniss 1991) and emotional (Glaser 1993) abuse. It is beyond the scope of this chapter to consider the relative merits of the therapeutic interventions available and their outcomes have been well reviewed by Jones (1991) and Gough (1993).

My intention is to discuss the factors that are essential prerequisites of any therapeutic help, irrespective of its style and setting or the nature of the parenting breakdown. These factors are able to be considered during overall assessments of parenting and act as guides to whether therapeutic interventions should be attempted before a court makes the final decision about placement of the child. I shall use examples from my work in the Emanuel Miller Day Unit and in Out-patients at St George's Hospital to illustrate that there are some cases in which it is evident that change is likely to occur and others in which it is equally clear that therapy is not possible. However, between these two extremes lie cases in which interventions need to be attempted and the outcome monitored, or else prolonged 'therapeutic assessments' are justified. I shall use as examples of this last situation cases in which young mothers had denied that they were pregnant and then abandoned or killed their newborn infant.

THEORETICAL PRINCIPLES

Three concepts that originated in the theory and practice of psychoanalysis form a useful basis for considering a person's capacity to benefit from any modality of treatment. They are *psychological conflict*, *denial* and *treatment alliance* (Sandler *et al.* 1973).

Psychological conflict can best be described as an inner battle between different agencies of the mind, usually between the impulse to do something and the acknowledgement that such actions would be socially or interpersonally unacceptable. Such conflicts are uncomfortable and give rise to anxiety. In order to reduce psychological discomfort, the unconscious mind compromises and sides with one element, while *denying* the other. Excessive anxiety is avoided by the original thought being relegated to unconsciousness. One manifestation of this denial is inability to recall certain events or thoughts. Another is the person's attribution of all problems to others, together with the belief that they themselves are trouble free.

In order for anyone to consider that there is a problem requiring resolution, they must acknowledge to some degree that they are conflicted; there must be some permeability to their denial; and they must have some ownership of their contribution to the problems. However, acknowledgement of psychological conflict and exploration of its origins (or feedback about its manifestation in problem behaviour) may provoke anxiety and a preference to retreat back into denial. The *treatment alliance* describes that part of a person which is able to side with the work of therapy and engage with it, despite any psychological discomfort that it releases. It is especially important at the beginning of treatment, after which the positive benefits of increased understanding, or behaviour change, are able to take over.

A 29 year old mother of two children, a girl aged 7 and a boy aged 5, had experienced physical and sexual abuse as a child and was now separated from her violent husband. She often responded angrily to her son's behaviour, culminating in an incident in which she put her hands around his neck and tried to strangle him. Realising what she was doing, she stopped and rang social services and the children were accommodated during assessment. The mother was able to acknowledge the problem in her relationship with her son, agreed that she might be confusing him with the absent father, wanted to work on it and asked for help. She had some sense that her own maltreatment as a child had an effect on her current parenting. Despite the difficulties that had led to the crisis, there was evidence of a good attachment between the children and their mother. The family were able to engage in recommended treatment in the day unit and made good use of it.

FACTORS RELEVANT TO TREATABILITY

The above principles, and example of successful therapy, point to a number of factors that need to be considered when assessing a parent's capacity to benefit from treatment.

Acknowledgement that caretaking problems have occurred

There must be sufficient acknowledgement by parents being considered for treatment that there are problems in their relationship with a child and that changes need to occur in that relationship. Some parents refuse to accept that their behaviour has been harmful to their child and instead believe that professionals have accused them of abuse without justification. They may suggest, for example, that if only social services 'went away' then everything would be fine. During assessment, it is useful to repeat to the parent details of the concerns expressed by others and ask the parent to explain why they think these people had become worried.

Other parents seem to cooperate with the assessment, but it becomes apparent that they are only complying with the court's request for a mental health opinion and they do not agree that there has been a problem. Hence, it is useful to start assessments by asking parents to describe what has happened to necessitate the assessment.

A young couple were referred to me for assessment and possible treatment. Their 4 month old son had been admitted to hospital with a fractured skull and skeletal survey showed old and healing fractures of ribs and one leg, which were considered to be the result of non-accidental injury. Both parents denied injuring the infant and could not give an account of how the injuries had occurred, even though he had never been out of their care. The couple gave unconvincingly 'bland' personal histories, saying they had come from normal happy families, that their relationship was a good one and they wanted their baby home. I offered a number of interviews to explore the issues further but, although they attended, we were unable to find common ground upon which to work and it was clear that therapeutic intervention was not possible because they could not agree its purpose.

However, assessors must be especially sensitive to the cultural variations in parenting styles. Parents who have grown up in a particular culture may not believe that their parenting has been a problem because that culture would view it as normal. This applies as much to variations between classes within a society as to immigrants into it. At the interview, the parents can be asked to describe expectations in the culture in which they grew up and education about the effects of particular child rearing practices on children's development may be necessary.

Ownership of their contribution to the problems

As well as acknowledging that there are problems, parents must accept the need for changes in the parent–child relationship. This requirement may contrast with the parents who believe that practical help, especially re-housing, is all that is needed. While such 'concrete solutions' (Reder *et al.* 1993) may go some way towards helping families with their social stress, they will not in themselves significantly alter the interrelationship between parent and child. Hence, there needs to be a recognition by the parents (and professionals working with them) that relationship problems require treatments that address the relationship.

Parents are unlikely to benefit from treatment if they deny responsibility for their contribution to the relationship problems and instead blame others for causing them. They may accuse professionals, such as social workers, of not having done enough for them, or for seeing problems that do not exist. Parents who persistently blame the child for the abuse that they suffered and believe that the child should change will not engage in treatment necessary to change their own contribution to the parent–child relationship.

A different form of denial of responsibility is the parents who experience events happening to them without any sense of personal involvement. They describe their lives as though they have been the passive and helpless victims of other people's whims, without any belief that they could take control of their lives. Often, they are mothers who were abused as children and later enter into relationships with violent men. Their view of themselves has a more pervasive quality from so-called 'disempowerment' in relation to men and the absence of a sense of 'personal agency' makes it extremely difficult for them to contribute to a treatment alliance.

One circumstance in which denial may be overcome is when an alleged sexual abuser is shown a video-recording of the child's disclosure. I believe that this is particularly helpful when the child has given a clear and coherent account of their abuse and I have known some fathers to change their plea once they had watched the video recording in the presence of an experienced professional worker. A few abusers will persist with their denial and remain adamant that the child is lying, in which case therapeutic intervention is contraindicated.

Most authors take the view that, until perpetrators acknowledge responsibility for their behaviour and the part they played in the child's abuse, the child remains at risk of further maltreatment (e.g. Green *et al.* 1981; Dale *et al.* 1986; Elton 1988; Bentovim 1992). For the most part, this is also true for treatability. However, I shall discuss later circumstances in which parental memory and acknowledgement of their part in the child's abuse is gradually recovered through 'therapeutic assessment'.

Internal motivation

An adequate treatment alliance depends on motivation for change that originates within the person rather than from external coercion. Internal motivation is suggested by a sense of distress that problems have occurred, genuine expressions of concern for the child and for the future of the parent–child relationship and some indication of wanting to deal with those issues.

By contrast, some parents say that they are willing to attend a treatment centre, but it becomes apparent that this is motivated by secondary gain. Sometimes, their legal advisor has suggested that they are more likely to win the court case if they make such a statement. Its genuineness can be tested by asking the parent what thoughts have gone into that decision, whether anyone has advised them to agree to it and what they know about the treatment they are willing to 'attend'. Suspicion should be raised by last minute agreements to go for treatment, just as the case is going to court, when all previous interviews have revealed an absence of motivation.

Alternatively, parents may be sent for treatment by professionals and only turn up for the assessment interviews in order to appear cooperative. Families have been referred to me as one action from a list of case conference decisions, yet their acknowledgement of problems and motivation for change is non-existent. It is essential to differentiate between cooperation and compliance. Courts may also develop an unreal belief that families can be helped and insist on their referral.

> I was involved with a single mother and her six children over a number of years. The family had a traumatic history, including the death of one child from cancer and severe burns (probably accidental) to another. The children were well known to social services with problems of staying away from home, failing to attend school, stealing, enuresis, encopresis and unsocialised aggression and all the children were on the child protection register for neglect. Despite several house moves and considerable social work input, the mother maintained that the local authority had not provided her with a satisfactory flat, with enough financial support, sufficient holidays for the children or good-enough day care for the younger ones. She saw these as her principal problems. Eventually, all the children became wards of court (under the old legislation), with care and control to their mother. At each court hearing, the mother claimed that she wished her children to have treatment with the local child psychiatrist and the court, probably sympathising with the mother's traumatic history, seemed to side with her point of view that it was someone else's responsibility to

meet the children's needs. The judge kept the children at home and ordered that the family should 'attend St George's Hospital for therapy by Dr Fitzpatrick'. Then, when I saw them, the mother said that she did not believe that she or her children had any problems. This was repeated on three occasions and each time I had to report to the court that treatment was contraindicated.

These cases place social workers in an unenviable position of trying to find *someone* to provide the treatment even though assessment indicates the parents are not motivated for change. Useful questions during assessment, therefore, are 'whose idea was it for you to come to see me?' and 'what was your reaction to that suggestion?'

However, not all maltreating parents can be expected to have a fully developed internal motivation for change from the outset. Wolfe *et al.* (1982) and Crimmins *et al.* (1984) report that court-mandated treatment can be effective, although high drop out rates are also mentioned (e.g. Famularo *et al.* 1989). I believe that treatment ordered by courts can only be effective when it is part of a well-prepared intervention plan and based on prior assessment that motivation and a treatment alliance are likely to develop as treatment progresses.

Ability to see professionals as potentially helpful

Some parents have a hostile and suspicious attitude to professionals which persists despite all attempts to help them. They do not think that anyone has helped them in the past and they do not expect anyone to prove helpful in the future. Occasionally, this is based upon actual experiences, but more commonly it stems from the parenting they received as children which was uncaring and unresponsive. They grow up unable to hold in mind a positive view of any other potential helper and it is rare for them to view professionals benignly.

This can be assessed by retracing the parent's history with them, asking about the professionals whom they have met and whether they proved helpful. Another guide is whether the parent has entered any formal treatment programme in the past, in which case they need to be asked about their attitude to it and its outcome.

Formal psychiatric disorder

It is commonly suggested that the presence of a formal psychiatric disorder, especially psychosis, contraindicates attempting to rehabilitate children and parents through psychological therapy (e.g. Jones 1987; Nicol 1988). The same is said of parents who abuse drugs or alcohol (e.g. Kempe and Kempe 1978; Gabinet 1983). In my experience, psychiatric disorders first need to be assessed by adult psychiatrists and treated with medication or other appropriate psychiatric interventions. Once the condition is under control, the parent's parenting skills and capacity to engage in therapeutic help can be assessed in the usual way. Hence, two separate, but interrelated, assessments are necessary – of the parent's psychiatric state and of the parenting relationship.

One difference is that the effects on the child of repeated parental hospitalisations need to be considered. The other is that treatment may need to be directed to the children to help them make sense of their parent's mental illness and not feel responsible for it. Conjoint sessions should also be considered in which the parent is encouraged to help the child understand about the illness.

Circumstances which are especially concerning, and mean that the child remains susceptible to emotional abuse, are when parents have withdrawn into a paranoid state that is unresponsive to psychiatric treatment. The child may have become included in the parent's delusions (Kempe and Kempe 1978), either seen as bad or else taught that the world is a dangerous place. In addition, if the parent is unwilling to attend for recommended psychiatric treatment, then rehabilitation is usually contraindicated.

> I was involved in the assessment of a single mother and her three children. The mother had had several psychotic episodes, during which she became paranoid about the outside world, withdrew into her flat, kept the curtains tightly closed and her children stopped attending school. On each occasion, the children were accommodated for the few weeks that their mother was a psychiatric in-patient and then returned to her care because she had responded well to medication. However, within a few months of discharge, the mother would stop taking her medication because she did not believe that she had been ill and she again withdrew into the flat with her children. During these episodes, the children increasingly saw the world as hostile and they were finally taken into care. Rehabilitation was not possible because the mother continued not to have insight into her psychiatric disorder.

The diagnosis of personality disorder is sometimes used as a 'catch all' to include anyone whose relationships are disordered and it is inferred that such people are inaccessible to treatment. This is unfortunate, since many parents who are so labelled have suffered severe emotional, sexual or physical abuse in childhood and they carry its effects into relationships in adult life. Many are able to be helped by psychological treatment that addresses their previous history. Indeed, it has been shown that psychotherapy is one of the factors that helps parents who were themselves maltreated break the intergenerational cycle of abuse (Egeland *et al*. 1988).

Similar arguments apply to parents with learning disability, who should not be dismissed automatically as being unable to benefit from treatment.

THERAPEUTIC ASSESSMENTS

There are some parents whose capacity to benefit from treatment and resume adequate care of their children only becomes evident over the course of a lengthy assessment process. These 'therapeutic assessments' are not the same as so-called 'trials of therapy'. Trials of therapy occur over a small number of sessions, perhaps two or three, during which the assessor clarifies whether good indicators for treatment are present and introduces the person to the process of therapy. If psychodynamic psychotherapy is being considered, the assessor suggests links between elements of the person's current experiences and previous relationships in order to assess their psychological mindedness and whether they are prepared to consider such hypotheses. In a sense, trials of therapy should be included in all assessments of parenting so that the likelihood of the parent using treatment can be reported to the court.

Therapeutic assessments, on the other hand, take more time, perhaps 6 months, because the process of unravelling the parent's conflicts is more complex. I consider recommending prolonged therapeutic assessments when faced with one or more of the following circumstances. The (usually) mothers are young and emotionally immature with flexibility in their personality, so that there is the potential to improve their parenting skills as they develop psychologically. It is possible to hypothesise that the parenting breakdown is linked to developmental crises or internal psychological conflicts, although their exact nature remains obscure at initial assessment. The parent herself is perplexed about her behaviour and unable to explain her predicament or why the abuse occurred: however, she is concerned to avoid any repetition. The nature of the parenting breakdown may be unusual and more often occurs as a result of acts of omission rather than commission. Often, the mothers are not clear in their own minds whether they wish to have the child returned to their care and this represents a general inability to resolve conflicts about themselves or the child without outside help. In addition, they acknowledge that there are problems and are willing to engage cooperatively with professional agencies.

The other group of cases in which I consider recommending therapeutic assessment is when there is clear evidence of a good attachment between the parent and child, because of islets of good-enough parenting, despite breakdown in other aspects of the parenting behaviour. Examples would be parents who recurrently abuse alcohol or repeatedly take overdoses, or mothers who function adequately when not in a relationship with a violent partner.

Initially, the assessment addresses whether modification is possible in the parent's perception of the problem and their contribution to it, as well as their ability to cooperate with a therapeutic approach. As it progresses, it addresses whether the parent can acknowledge the separate existence of the child as a person in its own right and their need to provide a safe physical environment for the child and ensure protection from harm. It is essential that therapeutic

assessments take place within a clear and effective child protection framework and that the assessment and treatment components remain interlinked,
since the assessment needs to address whether therapeutic input has led to
actual changes in parenting and therefore diminished risk to the child.

Therapeutic assessment following denial of pregnancy

The indicators for therapeutic assessments are well illustrated in a series of
mothers I have seen who had denied that they were pregnant and had either
abandoned or assaulted their newborn baby. The denial process needed to be
the focus of much of the work with them.

In giving their histories, the mothers claimed that they had never realised
that they were pregnant, or only became aware of it at a very late stage. Their
partner, family and friends were similarly unaware of the pregnancy. There
was no preparation for the babies, no antenatal care and after the births the
babies were either related to as unwelcomed, intrusive and persecutory beings
or else were ignored as though they did not exist. The babies suffered a range
of fates, from rejection and failure of mother–infant bonding, through
physical abuse, to abandonment and sometimes infanticide. The mothers
showed no evidence of puerperal psychosis or formal psychiatric disorder,
which is consistent with other reports in the literature (Brozovsky and Falit
1971; Wilkins 1985; Cherland and Matthews 1989; Bonnet 1993).

An 18 year old single mother was referred because she had been traced as
the mother of a baby found abandoned in a telephone box. She had never
acknowledged that she was pregnant, had given birth secretly and then
abandoned the baby as an attempt to conceal its existence. She and her own
mother now wanted the baby returned to her care. I assessed the mother as
immature, with a child-like naivity. Her denial did not have a fixed,
organised quality but was primarily based on her fear of the consequences
of police prosecution. I offered her psychotherapy, which lasted for 6
months, during which she gradually recovered memories of the pregnancy
and birth. This was followed by 6 months in a mother and baby unit. As a
result of her increased personal maturity and the child existing in her mind
as well as in the external world, the infant was successfully returned home.

A 23 year old woman was traced by the police as the mother of a baby
found in the rubbish chute of a block of flats where she lived with her
boyfriend. It was by chance that the baby was discovered by a man out
walking his dog. The dog had sniffed around a black rubbish sack and,
when the man went to investigate, he heard a whimper of the newborn baby
inside. The baby survived. The mother's boyfriend denied knowledge of
the pregnancy and birth and the mother herself at first denied to the police
all knowledge of her pregnancy, the birth or the infant's disposal. However,
when they later identified her as the infant's mother, she asked for him to

be returned to her care. This mother had a mild learning disability, but the most relevant finding at assessment was that she expressed no guilt about her act, or concern for its implications for the baby. She did not think of the baby as a person but as a doll which she could wheel around in a pram. The infant was eventually placed for adoption.

A 39 year old single professional parent had planned her pregnancy so that she could have the baby but no further contact with the father. She concealed the pregnancy from her family, friends and colleagues and deliberately went to France for the baby's birth, having resigned from her job. Mother and baby then returned to England when the baby was 1 week old, but no one in this country was aware of the baby's existence until she was admitted to hospital with fractures of her ribs and limbs. The mother's explanation was that she had dropped her when walking downstairs. At assessment, it was evident that the mother was depressed, with feelings and conflicts accessible to her, and she was in an emotional crisis. She received antidepressant medication and I also saw her for 5 months of weekly psychotherapy, after which the baby was successfully rehabilitated home, and the therapy continued for a further 18 months after this.

My understanding of these situations is that the mothers are unable to allow space in their minds for the pregnancy and the inevitability of the child. The child does not have an internal existence in the mother's mind and, when born, cannot exist externally for her. Underlying conflicts concern the mother's relationship with her own mother, with her father, with the baby's father, and/or with her own body, sexuality and femininity.

The following case study illustrates in more detail the intrapsychic conflicts of such mothers and how decisions about their capacity to parent may require many months of psychotherapeutic assessment. The work was carried out as part of a much wider intervention by social workers, health visitor, mother and baby unit and family resource centre. Importantly, it was sanctioned by a child protection framework which included repeated court hearings, regular case conferences and other meetings of the professional network in which I, as assessor/therapist, fully participated.

Sheila was a 21 year old woman who was referred to me by her social worker when she was 25 weeks pregnant, with the request to help social services make decisions about her ability to meet the needs of her unborn baby. Sheila had left home at the age of 18 to marry her (first) boyfriend of the same age. She soon became pregnant but had no knowledge of it until the child's birth. The baby was named Michelle and, when she was 6 weeks old, she was taken into casualty with a fractured skull, from which she died 8 months later. Both parents were initially charged with grievous bodily harm but the criminal case was dropped because of insufficient evidence. When Michelle died, the police arrested Sheila's husband on a charge of murder. Sheila told me during our initial meeting that neither she nor her husband had caused the injuries to the baby and she could not understand how they had happened. However, Sheila had not visited Michelle during the months that she had remained alive, nor had she enquired about her well-being. Following her husband's remand, Sheila 'discovered' that she was now 22 weeks pregnant and this led to the referral to me from social services.

At the initial interview, Sheila expressed little feeling about this second pregnancy, except to say that it filled up the emptiness inside her. Sheila's emotionally 'cut-off' state was exemplified by such statements as 'I can't think', 'I don't remember', 'I don't know how I feel'. She expressed some fears that the baby would be removed from her and said that she wanted to care for it. Five days after this interview, Sheila went into premature labour and a 2 lb 3 oz baby boy was born by emergency Caesarean section. My initial report to social services was that Sheila's capacity to care for her second child would require prolonged assessment and, as part of the child protection plan, I arranged to see Sheila for a number of weekly assessment meetings, which eventually extended into treatment lasting over a year.

In the early months, Sheila gave the impression of being a spectator in her own life. She spent a lot of time in the intensive care unit, not with her infant, but in an adjoining parent's suite. The staff reported a sense of disconnection between themselves and Sheila and Sheila and the baby. In her sessions with me, she rarely mentioned her baby unless I asked and it took her many weeks even to give him the name Robert.

Sheila seemed to accept passively everything that happened in her day-to-day life and expressed no emotion about it. The first time that she spontaneously expressed any emotion was in the fifth session. Robert had required surgery at another hospital and, when asked to accompany him, she had refused. Eventually she 'remembered' that Michelle had been treated at that particular hospital and she acknowledged that she could not face the thoughts and memories about Michelle. I felt that, until Michelle existed for Sheila, there was no possibility of Robert existing and that Michelle needed to 'come alive' psychologically for Sheila so that she could mourn her loss (as discussed by Lewis 1979). I therefore encouraged Sheila to talk about Michelle, to visit her grave and, with the aid of photographs and information from the social worker, pieced together details about her short life.

Alongside this aspect of the work, I also explored Sheila's relationships with her parents. Although there was no history of overt maltreatment, Sheila felt that she had not existed for either of her parents and there was no emotional contact between them now. Then, as a mother in her own right, Sheila 'never felt like a mother', 'didn't feel anything for her', 'it seemed she didn't belong to me', 'it seemed nothing but crying and feeding, crying and feeding'.

Over the next few months, Sheila tentatively approached owning a memory of Michelle, at one point saying, 'I wish I knew why it happened'. However, her handling of Robert remained distant and awkward with no eye contact and by the time he was ready to be leave hospital at 4 months of age, it was clear that he still had no place in his mother's mind and he was discharged to a foster home under an interim care order.

Sheila accepted this arrangement and visited him regularly, although she was reluctant to wash and feed him there. Instead, she quickly developed a dependent relationship on the foster mother and saw Robert as a rival for her attention. Sheila cast the social worker and me as withholding figures (just like her mother) who were depriving her of her child and she threatened to abandon the baby and move away. However, she did not carry out her threats and continued to see me and we were able to understand her fears that I, too, would not be interested in her and would forget about her.

We were also able to explore Sheila's feelings of being like an infant, a non-sexual child, who was quite disconnected from her adult physical and sexual body. She had no awareness of her menstrual cycle and could not tell me the dates of her periods. She confused sexuality with sentimentality and avidly read Mills and Boon romances. She experienced her baby as a 'doll' who had arrived unannounced and unexpected and was not the result of parental intercourse. Her thoughts about pregnancy and labour resembled the fantasies of a very young child and seemed disconnected from actual experience. These attitudes to sexuality gradually changed as we discussed them and Sheila became aware that she wanted her baby. However, she wanted him because he might love her, meet her emotional needs and fill up her emptiness inside.

Following this shift in Sheila's relationship to Robert, in which he began to be 'real' for her, the child protection network agreed for them to move together into a residential unit for 3 months. From there, they moved to an independent living unit combined with attendance at a family resource centre. This allowed her parenting skills to be assessed while her therapeutic assessment with me continued. It was Sheila who insisted on bringing Robert to these sessions rather than leave him with someone else for 3 hours and she talked constantly about him while feeding and changing him in my room. She talked with regret about the loss of their time together during the early weeks of his life when he was in special care, of having to get to know him and how alike, or unlike, Michelle he was.

Robert was not an easy baby and he had recurrent chest infections which required medication. Because of the previous history, I felt it was particularly important for Sheila to be aware of her negative feelings towards him so that she could find a way to deal with them and I was able to link her perception of Robert as a greedy and demanding baby with her own murderously angry infantile feelings.

When Robert was 11 months old, Sheila and he were rehoused in their own accommodation, after a court hearing that granted a 1-year supervision order to social services. I reported to the court that Sheila had managed to separate emotionally from her husband, was able to grieve the death of her first child and was able to acknowledge her failure to protect her. As a result, she was aware of her responsibility to protect Robert. The residential unit also reported on the observable improvement in her parenting skills. I continued to see Sheila for psychotherapy in her own right for a further 6 months, at decreasing intervals, during which time we further explored her relationship to her own mother.

Prolonged assessment of Sheila revealed many of the underlying conflicts that I have noted with mothers in similar cases and have also been reported by Bonnet (1993). Pregnancy triggers the re-emergence of traumatic childhood memories and, in order to protect the self from experiencing unbearable psychological conflict, the memories are repressed by denial and, with them, knowledge of the pregnancy. Memories may be of parental neglect, physical violence or sexual abuse and, because the associated intense psychic pain renders them unthinkable and unbearable, the pregnancy/foetus also becomes unthinkable, unbearable and unknowable. Instead, signs of pregnancy are rationalised, with weight gain attributed to changes in eating habits, for example.

The early traumatic experiences also leave the women with conflicts about their sexuality, their femininity and knowledge about fruitful parental intercourse. They deny their procreative potential and their actual pregnancy in order to protect them from these conflicts. These women did not consider contraception since, right up to the discovery of the foetus, they never imagined that they were capable of becoming pregnant. Becoming impregnated through sexual intercourse with a man was unthinkable. Their subsequent pregnancies were similarly unthinkable.

It also seemed clear that, in a number of these women, denial of the existence of the foetus protected it from their mother's violent fantasies that originated in their early traumatic upbringing. Once knowledge of the foetus/baby was allowed to enter the mind, there was a potential for murderous thoughts to become conscious and to be acted upon.

I therefore believe that, when considering whether rehabilitation of a mother and baby is possible in such cases, the psychological conflicts and fantasies of the mother need to be assessed. This should included addressing whether the child can be thought about (or, literally, borne) in the mother's mind and thereby acquire a psychological existence for her. Only when this occurs can the mother begin to address the actual emotional and physical needs of the child.

Although I have discussed the indicators and process of therapeutic assessments in cases of denial of pregnancy, the same principles apply to other examples of parenting breakdown. When it is uncertain whether a parent can successfully resume care of their physically, sexually or emotionally abused child because the conflictual basis for the caretaking problems are unclear but appear to be accessible, therapeutic assessment should be considered. The indications for persisting with such an intervention are that the parent continues to respond well to the therapy and shows improvement in their relationship with the child and in general parenting skills. Therapeutic assessment needs to continue until it is evident that the mother is meeting the child's needs and that the risk to the child is minimised. After that, continued therapy in its own right may be indicated.

COMMON ISSUES DURING TREATMENT

Sheila was offered psychodynamic psychotherapy in an out-patient setting, together with help for parenting skills in a mother and baby unit. In my experience, cases of severe maltreatment require an approach that simultaneously addresses different aspects of the problem and this is often best provided in settings such as a day or residential unit. Exploratory work can proceed alongside practical support and the learning of behavioural skills.

No matter what modality of treatment is offered, a number of issues commonly arise during its course. They need to be anticipated and measures taken to prevent them becoming a barrier to progress. If these measures are woven into the treatment programme, then an initial assessment for treatment will not consider the parent's liability to show them as a contraindication for treatment.

Because of their own history of deprivation and maltreatment, most parents attending a unit to resolve their abusing behaviour will eventually develop considerable dependency on the unit (Kennedy 1988). They value the care and concern shown by staff and the practical support that they receive. At some stage, a state of homeostasis develops, in which little progress occurs but little deterioration either. If left unacknowledged, the parents would continue attending and valuing the unit, but no further change would result. Because no further abuse is reported, anxiety abates in the professional network and there is little impetus for change.

Therefore, at the Emanuel Miller Unit, we integrate into the programme regular reviews in which we ask the parent(s) 'what issues do you want to work on?', we ask ourselves 'why is treatment still happening?' and we ask members of the professional network 'what external changes do you require in order for treatment to be considered successful?'

Another issue that some therapists find difficult is the possibility of being asked to write a report for court proceedings during the course of treatment. In my view, this should not pose any problem and therapists should always be prepared to write court reports. I consider this to be a measure of them acknowledging the interrelationship between the internal and external world and the need to integrate treatment with the demands of the real world.

CONCLUSIONS

There is no hierarchy of importance in the factors required for treatability. They are interdependent. Parents must show a willingness to engage with professionals, in trying to solve parenting problems that they believe exist, which they acknowledge that they have contributed to. Parents will not benefit from treatment if they persistently deny responsibility for their abusive behaviour, blame problems on to other people and have a suspicious or hostile attitude to professionals. Parents with a formal psychiatric disorder, who include the child in their delusional world and refuse to attend for psychiatric treatment, are also unlikely to benefit from any of the psychological therapies.

Prolonged therapeutic assessments are indicated for young and emotionally immature parents who are likely to develop parenting skills as they mature psychologically and when there is some indication that the underlying conflicts will become accessible.

REFERENCES

Asen, K., George, E., Piper, R. and Stevens, A. (1989) 'A systems approach to child abuse: management and treatment issues', *Child Abuse and Neglect*, **13**, 45–58.

Bentovim, A. (1992) *Trauma Organised Systems: Physical and Sexual Abuse in Families*, London: Karnac.

Bonnet, C. (1993) 'Adoption at birth: prevention against abandonment or neonaticide', *Child Abuse and Neglect*, **17**, 501–13.

Brozovsky, M. and Falit, H. (1971) 'Neonaticide: clinical and psychodynamic considerations', *Journal of the American Academy of Child Psychiatry*, **10**, 673–83.

Cherland, E. and Matthews, P.C. (1989) 'Attempted murder of a newborn: a case study', *Canadian Journal of Psychiatry*, **34**, 337–9.

Crimmins, D.B., Bradlyn, A.S., St Lawrence, J.S. and Kelly, J.A. (1984) 'A training programme for improving the parent–child interaction skills of an abusive-neglectful mother', *Child Abuse and Neglect*, **8**, 533–9.

Dale, P., Davies, M., Morrison, T. and Waters, J. (1986) *Dangerous Families*, London: Tavistock.

Egeland, B., Jacobvitz, B. and Sroufe, L.A. (1988) 'Breaking the cycle of abuse', *Child Development*, **59**, 1080–8.

Elton, A. (1988) 'Assessment of families for treatment', in A. Bentovim, A. Elton, J. Hildebrand, M. Tranter and E. Vizard (eds) *Child Sexual Abuse within the Family: Assessment and Treatment*, London: Wright.

Famularo, R., Kinscherff, R., Bunshaft, D., Spivak, G. and Fenton, T. (1989) 'Parental compliance to court-ordered treatment interventions in cases of child maltreatment', *Child Abuse and Neglect*, **13**, 507–14.

Furniss, T. (1991) *The Multi-Professional Handbook of Child Sexual Abuse: Integrated Management, Therapy and Legal Intervention*, London: Routledge.

Gabinet, L. (1983) 'Child abuse treatment failures reveal need for redefinition of the problem', *Child Abuse and Neglect*, **7**, 394–402.

Glaser, D. (1993) 'Emotional abuse', in C.J. Hobbs and J.M. Wynne (eds) *Clinical Paediatrics: International Practice and Research, Vol. 1, No. 1*, London: Baillière Tindall.

Gough, D. (1993) *Child Abuse Interventions: A Review of the Research Literature*, London: HMSO.

Green, A.H., Power, E., Steinbook, B. and Gaines, R. (1981) 'Factors associated with successful and unsuccessful intervention with child abusive families', *Child Abuse and Neglect*, **5**, 45–52.

Jones, D.P.H. (1987) 'The untreatable family', *Child Abuse and Neglect*, **11**, 409–20.

Jones, D.P.H. (1991) 'The effectiveness of intervention', in M. Adcock, R. White and A. Hollows (eds) *Significant Harm*, Croydon: Significant Publications.

Kempe, R.S. and Kempe, C.H. (1978) *Child Abuse*, London: Open Books.

Kennedy, R. (1988) 'The treatment of child abuse in an in-patient setting', *Bulletin of the Royal College of Psychiatrists*, **12**, 361–6.

Lewis, E. (1979) 'Two hidden predisposing factors in child abuse', *Child Abuse and Neglect*, **3**, 327–30.

Lynch, M.A. and Roberts, J. (1982) *Consequences of Child Abuse*, London: Academic Press.

Nicol, R. (1988) 'The treatment of child abuse in the home environment', in K. Browne, C. Davies and P. Stratton (eds) *Early Prediction and Prevention of Child Abuse*, Chichester: Wiley.

Reder, P., Duncan, S. and Gray, M. (1993) *Beyond Blame: Child Abuse Tragedies Revisited*, London: Routledge.

Sandler, J., Dare, C. and Holder, A. (1973) *The Patient and the Analyst: The Basis of the Psychoanalytic Process*, London: George Allen and Unwin.

Steele, B. (1980) 'Psychodynamic factors in child abuse', in C.H. Kempe and R.E. Helfer (eds) *The Battered Child*, 3rd edn, Chicago: University of Chicago Press.

Trepper, T.S. and Barrett, M.J. (1989) *Systemic Treatment of Incest: A Therapeutic Handbook*, New York: Brunner/Mazel.

Wilkins, A.J. (1985) 'Attempted infanticide', *British Journal of Psychiatry*, **146**, 206–8.

Wolfe, D.A., Sandler, J. and Kauffman, K. (1981) 'A competency-based parent training program for child abusers', *Journal of Consulting and Clinical Psychology*, **49**, 633–40.

Wolfe, D.A., Lawrence, J.S., Graves, K., Brehony, K., Bradlyn, D. and Kelly, J.A. (1982) 'Intensive behavioural parent training for a child abuse mother', *Behaviour Therapy*, **13**, 438–52.

Chapter 8

Predicting maltreatment
Kevin Browne

INTRODUCTION

The focus of this chapter is the assessment of risk in cases where parents are having emotional difficulties in caring for their children and the parent–child relationship is starting to break down. This is especially relevant for court work where difficult decisions have to be made in relation to care proceedings and, if the child is already on the child protection register, an assessment has to be made as to the risk of the family reabusing the child or abusing other children in the family.

At any one time, 4 in every 1,000 English children are currently listed on child protection registers. The majority of these children are under 5 years of age and males and females are equally represented (Department of Health 1994). Even after families have been referred to child protection agencies at least one in two abused children are reabused according to US estimates (Magura 1981). No such estimates exist for the UK, but a study by Hyman (1978) showed that 40 per cent of cases of child abuse coming up for case conference have already been known to the relevant authorities either on account of previous injury to the child under review or to one of his or her siblings. This is a common finding throughout the child abuse literature yet one apparently little appreciated by magistrates.

A study on child abuse in Ontario, Canada (cited in Greenland 1987) examined a small population of severely abused children requiring hospital admission. It was reported that 20 per cent of these children had been previously abused and that 10 per cent also had brothers and sisters who had been abused in previous incidents. In a later study, Greenland (1987) showed that 16 per cent of abused cases had a sibling who had either sustained a serious injury, or had died as a result of such an injury.

Risk factors to siblings

The dynamics of child abuse sometimes involves only one child but more often other children in the household will also be at risk. In some cases, the absence of the abused child may shift the focus of stress and frustration to another child in the family. In other families children are 'at risk' during a certain age, but if this is successfully passed the risk declines. Indeed, an older sibling of the abused child may have already been abused without detection.

According to an NSPCC study, *Child Abuse Trends in England and Wales 1983–1987* (Creighton and Noyes 1989), physical injury carries the least risk to siblings in comparison to other forms of child maltreatment. The percentage of siblings registered for the same type of abuse as the index child was as follows: 11 per cent physical injury; 14 per cent failure to thrive; 23 per cent sexual abuse; 39 per cent emotional abuse; 60 per cent neglect. It must be pointed out, however, that much earlier research in England (Baldwin and Oliver 1975) put the abuse risk to siblings at a much higher rate. Severe or moderate physical abuse was ascertained in 63 per cent of the siblings and suspected in a further 9 per cent.

Similar high figures were found in a more recent New York City study where 'lasting-harm or injury' to siblings was seen in 44 per cent of cases and suspected in a further 4 per cent (Greenland 1987).

In the book *Consequences of Child Abuse* Lynch and Roberts (1982) describe a study of 42 abused pre-school children, 23 of whom had been seriously injured, in comparison to their 27 siblings aged under 9 years. None of the siblings had any record of being abused, however there was evidence that the home environment and less than skilled parenting had had some effect on the abused children's brothers and sisters. Developmental assessments showed that 59 per cent of the abused children and 33 per cent of their siblings showed some developmental delay. In fact there was very little difference in the pre-school children's language delay (36 per cent of abused children and 28 per cent of siblings showing language delay).

Overall, the best developmental progress was shown in siblings born after the abuse incident i.e. brothers and sisters younger than the abused child. On follow-up, both abused children and their brothers and sisters showed behavioural problems (60 per cent of the abused and 40 per cent respectively) and there were no sex differences.

It might be suggested from the above that it is the abusive environment, rather than the abuse itself, which adversely affects child development and that it is in the best interests of a child to be removed from such living conditions whether or not they are the actual victims of physical violence. Alternatively, it might be pointed out that children who are taken into care and have 'lost' more than one family during their care history are also likely to show overt behavioural disturbances on follow-up (Lynch and Roberts 1982; Roberts 1993).

The dilemma is: will a child's development as an individual be enhanced by placing him/her in care? Placing children in care does *not* favour optimal development and only 6 per cent of children in long-term care receive any kind of help with their past experiences or rehabilitation with their natural parents (Rowe *et al*. 1984). Thus, one of the most important aspects to care proceedings is the assessment of risk to the child.

THE RISK APPROACH

As with other problems in child health and development, the risk approach to child maltreatment can be seen as a tool for the flexible and rational distribution of scarce resources and their maximal utilisation. This is based on the assessment of children and their families as high or low risk for child abuse and neglect. The aim of the risk strategy is to give special attention to those in the greatest need of help in parenting before child maltreatment occurs or reoccurs.

In the short term, intervention techniques aimed at the early prediction and identification of potential or actual abusing parents are more realistic than instigating changes in child care practice for all parents (primary prevention). This is considered to be secondary prevention and includes professionals involved in counselling, home visits and clinic, health centre or hospital care. Such professionals can be instructed routinely to screen for predicative characteristics in all families who come in contact with the service they are providing.

A number of articles have been written on the prediction of child abuse, many of which have presented a list of characteristics common to abusing parents and to abused children.

For example, it has been suggested that an 'early warning system' could begin in the labour room and that abusing parents can be predicted with 76 per cent accuracy from characteristics noted during the first 24 hours after birth (Gray *et al*. 1977). However, a recent review of the relative value of these characteristics for the practical and routine monitoring of potential child abusing families has emphasised a need for caution (Browne 1995).

Browne (1995) demonstrated the danger of predictive claims by evaluating a typical checklist completed by community nurses around the time of birth. The concept of the checklist was that, when applied to all families with a newborn child in a given locality, exceptional families with a high number of adverse risk factors were identified and visited more often. It was assumed that the higher the number of factors present, the greater the intervention required and the more 'at risk' the child. Evidence for the predominance of factors used for screening in abusing families had been already established (Browne and Saqi 1988a).

Community nurses completed a thirteen-item checklist (see Table 8.1) on all children under 5 years for whom a case conference was called on child physical abuse and neglect in the past year. In total, information was collected on 62 case-conferenced families. The community nurse concerned then identified two matched 'control' non-abusing families from the same district (i.e. 124 families) to whom the checklist was also applied.

The percentage of abusing and non-abusing families showing each risk factor is presented in Table 8.1. Most of the risk factors exhibit a significant difference between the two samples, with the abusing families invariably showing a higher percentage. The risk factors are presented in order of relative importance as determined by stepwise discriminant function analysis, which takes into account any confounding influences between factors. Thus, the contribution of each risk factor to discriminate between abusing (NAI) cases and their matched controls was determined. Table 8.1 shows that the observation of whether the parent was indifferent, intolerant or overanxious was the best predictor, followed by family violence and socio-legal-economic problems.

Using discriminant function analysis, the optimum performance of the whole checklist as a screening instrument was established. It was found that fully completed checklists, with the relative weighting for each factor taken into account, could correctly classify 86 per cent of cases, which is better than most studies (Starr 1982). The screening procedure was sensitive to 82 per cent of the abusing families and specified 88 per cent of the control families as non-abusing. However, if the checklist of risk factors is used in this way it will miss 18 per cent of the abusing families and incorrectly identify 12 per cent of the non-abusing families as potential NAI cases. This has grave implications when such a checklist is applied prospectively to a population of births.

The low prevalence of child abuse, combined with even the most optimistic estimates of screening effectiveness, implies that a screening programme would yield large numbers of false positives. The checklist detection rate of 82 per cent compared to 12 per cent false alarms suggests that for every 10,000 births screened it would be necessary to distinguish between 33 true risk cases and 1,195 false alarms. This would indicate the requirement of a second screening procedure, to be carried out only on the 1,228 or so families labelled 'high risk' (Browne 1989b).

A more lengthy assessment could be used on these high-risk families, based on the significant differences between abusing and non-abusing families found in parent–child interaction studies (e.g. Browne and Saqi 1987; 1988b). Thus, a second screening could possibly distinguish the true potential NAI cases from the false positives by the use of behavioural indicators. A more difficult problem would be to distinguish the 7 missed cases of potential child abuse from the 8,765 correctly identified non-abusers, as they would be mixed up in a low-risk population of 8,772 families.

When the checklist was applied prospectively to a sample of 14,252 births (Browne 1995) it was found that 6.8 per cent of families with a newborn had a high number of 'predisposing' factors for child abuse. On follow-up, only 1 in 12 (7.6 per cent) of these 'high-risk' families went on to abuse their child

Table 8.1 Relative importance of screening characteristics for child abuse (as determined by stepwise discriminate function analysis)[a]

Checklist: characteristics	Abusing families (N = 62) %	Non-abusing families (N = 124) %
1. Parent indifferent, intolerant or overanxious towards child	83.9	21.8*
2. History of family violence	51.6	5.6*
3. Socioeconomic problems such as unemployment	85.5	34.7*
4. Infant premature, low birth weight	24.2	3.2*
5. Parent abused or neglected as a child	43.5	6.5*
6. Step-parent or cohabitee present	35.5	4.8*
7. Single or separated parent	38.7	8.1*
8. Mother less than 21 years old at the time of birth	40.3	23.4*
9. History of mental illness, drug or alcohol addiction	61.3	21.8*
10. Infant separated from mother for greater than 24 hours post-delivery	17.7	5.6*
11. Infant mentally or physically handicapped	1.6	0.8
12. Less than 18 months between birth of children	22.6	15.3
13. Infant never breast fed	46.8	40.3

* Significant difference *p*< 0.05.
[a] From Browne and Saqi (1988a).

within 5 years of birth, in comparison to 1 in 391 (0.3 per cent) for the low-risk families. Thus, it can be concluded that risk factors significantly predispose families to child abuse, but are not sufficient actually to cause violence in the vast majority (92 per cent) of families under stress.

The chances of situational stressors (risk factors) resulting in child abuse and other forms of family violence are mediated by, and depend on, the interactive relationships within the family. A secure relationship between family members will 'buffer' any effects of stress and facilitate coping strategies on behalf of the family. In contrast, insecure or anxious relationships will not 'buffer' the family under stress and any overload, such as an argument or a child misbehaving, may result in a physical or emotional attack. Overall, this will have a negative effect on the existing interpersonal relationships and reduce any 'buffering' effects still further, making it easier for stressors to overload the family system once again. This may lead to a situation where stress results in repeated physical assaults on the child.

On a more positive note, Leventhal (1988) provides evidence from longitudinal cohort studies that suggests prediction is feasible. However, he concludes that improvements in the assessment of high-risk families are necessary, including the further development and use of a standardised clinical assessment of the parent–child relationship.

THE ASSESSMENT OF PARENT–CHILD RELATIONSHIPS

The move away from sociodemographic approaches to clinical forms of assessment for pathological parenting, requires detailed knowledge of parent–child interaction and attachment in child maltreating families.

Belsky (1980; 1988) conceptualises child maltreatment as a social-psychological phenomenon that is multiply determined by forces at work in the individual, the family, as well as in the community and the culture in which both the individual and the family are embedded. Given a particular combination of these factors, an interactional style develops within the family and it is in the context of this interaction that abuse occurs.

There are five important aspects to the assessment of parent–child relationships: (1) the evaluation of caretakers' knowledge and attitudes to parenting the child; (2) parental perceptions of the child's behaviour; (3) parental emotions and responses to stress; (4) the observation of parent–child interaction and behaviour; and (5) the quality of child to parent attachment.

Knowledge and attitudes to child rearing

Research suggests that abusing and non-abusing families have different attitudes about child development. Martin and Rodeheffer (1976) reported that abusers have distorted and unrealistically high expectations about their children's abilities and this influences discipline and punishment. For example, abusing parents may have unrealistic beliefs that babies should be able to sit alone at 12 weeks and take their first step at 40 weeks. More importantly, they may expect their infants to be able to recognise wrong-doing at 52 weeks. Therefore, a significant proportion of sexual and physical abusive incidents involve senseless attempts by parents to force a child to behave in a manner that is beyond the child's developmental limitations.

Some research has suggested that these deficits in parental knowledge or understanding were due to low adult intelligence (e.g. Smith 1975), but this has been refuted (Hyman 1977). The parents know what to expect and do with young children, they just do not apply this knowledge to their own children. Starr (1982) found that one of the differences between abusing and non-abusing parents is that the abusing group see child rearing as a simple rather than a complex task. Many of them show a lack of awareness of their child's abilities and needs.

Parental perceptions of child behaviour in abusing and non-abusing (high-risk and low-risk) families

Crittenden (1988a) discusses the role of the parents' thought processes in the distortion of interactive patterns in maltreating families. She found that two patterns, cooperation/interference and involved/withdrawn, significantly discriminated abusing and non-abusing families. Stratton and Swaffer (1988) also conclude that there are good theoretical grounds for supposing that the beliefs that abusive parents hold about their children are an important factor in determining whether, and in what ways, a child will be abused. The results of their work show that abusing mothers attribute more control and more internal causes to their children and less to themselves in comparison with a non-abusing group of mothers of handicapped children. They go on to suggest that causal attributions held by abusive parents, both in general and with respect to their children, should be a powerful indicator to the chances of child maltreatment.

It is believed that abusing parents have more negative conceptions of their children's behaviour than non-abusing parents; they perceive their children to be more irritable and demanding. This may be related to the fact that abused children are more likely to have health problems, eating or sleeping disturbances. Alternatively, it may be a direct result of the unrealistic expectations of abusing parents (Rosenberg and Reppucci 1983).

A study conducted by Browne and Saqi (1987) looked at mother–infant interaction in abusing families compared with high-risk and low-risk control groups. The control families with an infant of the same age and sex were designated high or low risk on the basis of their scores on the checklist of risk factors described earlier. The families were also matched for ages and occupation of parents, ethnic origin of child and type of housing. During four weekly home visits the mother and child were observed at play and the mother was asked to complete a questionnaire with reference to her child's behaviour. The questionnaire was based on the Behaviour Checklist devised by Richman et al. (1983) and covered four main areas of behaviour: sleeping and eating patterns, activity, controllability and interaction with others. The results showed a significant difference in responses. Abusers had significantly more negative perceptions than low-risk or high-risk mothers. The low-risk mothers had the most positive perceptions.

Fewer negative perceptions may be related to the fact that the low-risk group had experienced significantly fewer life stress events (from the Parenting Stress Index, Abidin 1983) over the previous 12 months. This confirms the validity of the 'social-situational' approach as the high-risk group mirror the abusers in the number of life stress events. However, a parent under stress still requires a certain level of misconception about their child to become a potential child abuser. Thus, high-risk parents who do not go on to abuse, have more positive perceptions about their children than do the abusing parents. This has also been confirmed by the work of Wood-Schuman and Cone (1986).

It has previously been suggested that the child contributes to its own abuse by placing stress on vulnerable parents (Kadushin and Martin 1981). Browne and Saqi (1987) do not support this notion, as they found no significant differences in children's health records. The abuse may be attributed to the fact that the parents have unrealistic expectations of their children. They interpret certain age-appropriate behaviours as deliberate non-compliance, concluding that this behaviour is an indication of the child's inherent 'bad' disposition.

Thus, abusive parents may see their child's behaviour as a threat to their own self-esteem, which then elicits a punitive attitude and an insensitive approach to parenting.

Assessing parental emotion and responses to stress

A factor common to many child abusers is heightened arousal in stressful situations. Frodi and Lamb (1980) showed video-taped scenes of crying and smiling infants to abusive parents and matched controls. They found that abusers showed greater discomfort, irritation and emotional arousal in response to infant cries and smiles. Abusive parents also showed greater physiological arousal, such as increased blood pressure and heart rate, and reported more annoyance, indifference and less sympathy to both the crying and smiling infants.

In a similar study conducted by Wolfe et al. (1983), abusive and non-abusive parents were presented with scenes of video-taped parent–child interaction, some of which were highly stressful (such as children screaming and refusing to comply with their parents) and some of which were non-stressful (e.g. a child watching television quietly). As expected, the abusive parents responded with greater negative arousal than did the non-abusive comparison group.

Thus, it may be suggested that poor responses to stress and emotional arousal play a crucial role in the manifestation of child abuse and neglect. Indeed, measures of stress, such as the Family Stress Checklist (Orkow 1985) and the Parenting Stress Index (PSI) (Abidin 1983) have previously been used for studies on child abuse (e.g. Browne and Saqi 1987). The PSI is a screening instrument that provides scores related to the parent's sense of attachment, competence, social isolation, relationship with spouse, mental and physical health. In addition to an assessment of life stress events, it also provides scores on the child's demands, mood, activity, adaptability and acceptability, as perceived by the parent.

In relation to physical child abuse, indicators of individual differences in impulsive aggression have also been developed, such as the irritability and emotional susceptibility scales (Capara *et al*. 1985). However, Edmunds and Kendrick (1980) conclude, from their study of the measurement of aggression, that indices of social interaction are required. For example, the ratio of positive to negative comments is an important indicator of affection in relationships (Browne 1986).

Trickett and Kuczynski (1986) studied the techniques of discipline chosen by parents and their effectiveness. They found that abusive parents reported using punitive approaches, such as yelling and threatening, regardless of the type of child misbehaviour. Non-abusive parents, on the other hand, used a variety of disciplinary techniques depending on the situation. Consequently, it was found that abused children were less likely than non-abused children to comply to their parents' commands.

The majority of incidents of physical abuse which come to the notice of the authorities arise from situations where parents are attempting to control or discipline their children. Abusive parents are significantly more harsh to their children on a day-to-day basis and are less appropriate in their choice of disciplinary methods compared to non-abusive parents. It is the ineffectiveness of the abusive parents' child management styles which contributes to the abuse. If the parents' initial command is ineffective and is ignored by the child the situation will escalate and become more and more stressful until the only way the abusive parents feel they can regain control is by resorting to violence.

Patterson (1986) described rejecting parents as very unclear on how to discipline their children. They punish for insignificant transgressions, whereas serious transgressions, such as stealing, go unpunished. Where threats are given, they are carried through unpredictably. Neglectful parents show very low rates of positive physical contact, touching and hugging and high levels of coercive, aversive interactions.

In contrast, effective parenting is characterised by a flexible attitude, so that parents respond to the needs of the child and the situation. House-rules are enforced in a consistent and firm manner, using commands or sanctions where necessary. In most situations, the child will comply with the wishes of the parent and conflict will not arise.

Observing parent–child interaction and behaviour

The reciprocal nature of the parent–child relationship, or lack of it, has been observed by methods broadly based on the Strange Situation Procedure (Ainsworth and Wittig 1969). The methods used involve at least three phases of observation of the child's behaviour and interaction: before separation from the mother; during separation; and on reunion.

Overall, research studies (Hyman *et al.* 1979; Lewis and Schaeffer 1981; Gaensbauer 1982; Browne and Saqi 1987; 1988b; Browne 1989a) indicate that, prior to separation, there is less interaction and less positive affect between abusing mother–child pairs in comparison with non-abusing pairs. During separation, abused infants show less interest in strangers and objects around the room and are less upset than their matched controls. However, abused infants that do display distress and discomfort persist in this, long after their mother's return. By contrast, the matched non-abused infants show immediate recovery. On reunion, the abused infants show less positive affect and greeting behaviour and, again, mother–infant interaction in abusing pairs is less reciprocal than controls, with fewer visual and vocal exchanges.

Therefore, one method of assessment is to look at the amount of interactive behaviour occurring between parent and child (Browne 1986; 1989a). At this basic level, the interest is in whether or not there is interaction at all and whether it receives a response (regardless of its content). Types of interaction have been analysed in the following manner. If a general interactive initiative is shown (i.e. behaviour directed towards another), it can have one of three possible outcomes: it may result in the respondent reacting with another interactive initiative (mutual or reciprocal interaction); it may result in the respondent reacting with a non-interactive behaviour (causal interaction); or it may receive no reaction at all (failed interaction). For example, if the mother is eating and the child reaches for the food (interactive initiative), the mother may give the child some food (mutual interaction), stop eating and attend to the child (causal interaction) or continue to eat (failed interaction).

Interaction assessments demonstrate that abused infants and their mothers have interactions that are less reciprocal and fewer in number than their matched controls, whether in the presence or absence of the stranger. In addition, abusive mothers actively interfere with their infants, adjusting posture and clothing and preventing play and exploration (Browne 1986; 1989a; Browne and Saqi 1987; 1988b).

Observational studies provide evidence that social behaviours and interactional patterns within abusing and non-abusing families are different. Abusing parents have been described as aversive, negative and controlling, with less prosocial behaviour (Wolfe 1985). They also show less interactive behaviour both in terms of sensitivity and responsiveness to their children. This may result in infants developing an insecure attachment to their abusive caretakers, which in turn produces marked changes in the abused children's social and emotional behaviour. Nevertheless, the consequences of maltreatment are not the same for all children. Findings suggest there are more behaviour problems in children who are both abused and neglected (Crittenden 1988b). Abusing and neglecting parents, together with their children, suffer from pervasive confusion and ambivalence in their relations with each other. This is not the same as simple parental rejection. It reflects more an uncertainty in the relationship which leaves the child vulnerable and perplexed as to what is expected.

Assessing infant attachment to the parent

The view that children are predisposed to form attachments during infancy (Bowlby 1969) has considerable importance for the study of child abuse. The literature contains numerous reports regarding the high number of abusive parents who were themselves victims of abuse as children (e.g. Egeland 1988). It has been suggested that, in some cases, the link between experiences of abuse as a child and abusing as a parent is likely to be the result of an unsatisfactory early relationship with the principal caretaker and a failure to form a secure attachment (Browne and Parr 1980; DeLozier 1982; Bowlby 1984).

Evidence for this notion has been provided by Crittenden (1985), who found that all of the abused and neglected infants in her study showed an insecure pattern of attachment towards their mother. However, Browne and Saqi (1988b) have demonstrated that only a greater proportion of maltreated infants are insecurely attached to their caregiver (70 per cent) in comparison with infants who have no record of maltreatment (26 per cent). Despite the maltreatment, 30 per cent of abused children are resilient to their experience and are securely attached. Schneider-Rosen et al. (1985) report similar findings and suggest that, even for abused infants, compensatory background factors will increase the probability of a secure attachment, while, under normal circumstances, stressful environmental factors will increase the likelihood of an insecure attachment.

Each individual infant can be assessed for the quality of attachment to the parent, using the Strange Situation Procedure, described above. The infant to parent attachment can be described using four broad categories of the infant's response to the presence and absence of the mother (Browne and Saqi 1988b, adapted from Ainsworth et al. 1978).

1 Avoidant infants (Insecurely Attached Type I): show high levels of play behaviour throughout and tend not to seek interaction with the parent or

stranger. They do not become distressed at being left alone with the stranger. On reunion with their parent, they frequently resist her physical contact or interaction.

2 Independent infants (Securely Attached Type I): demonstrate a strong initiative to interact with their parent and to a lesser extent, the stranger. They do not especially seek physical contact with their parent and are rarely distressed on separation. They greet their parent upon reunion by smiling and reaching for her.

3 Dependent infants (Securely Attached Type II): actively seek physical contact and interaction with their parent. They are usually distressed and often cry when left alone with the stranger. On their parent's return, they reach for her and maintain physical contact, sometimes by resisting her release. Generally they exhibit a desire for interaction with the parent in preference to the stranger.

4 Ambivalent infants (Insecurely Attached Type II): show low levels of play behaviour throughout and sometimes cry prior to separation. They demonstrate an obvious wariness of the stranger and intense distress at separation. They are also more prone to crying while left alone with the stranger. They are ambivalent and frequently mix contact-seeking behaviours with active resistance to contact or interaction. This is especially evident on the parent's return: on reunion, these infants continue to be distressed as usually the parent fails to comfort them.

Ainsworth *et al.* (1978) have examined the relationship between the infant's response to separation and reunion and the behaviour of both mother and child in the home environment. Their findings suggest that maternal sensitivity is most influential in affecting the child's reactions. In the homes of the securely attached infants sensitive mothering was exhibited to the infants' behaviour. While insecurely attached, avoidant infants were found to be rejected by the mothers in terms of interaction and it was suggested that the enhanced exploratory behaviours shown by these infants were an attempt to block attachment behaviours which had been rejected in the past. In the home environments of the insecurely attached ambivalent infants, a disharmonious mother–infant relationship was evident and the ambivalent behaviours shown were seen as a result of inconsistent parenting.

Maccoby (1980) concludes from the above findings that the parents' contribution to attachment can be identified within four dimensions of caretaking style.

1 *Sensitivity/insensitivity.* Sensitive parents 'mesh' their responses to the infant's signals and communications to form a cyclic turn-taking pattern of interaction. In contrast, insensitive parents intervene arbitrarily and these intrusions reflect their own wishes and mood.

2 *Acceptance/rejection.* Accepting parents accept in general the responsibility of child care. They show few signs of irritation with the child.

However, rejecting parents have feelings of anger and resentment that eclipse their affection for the child. They often find the child irritating and resort to punitive control.

3 *Cooperation/interference*. Cooperative parents respect the child's autonomy and rarely exert direct control. Interfering parents impose their wishes on the child with little concern for the child's current mood or activity.

4 *Accessibility/ignoring*. Accessible parents are familiar with their child's communications and notice them at some distance, hence they are easily distracted by the child. Ignoring parents are preoccupied with their own activities and thoughts. They often fail to notice the child's communications unless they are obvious through intensification. They may even forget about the child outside the scheduled times for caretaking.

The four dimensions are heavily influenced by parental attitudes, emotions and perceptions of the child, as discussed earlier. The dimensions are interrelated and together they determine how 'warm' the parent is to the child. Indeed, Rohner (1986) has developed a description of parental warmth and rejection, which he terms the 'Warmth Dimension', which integrates Maccoby's four dimensions (see Figure 8.1).

Browne (1989b) suggests that the behavioural responses of the parent and the infant to an observer/stranger will be similar to their reactions to a community worker. Thus, the precise determination of behavioural characteristics is considered to be of value, to provide indicators that will help to recognise families needing extra support and help in parenting.

TURNING RESEARCH INTO PRACTICE

For social and background risk factors to be of use in the recognition and prediction of child abuse and neglect they must be considered within the context of the family's interpersonal network, which takes into account poor parenting, family violence, social isolation, mental illness and chemical dependency. These factors have been shown by research to be strong predictors for child maltreatment. Indeed, Ayoub *et al.* (1995) claim from their work in Boston that families presenting with depression, withdrawal, low self-esteem, limited parenting skills and unrealistic expectations of their children are most unlikely to show change with home-based interventions. In the presence of family violence and chemical dependency there is a tendency for these families to deteriorate and the child's safety must be carefully monitored.

Child maltreatment is a complex problem with no quick-fix solutions. The majority of facets appear to respond better to prevention than treatment and the research of Olds *et al.* (1986) in the USA provides a good example of effective interventions in promoting parental confidence and self-confidence in the management and care of the child. These interventions have been

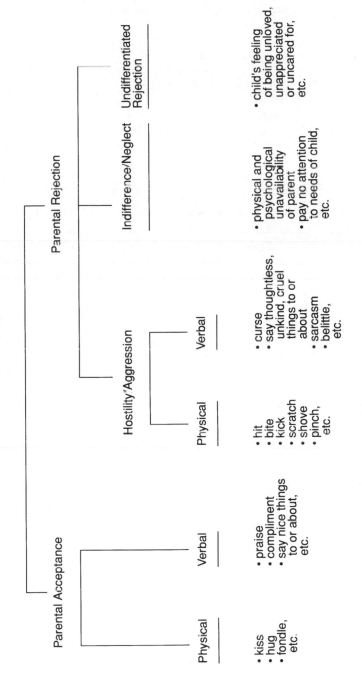

Figure 8.1 Conceptual framework of principal parenting concepts in parental acceptance–rejection theory
Source: Rohner 1986

shown to improve mother–child play and reduce physical punishment and the incidence of child abuse and neglect.

CONCLUSIONS

In the past 20 years there has been much debate on what services can be delivered to minimise the maltreatment of children. This debate has been limited by a poor understanding of intervention strategies for child abuse and neglect and of what constitutes a desirable outcome. Reviews on the causes of maltreatment (e.g. Browne 1988) have emphasised a growing recognition that child abuse and neglect is a product of a poor parent–child relationship, which often occurs in the context of other forms of family breakdown. Therefore, child maltreatment is often associated with other forms of family violence which also need to be addressed (Stanley and Goddard 1993; Browne 1993; Carroll 1994).

Wolfe (1993) observes that there have been promising developments in early interventions which address parental competency and family support to promote more positive parental knowledge, attitudes, skills and behaviour. Given that the prediction of child abuse and neglect in families has met with limited success and a high number of false alarms, such positively orientated interventions are preferable with the child remaining in the family. Never-theless, it should be recognised that some children are in danger if they remain in a violent family. Despite the costs to these children of being taken into care, their immediate safety must take precedence over intervention strategies. Hence, the careful and accurate assessment of the potential for change in family interactions and relationships is essential. Health and social service resources must be adequately provided to meet this need.

REFERENCES

Abidin, R. (1983) *Manual of the Parenting Stress Index (PSI)*, Charlottesville, VA: Psychology Press.

Ainsworth, M.D.S. and Wittig, B.A. (1969) 'Attachment and exploratory behaviour in one-year-olds in a strange situation', in B.M. Foss (ed.) *Determinants of Infant Behaviour*, London: Methuen.

Ainsworth, M.D.S., Blehar, M.C., Waters, E. and Wall, S. (1978) *Patterns of Attachment: A Psychological Study of the Strange Situation*, Hillsdale NJ: Erlbaum.

Ayoub, C., Willett, J. and Robinson, D. (1995) 'Families at risk of child maltreatment: entry level characteristics and growth in family functioning during treatment', *Child Abuse and Neglect* (in press).

Baldwin, J.A. and Oliver, J.E. (1975) 'Epidemiology and family characteristics of severely-abused children', *British Journal of Preventive and Social Medicine*, **29**, 205–21.

Belsky, J. (1980) 'Child maltreatment: an ecological integration', *American Psychologist*, **35**, 320–35.

Belsky, J. (1988) 'Child maltreatment and the emergent family system', in K.D.

Browne, C. Davies and P. Stratton (eds) *Early Prediction and Prevention of Child Abuse*, Chichester: Wiley.

Bowlby, J. (1969) *Attachment and Loss. Vol. 1: Attachment*, London: Hogarth.

Bowlby, J. (1984) 'Violence in the family as a disorder of the attachment and care giving systems', *American Journal of Psychoanalysis*, **44**, 9–31.

Browne, K.D. (1986) 'Methods and approaches to the study of parenting', in W. Sluckin and M. Herbert (eds) *Parental Behaviour*, Oxford: Blackwell.

Browne, K.D. (1988) 'The nature of child abuse and neglect: an overview', in K. Browne, C. Davies and P. Stratton (eds) *Early Prediction and Prevention of Child Abuse*, Chichester: Wiley.

Browne, K.D. (1989a) 'The naturalistic context of family violence and child abuse', in J. Archer and K. Browne (eds) *Human Aggression: Naturalistic Approaches*, London: Routledge.

Browne, K.D. (1989b) 'The health visitor's role in screening for child abuse', *Health Visitor*, **62**, 275–7.

Browne, K.D. (1993) 'Violence in the family and its links to child abuse', *Balliere s Clinical Paediatrics*, **1**, 149–64.

Browne, K.D. (1995) 'Preventing child maltreatment through community nursing', *Journal of Advanced Nursing*, **21**, 57–63.

Browne, K.D. and Parr, R. (1980) 'Contributions of an ethological approach to the study of abuse', in N. Frude (ed.) *Psychological Approaches to Child Abuse*, London: Batsford.

Browne, K.D. and Saqi, S. (1987) 'Parent–child interaction in abusing families: possible causes and consequences', in P. Maher (ed.) *Child Abuse: An Educational Perspective*, Oxford: Blackwell.

Browne, K.D. and Saqi, S. (1988a) 'Approaches to screening families high risk for child abuse', in K.D. Browne, C. Davies and P. Stratton (eds) *Early Prediction and Prevention of Child Abuse*, Chichester: Wiley.

Browne, K.D. and Saqi, S. (1988b) 'Mother–infant interactions and attachment in physically abusing families', *Journal of Reproductive and Infant Psychology*, **6**, 163–82.

Capara, G., Cinanni, V., D'Imperior, G., Passerini, S., Renzi, P. and Travaglia, G. (1985) 'Indicators of impulsive aggression: present status of research on irritability and emotional susceptibility scales', *Personality and Individual Differences*, **6**, 665–74.

Carroll, J. (1994) 'The protection of children exposed to marital violence', *Child Abuse Review*, **3**, 6–14.

Creighton, S. and Noyes, P. (1989) *Child Abuse Trends in England and Wales 1983–1987*, London: NSPCC.

Crittenden, P.M. (1985) 'Maltreated infants: vulnerability and resilience', *Journal of Child Psychology and Psychiatry*, **26**, 85–96.

Crittenden, P.M. (1988a) 'Distorted patterns of relationship in maltreating families: the role of internal representational models', *Journal of Reproductive and Infant Psychology*, **6**, 183–99.

Crittenden, P.M. (1988b) 'Family and dyadic patterns of functioning in maltreating families', in K.D. Browne, C. Davies and P. Stratton (eds) *Early Prediction and Prevention of Child Abuse*, Chichester: Wiley.

DeLozier, P. (1982) 'Attachment theory and child abuse', in C. M. Parkes and J. Stevenson-Hinde (eds) *The Place of Attachment in Human Behaviour*, London: Tavistock.

Department of Health (1994) *Children and Young Persons on Child Protection Registers – Year Ending 31 March 1993, England*, Personal Social Services Local Authority Statistics, London: HMSO.

Edmunds, G. and Kendrick, D.C. (1980) *The Measurement of Human Aggressiveness*, Chichester: Ellis Horwood (Wiley).

Egeland, B. (1988) 'Breaking the cycle of abuse: implications for prevention and intervention', in K.D. Browne, C. Davies and P. Stratton (eds) *Early Prediction and Prevention of Child Abuse*, Chichester: Wiley.

Frodi, A.M. and Lamb, M.E. (1980) 'Child abusers' responses to infant smiles and cries', *Child Development*, **51**, 238–41.

Gaensbauer, T.J. (1982) 'Regulations of emotional expression in infants from two contrasting caretaking environments', *Journal of American Academy of Child Psychiatry*, **21**, 163–71.

Gray, J.O., Cutler, C.A., Dean, J. and Kempe, C.H. (1977) 'Prediction and prevention of child abuse', *Child Abuse and Neglect*, **1**, 45–58.

Greenland, C. (1987) *Preventing CAN Deaths*, London: Tavistock.

Hyman, C.A. (1977) 'A report on the psychological test results of battering parents', *British Journal of Social and Clinical Psychology*, **16**, 221–4.

Hyman, C.A. (1978) 'Non-accidental injury' (A research report to the Surrey Area Review Committee on non-accidental injury), *Health Visitor*, **51**, 168–74.

Hyman, C.A., Parr, R. and Browne, K.D. (1979) 'An observation study of mother–infant interaction in abusing families', *Child Abuse and Neglect*, **3**, 241–6.

Kadushin, A. and Martin, J. (1981) *Child Abuse: An Interactional Event*, New York: Columbia University Press.

Leventhal, J. (1988) 'Can child maltreatment be predicted during the perinatal period: evidence from longitudinal cohort studies', *Journal of Reproductive and Infant Psychology*, **6**, 139–61.

Lewis, M. and Schaeffer, S. (1981) 'Peer behaviour and mother–infant interaction in maltreated children', in M. Lewis and L.A. Rosenblum (eds) *The Uncommon Child*, New York: Plenum Press.

Lynch, M. and Roberts, J. (1982) *Consequences of Child Abuse*, London: Academic Press.

Maccoby, E.E. (1980) *Social Development: Psychology Growth and the Parent–Child Relationship*, New York: Harcourt Brace Jovanovich.

Magura, M. (1981) 'Are services to protect children effective?', *Children and Youth Services Review*, **3**, 193.

Martin, H.P. and Rodeheffer, M. (1976) 'Learning and intelligence', in H.P. Martin (ed.) *The Abused Child: A Multidisciplinary Approach to Developmental Issues and Treatment*, Cambridge MA: Ballinger.

Olds, D., Henderson, C., Chamberlin, R. and Tatelbaum, R. (1986) 'Preventing child abuse and neglect: randomized trial of nurse home visiting', *Pediatrics*, **78**, 65–78.

Orkow, B. (1985) 'Implementation of a family stress checklist', *Child Abuse and Neglect*, **9**, 405–10.

Patterson, G.R. (1986) 'Maternal rejection: determining or product for deviant child behaviour', in W.W. Hartup and Z. Rubin (eds) *Relationships and Development*, Hillsdale NJ: Erlbaum.

Richman, N., Stevenson, J. and Graham, P. (1983) *Pre-School to School: A Behavioural Study*, London: Academic Press.

Roberts, J. (1993) 'Abused children and foster care: the need for specialist resources', *Child Abuse Review*, **2**, 3–14.

Rohner, R.P. (1986) *The Warmth Dimension: Foundations of Parental Acceptance – Rejection Theory*, Beverly Hills CA: Sage.

Rosenberg, M.S. and Reppucci, N.D. (1983) 'Abusive mothers: perceptions of their own and their children's behaviour', *Journal of Consulting and Clinical Psychology*, **51**, 674–82.

Rowe, J., Cain, H., Hundleby, M. and Keane, A. (1984) *Long-Term Foster Care*, London: Batsford.

Schneider-Rosen, K., Braunwald, K.G., Carlson V. and Cicchetti, D. (1985) 'Current perspectives in attachment: illustrations from the study of maltreated infants', in I. Bretherton and R. Waters (eds) *Growing Points in Attachment Theory and Research*, Monographs of the Society for Research in Child Development (No. 209).

Smith, S. (1975) *The Battered Child Syndrome*, London: Butterworths.

Stanley, J. and Goddard, C. (1993) 'The association between child abuse and other family violence', *Australian Social Work*, **46**, 3–8.

Starr, R.H. (1982) *Child Abuse and Prediction: Policy Implications*, Cambridge MA: Ballinger.

Stratton, P. and Swaffer, A. (1988) 'Maternal causal beliefs for abused and handicapped children', *Journal of Reproductive and Infant Psychology*, **6**, 201–16.

Trickett, P.K. and Kuczynski (1986) 'Children's misbehaviours and parental discipline strategies in abusive and non-abusive families', *Developmental Psychology*, **22**, 115–23.

Wolfe, D.A. (1985) 'Child-abusive parents: an empirical review and analysis', *Psychological Bulletin*, **97**, 462–82.

Wolfe, D.A. (1993) 'Child abuse prevention: blending research and practice', *Child Abuse Review*, **2**, 153–65.

Wolfe, D.A., Fairbank, J., Kelly, J.A. and Bradly, A.S. (1983) 'Child abusive parents and physiological responses to stressful and nonstressful behaviour in children', *Behavioural Assessment*, **5**, 363–71.

Wood-Schuman, S. and Cone, J. (1986) 'Differences in abusive, at risk for abuse and control mothers' descriptions of normal child behaviour', *Child Abuse and Neglect*, **10**, 397–405.

Chapter 9

Quantitative measures of parenting: a clinical-developmental perspective

Sue Jenner and Gerard McCarthy

INTRODUCTION

An increasing proportion of child mental health time is taken up with attempting to assess and, where possible, improve the quality of parenting children experience in their families and to assess whether children should be removed from, or returned to their parents. Often, the recommendations are given considerable weight in court and are likely to have profound consequences. Given this heavy responsibility, there is interest in whether quantitative measures might be able to help clinicians assess the quality of parenting a child is receiving, how this is impacting on the child's functioning and development, and the parent's potential for change.

In contrast to clinical judgements, where little is known about their reliability, validity or the processes by which they are arrived at, the properties of quantitative measures are established. The reliability, validity and limitations of quantitative measures are known and they have been tested in various ways, against criteria other than clinical judgement.

However, while quantitative measures of parental functioning have been developed in the field of developmental psychology, to our knowledge very few such measures have been developed specifically for use in assessing parenting in clinical settings and for use in the assessments increasingly required by courts. Given this situation, we would like to suggest that clinicians might increasingly be able to use some of the theoretical and methodological advances that have taken place in developmental psychology in understanding parenting to help them in their parenting assessments. While many of the quantitative measures used in this field have not been applied in a clinical context, recent work in developmental psychology can provide clinicians with a framework for thinking about parenting and, more specifically, it can help clinicians identify factors that are known to play an important role in the parenting process. It also alerts clinicians to areas of research on parenting being undertaken by developmental psychologists and to how researchers are attempting to measure quantitatively these processes.

In this chapter we shall therefore briefly consider some of these recent developments. In particular we shall focus on recent work on the attachment relationships of children and parents. In the second half of the chapter we shall move on to outline a quantitative procedure that has recently been developed to enable the assessment and treatment of parenting skills and deficits in the context of child protection (Jenner 1992).

In the model of parenting we shall use here, we suggest that a useful definition of parenting needs to include two main elements. First, it needs to include a notion about the kind of parenting that appears to promote or hinder child functioning throughout childhood and adulthood. Second, it includes a notion about the factors that determine a particular adult's style of parenting (Belsky 1984). Drawing such a distinction enables clinicians and researchers to look not only at the quality of current parental functioning but also to be aware of the factors that determine the quality of parental functioning. It also draws attention to the issues that need to be assessed when attempting to understand and change the quality of parental functioning. Given the important role that determining factors play in understanding the parenting process, we shall look in this chapter at how theoretical and methodological advances from the field of developmental psychology can be applied to addressing both the quality of parental functioning and its determinants.

DETERMINANTS OF PARENTING

Current theories of parental functioning hold that it is multiply determined. For the purpose of this review, we follow Belsky (1984) in grouping the important determining factors under three main headings. These will be: (1) characteristics of the parent, (2) characteristics of the child, (3) sources of stress and support in the wider social environment.

Characteristics of the parent: parents' internal working model of attachment relationships

Parents' mental representations of their childhood experiences with attachment relationships or 'internal working models' of attachment relationships are thought to determine their sensitivity to their child's attachment needs and behaviour and to influence the quality of parenting a child receives (Bowlby 1973). Parents who have insecure internal working models are thought to block or distort their infant's attachment-related signals because they find these signals threatening to their current state of mind with respect to attachment. Parents with secure internal working models are believed to have either worked through their past negative attachment experiences or to have had secure experiences. These secure parents are able to receive and respond to their children's attachment-related signals without experiencing mental conflict and anxiety and without having to block or distort the processing of signals of distress, fear and anxiety. Interestingly, parents who

have experienced insecure and/or traumatic childhood attachment relationships with their own parents, but who are able to give a coherent account
when discussing and evaluating these experiences, also tend to have infants
who are securely attached to them. This is an important finding and suggests
that a parent's capacity for self-reflection in relation to attachment-related
issues plays a very powerful role in determining the quality of their own
infant's attachment to them (Fonagy *et al.* 1994).

This clinically relevant body of research is largely based on Main and her
colleagues' development of the Adult Attachment Interview (AAI). This is
used to assess an adult's internal working model or affective-cognitive
representation of attachment. The AAI is a standardised semi-structured
interview which is designed to elicit the subject's accounts of his/her
attachment experiences in childhood and how these relationships have
changed over time and how they have influenced their adult personality (Main
and Goldwyn 1991). By looking at the thoughtfulness and the coherency with
which the adult is able to describe these childhood experiences and their
effects, the interview aims to assess the subject's current state of mind with
respect to attachment in general. In this way, the interview aims to assess
how each individual thinks, reflects and organises his or her mind in relation
to early experience, and not simply through what the person remembers. The
coding system of the AAI leads to adult attachment classification in three
main categories. These are Autonomous or Secure (F), Insecure-Dismissing
of attachment (D) and Insecure-Preoccupied in relation to attachment (E).
Also, adults who show the presence of unresolved responses to loss and
trauma receive the additional classification Unresolved (U), which is superimposed on their main classification.

It is our impression that parents who have experienced abuse and/or neglect
in their childhood attachment relationships, and who have been unable to
come to terms with and resolve these painful emotional experiences, are least
able to provide their own children with the secure parenting they require and
are least able to respond to psychological treatments. Importantly, these
parents appear to be unable to remember the affective experiences associated
with the painful childhood experiences and, where these original affects are
unavailable to them, the parent is more likely to repeat their adverse
childhood experiences with their own children. In such situations, only when
the parent is able to be in touch with their own often overwhelmingly painful
feelings from childhood are they able to be sensitive to, and aware of, the
emotional needs and suffering of their own children (Fraiberg *et al.* 1975).

Research is currently underway to investigate in more detail the way
parents' internal working models of attachment are related to parenting
behaviour and parents' ability to use psychological treatment. Findings from
these studies will provide clinicians with information about the way internal
working models of attachment influence parenting behaviour and hopefully
then there may be ways of adapting the AAI for use in a clinical context. At

the present, the AAI requires specialist training to use, and its usefulness and reliability in clinical settings have not been established. However, given the importance of the above set of findings it seems important that clinicians are aware of this body of research.

Characteristics of the child: children's internal working models of attachment relationships

Towards the end of the first year, the infant is thought to be constructing cognitive-affective representations of its relationships with attachment figures. These internal working models are thought to be built on the basis of the child's actual experiences with its attachment figures and are increasingly used by the child to appraise and guide its behaviour, both with parents and with teachers and peers. In this way, the thoughts and feelings that children develop about themselves and their attachment figures play an increasingly important role in influencing the way they relate to their parents (Bretherton 1985). Children who have experienced rejection and/or abuse and neglect develop negative thoughts and feelings about themselves and their parents. For example, a child who expects his/her attachment figure to be unavailable in times of emotional need is unlikely to confide in them and may learn to avoid them. This in turn can lead to the parent feeling rejected by the child. One important consequence of this is that these children come to feel very insecure in their attachments to their caregivers.

This important body of research on the development of secure and insecure childhood attachment relationships has largely been based on a procedure devised by Ainsworth and her colleagues known as the Strange Situation (Ainsworth *et al.* 1978). This procedure can be used to assess and classify the quality of infants' and toddlers' attachments to their caregivers. The Strange Situation consists of eight 3-minute episodes involving two separations and reunions of the parent and child in an unfamiliar setting. The 20-minute procedure is designed to activate the child's attachment system so that the organisation of this system in relation to the particular caregiver and the quality of this attachment can be assessed. Infants classified as secure (Pattern B) use the mother as a secure base from which to explore, become distressed by her absence, but greet her positively on her return, and then return to exploration. Until recently, only two patterns of insecurity had been identified using the Strange Situation. Infants classified as insecure-avoidant (Pattern A) explore with minimal reference to the mother, show little distress on separation and avoid or ignore the mother at reunion. Infants classified as insecure-ambivalent/resistant (Pattern C) are highly distressed on separation and are difficult to settle on reunion. In normative samples, 66 per cent of infants are classified as secure, 20 per cent as insecure-avoidant and 14 per cent as insecure-ambivalent. As a result of recent research on clinical populations, a fourth pattern has been identified, known as insecure-disorganised (Pattern D). High rates of disorganised attachments have been found with a number of serious maternal risk factors, such as child maltreatment, maternal unipolar or bipolar depression and multi-problem family status. The disorganised classification has also been associated with a maternal history of loss of an attachment figure in childhood and, more specifically, to unresolved mourning of prior losses (Belsky and Cassidy 1994).

Importantly, the quality of the child's attachment relationship as assessed in the Strange Situation has been found to reflect the quality of the attachment relationship as experienced by the child over the first year of life. Attachment security at age 12 and 18 months is related to ratings of maternal sensitivity, warmth, responsiveness and involvement made over the first year of life. Insecure-avoidant attachment is correlated with intrusive, excessively stimulating interactional styles of mothering, whereas insecure-resistant/ambivalent attachment is related to an unresponsive, unpredictable and underinvolved approach to caregiving.

Recently, attachment researchers have found that children with histories of parental maltreatment are more than twice as likely as non-maltreated children from similar socioeconomic circumstances to be classified as insecure (Belsky and Cassidy 1994). They have also found specificity between the type of maltreatment and type of insecurity experienced by the children. Children who have experienced physical abuse are more likely to develop insecure-avoidant attachments, whereas neglected children are more likely to develop insecure-ambivalent attachments. More recently, investigators have discovered that maltreated youngsters often develop atypical patterns of attachment to their caregivers. These attachment patterns are characterised in part by a co-mingling of patterns of avoidance and ambivalence and are classified as insecure-disorganised (Main and Soloman 1986).

The quality of a child's early attachments plays a powerful role in influencing the child's subsequent social and emotional development. A secure attachment history has been shown to provide a foundation upon which subsequent harmonious relations with adults and peers are built (Bretherton 1985). Children with an insecure attachment history have more dependent relationships with their teachers, are less popular, more unsociable and more aggressive in their peer relationships and experience more difficulty in establishing close relationships with friends than children with secure histories. They are also less compliant, less able to tolerate frustration and experience more conflict and disharmony in their relationships with their parents. More recently, insecure-disorganised attachments have been found to be a strong predictor of hostile-aggressive behaviour in the classroom and to be significantly related to the presence of externalising behaviour problems in children.

More recently, Cassidy and Marvin (1992), working with the MacArthur

Working Group on Attachment, have produced a procedure for classifying the quality of attachment in 3–4 year olds using a modified separation and reunion procedure. Main and Cassidy (1988) have also produced a similar system for 6 year olds.

Researchers have also developed ways of measuring attachment using representational rather than the behavioural methods of the Strange Situation. Cassidy (1988) has developed a procedure to assess quantitatively the quality of a child's internal working model of attachment using an incomplete doll play procedure.

Clinicians are increasingly being asked to assess and give an opinion on the quality of a child's attachment to their parents or caregivers, how the security of the child is being affected by the quality of the parenting they are receiving and to assess how the child's social and emotional development is likely to be affected by various placement alternatives. Given the current lack of valid and reliable ways of assessing attachment-related issues in a clinical context, we suggest that clinicians might increasingly use these theoretical and quantitative advances in the study of childhood attachment in their work.

Sources of social support in the parent's wider social environment

Current theories of parental functioning highlight that the quality of a parent's close relationships, both love relationships and wider social supports, plays an important role in influencing the quality of parenting a child receives. The availability to parents of support from other adults and their ability to use this has a major effect on the parenting process (Rutter *et al.* 1983).

Parents who experience difficulty in dealing with their own needs for security and support and who have difficulties in establishing secure and supportive relationships with other adults appear to experience difficulty in dealing with stressors such as life events. The lack of secure support makes them more vulnerable to external stressors and to parenting breakdown and mental health problems (Brown and Harris 1978; Rutter *et al.* 1983). It also increases the likelihood they will form overly dependent relationships with their children, which in turn may inhibit the child's healthy social and emotional development. Bowlby (1973) has clearly described the way in which parent–child attachment relationships can become inverted where the child comes to serve as an attachment figure for the parent.

The quality of the marital relationship has been found to be related to a number of aspects of parental functioning. These include the quality of mother–infant and father–infant interaction, maternal and paternal competence, infant–mother attachment and a host of positive infant behaviours (Belsky 1984). Two useful measures are the Dyadic Adjustment Scale (Spanier 1976) and the Marital Adjustment Test (Lock and Wallace 1959).

The availability of significant others and the support received from them have been found to exert a positive impact on parental functioning. In their study of divorce, Hetherington *et al.* (1978) found that the adequacy of the mother's social support network was positively related to her effectiveness with her children. Also, Crittenden (1985) has found that the utilisation of social support is related to the quality of infant–mother attachment.

A useful measure is the Significant Others Scale (Power *et al.* 1988). This scale measures different functional resources of social support that are provided by a number of significant role relationships within an individual's social network. This scale can be used, along with a clinical interview, to map and assess the quality of a parent's social support network.

QUANTITATIVE MEASURES OF PARENTING BEHAVIOUR

Over the past 30 years, major changes have taken place in the way researchers have conceptualised the relevant skills and important functions of parenting. They have moved away both from studying such things as particular disciplinary techniques and from seeing parenting as a one-way process where children are the passive recipients of things done to them by parents. Nowadays, parenting is seen as being a two-way process in which reciprocal interactions between parents and children are central. Consequently, research has shifted to looking at patterns of family communication and the quality of family relationships. This research has shown that the kind of parenting that promotes optimal child development is sensitive parenting. That is, parenting that is attuned to children's capabilities and needs as they face the various developmental tasks of growing up (Belsky 1984).

In parallel with a change in the way parenting skills and functions have been conceptualised during the past 30 years, there has been a shift in the methods that have been used for the assessment of parenting. Associated with this shift in interest to the processes of family interactions, has come a decreasing reliance on questionnaires and self-reports and an increase in the use of observational procedures and interview techniques.

In the next section, we shall look at an observational procedure known as the Parent–Child Game that has been adapted for use in the assessment and treatment of parenting skills and deficits in the context of child protection (Jenner 1992).

The Parent–Child Game (Forehand and McMahon 1981) was originally designed as a psychological treatment intervention to be used as a parent training technique. The theoretical model from which the Parent–Child Game was derived involved central concepts from social learning theory, developmental psychopathology, normal child development and cognitive behavioural psychotherapy. It has subsequently been adapted to function as an assessment approach (Jenner 1992) and has proved particularly useful within the area of child protection. In terms of treatment, the Parent–Child Game functions as a powerful parent training intervention, capable of producing desirable change in an adult's child management and interaction styles, by teaching an increased use of child-centred parenting behaviours and a reduced frequency of child-directive behaviours. Parental child-centred behaviours, as defined by Forehand and McMahon (1981), consist of praise, smiles, imitation, ignoring minor naughtiness, positive touches and attention, where a parent speaks enthusiastically about what the child is doing or how they are feeling. Child-directive behaviours include commands, saying no, teaching, questions, criticism and negative touches. An excess of child-centred parental behaviours is considered to enhance a child's individual development, reduce their non-compliance and improve the quality of the parent–child relationship. Similarly, an excess of child-directive behaviours can be associated with an adverse developmental impact on the child, raised levels of non-compliance and an improvised/coercive pattern of parent–child interactions (Patterson 1982). As an assessment tool, the Parent–Child Game can provide initial baseline measures of current functioning, while a comparison between pre- and post-treatment baselines can indicate potential for change. A wealth of clinical experience strongly indicates that an excess of child-directive behaviours are positively correlated with an increased likelihood of child abuse, particularly in the areas of social and emotional development. Multi-centre comparative treatment projects are currently collecting data to test this clinical experience. Research carried out in the United States (Forehand and McMahon 1981; Forehand and Long 1988) indicates that positive changes in parenting consequent upon treatment with the Parent–Child Game are still maintained at a 10-year follow-up point.

In the quantitative assessment of parenting it is necessary to have profiles of normal parenting style in order to establish valid comparisons with abnormal/clinical parenting behaviour. It has been shown (McMahon and Forehand 1984) that the following scores on the Parent–Child Game categories of child-centred and child-directive behaviours are characteristic of non-clinical parents' behaviour over a 10-minute period:

Child centred (CC)	Child directive (CD)	Ratio of CC:CD
40–50	60–70	1:1.3–1.75

By contrast, clinic-referred parents scores on the Parent–Child Game pre-treatment are found to be:

Child centred (CC)	Child directive (CD)	Ratio of CC:CD
10–20	50–100+	1:5+

Criteria for the successful outcome of treatment have been set by Forehand and McMahon (1981) and are shown below, although research is awaited to confirm a positive correlation between a CC:CD ratio of this magnitude and the reduction in the risk of child abuse. The prevailing clinical impression, however, is that it does.

Child centred (CC)	Child directive (CD)	Ratio of CC:CD
60+	10	6:1

Thus a complete reversal of the scores and ratios of CC and CD behaviours is often required before treatment with the Parent–Child Game can be evaluated as having achieved its aim.

The Parent–Child Game, whether used as an assessment and/or treatment approach, therefore provides quantitative data demonstrating a clinic parent's current level of functioning, which can then be contrasted with that of the non-clinic parent, and can also produce single case design quantitative information on a referred parent's pre- and post-treatment scores. Both these types of data are extremely useful in generating accurate assessments of parenting and the potential for change in the desired direction (Jenner and Gent 1995).

Rather than providing details on the psychological techniques and exact behaviour categories involved in the Parent–Child Game, which are readily available elsewhere (Forehand and McMahon 1981; Jenner 1992; Jenner and Gent 1995), the brief presentation of one clinical case, and the more detailed discussion of one statutory referral should serve to clarify many of the issues relating to this approach and its use in the assessment of parenting.

Case A: a clinical referral

The Puttnam family were referred via their GP following a series of consultations where Mrs Puttnam complained of feeling 'desperate and depressed' because neither she nor her husband could control the behaviour of their four-and-a-half year old son Nick. The two other children in the family, Bernie, a 7 year old girl, and Jamie, a 10 year old boy, had proved relatively easy to care for and both parents felt overwhelmed by the management problems presented by their youngest son and undermined by their lack of success in attempting to use firm limits to regulate his behaviour.

The assessment and treatment approaches used with the Puttnam family contained the following elements: developmental assessment of Nick; family and marital history, including life events and social supports; psychiatric history and status of Mr and Mrs Puttnam; interviews with Bernie and Jamie; Parent–Child Game baseline measures; Parent–Child Game treatment with both parents and Nick; play therapy for Nick; sibling group play sessions; marital therapy for Mr and Mrs Puttnam; and cognitive behaviour therapy for Mrs Puttnam. The choice of the Parent–Child Game treatment intervention followed assessment that the interactions between the parents and Nick contained a significant excess of child-directive behaviours and coercive sequences which resulted in each of the participants finding the time spent together distinctly unrewarding.

The assessment baseline of the Parent–Child Game parental behaviour categories of child-centred and child-directive behaviours showed that Mr and Mrs Puttnam's interactions with Nick were characterised by an excess of the latter, with a CC:CD ratio of approximately 1:3.5–4.

As this pattern of scores was significantly different from that found in non-clinic families, six sessions of the Parent–Child Game were carried out. Each treatment session lasted for one-and-a-half hours and took place in a controlled learning environment consisting of a video suite with a one-way mirror and an inductive audio feedback loop through which the therapist used instruction, verbal prompts, verbal modelling, praise and labelling of child-centred behaviours and reminders to avoid child-directive behaviours, all within a shaping framework. Mr and Mrs Puttnam each had 10 minutes' treatment using an earbug whilst playing with Nick, who had chosen the toy materials himself. The remaining portion of each session was used as an interview and discussion opportunity with both parents together, the focus being on problem solving, generalisation and the rationale of the Parent–Child Game. At the end of the sixth session, Mr and Mrs Puttnam's parenting behaviours were once more assessed, using the same baseline format as before, demonstrating that Mrs Puttnam had dramatically improved her ratio of CC:CD parenting behaviours to 11:1, while Mr Puttnam, though not quite meeting the official criteria of successful treatment of a 6:1 ratio of CC to CD behaviours, had nonetheless made very significant and desirable changes in his parenting style, shown by a post-treatment CC:CD ratio of 4:1. Both parents stated that Nick's behaviour was vastly improved, that they felt they were 'winning' and that everyone in the family was much happier. It is naturally acknowledged that the other treatment elements used with the Puttnam family members doubtless also played an important part in their progress, though the comparison between baseline 1 and baseline 2 scores on the Parent–Child Game gave unequivocally clear quantitative, causal data on the changes in parenting style from a type known to damage a child's development to one which is acknowledged to encourage and enhance their progress.

Case B: a statutory referral

Ms Terry, Mr Farley, their one-and-a-half year old daughter Jemma and Ms Terry's 6 year old son Lyle, were referred by their local social services child protection team. Both children were being fostered following interim care orders granted because of a history of parental violence, alcohol abuse by Ms Terry, neglect, emotional abuse and non-accidental injury to Jemma. Ms

Terry denied any abuse of alcohol, claimed that her parenting of both children had always been successful and blamed any problems on Mr Farley's change of personality due to drug abuse. Mr Farley denied any personal responsibility for the children being taken into care and stated that he had been disturbed by Ms Terry's alcoholism and violence towards him and her inadequate care of the children. The children were considered to have suffered significant harm, though the precise impact on their development had not been established. Both parents were making separate applications for care of the children and, whilst continuing to be very highly critical of each other and living apart, each said they still felt very deeply for the other and wanted to have relationship counselling to deal with all the 'hatred and resentment'. Lyle had variously said he wanted a 'new mummy and daddy' or wanted to live with his mother and loved Jemma more than anyone; while Jemma's delayed language development prevented her saying anything except 'mum' to any adult female with whom she came into contact. The referrers requested an assessment of the parental relationship, their intellectual abilities, the pattern of attachments within the family, the children's development and Ms Terry and Mr Farley's parenting abilities and potential for change.

The assessment via treatment approach was used with this family. The assessment via treatment approach follows a single case design methodology where baseline scores are taken prior to and after treatment. Here it included the following components: Parent–Child Game, involving both adults and the two children; play therapy with Lyle; sibling sessions with Lyle and Jemma; marital therapy; observation of separations and reunions between parents and children; observation of unstructured family play sessions and family meal times.

The Parent–Child Game intervention was implemented, as both Ms Terry and Mr Farley's baseline 1 scores showed an excess of child-directive behaviours and a low frequency of praise towards Lyle and Jemma. Play therapy with Lyle was provided in an attempt to help him clarify his feelings about the significant adults in his life. Sibling sessions, involving observation of the two children's affect towards one another, their ability to play in a mutually rewarding and cooperative fashion and their protective/dependent behaviour in their interactions, were used to assess the attachment between Lyle and Jemma. Marital therapy was seen to be appropriate for the parents, the aim being to assess their ability to either resolve their differences or separate in a less damaging fashion than they had so far demonstrated. Observation of separations and reunions provided information on family attachment patterns and the parents' sensitivity to Lyle and Jemma's differing developmental needs in this area. Observation of family play sessions and meal times was used to establish the degree of generalisation of any newly learnt Parent–Child Game behaviours to the more natural environment of those two activities.

The Parent–Child Game initial baseline scores of Ms Terry and Mr Farley, in terms of their use of child-centred and child-directive behaviours with Lyle and Jemma, were as follows:

Ms Terry	Child centred CC	Child directive CD	Ratio of CC:CD
Lyle	14	62	1:4.5
Jemma	20	73	1:3.5

Mr Farley	Child centred CC	Child directive CD	Ratio of CC:CD
Lyle	24	76	1:3
Jemma	33	88	1:2.6

This pattern of scores was considered to be sufficiently discrepant to the profile of non-clinical parents to warrant six sessions of the Parent–Child Game in order to establish Ms Terry and Mr Farley's potential for change in their parenting style. The format of the treatment sessions was as for the Puttnam family, although rather more complex because all possible combinations of parents and children were used: i.e. Ms Terry and Lyle; Ms Terry and Jemma; Ms Terry and both Lyle and Jemma; Mr Farley and Lyle; Mr Farley and Jemma; and Mr Farley with both children. The length of the sessions was extended to 2 hours to accommodate these arrangements. The interview section of each session was similar to that used with the Puttnam family. At the end of the sixth session, Ms Terry and Mr Farley were again assessed using the same baseline format as before, showing the following scores:

Ms Terry	Child centred CC	Child directive CD	Ratio of CC:CD
Lyle	21	49	1:2.3
Jemma	34	50	1:1.5

Mr Farley	Child centred CC	Child directive CD	Ratio of CC:CD
Lyle	40	58	1:1.5
Jemma	52	67	1:1.4

The scores at second baseline indicated that Ms Terry had shown a degree of improvement, though, while the ratio of CC:CD had improved to the point where it was comparable with that of non-clinic parents, she had not achieved the post-treatment criteria of a 6:1 CC:CD ratio characteristic of a successful outcome (Forehand and McMahon 1981). Ms Terry was considered to have demonstrated only a limited potential for change. This was also underlined by the relative lack of generalisation of Parent–Child Game behaviours to play and meal times. Mr Farley's progress was construed in a similar fashion. Both Ms Terry and Mr Farley expressed their enthusiasm for the Parent–Child Game and said that, had they received such 'practical' help before, social services need never have become involved. This response demonstrates, firstly, a common reaction by the vast majority of parents to the Parent–Child Game and, secondly, Ms Terry and Mr Farley's rather limited understanding of the involved professionals' serious concerns. It was also apparent that the children had found the more child-centred attention from Ms Terry and Mr Farley distinctly more rewarding and enjoyable than their parents' former style of interaction. However, Ms Terry and Mr Farley also stated that it 'felt strange' to be 'lavishing' such praise on the children as they themselves had experienced physical and emotional abuse as children.

Information from the other elements of the assessment via treatment package indicated that both children were insecurely attached to their parents. Lyle was helped to clarify his wishes, becoming able to say that 'me and J would like a new mummy and daddy, please, cos the fighting [between Ms Terry and Mr Farley] is scary'. Marital therapy showed that Ms Terry and Mr Farley were locked into a pathological and mutually destructive relationship which they were apparently unable to modify. The conclusions drawn from the above information and extensive documentation available regarding past events, led to a recommendation that Lyle and Jemma should be placed together within an alternative, permanent family. The specific contribution of the Parent–Child Game to this recommendation lay in the technique's ability, when used in the single case design format, to provide a quantitative estimate of an adult's potential for change in their parenting style. However, scores from the Parent–Child Game do not qualify as a valid or reliable measure of overall functioning and must always be considered in conjunction with information on a parent's ability to protect and nurture all aspects of their child's development. Integrating the findings from the Parent–Child Game with other measures used, and the information derived from interviews, seems best achieved through multidisciplinary team work.

CONCLUSIONS

It is hoped that this description of a selection of the quantitative measures available for use in the assessment of parenting has shown the importance of gathering accurate and reliable information on the determinants of parenting. It is clear that a great deal of applied research will be needed in order to identify the most effective combinations of the numerous standardised assessment instruments available from both the developmental and clinical fields in the assessment of parenting. Meanwhile, the quantitative measures of parenting used in current practice in child protection provide objective data for professionals whose aim is to gather relevant and representative information in the taxing task of assessing parenting in a legal framework.

REFERENCES

Ainsworth, M.D.S., Blehar, M.C., Waters, E. and Wall, S. (1978) *Patterns of Attachment: A Psychological Study in the Strange Situation*. Hillsdale NJ: Erlbaum.

Belsky, J. (1984) 'The determinants of parenting: a process model', *Child Development*, **55**, 83–96.

Belsky, J. and Cassidy, J. (1994) 'Attachment: theory and evidence', in M. Rutter and D. Hay (eds) *Developmental Principles and Clinical Issues in Psychology and Psychiatry*, Oxford: Blackwell.

Bowlby, J. (1973) *Attachment and Loss. Vol. 2: Separation*, New York: Basic Books.

Bretherton, I. (1985) 'Attachment theory: retrospect and prospect', in I. Bretherton and E. Waters (eds) *Growing Points of Attachment Theory and Research*, Monographs of the Society for Research in Child Development (No. 50).

Brown, G.W. and Harris, T. (1978) *Social Origins of Depression: A Study of Psychiatric Disorder in Women*, London: Tavistock.

Cassidy, J. (1988) 'Child–mother attachment and the self in six-year olds', *Child Development*, **59**, 121–34.

Cassidy, J. and Marvin, R.S. (1992) 'Attachment Organisation in Three and Four Year Olds: Guidelines for Classification', unpublished scoring manual, The Pennsylvania State University.

Crittenden, P.M. (1985) 'Social networks, quality of child rearing and child development', *Child Development*, **56**, 1299–313.

Fonagy, P., Steele, M., Steele, H., Higgitt, A. and Target, M. (1994) 'The theory and practice of resilience', *Journal of Child Psychology and Psychiatry*, **35**, 231–57.

Forehand, R.L. and Long, N. (1988) 'Out-patient treatment for the acting out child: procedures, long term follow-up data and clinical problems', *Advances in Behavioural Research and Therapy*, **10**, 129–77.

Forehand, R.L. and McMahon, R.J. (1981) *Helping the Non-Compliant Child: A Clinicians Guide to Parent Training*, New York: Guildford.

Fraiberg, S., Adelson, E. and Shapiro, V. (1975) 'Ghosts in the nursery: a psychoanalytic approach to the problem of impaired infant–mother relationships', *Journal of the American Academy of Child Psychiatry*, **14**, 387–422.

Hetherington, E.M., Cox, M. and Cox, R. (1978) 'Effects of development on parents and children', in M.E. Lamb (ed.) *Nontraditional Families*, Hillsdale NJ: Erlbaum.

Jenner, S. (1992) 'The assessment and treatment of parenting skills and deficits: within the framework of child protection', *ACPP Newsletter*, **14**, 228–33.

Jenner, S. and Gent, M. (1995) 'Evaluating the contribution of a parent training technique to a parenting assessment package for parenting skills and deficits, in the context of child protection', *ACPP Review and Newsletter* (in press).

Lock, H.J. and Wallace, K. (1959) 'Short marital-adjustment and prediction tests: their reliability and validity', *Marriage and Family Living*, **43**, 251–5.

McMahon, R.J. and Forehand, R.L. (1984) 'Parent training for the non-compliant child: treatment outcome, generalization and adjunctive therapy procedures', in R.F. Dangel and R.A. Polster (eds) *Parent Training: Foundations of Research and Practice*, New York: Guildford.

Main, M. and Cassidy, J. (1988) 'Categories of response with the parent at age six: predicted from infant attachment classification and stable over a one month period', *Developmental Psychology*, **24**, 415–26.

Main, M. and Goldwyn, R. (1991) 'Adult Attachment Classification System, Version 5', unpublished manuscript, Department of Psychology, University of California, Berkeley.

Main, M. and Soloman, J. (1986) 'Discovery of an insecure-disorganized/disoriented attachment pattern: procedures, findings and implications for the classification of behaviour', in T.B. Brazleton and M. Yogman (eds) *Affective Development in Infancy*, Norwood NJ: Ablex.

Patterson, G. (1982) *Coercive Family Processes*, Eugene OR: Castalia Publications.

Power, M.J., Champion, L.A. and Aris, S.J. (1988) 'The development of a measure of social support: the significant others scale (SOS)', *British Journal of Clinical Psychology*, **27**, 349–58.

Rutter, M., Quinton, D. and Liddle, C. (1983) 'Parenting in two generations: looking backwards and looking forwards', in N. Madge (ed.) *Families at Risk*, London: Heinemann Educational.

Spanier, G.B. (1976) 'Measuring dyadic adjustment: new scales for assessing the quality of marriage and similar dyads', *Journal of Marriage and the Family*, **38**, 15–28.

Chapter 10

Giving due consideration to the family's racial and cultural background
Begum Maitra

INTRODUCTION

> They sought it with thimbles, they sought it with care;
> They pursued it with forks and hope;
> They threatened its life with a railway share;
> They charmed it with smiles and soap.
>
> (Lewis Carroll, The Annotated Snark)

Discussions about race and culture are clearly powerfully emotive. They often begin with disagreements about definitions, get hopelessly stuck between what is common to all groups and what is specific, and end in hostile silence or in cries of 'racism'. Lewis Carroll's mythical beast, the Snark, arouses both dread and curiosity, and is an apt metaphor for professional attitudes to 'difference'; perhaps especially to difference based on 'race' or 'culture'. The tolerance of racial/cultural difference often encounters major obstacles exactly at the point at which professionals believe that they are acting to protect vulnerable individuals or groups, such as in child protection work.

Repeated experiences of cross-cultural confusion, of race awareness or anti-racist trainings, or the sheer discomfort of requiring to re-examine one's professional beliefs and practice may lead professionals to adopt a variety of positions. Some focus on racism and its effects on non-white groups, others adopt a 'colour blind' approach in the belief that a professional (Western) training and a liberal political view are sufficient to ensure non-discriminatory practice. The result is to make race too 'political' an issue for clinical groups and, by implication, of little interest outside the concerns of anthropologists. This is not to claim, however, that 'black' professionals hold a unified view on the subject.

This chapter contains material from my clinical experience as a black/Bengali/Indian child psychiatrist in Britain. These are drawn mainly from the cultural groups of the Indian subcontinent, with whom I have the closest experience. (Words in Bengali/Urdu have been translated both literally, and figuratively.) I have included cases in which child protection was not the main concern, hoping to illustrate the importance of a number of subjects that are vital to the frame of reference within which cross-cultural understanding and assessment of parenting needs to take place. These include immigration, racism, class and gender. I have then considered data on families from a variety of cultural sources. It is not my intention to present factual or exhaustive information about any specific group, but to make some general points about variations in beliefs and behaviour and to raise the question of whether, and under which circumstances, the 'best interests' of a child can be separated from its familial/cultural context. The chapter ends with some strategies that I have found useful in my own assessments of minority ethnic families; I imagine that in the individual case these will vary in importance with the 'cultural distance' between observer and subject.

Case example – Hasina and her Bangladeshi family

I was asked to assess Hasina Begum (aged 12 years) by her social worker who was extremely concerned about Hasina's repeated disappearances from home and her wild stories of days spent with unnamed men in hotels all over London. The social worker had observed Hasina's father beat her in a great rage when she returned from one of these disappearances and was also concerned about emotional abuse and neglect. She (the social worker) thought that the parents showed little warmth or affection towards Hasina, or appreciation of her needs for education, peer relationships and so on. Mother was pregnant with their seventh child and had little time to devote to her oldest daughter. Hasina was expected instead to miss school and help look after the younger children. At a meeting of professionals, a vague concern was also voiced about the possibility of sexual abuse in the family. Furthermore, in response to her behaviour, Hasina's parents had threatened to take her to Bangladesh and give her in arranged marriage there. This caused so much professional anxiety that an emergency prohibited steps order was sought in court, and granted. Among other things it forbade the parents 'to plan' Hasina's marriage and asked for Hasina's and her father's passports to be handed over to the court.

I met with the family in their home. I found a home that was rather more untidy and disorganised than other Bangladeshi homes of comparable socio-economic status that I have visited. Hasina's mother's background in Sylhet was rural but the family owned land and had a *paka bari* (house of brick or cement as opposed to peasant homes of mud and thatch). These details are relevant as they helped me place the family within a rural socioeconomic frame, and to understand that the family's sense of self-esteem, and therefore of shame at public embarrassment, remained linked with markers of status in Bangladesh rather than with their life in Britain. Hasina's mother wept as she showed me photographs of well-dressed groups of relatives within the spacious courtyard of her family home. Hasina's father was reluctant to say much about his family; his wife indicated that her family was of higher status than his. Though the parents seemed to have no wish to return to Bangladesh I had the impression that they had little enthusiasm for, or interest in, life in London beyond the barest essentials.

During my first visit, Hasina's mother, almost full-term pregnant, struggled with decreasing success to keep the three youngest children under some supervision. Her husband had been unemployed for some years and spent much of his time in bed or out of the home. The settee was stained and most of the furniture covered with crumbs of food. Both parents were furious with Hasina and very bitter about what they saw as the social worker's collusion with Hasina in not reprimanding her for her behaviour. The parents argued loudly and unceasingly about what should be done about Hasina. I interpreted father's vague but impressively global threats towards Hasina as indication of helpless frustration rather than dangerous intent. Hasina, leaning against the living room door, was not particularly intimidated and scowled back at him. Hasina's mother bemoaned their fate for having a disobedient daughter – "Is there any sorrow so great as a child that disobeys and dishonours her parents?"

My assessment of the meaning of both verbal and non-verbal material – its volume, intensity, dramatic impact and interactional intent – was based on my experience of other Bangladeshi families of equivalent social position and on series of questions to check whether, and to what extent, this family varied from what may be thought of as the 'normal' pattern for that group.

The mother confided in me that Hasina was very probably nearer 16 years than the 12 years stated in her passport. Perhaps this was why she had developed such a keen interest in men, and, if this was what she wished, then the best solution would be to find a husband who would cool/calm (*thanda*) her disturbed/heated (*uttejito*) state. However, the neighbours had heard Hasina's stories and there had been abusive telephone calls from Bangladeshi families telling Hasina's mother to keep her away from their sons. The scandal was unlikely to allow a match to be found in London. She appealed to me, as a woman and her sister (*boyin*), to help them get Hasina back to Bangladesh. With regard to Hasina's rudeness towards them and her recent refusal to help with housework they blamed television for teaching her to disobey her parents.

I talked with the parents about how they might help to calm their daughter. They wanted to take her to a *mullah* (religious healer) in East London and expected that he would give her a *tabiz* (amulet containing writing from the Holy Koran) or use other religious means to rid Hasina of her angry disobedience and her shameful behaviour. However, they were unable to arrange the trip without someone to take care of the younger children. There was little support in the neighbourhood because of regional rivalries within the Bangladeshi community, and, besides, other parents did not want Hasina influencing their children.

Halfway through my interviews Hasina disappeared again. Her parents said they were fed up, and did not care any more. The social worker suspected they knew where she was because her mother was not at their office every morning, demanding that something be done. Weeks passed and professional anxieties grew – perhaps she had been smuggled out of the country, or secretly married off. The new baby was born and at my next visit I found the home much more organised. Hasina's father cooked lunch while his wife nursed the baby. They amicably discussed their older son's progress at school and mother's childhood in Bangladesh.

Shortly afterwards Hasina reappeared, and she was greatly changed. No longer the sullen, provocatively dishevelled adolescent, she explained that she had been with relatives, studying the Koran with a favourite great-uncle. She described to me with great earnestness the horrors of hell that awaited a disobedient child. She did not wish to return to school, she had been bullied there, and she felt she would rather learn to keep house instead, in preparation for marriage. I was somewhat sceptical about the lasting nature of this change, but very impressed. Her parents asked me again to explain to the court that they wished to take Hasina 'home' – it would bring her peace of mind (literally – her mind/heart would be cooled), as she was really too immature still for marriage.

My preliminary report to social services offered an alternative view of Hasina's parents – as a couple that were coping poorly (when compared with other parents in a similar position) with the gap between their fantasies of 'benefits' in Britain and the reality, rather than as wilful or malicious abusers of services. Their initially ineffectual attempts to 'protect' their daughter's welfare and interests revealed a similar difficulty in adapting to the psychological realities of their immigrant status, on its impact on their relationships with their adolescent child, and the need to harness what resources there were in the local Bangladeshi community.

RACE, ETHNICITY AND CULTURE

The referral of this family to me was ostensibly based on the 'ethnic' and cultural common ground we shared. Social services had struggled with interpreters and made little headway in communicating with the family. The social worker had worried about the 'lies' both parents told them; mother had claimed to be ill and unable to attend an appointment but she was seen that day at the local market. The social worker had asked (through the interpreter) what would happen if Hasina behaved in a promiscuous manner in Bangladesh. Mother had gestured that her throat would be cut, but insisted that taking Hasina there was the only solution; the social worker was uncertain whether the threat was metaphorical or real in the context of the family's culture. Referrals on cultural grounds often mask intractable personal circumstances or just difficult people (Littlewood 1993a) and frequently mark a breakdown in the relationship between an agency and a family, which is then construed as lying within the culture of the client/family. For example, Hasina's parents' attempts to exert parental control may be incorrectly interpreted using received ideas about the supposed oppression of women in traditional/Islamic culture.

'Ethnicity' is a relatively recent term used loosely to replace the more contentious 'race', but most often used to mean 'non-white', e.g. the children of immigrants from Europe tend to lose their ethnic colouring more easily than 'second generation Asians' who remain an ethnic group. 'Race', as a term indicating group difference based on genetically distinct identity, has been discredited. Rapid changes in national boundaries, vast migrations across these boundaries, legal, illegal and refugee, and mixed-race marriages and children – all of these render old concepts of 'racial' identity obsolete. 'Culture' has been defined in innumerable ways and, for the purposes of this discussion, I mean the 'total of non-biologically inherited patterns of shared experience and behaviour through which personal identity and social structures are attained in each generation in a particular society, whether ethnic group or a nation' (Littlewood 1989). While containing elements that link a group with its historical past it is important to remember that cultures are dynamic and responsive to local events.

Minority groups, by virtue of their minority status, experience certain pressures from the dominant majority, that may be experienced as threats to their unity, resources, or to their 'cultural' identity. In the case of immigrant groups this may include racism, and competition with other minority groups for scant resources. Sociologists speak of the 'imagined communities' that groups create in the face of such threat, motivated by the desire to unite disparate language or religious subgroups for a common purpose, or to mark their separation from others. The ethnic minority group may seek an 'authentic' identity through selective reinterpretations of its history. Eade (1992) has written about the Bangladeshi community in Britain and the ways in which Bengali nationalist and Islamic factions interpret the history of the community in different ways and imply diverging allegiances (to the powerful Islamic Middle East and to the cultural history of Bengal in the Indian subcontinent respectively). It is necessary to remember, however, that the individual may choose a 'reference group' (De Vos 1990) that is other than its ethnic group, or choose more than one, e.g. children of Bangladeshi parents may identify themselves as British, black, Islamic and/or Bangladeshi.

'Race' or 'culture'?

There is a debate among some black professionals about the use of the very term 'black' – namely, its use to mean 'non-white', and to indicate the shared experiences of all non-white groups in Britain. In this desire to encourage a united stand against racial discrimination, institutional and personal, the consideration of cultural variation may seem self-indulgent, even dangerously 'separatist', and I share with black colleagues an anxiety that a focus on culture may divert attention from a consideration of racism. Despite these concerns, the significance of culture must not be underestimated, particularly when attempting to understand the influences upon internal structures within the individual which govern how she or he experiences and interacts with the world. Without an examination of the interactive effects of racism, minority status and socioeconomic disadvantage with each group's cultural systems, a focus on racial discrimination alone runs the risk of confining the minority person within two stereotypes – of victim, or its mirror-image, the rigidly idealised 'black' identity. On the other hand, a focus on culture alone will merely serve to keep minority groups in the position of exotic curiosities, rather like 'natives' to early explorers.

THE LARGER CONTEXT OF ASSESSMENT

British cultural systems, professional or lay, are imbued with beliefs about the individual, the family and society, and the orbits of authority and influence of each of these. They also contain influences from earlier periods of British history – from Britain's position as a colonial power over parts of the world from which many of its current minority groups originate. The scope of this chapter prevents a fuller discussion of the psychological impact of colonialism, racism and immigration on current attitudes, both professional and lay, which must necessarily affect both the assessing professional and the parent/family under assessment. It is my contention that for those who are interested in cross-cultural assessment, or work in areas of high immigrant density, an examination of the relevant literature is essential.

I include a very brief, and possibly idiosyncratic, list of the literature that I have found useful on how the processes named above influence British psychiatry (Littlewood 1993b); on the psychological effects of colonialism and racism (Fanon 1967); on acculturation and the mental health of the immigrant (Berry and Kim 1988); on culture, health and help seeking (Helman 1984); on beliefs about race and culture that are inherent in the theory and practice of psychoanalysis (Kakar 1985; Gordon 1993) and in the Western social sciences (De Vos and Suarez-Orozco 1990).

Case example

Shortly after the Gulf War, a 10 year old Iranian girl was referred with episodic weakness of the legs that prevented her from attending school. I discovered that her reluctance had begun around her ninth birthday when she was required by religious custom to start wearing a headscarf. Her parents were sympathetic when she was teased at school and suggested that she could defer wearing a scarf for a few more years. They also tried to brush off the significance of attacks on their own flat in London during the Gulf War; clearly, they explained, this was based on the assailants' ignorance about the difference between Iran and Iraq. The presenting problem was significantly alleviated when the child transferred to an Islamic school, at which her headscarf was the norm rather than yet another marker of her difference.

Cultural relativism, or the idea that each cultural system of belief and behaviour is governed by a coherent internal structure of logic and meaning, encourages respect for alternate world views and ways of being. However, this is a much more difficult stance to maintain when one's own autonomy is threatened, or when one believes that another is threatened. To Hasina's social worker the threat of Hasina having her throat cut by outraged relatives in Bangladesh appeared real enough to warrant immediate legal sanctions. To her parents, the risk Hasina placed herself at (both sexual and physical) was not all, there was also a threat to the family's viability as respected members of their community. This warranted urgent action too, i.e. removal from the permissiveness of British society to Bangladesh where socially acceptable responses might be found to Hasina's wishes.

Class and gender

The temptation to speak of cultures in broad-brush categorisations often overlooks the significance of gender and class. Mirza (1992) points out how stereotypes of the black Afro-Caribbean family (of strong matriarchal women and feckless men) are derived from a focus on working-class families and from the methodological bias in social class data. The accepted practice of rating social class by using the occupational status of the male as head of the family reflects European patriarchal norms and social realities. Unequal employment opportunities, particularly at non-manual jobs, affect black men more than women, and even more severely so in areas of high unemployment. When the higher rates of family breakup and single mothers in working-class British families is added to this picture, the black working classes are likely to contain fewer employed male heads. Social class ratings derived from such data may not adequately reflect the education and employment status of black women who, in fact, head the household. O'Donovan (1984) notes the persistence of patriarchal notions of authority and gender role allocation in the British legal system despite changes in the status of women in the West; in other parts of the world, urbanisation and industrialisation are effecting major changes in the traditional relationships between men and women (Kayongo-Male and Onyango 1984).

Within cultures, social class may also account for much of the variability in parental behaviour. Cook-Gumperz's study (1973) of British mothers confirms clinical impressions concerning the influence of social class upon styles of control: that middle-class mothers are more likely to give verbal explanation of rules to children, with discussion of context and individual responsibility; working-class mothers are more likely to use punishment and to convey rules as fixed and unrelated to context. The difficulty in correctly judging what is appropriate parental control and what is not, becomes more complex the greater the distance in terms of social class and culture between the family under assessment and the observer. This is complicated even further by the effects of the acculturation process as the immigrant family chooses to adopt certain patterns of behaviour from the host culture but not others.

CULTURE AND 'THE FAMILY'

There has been much discussion about notions of 'the child', 'childhood' and 'the family' being cultural inventions influenced by historical factors, rather than reflective of general truths about human societies (Kessel and Siegel 1983). In the modern West, technical procedures and social phenomena, such as surrogate motherhood, and gay/lesbian marriage and parenthood, continue to redefine sexuality, gender and familial relationships and roles. Stimulated by *in vitro* fertilisation technology, a government inquiry (Department of Health 1984) struggled with biological and legal definitions of 'mother' and 'father', revealing important assumptions within Western culture (Rivière 1985). Though the circumstances and strategies of other cultures may appear alien they deal with similar desires and concerns – the legitimacy of the child, paternity, the inheritance of property, and the relative positions of the range of women that may be 'mothers' to a child.

Studies of households around the world illustrate the variety of structures possible – from single-parent, nuclear, extended to 'joint' families (in which several married sons and their families may live with elderly parents and unmarried siblings). Whether such structures are more or less stable for each culture, or whether families pass through nuclear and extended phases, what is more relevant to ethnic minority families in Britain is the impact of British systems, such as immigration laws and housing regulations, upon the desired family structure and the experience of this by particular families.

Case example

Eight year old Hassan worried his teachers with the violently aggressive fantasies he repeatedly voiced in play. His father had died within a year of his mother arriving with Hassan and three older daughters from Bangladesh. The family had succeeded in also bringing Hassan's ailing *Boro-ma* (his father's senior wife; literally – bigger/older mother) and her two adult unmarried daughters over but could find no way to do the same for Boro-ma's oldest son. With the father's death he, though only 26 years old, was the male head of the family and in his absence Hassan could not be convinced that he did not need to carry the burden of protecting the women from the repeated harassment they faced on their council estate.

Marriage in Western tradition has only relatively recently given to romantic love the central position it currently enjoys. The power of this ideal, greatly supported by popular culture, is interlinked with the imperatives of individualism and free choice. From such a viewpoint, the traditional functions of marriage in non-Western cultures – of procreation and of uniting family resources (e.g. Gil'adi 1992; Linzer 1984) – may appear oppressive, even immoral, in their attitude to the individual.

An important correlate of this dimension of the romantic marital bond is the nature of the subsequent relationship between the parental couple. In assessing how a couple behaves as parents much attention is paid in Western professional practice to factors such as the time parents spend together, whether parents discuss and jointly implement rules, rewards and 'punishments' for their children, whether the boundaries and hierarchical relationships between the parental and child 'subunits' are maintained. While it is clear that these may all be influenced by cultural expectations, it is harder to accept that the most cherished notions of motherhood, parental love and parental roles may be dictated by historical economic events. Kessen (1983) describes the creation of the 'good mother' in Western cultures when industrialisation made it no longer necessary to use women and children as cheap labour. Cast in a sentimentalised vision of purity and vulnerability, women and children were confined to the home; men controlled the public domain but gradually lost authority in the home. However, the decay of the extended family and intrafamilial support networks for women, and the return of women to paid employment, has resulted in the declining prestige of motherhood and child care. Studies of depression in Western women point to the stressful nature of child care and the significance of a confiding relationship with the spouse/partner.

From the point of view of the non-Western family, of course, a marriage that places romantic choice above the good of the family is likely to seem immoral because it is self-centred and closer to animal than human nature in that it accords such influence to something as transient as sexual desire and choice. Mirza (1992), writing about a different historical chain of events, links the relative absence of patriarchal systems in the Caribbean to its history of slavery; women in such contexts did not rely on men, but developed a strong sense of equality and independence. By contrast, in Asian families within patriarchal cultures economic power rests with the father, who wields almost complete authority as disciplinarian and teacher in the home; the mother is almost exclusively responsible for the care of young children and the socialisation of older daughters. Extended female kin provide support and practical assistance in day-to-day tasks and joint parental decision-making may rarely be necessary. The separation into nuclear family units after migration, depending upon the availability of accommodation and employment, entails major changes to this gender allocation of tasks and the nature and functions of the marital relationship. The authority of the father may also be undermined by experiences of powerlessness in the outer world, as was strikingly evident in Hasina's father's relationships with her mother and with Hasina. It was only when his authority was effectively supported by both religious tradition and male elders that the marital and family relationships improved.

The 'meaning of the child', child rearing and the responsibilities of parents

The influence of cultural beliefs about the human infant on its earliest treatment is visible in ancient practices in Europe and the Middle East, such as swaddling. According to De Mause (1974), it was meant to restrain the animal nature of the infant, just as later excessively harsh punishments were intended to compensate for its intrinsically sinful nature. In a different religious context, far removed from Christian notions of original sin, is found the permissive indulgence of childhood in the Indian subcontinent (Kakar 1981).

Despite such variation it is important to note that child abuse has been prevalent in cultures around the world, both Western and non-Western (De Mause 1974; Gil'adi 1992), and continues in many poverty-ridden parts of the world, where infant mortality is also high. In extreme form it appears as infanticide, abandonment and exposure, in lesser forms as selective with-holding of food or care; in many parts of the world more female infants are subjected to such treatments. Scheper-Hughes (1987) questions the tendency to judge these parents (and overwhelmingly this falls upon mothers) as inhumanly callous, or these cultures as inclined to the view of children as interchangeable commodities.

Violence to female children, as in genital mutilation, must be viewed within the context of the position of women within the culture. Where women continue to be seen as the property of the male head, the family or the clan, female sexuality and desire is often construed as dangerous to male authority and women are socialised into acceptance of virginity/chastity as essential feminine virtues. Levinson's (1989) record of the African tribal viewpoint suggests that genital mutilation is a mark of ethnic identity that is more important than any pain or suffering that the operation may bring. Whether this practice is seen as a culturally sanctioned means of controlling female sexual autonomy or as a highly valued marker of identity, it is unrealistic to expect that these practices are readily available to change. Indeed the very experiences of isolation, racial discrimination and feared loss of cultural identity in minority ethnic groups may cause parents to cling harder to traditional practices, providing an illusion of some control over their lives. Real freedom to change is available only when a community has achieved a measure of security and self-determination. This must be distinguished from the adoption of Western customs that is motivated by a wish merely to conform, or the internalisation of negative stereotypes of the individual's cultural group.

The issue of whether ethnic minority parents must be compelled to obey the laws of their adoptive country is a complex issue and may best be examined within the discussion of what constitutes the best interests of the child. For example, the fact of sexual activity among Western adolescents below the legal age of consent is a matter of concern to society and has stimulated discussion and decisions that alter the criminal significance of breaches of this particular law. The need to prevent pregnancy in these youngsters is seen as more important than parental authority in this area, or the need to charge the child with breaking the law. It is certainly more easily attainable than altering peer pressures that may lead to sexual activity against the child's own inclination. Indeed, the debate about the lowering of the age of homosexual consent points to the way in which sexual, social and legal norms influence each other.

With ethnic minority children, parenting assessments are often required when the manifest conflict appears to be between parental authority, in its insistence on some traditional practice, and either the child's reluctance to comply or the belief of the Western professional that the practice would harm the child in some way. The important issue must be, as always, the child's long-term interests and these include its place within its community *in Britain*. Where a cultural practice, such as female genital mutilation, may carry serious long-term physical and psychological ill-effects, the assessment of parental attitudes must include their openness to discuss the benefits and risks of the procedure with professionals. This discussion may be greatly facilitated by enlisting the assistance of respected bicultural members of the parents' community. Legal safeguards may be necessary to ensure that hasty action is prevented and a realistic time period allowed for parents to explore the implications of their wishes upon the lives of their children. The task of the professional is to be open to the parents' view, and to attempt to understand parental wishes as largely motivated by their concerns for their child's welfare, although influenced by their personal experiences and feelings as parents within a minority culture. To lose sight of this process in excessive professional haste to 'protect' ethnic minority children may create or exacerbate transgenerational family conflict, further destabilising joint parental authority in a manner, and at a time, that is least helpful to the child.

In a study spanning six cultures, Whiting and Edwards (1988) found important cultural differences between styles of mother–child interaction and the varying patterns of reciprocal behaviours that children develop. They show that children have very different socialising experiences depending upon the companions they have at different ages, a most notable variable being whether or not they are required to go to school. These experiences are then likely to have far-reaching consequences on the community; for example, the early experience of caring for younger siblings, through the immediate emotional rewards that it provides, imparts a sense of self-esteem and of responsibility for other members of the family, as well as mitigating the egoistic motives that derive from the more individualistic and competitive strivings of the school context. Roland (1988) suggests that societies that foster nurturance, dependence (and 'overstimulation') create a sense of self that is familial rather than individual and, as a whole, may have less drive to technological advancement. For ethnic minority children growing up in Britain it may well be thought that an upbringing that does not foster individualistic and competitive desires is a distinct handicap. However, variations in the value placed on individual versus community goals exist between the social classes in white British culture too and may only seem repressive and restrictive when couched in an alien idiom.

Other important variations exist between beliefs in Western professional and 'ethnic' cultures about the demarcation of the roles of parents and children. One such is indicated by the idea of the 'parentified child', implying undesirable role reversal with the child in the caring/nurturing role. Several South-East Asian cultures permit, and even value, much greater degrees of variability in daughter–parent (Lau 1984; Guzder and Krishna 1991) and mother–son roles and interactions (Nandy 1980).

The manner in which children are socialised into full and effective membership of the group may vary with culture, but implies always the expertise and authority of parents and the dependence of children. Parents must exert control and expect obedience from their children. It is interesting to note that secular and egalitarian ideals in the West have replaced the idea of 'obedience' with the concept of 'internalised' control. However, the Children Act re-establishes the significance of external controls from parents upon children, as implied by its absence or failure in the child who is 'out of parental control'. Other cultures may require obedience not only to parents, but also to all elders and to religious precepts.

Among the obligations of parents in all cultures is the duty to educate the child so that it will be equipped to fulfil the demands of adult roles within its cultural group. Formal education may be highly valued by many immigrant groups, particularly as a means of bettering their chances of employment and income. However, this may seem less relevant to others, particularly for daughters who may be expected instead to acquire domestic skills in preparation for marriage and motherhood. In several traditional cultures, in which religion retains the central position it has lost in much of the West, the additional duty to introduce the child to its cultural and religious heritage is a particular aspect of the father's role. Linzer (1984) speaks of the duty of *pidyon ha-ben*, the duty to introduce the Jewish child to 'the memory of Egypt', that is to the history of the group. The significance of such parental tasks in the development of the social identity of a child is likely to be particularly relevant to ethnic minority children, to whom positive public images of their group may be infrequently available. Despite this, it has been accorded relatively little importance in the literature on parenting. While there has been much debate on the subject, particularly in relation to the transracial adoption and fostering of black children, the relevance of racial and cultural identity to minority group children cannot be ignored (Larson 1989; Phinney and Alipuria 1990; Maxime 1993) and is reflected in the encouragement given by the Children Act to consider the race, culture, religion and language of the child in assessing his or her needs and welfare.

CONCLUSIONS

In conclusion I would like to make some general points about common pitfalls in cross-cultural assessments, and some strategies that I have found useful in my work in this area.

Some assumptions to beware of

1 That a smattering of English words implies the ability to understand or express complex psychological issues.
2 That Western dress implies a grasp of Western ideas, beliefs or systems.
3 That wives/mothers who do not speak in the presence of their husbands, or who walk five steps behind their husbands, are necessarily timid or do not wield much power in the home.
4 That the submissiveness and excessive politeness of ethnic minority clients, the "yassuh boss" response set (Griffith 1977), indicates agreement; this may be a way of testing the interviewer's attitude and interest.
5 That non-verbal behaviours and the intensity of facial expressions of emotion have equivalent meanings across cultures.
6 That certain Western patterns of thought, such as introspection (Kakar 1982), and hypothetical questions (as in the circular questioning of systemic family therapy), are universally applicable, relevant or even comprehensible to other cultural groups.
7 That Western-style 'liberation' is uniformly desirable to individuals, particularly women, despite what appear to be clearly oppressive socio-cultural settings. It is useful to remember that the exhortations of well-meaning professionals may be experienced as coercive; liberation needs to be seen within the social context of the individual and also to keep pace with the individual's ability to tolerate possible alienation from the group.
8 That cultural rules may not be broken; it must be emphasised that it requires great patience, ingenuity and consultation with bicultural colleagues to discover culturally sanctioned 'get-out' clauses.

9 That interpreters have the necessary knowledge about the beliefs of the 'child care culture'.
10 That all black professionals are equally interested in cultural issues and willing to enter this area of professional conflict.
11 That invitations to the client/patient's home, offers of food and such other behaviours, are insidious attempts to manipulate or bribe; this may be the family's attempt to feel more the social equals of professionals, rather than their racial and social inferiors.

Suggestions

1 Anticipate and plan for a greater number of interviews than usual, possibly of somewhat longer duration if other professionals are to be present.
2 Consider making at least one assessment interview in the family home; this has enormous advantages that may well outweigh the discomfort of feeling the intruder, of difficult interview conditions, sometimes amidst the chaos and noise of large families.
3 Be aware that the family will 'check you out' in a variety of ways to assess your attitude towards their cultural/ethnic group, and to assess your independence from other professional agencies.
4 Repeated explanations are likely to be necessary to explain the entire process of assessment, your part in it, as well as the specific responsibility you may have in making reports to the court. Asian families are often confused by the contradictions that I, as an Asian woman and child psychiatrist, embody to them and may feel a sense of betrayal when at the end of a series of emotive interviews, made more so by our common mother tongue, I make a decision about their child that contradicts cultural notions of the child's best interests.
5 Use a professional interpreter rather than a child, member of the family or family friend. This is not a simple matter as the interpreter, too, may arouse anxieties about confidential family matters being made available to the minority community. It is very important to confirm for yourself the training and experience of the interpreter. I am keenly aware of the difficulties in translating cultural constructs, both professional and 'Asian' and confess to struggling particularly with sexual terminology in the Indian languages I speak, as equivalent colloquial terms may have nuances that are inappropriate to the professional nature of the interview. Interpreters may be less aware of the significance of certain issues and may be tempted to abbreviate or condense when equivalents are clumsy, or when they wish to avoid causing offence or pain.
6 Several voluntary organisations and social services departments hold lists of bicultural bilingual professionals. Consider joint interviews, consultations, supervision arrangements. Again, this is not without its own problems

and I would be wary of setting up 'cultural experts' as there are wide intracultural variations by subgroup, class, etc.

7 The inclusion of cultural contexts at all levels of training, and at least the consideration of systems of oppression, such as racism, in how these might affect bodies of knowledge and theory.

REFERENCES

Berry, J.W. and Kim, U. (1988) 'Acculturation and mental health', in P.R. Dasen (ed.) *Health and Cross-Cultural Psychology*, Beverly Hills CA: Sage.

Cook-Gumperz, J. (1973) *Social Control and Socialization*, London: Routledge and Kegan Paul.

De Mause, L. (1974) *The History of Childhood*, London: Bellew.

Department of Health (1984) *Report of the Committee of Inquiry into Human Fertilization and Embryology*, London: HMSO.

De Vos, G.A. (1990) 'Self in society: a multilevel, psychocultural analysis', in G. A. De Vos and M. Suarez-Orozco (eds) *Status Inequality. The Self in Culture*, Newbury Park CA: Sage.

De Vos, G.A. and Suarez-Orozco, M. (eds) (1990) *Status Inequality – The Self in Culture*, Newbury Park CA: Sage.

Eade, J. (1992) 'Quests for belonging', in A.X. Cambridge and S. Feuchtwang (eds) *Where You Belong*, Aldershot: Avebury Macmillan.

Fanon, F. (1967) *Black Skins, White Masks* (translation of French edition), Harmondsworth: Penguin.

Gil'adi, A. (1992) *Children of Islam: Concepts of Childhood in Medieval Muslim Society*, London: Macmillan.

Gordon, P. (1993) 'Souls in armour: thoughts on psychoanalysis and racism', *British Journal of Psychotherapy*, **10**, 62–76.

Griffith, M.S. (1977) 'The influences of race on the psychotherapeutic relationship', *Psychiatry*, **40**, 27–40.

Guzder, J. and Krishna, M. (1991) 'Sita-Shakti: cultural paradigms for Indian women', *Transcultural Psychiatry Research Review*, **28**, 257–301.

Helman, C. (1984) *Culture, Health and Illness – An Introduction for Health Professionals*, Bristol: John Wright.

Kakar, S. (1981) *The Inner World: A Psychoanalytic Study of Childhood and Society in India*, Delhi: Oxford University Press.

Kakar, S. (1982) *Shamans, Mystics and Doctors: A Psychological Inquiry into India and its Healing Traditions*, London: Unwin.

Kakar, S. (1985) 'Psychoanalysis and non-western cultures', *International Review of Psycho-Analysis*, **12**, 441–8.

Kayongo-Male, D. and Onyango, P. (1984) *The Sociology of the African Family*, New York: Longman.

Kessel, F.S. and Siegel, A.W. (eds) (1983) *The Child and Other Cultural Inventions*, New York: Praeger.

Kessen, W. (1983) 'The American child and other inventions', in F.S. Kessel and A.W. Siegel (eds) *The Child and Other Cultural Inventions*, New York: Praeger.

Larson, H. (1989) *Culture at Play: Pakistani Children, British Childhood*, Berkeley: Department of Anthropology, University of California.

Lau, A. (1984) 'Transcultural issues in family therapy', *Journal of Family Therapy*, **6**, 91–112.

Levinson, D. (1989) *Family Violence in Cross-Cultural Perspective*, Newbury Park CA: Sage.

Linzer, N. (1984) *The Jewish Family – Authority and Tradition in Modern Perspective*, New York: Human Sciences Press.

Littlewood, R. (1989) 'Glossary' in *Report of the Royal College of Psychiatrists Special (Ethnic Issues) Committee*, London: Royal College of Psychiatrists.

Littlewood, R. (1993a) 'Towards an intercultural therapy', in J. Kareem and R. Littlewood (eds) *Intercultural Therapy: Themes, Interpretations and Practice*, London: Blackwell Scientific.

Littlewood, R. (1993b) 'Overview: ideology, camouflage or contingency? Racism in British psychiatry', *Transcultural Psychiatric Research Review*, **30**, 243–90.

Maxime, J. E. (1993) 'The importance of racial identity for the psychological well-being of black children', *ACPP Review and Newsletter*, **15**, 173–9.

Mirza, H. S. (1992) *Young, Female and Black*, London: Routledge.

Nandy, A. (1980) 'Woman versus womanliness in India: an essay in cultural and political psychology', in *At the Edge of Psychology: Essays in Politics and Culture*, Delhi: Oxford University Press.

O'Donovan, K. (1984) 'Protection and paternalism', in M.D.A. Freeman (ed.) *State, Law and the Family – Critical Perspectives*, London: Tavistock.

Phinney, J.S. and Alipuria, L.L. (1990) 'Ethnic identity in college students from four ethnic groups', *Journal of Adolescence*, **13**, 171–83.

Rivière, P. (1985) 'Unscrambling parenthood: the Warnock report', *Anthropology Today*, **4**, 2–7.

Roland, A. (1988) *In Search of Self in India and Japan: Toward a Cross-Cultural Psychology*, Princeton NJ: Princeton University Press.

Scheper-Hughes, N. (1987) 'Culture, scarcity, and maternal thinking: mother love and child death in Northeast Brazil', in N. Scheper-Hughes (ed.) *Child Survival: Anthropological Perspectives on the Treatment and Maltreatment of Children*, Dordrecht: Reidel.

Whiting, B.B. and Edwards, C.P. (1988) *Children of Different Worlds: The Formation of Social Behaviour*, Cambridge MA: Harvard University Press.

Part III

Specific circumstances

Chapter 11

Parents with psychiatric problems
Diana Cassell and Rosalyn Coleman

INTRODUCTION

There is a wide spectrum of beliefs about what should happen when a child's parent has a major psychiatric disorder. Some professionals are mindful of the potential for emotional damage or abuse and suggest that most children should be separated from such parents. Others believe that the damage caused by moving children is to be avoided at all costs and advocate keeping them with their ill parents. Sometimes, professionals feel that the parents should not be blamed or disadvantaged because of their problems and the poignancy of the parent's suffering can mean that professionals do not focus on the issues for the child. The dilemma is especially difficult in these cases because the effects on the child are often subtle and concern the potential for emotional or physical harm, rather than proven abuse. Thus, professionals may be unsure whether they can achieve the level of proof that is needed in court.

There is a need to address the concept of 'significant harm' in this context. Consideration of whether damage is, or will be, occurring depends on the likely effects on the child if the situation does not improve and the likelihood of change in the parent. An assessment of whether the parents can meet the child's needs should be balanced against the likely outcomes for the child, if removed. This process may need to be separated into stages: short term, when physical protection might be required; and longer term, when professionals are able to focus on emotional factors.

The principal questions put to psychiatrists are about the extent to which the parent's problems are interfering with their parenting skills and harming the child. In this review, we shall include the major findings about child psychopathology as it relates to parental diagnosis and consider when these problems constitute significant harm.

There is a large literature about the influence of parental psychiatric disorder on children, summarised by Beardslee *et al.* (1983) and Rutter and Quinton (1984). Generally, however, authors have not considered whether the identified psychological effects reach the level of significant harm to the child's psychological development. Similarly, little has been written about the risks of physical abuse or neglect when a child is living with a disturbed parent. However, some inferences can be drawn from descriptions of the ways in which psychiatric problems affect parenting behaviour.

Depression has received the greatest attention in the research literature and we shall therefore review this in more detail. Similar symptoms occur with other diagnoses, allowing some inferences to be drawn about parents with other problems. We shall not consider parents with psychopathic personalities, because the assessment will be guided by consideration of their relationships, by their insight into their situation and their motivation for change. Problems associated with parents who misuse alcohol or drugs are discussed separately in Chapter 12.

Most studies have looked at mothers. However, there is no reason to believe that the risk of child psychopathology is any different when fathers are psychiatrically disturbed (Phares and Compas 1992). We feel that it is reasonable to conclude that assessments of fathers should be guided by the same principles and, where we refer to mothers, the same would apply to any carer of a child.

DEPRESSION

Puckering (1989) suggests that mothers who first experience depression postnatally have greater difficulties attending to, and interacting with, their infants than those who have had prior episodes of depression. The mother's feelings about being a mother may contribute to the depression (Wrate *et al.* 1985) and ambivalence about the child or their transition to the new role might make parenting difficulties more likely to occur. The relationship between the mother and child will clearly be affected if the mother blames her child for her suffering.

Parental depression is often manifested by insensitivity and unavailability, provoking anger and distress in the infant and disruption of the infant's developing ability to modulate affect and arousal (Cummings and Davies 1994). Cox (1988) found depressed mothers had particular difficulties managing distressed infants, compounding the problem. The insecure attachments that may result would also render the child more difficult to parent. Depressed parents are more sensitive to negative behaviour in the children and tend to be more coercive, inconsistent and likely to avoid confrontations with them (Cummings and Davies 1994). Puckering (1989) emphasised the importance of maternal irritability, because children who are criticised are more likely to become self-critical, undermining development of their self-esteem.

Similarities of parenting style have been described between depressed parents and parents who have abused their children. These are: inconsistency, hostility and anxiety-provoking or guilt-inducing means of child rearing;

except that depressed parents do not use harsh, authoritarian discipline (Susman *et al.* 1985). Kinnard (1982) found high rates of depressive symptomatology in parents who had abused their children. This is perhaps not surprising, because parents who are struggling to maintain control of their child, or who are maltreating a child, tend to feel hopeless and guilty.

Some parents experience depression related to their own poor parenting and adversities in childhood, resulting in conflicts about managing the demands of parenthood and lack of role models. A crisis may be precipitated when their child approaches the age at which the parent experienced major traumatic events. One depressed mother who had been sexually abused by her father in early childhood, described her 4 year old as being as difficult and unhappy as she had been at that age. The mother had become frightened by her impulses to harm her child. Through therapy, she dealt with the memories which surfaced and was able to increase her ability to care for her child. This programme required intensive input from both adult and child mental health services and the child was successively rehabilitated.

Children of depressed parents may fail to thrive because of chaotic meal times, parental expression of hostility and difficulty controlling them (Cox 1988). Evans *et al.* (1972) found a pattern of failure to thrive in babies who were unplanned and unwanted by their depressed mothers. In many of these cases, support and casework were effective in helping the child's care.

The quality of a young child's attachments and interactions with the parent are an important part of the assessment. The mother's level of engagement in interactions should be assessed, especially her sensitivity, emotional availability and ability to cope when her child is distressed. Other components of the assessment should include her ability to manage the child's behaviour through strategies that are appropriate, consistent and effective. Kinnard (1982) found that the depth of depression related to the extent of any parenting problems, so that a recent assessment of the parent's mental state will be a useful guide to the child's current welfare.

It is evident that children living with depressed parents may have problems with their physical growth, development of self-esteem, capacity to form secure relationships and ability to manage their feelings. These are more liable to reach the threshold of significant harm if the parent's depression pervades all aspects of family life, when relationships are unreliable or when the parent's hopelessness and lack of energy lead to neglect. In addition, the parent may feel so irritated by their child's needs that physical abuse occurs.

PSYCHOSIS

Parents with chronic schizophrenia show some similarities to depressed parents but, in addition, the effects of 'negative symptoms' (lack of motivation and withdrawal) are particularly important. Withdrawal and detachment are especially damaging to the parent–child relationship (Downey and Coyne

1990). For example, parents may spend so much time sitting absorbed in their own thoughts that the child feels abandoned and their basic needs remain unmet. One schizophrenic mother did not respond to most of her child's communications and never initiated any. She rarely fed the child herself or played with him, relying instead on neighbours and relatives.

During episodes of florid psychosis, the problems for the family change as the parent becomes unpredictable and chaotic. Their lack of judgement may result in accidents or neglect of the child. One mother, who had recently separated, became hypomanic and requested admission to hospital. When asked about her 8 year old son, she said he was 'alright', but the social worker found him sitting on the doorstep. Between episodes, she was a satisfactory parent and had a good relationship with her son. The more severe a parent's psychosis and lack of contact with reality, the greater is the risk to the child's immediate safety. One mother believed that she had continuous spiritual communication with her toddler and so would leave him alone all day. After she was treated, she agreed to close monitoring of herself and the child and, although she did not make a complete recovery, the child remained safe and showed no lasting adverse effects.

If the child is included in the content of the parent's delusions, the risk to the child's emotional development and the potential for physical harm are much greater (Rutter and Quinton 1984). The parent's altered beliefs can include any facet of the child. One mother believed that her son was a little girl and raised him as a girl, damaging his psychosexual development, sense of identity and self-esteem. We shall consider this issue further in the section on dangerousness.

If socially isolated, there is the risk of *folie à deux* developing, especially if the parent and child have a highly dependent relationship and the child is included in the parent's delusion. One father believed his son was a member of the Holy Trinity. They lived a secluded existence and the boy expressed ideas that he was different from other children and was unable to make relationships with peers or adults. Fortunately, when a *folie à deux* occurs, the child's abnormal beliefs will recede following removal from the parent. If the child remains at home and continues to be influenced by the parent's delusions, there is a strong likelihood of damage to the child's psychological development. Hence, if the parent cannot be treated because of poor compliance or lack of response to medication, it is likely that the child will need to be removed into care.

Therefore, in addition to the effects on development that have been identified in the previous section on depression, children of psychotic parents may also suffer through feeling abandoned or neglected and because of lack of awareness of their safety needs while their parent has florid symptoms. Their sense of identity and successful psychological differentiation can also be jeopardised.

In assessment, it is important to consider the history of the relationship between the ill parent and child. Some parents do manage warm relationships despite severe symptoms, enabling the child's development to progress satisfactorily. Downey and Coyne (1990) describe how such positive contact can protect the child against emotional damage, but warn that increasing behaviour problems in the children of schizophrenic parents may indicate maltreatment.

Useful factors to consider in assessment are the quality and quantity of eye contact, the parent's responsiveness to the child's needs, the content of the psychotic ideation, the history of the parent's ability to manage their anger safely during previous breakdowns and the availability of another responsible adult. The parent's judgement can be assessed by asking them for their views about the child's needs. The diagnosis and prognosis should be clarified, including the treatment or hospitalisations required.

Psychosis and dangerousness

If the parent shows florid psychotic symptoms, some assessment of dangerousness must be made. Most children who are murdered by their parents are between 1 and 5 years old (d'Orban 1979), so that considerations of risk must extend beyond the puerperium. Many of these killings are 'altruistic' in that the parent believes they are protecting the child from other dangers. Resnick (1969) cautions that the danger is increased for a child who is the favourite of a loathed partner. Murderous violence can occur in those with no previous history of child maltreatment and hence it is essential to consider the content and nature of any delusions. Rodenburg (1971) emphasises the importance of also assessing the parent's personality and general interpersonal functioning as a guide to their potential to enact murderous ideas.

If the parent's symptoms include hallucinations that directly command them to do certain things, or distressing persecutory delusions, the physical risk to the child is significantly increased. This is even more so if the child is incorporated into the psychotic ideation. Similarly, if a psychotic parent is suicidal, or mentions harm occurring to the child, assessment is needed of the content of the delusions.

The child's safety must be monitored during assessment and treatment of the parent and is guided by the parent's mental state. For example, in reviewing parents who had attacked their children while psychotically disturbed, Anthony (1986) found a pattern of deterioration of judgement prior to the attack. Other factors of relevance are any history of aggression or suicidal behaviour and whether there is anyone able to monitor the situation.

In morbid jealousy, the level of violence can be extreme, even leading to murder, with the ill parent totally preoccupied by worries about what their partner is doing. The children will be at significant physical or emotional risk. The family environment will be dominated by the ill parent's worries and other members of the family may feel terrorised and confused. One father believed that his wife was having sex, even when she went to attend to their child. He would follow her, waking the boy, so that the child was exhausted and continuously distressed.

Puerperal psychosis and dangerousness

Assessment of risk in puerperal psychosis, particularly during the acute episode, requires particular attention. We know of one mother who threw her baby out of the window when left alone with him momentarily. The study by Oates (1988) of home-based nursing for puerperal illness suggested that assessment of risk can be based on three factors: whether a relative is available to monitor and supervise; whether the baby is included in the delusional symptoms; and absence of rough handling or inappropriate actions towards the baby that imply physical aggression. This requires a considerable period of observation of the mother handling her baby, during which they should be adequately supervised. In addition, the finding by Bluglass (1978) that mothers may kill older children during puerperal illnesses indicates that there should always be consideration of the potential risk to other siblings.

If a mother has no prior psychiatric history, then a mother with puerperal psychosis may have no further episodes and there need be few concerns about her recovery. However, some mothers remain disturbed and poor parenting skills result because of the disruption at a critical period when the mother is learning about her baby and adjusting to motherhood. The baby of one mother with puerperal psychosis was seriously dehydrated because she had changed to breast feeding at 8 days and was not lactating, but offered no other feeds.

Appleby and Dickens (1993) emphasise the need for detailed assessments of parenting once the mother recovers. It is important that future planning about the child's life only occurs following recovery, so that the emerging mother–child relationship can be assessed.

NEUROTIC DISORDERS

Parents with neurotic disorders include those who had unhappy or deprived childhoods and who have difficulty forming appropriate relationships with their own children. For example, the child may develop concern about the parent's problems and so act as their carer, or the parent may be irritable with the child when troubled by neurotic worries or ritualistic obsessions. We shall consider child care issues that may be associated with particular neurotic problems.

Anxiety

Maternal anxiety can contribute to poor child adjustment and behaviour problems because of the mother's emotional unavailability or conflict about managing the child behaviour (Barnett *et al.* 1991). Berg and McGuire (1974) linked school refusal to maternal anxiety, especially agoraphobia. We once saw a 7 year old school-refusing boy whose family had avoided acknowledging to professionals that the mother never left the house. Specific help for the mother led to the child returning to school, facilitated by a supervision order.

Other phobias can have a profound effect upon the family's lifestyle, particularly if there is pronounced avoidance of the feared object. However, many families use a variety of coping strategies to limit the impact upon the child and there is little evidence that such children suffer significant harm.

Obsessive-compulsive disorder

There is particular risk of harm when obsessions involve the child directly. However, these parents often acknowledge the child's plight and can be very motivated to seek treatment. One mother was unable to prepare food because of obsessive worries about hygiene. She accepted the need for treatment whilst her child's care was monitored. Another mother was fearful of contamination and regularly spray-hosed her child until his skin was raw. He needed immediate protection by removal from home, whilst his mother was treated.

Rodenburg (1971) described parents with obsessive thoughts about killing their child and who feared acting upon this or going insane in their attempts to stop themselves. They usually had problems expressing anger generally and controlling their children. Such parents tend to tell others about the problem rather than enact their thoughts and to be highly motivated to receive treatment, but specific assessment of their impulse control and history of violence is also required.

Eating disorders

It is unusual for children of parents with eating disorders to come to care proceedings. These families readily conceal problems, so that professionals are not aware of the possible risks to the child. However, in two investigations of mothers with bulimia nervosa, many of the mothers expressed concerns about their child's weight and body shape (Lacey and Smith 1987; Stein and Fairburn 1989). Lacey and Smith found that some mothers had tried to slim their children by restricting food and Stein and Fairburn report mothers' accounts that, during binges, they tended to ignore or physically punish their children. Both studies revealed children with non-organic failure to thrive, whose mothers described difficulty keeping food available for their children's meal times because of their binge eating.

We have seen two children of bulimic mothers who had non-organic failure to thrive. In each case, once it was established that the child was underfed and this was reflected back to the parents, they were able to work together to ensure the child's nutrition. Interestingly, this acted as a trigger for each mother to start to take control over her own eating.

Somatising disorder

Zoccolillo and Cloninger (1985) found that children of parents with somatising disorder were more likely to suffer abuse or be received into care than children of parents with depression. They also had high rates of psychiatric disorders. People with somatising disorders often have antisocial symptoms and psychosomatic complaints that started during childhood and progressed to difficulties with relationships and impulse control. Thus, they experience parenting as problematic because of the stresses involved and the need, at times, to prioritise the child over themselves. Livingstone (1993) has shown that a child with behaviour problems is at heightened risk of physical abuse from a somatising parent.

Mogielnicki *et al.* (1977) suggest that, by presenting to emergency medical services with a psychosomatic complaint, parents are giving a clue that they are worried they might abuse their child and are seeking to prevent this.

DELIBERATE SELF-HARM

Some parents who deliberately harm themselves have a psychiatric disorder, in which case the implications for the child are more those associated with the underlying disorder, as discussed above. Otherwise, self-harm usually reflects more general stresses and relationship difficulties, which may affect the child's safety and well-being.

Suicidal behaviour may be a forewarning of child abuse, as described by Ounsted (1975), although it is more frequent that a suicide attempt follows an incident of child abuse. When a parent feels guilty about what has happened, they may attempt to avoid facing the consequences or to punish themselves. A small number of parents who attempt suicide also try to kill their child and Rodenburg (1971) found that the child had often been rejected previously. Parents who are preoccupied with suicidal ideation may conclude that, in order not to leave their child, it is necessary to kill them too.

Assessment needs to focus on the parent's ability to recognise the seriousness of the concerns and their motivation to resolve any underlying difficulties. One mother, who had killed her first baby during an episode of puerperal psychosis, cut her 3 year old's wrists and then her own after a period of relationship difficulties and heavy drinking. Neither died and, on release from custodial sentence, the mother requested to have her child again. She was returning to the same relationship stresses, denied that there could be any risk to the child and accepted little responsibility for what had happened. As a result, the child was placed with alternative long-term caretakers.

When a parent is communicating suicidal ideation, assessment should include exploration of their history of aggressive behaviour, any concerns they may have about harming the child and whether they are feeling guilty, as well as the quality of their relationship with the child (Hawton *et al.* 1985). It can also be helpful to ask the suicidal parent what they believe would happen to the child if they died.

OTHER FACTORS TO CONSIDER IN THE ASSESSMENT

A number of factors need to be considered in assessments of parents with psychiatric problems in addition to those specific to the particular condition.

If the parent's symptoms include aggression, then the child is more at risk of both emotional and physical harm (Rutter and Quinton 1984) and children who witness parental aggression show higher rates of psychiatric disturbance. There is a particular risk to the child's physical safety from aggressive manic parents because of their disinhibition.

The way that parents express their problems is important to the impact on the children. For example, Cox (1988) discusses that the effects are less when depressed parents manifest despair and misery than if they show irritability and hostility to the child. Some parents are able to modify their behaviours in the presence of the child, especially for short periods, and this information should be sought during assessment.

It must be remembered that the nature of particular symptoms may lead a parent to behave in a manner that would suggest ambivalence about their children. For instance, the negative thinking during depression can lead a parent to feel that they will never be able to manage their children and to request accommodation (Sheppard 1993). Decisions about care should be based on careful assessment of the parent's motivation and mental state, as well as their relationship with the child.

In considering the parent's psychiatric state, the focus can sometimes become too narrow and important areas of the assessment, such as a detailed account of the parent's own experiences of childhood and being parented, may be missed. Likewise, clues about the general coping ability of the parent, from information about housing, finances, hygiene, etc., can be equally important.

Assessment must include an opinion about the likely prognosis for the parent's disorder. Factors such as the chronicity and severity of the illness are relevant to the impact on the child. Parents who have discrete episodes of illness, with good functioning and relationships in between, pose fewer risks to the child than those who have chronic and persistent symptoms.

Assessment should include consideration of the effects of any separations necessitated by admission of the ill parent to hospital. Psychiatric admissions tend to occur as an emergency and so children experience sudden disruptions. Previous good experiences of separations help the child cope. Clearly, families without partners or relatives to help are more likely to suffer. If a parent does have a pattern of repeated hospitalisations, then it is important to consider whether the child's needs would best be met by alternative care just during future acute episodes, or alternatively, whether more permanent separation from the parent might offer greater stability and security for the child.

The availability of family support is an important factor, since a relative can sometimes be ascribed a role of monitoring the child's safety. Other trusting relationships are helpful in promoting the child's welfare, as is the availability of someone to take over when the parent is unwell or feels overwhelmed or frustrated.

The effects of medication upon a parent's ability to care for their child should be enquired about, especially if the parent is likely to remain on those drugs for a long time. For example, many parents on major tranquillizers find they cannot wake at night to feed a baby. Some find medication with sedative side-effects makes it difficult for them to attend to their children adequately and may stop the treatment.

Exploration of the parent's understanding of their problems yields important information about their likely commitment to change. For instance, parents who can prioritise the order in which to tackle problems are more likely to be able to improve their parenting skills. Similarly, it will be easier for professionals to work in partnership with them over plans to protect the child. Their level of insight into the illness is often linked to this. Those who insist that they have no problems tend not to acknowledge their child's plight and also fail to comply with treatment. Lack of insight may imply that the parent is in a more severe phase of their illness and requires review, perhaps even compulsory admission to hospital, by those responsible for their treatment.

The child's age is particularly significant. Children have different emotional and physical needs at different ages and so the impact of illness on parenting will vary with the various developmental stages. Generally, if a child's parenting has been good enough during infancy, or if the child was older at the onset of their parent's illness, then the psychological risks are less. Early infancy and adolescence will be periods of heightened vulnerability to adverse parenting (Beardslee *et al*. 1983). One to three year olds are at an especially sensitive period in the development of attachment, while adolescents may have problems separating from depressed parents and developing autonomy (Cummings and Davies 1994). The child's temperament also plays a part and Murray *et al*. (1993) have shown that a child with a difficult temperament is more affected by adversity.

THE ASSESSMENT PROCESS

Two distinct legal statutes, each with a different basic premise, may be invoked if concerns arise about the welfare of a child whose parent has a mental health problem. The Mental Health Act is concerned with psychiatric diagnosis and the adult's civil rights, whilst the Children Act considers the balance between the child's needs and the parent's responsibilities. There can be a choice of legal interventions when working with these families. The Mental Health Act is appropriate if compulsory admission and treatment of the parent will improve the situation for the child. If not, or if the social support is not adequate or concerns for the child are likely to continue, then using the Mental Health Act will not, in itself, protect the child.

For the principle of paramountcy of the child's interests to be followed, as directed by the Children Act, those involved in the decision-making process need to be free from professional dilemmas. It should be remembered that requesting an adult psychiatrist to give an opinion about whether the child should be removed from the parent may jeopardise their therapeutic relationship with the ill parent. This conflict of interests can lead the professional concerned into difficulty over what to say and could mean that a traumatised parent, already in a highly vulnerable state, trusts no one.

It is therefore helpful to clarify which professionals have a primary responsibility for the child(ren) and who is attending to the needs of the ill parent. But, in addition, the adult psychiatrist needs to combine treatment of the parent and advocacy of the parent's rights with recognition of the child welfare issues. Oates (1984) describes how adult psychiatrists tend to approach these situations in terms of the therapeutic usefulness *to the parent* of having a parenting role. We believe that clear enough distinctions between roles is both necessary and possible and, if combined with appreciation of the respective needs of the parent and the child, will allow complementary assessments to be made to the benefit of both. Network meetings can help address many of these issues and ensure that professionals are working in parallel.

The model we suggest is for adult psychiatrists to contribute by providing information about their assessment of the ill parent, with a focus on the diagnosis and prognosis. Informing other professionals of the terminology, treatment plans, expected time scale for recovery and some indication of the effects of the illness and medication on the parent's general functioning will help them formulate plans for the child. The child psychiatrist needs to assess the child's needs, the impact upon the child of the parent's problems, the parent–child relationship, parenting skills or capacity, family functioning, possible risks to the child and the capacity for change in the family relationships. The child psychiatrist can help interpret the mental health problems and explain their implications for the child. In order to make a valid recommendation about the child's future to a court, the child psychiatrist needs to be informed by the adult psychiatrist's assessment of the parent's diagnosis and prognosis.

CONCLUSIONS

In general, it is evident that children can live with a parent who has a psychiatric disorder without significant suffering. However, there are particular factors that lead one to worry, including hostile and aggressive behaviour (especially if there is a previous history of aggression), repeated deliberate self-harm, threatening delusions and hallucinations, a rapidly changing mental state, when a child is involved in the parent's symptoms (especially delusional thinking) and when the symptoms (such as irritability or withdrawal) or treatment interfere with parenting tasks (particularly ensuring the child's safety or providing for the child's basic needs). From the child's perspective, professional concerns should also be raised when the child is burdened by caring for the parent, or shows significant problems with attachment, psychological differentiation, identity formation, capacity for peer relationships, self-esteem, or ability to handle conflict.

REFERENCES

Anthony, E.J. (1986) 'Terrorizing attacks on children by psychotic parents', *Journal of the American Academy of Child Psychiatry*, **25**, 326–35.

Appleby, L. and Dickens, C. (1993) 'Mothering skills of women with mental illness', *British Medical Journal*, **306**, 348–9.

Barnett, B., Schaafsma, M.F., Guzman, A.-M. and Parker, G.B. (1991) 'Maternal anxiety: a 5 year review of an intervention study', *Journal of Child Psychology and Psychiatry*, **32**, 423–38.

Beardslee, W.R., Bemporad, J., Keller, M.B. and Klerman, G.L. (1983) 'Children of parents with major affective disorder: a review', *American Journal of Psychiatry*, **140**, 825–32.

Berg, I. and McGuire, R. (1974) 'Are mothers of school phobic adolescents overprotective?', *British Journal of Psychiatry*, **124**, 10–13.

Bluglass, R. (1978) 'Infanticide', *Bulletin of the Royal College of Psychiatrists*, **2**, 139–41.

Cox, A.D. (1988) 'Maternal depression and impact on children's development', *Archives of Disease in Childhood*, **63**, 90–5.

Cummings, E.M. and Davies, P.T. (1994) 'Maternal depression and child development', *Journal of Child Psychology and Psychiatry*, **35**, 73–112.

d'Orban, P.T. (1979) 'Women who kill their children', *British Journal of Psychiatry*, **134**, 560–71.

Downey, G. and Coyne, J.C. (1990) 'Children of depressed parents: an integrative review', *Psychological Bulletin*, **108**, 50–76.

Evans, S.L., Reinhart, J.B. and Succop, R.A. (1972) 'Failure to thrive', *Journal of the American Academy of Child Psychiatry*, **11**, 440–57.

Hawton, K., Roberts, J. and Goodwin, G. (1985) 'The risk of child abuse among mothers who attempt suicide', *British Journal of Psychiatry*, **146**, 486–9.

Kinnard, E.M. (1982) 'Child abuse and depression: cause or consequence', *Child Welfare*, **61**, 403–13.

Lacey, J.H. and Smith, G. (1987) 'Bulimia nervosa: the impact of pregnancy on mother and baby', *British Journal of Psychiatry*, **150**, 777–81.

Livingstone, R. (1993) 'Children of people with somatisation disorder', *Journal of the American Academy of Child and Adolescent Psychiatry*, **32**, 536–44.

Mogielnicki, R.P., Mogielnicki, N.P., Chandler, J.E. and Weissberg, M.P. (1977) 'Impending child abuse: psychosomatic symptoms in adults as a clue', *Journal of the American Medical Association*, **237**, 1109–11.

Murray, L., Kempton, C., Woolgar, M. and Hooper, R. (1993) 'Depressed mothers' speech to their infants and its relation to infant gender and cognitive development', *Journal of Child Psychology and Psychiatry*, **34**, 1083–102.

Oates, M. (1984) 'Assessing fitness to parent', in *Taking a Stand*, London: British Agencies for Adoption and Fostering.

Oates, M. (1988) 'The development of an integrated community-orientated service for severe postnatal mental illness', in R. Kumar and I.F. Brockington (eds) *Motherhood and Mental Illness: Vol. 2*, London: Wright.

Ounsted, C. (1975) 'Gaze aversion and child abuse', *World Medicine*, **10**, 27.

Phares, V.E. and Compas, B.E. (1992) 'The role of fathers in child and adolescent psychopathology', *Psychological Bulletin*, **111**, 387–412.

Puckering, C. (1989) 'Annotation: maternal depression', *Journal of Child Psychology and Psychiatry*, **30**, 807–17.

Resnick, P.J. (1969) 'Child murder by parents: a psychiatric review of filicide', *American Journal of Psychiatry*, **126**, 325–34.

Rodenburg, M. (1971) 'Child murder by depressed parents', *Canadian Psychiatric Association Journal*, **16**, 41–8.

Rutter, M. and Quinton, D. (1984) 'Parental psychiatric disorder: effects on children', *Psychological Medicine*, **14**, 853–80.

Sheppard, M. (1993) 'Maternal depression and child care: the significance for social work research', *Adoption and Fostering*, **17**, 10–15.

Stein, A. and Fairburn, C.G. (1989) 'Children of mothers with bulimia nervosa', *British Medical Journal*, **299**, 777–8.

Susman, E.J., Trickett, P.K., Ianotti, R.J., Hollenbeck, B.S. and Zahn-Waxler, C. (1985) 'Child-rearing patterns in depressed, abusive and normal mothers', *American Journal of Orthopsychiatry*, **55**, 237–51.

Wrate, R.M., Rooney, A.C., Thomas, P.F. and Cox, J.L. (1985) 'Postnatal depression and child development', *British Journal of Psychiatry*, **146**, 622–7.

Zoccolillo, M. and Cloninger, R. (1985) 'Parental breakdown associated with somatisation disorder (hysteria)', *British Journal of Psychiatry*, **147**, 443–6.

Chapter 12

Parents who misuse drugs and alcohol
Rosalyn Coleman and Diana Cassell

INTRODUCTION

We have shown in the previous chapter that the risk to children who live with a parent suffering from a psychiatric disorder is not significantly high. The picture appears to be different when parents regularly misuse drugs or alcohol, but care must be taken in interpreting the literature because of the limited and varied groups examined.

Substance misuse is not the same as recreational drug and alcohol use. Most people have tried alcohol. Ten per cent of young men drink to excess but few of them present for help with their drinking (Office of Population Censuses and Surveys 1992). Instead, they are likely to come into contact with professionals through casualty departments or the legal system after committing a crime. Of these young men, most become moderate in their drinking habits as they grow older. In 1981, a population survey showed that one in five men and one in ten women aged 20 use cannabis (Mott 1985). A study of crack users in a London borough (Mirza *et al*. 1991) showed that the populations presenting to police and drug agencies were very different, with almost no overlap. Thus, it is important to compare like with like and, unfortunately, some reports in the literature do not clarify the severity of the substance misuse studied.

In this chapter, we shall consider the relevance of drug and alcohol misuse in cases of parenting breakdown and review whether there is a link between substance misuse and child abuse. Although there is a larger number of reports whose findings imply a poor prognosis for children of substance misusers, we shall attempt to balance this with other evidence in the literature. Finally, we shall suggest how the risk to the children can be assessed.

DIRECT EFFECTS OF DRUGS AND ALCOHOL

Drugs affect mood, emotions, behaviour and social relationships and these, in turn, can impinge on parents' care of their children. Drugs may be used by parents for enjoyment, to block out unpleasant feelings, or, more rarely, to give them the courage to do things they otherwise might not, including acts of abuse. For ease of discussion, the drugs will be divided into groups which are not entirely equivalent.

Depressant drugs

Depressant drugs include alcohol, sedatives (such as barbiturates and benzo-diazepines), tranquillizers and solvents (such as glue). Their effects are to depress the functioning of the nervous system, which relieves tension and anxiety but, in addition, impairs mental and physical performance. As the higher functions of the brain are depressed, there is a tendency for social disinhibition, which can vary from an ability to become more outgoing with people to loss of self-control and violence. High intake leads to drowsiness, stupor or unconsciousness. With habitual usage, the body becomes tolerant to the sedatives, necessitating higher doses for the same effect and dependence is liable to develop if they are used on a regular basis. Withdrawal produces irritability, overarousal and difficulty sleeping and may induce more serious physical side-effects that require medical intervention.

As an example, when one parent 'binge drinks', family life can be characterised by alternate episodes of loving, caring behaviour to the child and fearsome rows between parents which occasionally erupt into violence.

Opiates

Heroin is the most common opiate of misuse but there are many others, such as methadone, DF118 and codeine linctus, which can be obtained on the black market or prescribed. The effects of opiates are to reduce emotional responsiveness, discomfort or anxiety, bringing feelings of warmth and contentment. Until high doses are reached, the person's mental faculties and physical abilities remain intact, although, at higher levels, there is some sedation, sleepiness and maybe unconsciousness. Again, regular use produces tolerance and physical dependence. The withdrawal reaction is unpleasant, but less severe than some of the depressant drugs and less life threatening.

A common clinical picture is the parent who is able to cope when 'using' regular doses, although sometimes is late getting up, and only becomes irritated with their child when withdrawing or using fluctuating amounts.

Stimulants

Stimulants include amphetamines, cocaine and ecstasy (which can also have similar effects to LSD). They increase the wakefulness of the person, so that fatigue and sleep are delayed. Performance is increased and mood elevated. Withdrawal primarily produces feelings of anxiety, but can induce severe depression. Repeated use may cause a paranoid reaction and, on occasion, a paranoid psychosis.

In one case, when a father visited his baby daughter, he jumped up and down in agitation, even when giving her toys and moving her from danger. He could not sit still and left in the middle of a conversation.

Hallucinogenic drugs

Drugs affecting perceptual functions include cannabis and LSD. Cannabis can be used to such excess that it causes severe problems, including psychosis. LSD produces a change in sensory phenomena: the person going through the 'trip' experiences distorted reality, particularly visual, and sometimes feels cut off from their experiences and surroundings. On occasion, the person can be out of contact with reality, not realising that their experiences are hallucinations. There is little withdrawal reaction, but users may suffer from flashbacks.

The effects of LSD on child care will most likely depend on whether the person takes it while caring for their child, as each 'trip' is unpredictable.

Perinatal problems

Substance misusers are at higher risk of problems during delivery and perinatal morbidity is increased. Opiate-dependent women have many more complications of pregnancy (Dattel 1990), including low birth weight, toxaemia, third trimester bleeding, malpresentation and foetal distress (Lawson and Wilson 1979). The neonates may show withdrawal signs of irritability, distress or fits (Strauss *et al.* 1976; Householder *et al.* 1982). There may be slow growth and occasionally microcephaly (Rosen and Johnson 1982; 1985). Cocaine has been associated with congenital abnormalities (Chasnoff *et al.* 1987; 1989). Alcohol can have a significant effect on infant development, including growth retardation and developmental delay. The foetal alcohol syndrome describes the severest end of the spectrum (Lemoine *et al.* 1968). Studies of a wider group of mothers with less severe alcohol problems, but who were nevertheless drinking excessively, indicated some developmental delay in the children, although unfortunately these studies were not well controlled (Zuckerman and Bresnahan 1991).

The parents are therefore faced with children who need extra care, may initially be in hospital, and therefore separated from them, for long periods and who show jittery responses when cuddled or played with. These features in themselves are known to predispose children to maltreatment (Herrenkohl and Herrenkohl 1979).

For example, a young couple, who were both heroin users, had a baby girl. The mother had been taking methadone but, prior to delivery, had become frightened at the prospect of being a parent and started also using heroin. The baby was born with withdrawal reactions and was jittery, restless and unable to sleep. For the first week, the parents visited daily, but, in the second week, the baby started fitting and became even harder to feed. She looked unwell and could not be picked up easily without fear of increased jitteriness. The father stopped attending the ward totally and the mother found the baby harder to handle and became increasingly anxious. Her visiting dropped off over the next month until she only came in briefly once a week. The case conference decided to place the child with a foster family, with a view to rehabilitation. However, despite attempts to help them, the couple failed to improve their relationship with the baby and she was eventually adopted.

INDIRECT EFFECTS OF DRUGS AND ALCOHOL MISUSE

Drug-related activity

Maintaining an addiction is expensive. At 1994 prices, a parent addicted to alcohol could spend from £40 a week on alcohol; it costs £35 a week to satisfy a modest methadone habit, bought on the black market; the equivalent dose of heroin would be £560 a week and a cocaine habit costs between £600 and £1,000 a week. Resourcing drug usage depends on income and whether the user has lost their job as a result of the dependency. People on a reasonable income can support alcohol or methadone habits by diverting resources away from the family budget. Only the very rich can continue to fund a heroin or cocaine addiction and most people need to find alternative sources of income, such as by theft, organised crime, prostitution, fraud or drug dealing. The effect on family life is considerable for people using illegal drugs which they cannot afford.

Families who misuse drugs and alcohol tend to become separated from normal support systems. They may be fearful of seeking help in case their children are taken into care. They sometimes cut themselves off from the extended family because they do not want to bring shame upon them or they may have stolen from them. Parents might show odd behaviour at the school, either through usage or withdrawal, which prevents the children being asked to others' homes, further decreasing their social network. Custodial sentences lead to additional disruption of family life, with children being accommodated out of the family.

Exposure to aggression and violence

The criminal behaviours that are sometimes used to resource an addiction can have a variety of effects on child care. In some families, crime or prostitution occurs in front of the children and possibly involves large numbers of people coming to the home, exposing children to violence or sexual activity. One 4 year old boy who was wandering through the house looking for his mother, a dependent heroin dealer, was severely assaulted by an addict looking for drugs.

Tracy and Williams (1991) cite studies which show that 70 per cent of substance abusing pregnant women had been beaten as adults: of these, 86 per cent were assaulted by their partner and the remainder were beaten by other family members or acquaintances. Reed (1985) describes the lives of chemically dependent women as violent, isolated and dysfunctional and that they do not sustain relationships with non-substance misusing men. Leonard and Jacob (1988) also conclude that alcoholism and acute alcohol consumption is associated with marital violence.

In one case of ours, a man who was a heavy drinker came home to find his wife was preparing to leave him. A confrontation developed in which the mother left but the father held their child hostage and then held the police, neighbours and his wife at bay with a knife. The child was asleep for part of this time and the father claimed that he had no intention of harming him. He considered the incident to be between himself and his wife and not to involve the child. His willingness to use aggression and his inability to see things from the child's point of view was clearly dangerous to the child's physical and emotional welfare.

Accidents and illnesses

Some children of substance misusers experience loss and separation from parents, as both illness and early death occur more frequently in these families. Alcohol misusers have twice the expected mortality rate and women of child bearing age who drink excessively have a mortality rate seventeen times that expected (Adelstein and White 1976). Fraser and Cavanagh (1991) attempted to follow up over a protracted time mothers who continued to use heroin after delivery, and found that 11 per cent had died.

HIV may be passed on to a child or spouse by an infected addict. Parents who are HIV positive have to cope with this stress as well as negotiating their own illness and making plans for their children's future.

There is also an association between substance misuse and parental mental illness, including affective disorder (Gibson and Becker 1973), alcohol hallucinosis (Benedetti 1952) and suicidal behaviour (Kessel and Grossman 1961), the implications of which are discussed in Chapter 11.

Accidents are more common in opiate users' households and children also have an increased risk of sustaining accidents if they have an alcoholic parent. In an unpublished retrospective audit, Williams (personal communication) found that approximately 7 per cent of children of opiate users had died from all causes.

We are not aware of any research that has examined the link between parental risk taking, self-neglect and negligence of the child's health and safety. In one case of ours, when parents who denied that they used drugs were visited, they were found to have left needles and syringes lying within easy reach of their children.

Effects on family life

Children of substance misusers may be put in reverse caring roles, in which they have to look after their parents instead of their own needs being met. For example, a 6 year old girl regularly brought her father to his psychiatric appointments because he could not always find his way and needed prompting about time. The little girl was anxious for her father's welfare, tearful and pale. He drank excessively and suffered from a liver disorder. On one occasion he had taken his daughter to the DHSS to claim for a new mattress, as his was covered in blood. He had not sought help for the bleeding and was continuing to drink, even though he had been told that, if he had another bleed, he had only a fifty-fifty chance of survival.

The effect on the quality of family life will depend on how often the drug is taken, in what quantities and in what context. Some addicted parents demonstrate concern for their children's welfare and are able to predict, and therefore avoid, adverse effects, but others fail to prioritise the children's needs in this way. A 35 year old mother of three young children had been using methadone for 5 years as treatment for heroin dependency. During the day, she only used methadone to 'keep her straight' (i.e. so that she would not have withdrawal effects), but on some evenings, or after a row with her husband, she used heroin, which made her drowsy. When this occurred, she would ask her husband to be available for the children. Thus, despite dependency, the possible consequences of her drug use were kept within limits, somewhat reducing the risk to her children.

This is in contrast to a 26 year old woman, who was trying to get her baby back from care and was glue sniffing throughout the day. She repeatedly failed to attend contact visits because she took drugs instead and was often unable to converse rationally. On the rare visits when she took no drugs at all, she was sociable and competent with the child. Decisions about the child's future had to be based on the likelihood that she would rearrange her habit and lifestyle sufficiently to be consistently and safely available for the baby. However, she said that she could not imagine a life without drugs, nor could she control them.

SUBSTANCE MISUSE AND PARENTING BREAKDOWN

Given the number of problems faced by substance misusing parents, it is not surprising that they also show a range of parenting difficulties. These include providing a daily structure, being consistent, managing their children's anger and coping with their children's transition into adolescence, especially if it involves experimentation with drugs (Greif and Drechsler 1993). One study (Johnson and Rosen 1990) found that the more intense the mother's drug abuse, the fewer her reports of 'easy baby' characteristics, suggesting that such mothers have different perceptions from other parents. Substance misusing parents have been reported to use more aversive behaviour (Bauman and Dougherty 1983), to feel inadequate (Deren 1986) and to have higher levels of stress than comparison mothers (Kelley 1992).

von Knorring (1991) reviewed a number of papers showing that children suffer from increased problems when their parents misuse alcohol, including hyperactivity, behavioural disorders, delinquency, depression and anxiety. Mathew *et al.* (1993) found an increase in agoraphobia, depression and antisocial behaviour among children of alcohol users. Much of the work on children of drug users is of short-term follow-up and it remains unclear whether the increase in referrals for specialist help with parenting problems and increased numbers taken into care (Larsson 1980; Fiks *et al.* 1985) is due to exposure to the drugs *in utero*, with neurological sequelae, or to the nature of the parenting.

The relationship between substance misuse and child maltreatment has been examined in a number of ways. In child care cases that came to court, Young (1964) found that 62 per cent of the parents were drinkers, while in the study of Fitch *et al.* (1975), 37 per cent were alcohol abusers. Chasnoff *et al.* (1987) found 34 per cent were drug users and 50 per cent substance misusers. Murphy *et al.* (1991) followed up 206 court cases and discovered that 43 per cent of the parents were substance misusers: children of these parents were more likely to be removed into care than the children of non-substance misusing parents (56 per cent compared with 35 per cent) and this was independent of economic status. A case-controlled study comparing parents who had abused their children with matched non-abusing parents (Famularo *et al.* 1986), found levels of current alcoholism of 42 per cent, compared with 12 per cent in the control group.

Not all studies, however, show the same trend and Simons *et al.* (1966) and Steele and Pollock (1974) report that only around 10 per cent of parents who come to the attention of services because of child abuse have drug or alcohol problems. This figure is not significantly different from the normal population, since Dawson (1992) identified 8 per cent of fathers, 2 per cent of mothers and 3 per cent of other adult family members in city areas as substance abusers. Variations in definition and reporting might explain the differences between these findings.

Schetky *et al.* (1979) examined parents whose children had been taken into care and found a significant history of alcoholism among them. Famularo *et al.* (1986) studied a group of severely maltreated children who had been removed from their parents' care and found that 50 per cent of their fathers and 30 per cent of their mothers had a history of alcoholism, compared with 6 per cent and 9 per cent respectively of a control group.

Julian and Mohr (1979) compared father–daughter incest cases with sexual abusers who were not the parent and showed that perpetrators were alcohol users in 32 per cent of the former and 14 per cent of the latter. Rada *et al.* (1978) compared adults who had committed incest with those who had been convicted of child molestation and found 50 per cent of both groups were alcoholic. In a sample of adults undertaking therapy for previous sexual abuse by their fathers, 35 per cent reported that the abuser had had a drinking problem (Herman and Hirschman 1981).

Other studies have attempted to see if there is any relationship between the type of substance misused and the type of abuse. In a series of cases where the children were taken into care (Famularo *et al.* 1992), alcohol was significantly related to physical abuse and cocaine to sexual abuse. There were fewer heroin users and neither physical nor sexual abuse was significantly related to opiate use.

Studies have also examined samples of known substance misusers. Sowder and Burt (1980) compared experiences of parenting as reported by children living with addicted and non-addicted parents. Abuse was reported four times more frequently in addicted families than in the controls. An interview study of parents who abused either alcohol or opiate drugs (Black and Mayer 1980) suggested that all their children had suffered some degree of neglect and 30 per cent had shown serious neglect. In addition, 27 per cent of the alcohol misusers had abused their children, as had 19 per cent of the opiate users. There was no control group for this study and there is some question why such a high degree of neglect was found.

Several studies have considered whether substance misuse could act as a predictor for child abuse but, unfortunately, only one considered substance abuse on its own. Murphy *et al.* (1991) found that substance misuse specifically indicated a worse outcome. Leventhal *et al.* (1989) showed that maternal drug use, previous sibling abuse and father being in gaol all predicted high incidence of abuse and Julian and Mohr (1979) reported that promiscuity and alcohol use in either parent predicted a poor outcome.

Overall, the community studies give a gloomy picture and suggest a poor outlook for many children of substance misusing parents. However, not all children in the investigations were maltreated and clinical experience indicates that some alcohol or drug misusing parents can provide satisfactory child care and a few children manage to flourish, despite their parents' substance misuse (Clair and Genest 1987; el Guebaly and Offord 1979; 1980). Some of the children studied by Seilhammer *et al.* (1992) commented that their father was more amiable when drinking and the authors speculate that drinking may temporarily reduce stress in certain families.

THE ASSESSMENT AND OPINION

How can we use this information to protect children? There is clearly an increased risk to children whose parents misuse drugs and alcohol. However, we are living in a society in which most people take alcohol and a significant proportion use illegal drugs. Furthermore, we know from clinical experience that such parents can provide good child care. Therefore, substance misuse on its own should not be a reason for removing a child from its family, even though it may be a cause for concern. It is important to note that those studies which show increased incidence of harm to the children are of parents who were addicted to drugs or alcohol, used it to excess and in an out of control manner and/or were resistant to treatment.

In assessing the child's needs, it will be necessary to look at a range of parenting behaviours that may be affected by substance misuse, including the day-to-day child care, the nature and extent of the substance misuse and any accompanying interpersonal problems and social difficulties. Swadi (1994) describes an approach to assessment which considers the substance misusing behaviour within the context of overall parenting. He suggests basing the assessment of drug misuse and its possible implications for the child on a series of questions. These include:

- How is money obtained to sustain the misuse and does the parent ensure that bills are paid?
- Is the home adequately clean and is there sufficient food?
- Do other substance misusers live in the same household?
- How dependent is the parent on other drug users for their social inter-action?
- Are the premises used for selling drugs or for prostitution?
- How dependent is the provision of basic necessities on whether or not the parent is misusing psychoactive substances?
- What is the pattern, frequency, type, quantity and method of substance use?
- Are the children protected from exposure to needles and other potential sources of HIV infection?
- Is the misuse stable, or is it chaotic, with swings between states of severe intoxication and periods of withdrawal?
- What is the pattern of child care when the parent is under the influence of psychoactive substances?
- What attempts have been made towards treatment and with what results?
- What is the effect on child care of any criminal activity or imprisonment, or of absences while procuring substances?
- Is the substance misuse accompanied by a psychiatric disorder and what effect does either have on the parent's cognitive state and judgements?
- Are the children involved in substance misuse?

These questions address issues specific to the substance misuse. Swadi also poses a series of other questions (similar to those discussed elsewhere in this book) which focus on the general parenting relationship and emphasises that the quality of the parent–child relationship should be the principal guide to the child's welfare. Our review indicates that if significant problems with parenting are identified, then children of substance misusing parents are at greater risk of serious harm than others.

Interim treatment measures may be suggested by the court and they will need to be guided by the likelihood of a positive response. Reports of the efficacy of methadone treatment programmes on parenting are mixed (Wilson 1989). A better outcome is reported from programmes which include a specific focus on parenting behaviours (Chang et al. 1992). Fiks et al. (1985) found improved benefit when day care was also obtained for the children. However, substance misusing parents were less cooperative with attempts at rehabilitation of their abused children than non-misusing parents (Famularo et al. 1989).

The overriding goal of parenting assessment is to establish whether the child is safe. If the court considers that the best interests of the child are served by treatment of their parents, the wording of the court decisions is important. According to Larsson (1980), 'If drugs become the focus of court orders the parents will conceal relapse to retain custody, and the beneficial effects of treatment for both their parenting and the drug abuse become seriously reduced.' A two-step procedure can be more useful, in which social services address the parenting issues, while the substance misuse services focus on the addiction, if necessary under a treatment order. The parent's motivation may be enhanced by the possibility of losing their child and the substance misuse service can then link the effects of their substance misuse with the changes needed for better parenting as laid down by the child protection services.

REFERENCES

Adelstein, A. and White, G. (1976) 'Alcoholism and mortality', *Population Trends*, **6**, 7–13.

Bauman, P.S. and Dougherty, F.E. (1983) 'Drug-addicted mothers' parenting and their children's development', *International Journal of the Addictions*, **18**, 291–302.

Benedetti, G. (1952) *Die Alkohol Halluzinaren*, Stuttgart: Thieme.

Black, R. and Mayer, J. (1980) 'Parents with special problems: alcoholism and opiate addiction', *Child Abuse and Neglect*, **4**, 45–54.

Chang, G., Carroll, K.M., Behr, H.M. and Kosten, T.R. (1992) 'Improving treatment outcome in pregnant opiate dependent women', *Journal of Substance Abuse Treatment*, **9**, 327–30.

Chasnoff, I.J., Burns, K.A. and Burns, W.J. (1987) 'Cocaine use in pregnancy: perinatal morbidity and mortality', *Neurotoxicology and Teratology*, **9**, 291–3.

Chasnoff, I.J., Lewis, D.E., Griffith, D.R. and Willey, S. (1989) 'Cocaine and pregnancy: clinical and toxicological implications for the neonate', *Clinical Chemistry*, **35**, 1276–8.

Clair, D. and Genest, M. (1987) 'Variables associated with the adjustment of offspring of alcoholic fathers', *Journal of Studies on Alcohol*, **48**, 345–55.

Dattel, B.J. (1990) 'Substance abuse in pregnancy', *Seminars in Perinatology*, **14**, 179–87.

Dawson, D.A. (1992) 'The effect of parental alcohol dependence on perceived children's behavior', *Journal of Substance Abuse*, **4**, 329–40.

Deren, S. (1986) 'Children of substance abusers: a review of the literature', *Journal of Substance Abuse Treatment*, **3**, 77–94.

el Guebaly, N. and Offord, D.R. (1979) 'On being the offspring of an alcoholic: an update', *Alcoholism: Clinical and Experimental Research*, **3**, 148–57.

el Guebaly, N. and Offord, D.R. (1980) 'The competent offspring of psychiatrically ill parents. Part 1: a literature review', *Canadian Journal of Psychiatry*, **25**, 457–63.

Famularo, R., Stone, K., Barnum, R. and Wharton, R. (1986) 'Alcoholism and severe child maltreatment', *American Journal of Orthopsychiatry*, **56**, 481–5.

Famularo, R., Kinscherff, R., Bunshaft, D., Spivak, G. and Fenton, T. (1989) 'Parental compliance to court-ordered treatment interventions in cases of child maltreatment', *Child Abuse and Neglect*, **13**, 507–14.

Famularo, R., Kinscherff, R. and Fenton, T. (1992) 'Parental substance abuse and the nature of child maltreatment', *Child Abuse and Neglect*, **16**, 475–83.

Fiks, K.B., Johnson, H.L. and Rosen, T.S. (1985) 'Methadone-maintained mothers: 3-year follow-up of parental functioning', *International Journal of the Addictions*, **20**, 651–60.

Fitch, M.J., Cadol, R.V., Goldson, E.J., Jackson, E.K. and Swarth, D.P. (1975) 'Prospective study in child abuse', paper presented at the Convention of America Public Health Association, Chicago.

Fraser, A.C. and Cavanagh, S. (1991) 'Pregnancy and drug addiction: long-term consequences', *Journal of the Royal Society of Medicine*, **84**, 530–2.

Gibson, S. and Becker, J. (1973) 'Changes in alcoholics self reported depression', *Quarterly Journal of Studies on Alcohol*, **34**, 829–36.

Greif, G.L. and Drechsler, M. (1993) 'Common issues for parents in a methadone maintenance group', *Journal of Substance Abuse Treatment*, **10**, 339–43.

Herman, J. and Hirschman, L. (1981) 'Families at risk for father–daughter incest', *American Journal of Psychiatry*, **138**, 967–70.

Herrenkohl, E.C. and Herrenkohl, R.C. (1979) 'A comparison of abused children with their nonabused siblings', *Journal of the American Academy of Child Psychiatry*, **18**, 260–9.

Householder, J., Hatcher, R., Burns, W. and Chasnoff, J. (1982) 'Infants born to narcotic-addicted mothers', *Psychological Bulletin*, **92**, 453–68.

Johnson, H.L. and Rosen, T.S. (1990) 'Mother-infant interaction in a multirisk population', *American Journal of Orthopsychiatry*, **60**, 281–8.

Julian, V. and Mohr, C. (1979) 'Father–daughter incest: profile of the offender', *Victimology*, **4**, 348–60.

Kelley, S.J. (1992) 'Parenting stress and child maltreatment in drug exposed children', *Child Abuse and Neglect*, **16**, 317–28.

Kessel, N. and Grossman, G. (1961) 'Suicide in alcoholics', *British Medical Journal*, **ii**, 1671–2.

Larsson, G. (1980) 'Amphetamine addiction and pregnancy. iv. Analysis of basic information concerning measures taken by social welfare agencies', *Child Abuse and Neglect*, **4**, 89–99.

Lawson, M.S. and Wilson, G.S. (1979) 'Addiction and pregnancy: two lives in crisis', *Social Work in Health Care*, **4**, 445–57.

Lemoine, P., Harousseau, H., Borleyru, J.-P. and Menuet, J.-C. (1968) 'Les enfants des parents alcooliques: anomalies observées à propos de 127 cas', *Ouest Médical*, **25**, 477–82.

Leonard, K.E. and Jacob, T. (1988) 'Alcoholism and family violence', in V.R. van Hasselt, R.C. Morrison and A.S. Bellack (eds) *Handbook of Family Violence*, New York: Plenum Press.

Leventhal, J.M., Garber, R.B. and Brady, C.A. (1989) 'Identification during the post partum period of infants who are at high-risk of child maltreatment', *Journal of Pediatrics*, **114**, 481–7.

Mathew, R.J., Wilson, W.H., Blazer, D.G. and George, L.K. (1993) 'Psychiatric disorders in adult children of alcoholics: data from the epidemiologic catchment area project', *American Journal of Psychiatry*, **150**, 793–800.

Mirza, H.S., Pearson, G. and Phillips, S. (1991) *Drugs, People and Services in Lewisham: Final Report of the Drug Information Project*, London: Goldsmith's College.

Mott, J. (1985) 'Self-reported cannabis use in Great Britain in 1981', *British Journal of Addiction*, **80**, 37–43.

Murphy, J.M., Jellinek, M., Quinn, D., Smith, G., Poitrast, F.G. and Gashko, M. (1991) 'Substance abuse and serious child mistreatment: prevalence, risk, and outcome in a court sample', *Child Abuse and Neglect*, **15**, 197–211.

Office of Population Censuses and Surveys (1992) *General Household Survey: 1990*, London: HMSO.

Rada, R.T., Kellner, R., Laws, D.R. and Winslow, W.W. (1978) 'Drinking, alcoholism and the mentally disordered sex offender', *Bulletin of the American Academy of Psychiatry and the Law*, **6**, 296–300.

Reed, B.G. (1985) 'Drug misuse and dependency in women: the meaning and implication of being considered a special population or minority group', *International Journal of the Addictions*, **20**, 13–62.

Rosen, T.S. and Johnson, H.L. (1982) 'Children of methadone-maintained mothers: follow-up to 18 months of age', *Journal of Pediatrics*, **101**, 192–6.

Rosen, T.S. and Johnson, H.L. (1985) 'Long-term effects of prenatal methadone maintenance', *National Institute of Drug Abuse Research Monograph*, **59**, 73–83.

Schetky, D.H., Angell, R., Morrison, C.V. and Sack, W.H. (1979) 'Parents who fail: a study of 51 cases of termination of parental rights', *Journal of the American Academy of Child Psychiatry*, **18**, 366–83.

Seilhammer, R.A., Jacob, T. and Dunn, N.J. (1992) 'The impact of alcohol consumption on parent–child relationships in families of alcoholics', *Journal of Studies on Alcohol*, **54**, 189–98.

Simons, B., Downs, E.F., Hurster, M.M. and Archer, M. (1966) 'Child abuse: epidemiologic study of medically reported cases', *New York State Journal of Medicine*, **66**, 2783–8.

Sowder, B. and Burt, M.R. (1980) 'Children of addicts and non addicts: a comparative investigation of five urban sites', in *Heroin Addicted Parents and their Children*, Rockville, MD: National Institute of Drug Abuse.

Steele, B.F. and Pollock, C.P. (1974) 'A psychiatric study of parents who abuse infants and small children', in R.E. Helfer, and C.H. Kempe (eds) *The Battered Child*, 2nd edn, Chicago: University of Chicago Press.

Strauss, M.E., Starr, R.H., Ostrea, E.M., Chavez, C.J. and Stryker, J.C. (1976) 'Behavioral concomitants of prenatal addiction to narcotics', *Journal of Pediatrics*, **89**, 842–6.

Swadi, H. (1994) 'Parenting capacity and substance misuse: an assessment scheme', *ACPP Review and Newsletter*, **16**, 237–44.

Tracy, C.E. and Williams, H.C. (1991) 'Social consequences of substance abuse among pregnant and parenting women', *Pediatric Annals*, **20**, 548–53.

von Knorring, A.-L. (1991) Annotation: 'Children of alcoholics', *Journal of Child Psychology and Psychiatry*, **32**, 411–21.

Wilson, G.S. (1989) 'Clinical studies of infants and children exposed prenatally to heroin', *Annals of the New York Academy of Sciences*, **562**, 183–94.

Young, L. (1964) *Wednesday's Children: A Study of Child Neglect and Abuse*, New York: McGraw-Hill.

Zuckerman, B. and Bresnahan, K. (1991) 'Developmental and behavioral consequences of prenatal drug and alcohol exposure', *Pediatric Clinics of North America*, **38**, 1387–406.

Chapter 13

Parents with learning disability
Ann Gath

INTRODUCTION

Early research on the children of parents labelled as mentally subnormal was universely pessimistic. It relied on samples of women who had lived in institutions all their lives often until the birth of the child. Findings from the various studies agreed that the children themselves were unlikely to be as retarded as their mothers but there was a high risk of family breakdown, including removal of children on grounds of neglect and cruelty. The sampling was strongly biased towards those women who continued to have problems themselves, as those who had escaped the net and become assimilated into the general community also escaped the scrutiny of the follow-up. Later studies concentrated on those families who had been before the courts, but it has been shown (Tymchuk and Andron 1990) that the courts deal very differently with parents who have learning disability from the general population. This finding mirrors the situation in the criminal court where people with a learning disability are more likely to confess to crimes, even if they have not committed them, because of their lower tolerance of prolonged interview sessions and the desire to please those in authority even if it is against their own interests (Gunn 1990). It can also be shown that people with learning disability are often disproportionately punished for relatively minor offences.

All studies have shown that parenting is a problem of those with mild or borderline learning disability. Rarely do women of moderate or more severe degree of disability become pregnant. In Down's syndrome, the range of intellectual ability is wide. The numbers of cases reported where a Down's syndrome woman has given birth are small (Rogers and Coleman 1992). In the majority of the cases where the paternity of the child was established it was found that the father was a close relative, the woman's own father, brother or maternal uncle. Sexual abuse is common in women with moderate or even more severe handicap, in both institutions and also at the hands of relatives or carers in the community (Turk and Brown 1993). Pregnancy is not a common result of such abuse.

There is no evidence to support the notion that mild learning disability is itself an absolute bar to the Winnicottian standard of 'good-enough parenting' (Gath 1988). Clearly, a person with such severe learning disability that they are unable to cater for their own basic care needs will not be able to care for another, especially one that is very young and totally dependent. Similarly, classic autism in which someone has no appreciation of interpersonal relationships would be incompatible with parenting, but pregnancy is extremely rare in such cases.

THE EFFECT OF DEPRIVATION AND INSTITUTIONAL LIVING

The studies reported by Gillberg and Geiger-Karlsson (1983) did appear to indicate that the women coming out of institutions to try to rear a child without having any experience of family life themselves did not do well. Such institutions offered little in the way of training and very little after care. Those cases are now rare in this country, but in parts of Eastern Europe, many women of mild retardation are in institutions, get no sex education and not surprisingly form attachments to others of comparable ability similarly incarcerated. When children are born, there is no attempt to assist the mothers but the children are taken to a separate institution to begin the cycle of severe deprivation all over again (Gath 1993).

It is some years since children have been admitted to long-stay hospitals. Thus the young women who are the parents of today and on whom the courts have requested an assessment are unlikely to have had an institutional background. Those who have been sent to boarding schools by local educational authorities for reason of their learning disability primarily, and behaviour problems in addition, are highly likely to remain in care of some sort in early adult life, being given little opportunity to form relationships and are also often put routinely on oral contraception from soon after the menarche.

Much more common is the girl of borderline ability who has been in care since her early teens and who has had poor relationships with her family of origin. For these girls, their borderline level of intellectual functioning is only one of many disadvantages and deprivations that they have suffered. Their own experience of mothering behaviour is a harsh one, often with early abuse and later rejection. As so often foster parents find out, the process of learning new parental models is a long process that can be painful for both parties. For many deprived girls, not only those with learning disability, the second chance to experience good parenting is never given. The ill-effects of poor childhood experiences in those of normal intelligence were ameliorated by later good experiences, particularly a stable spouse and good living conditions (Quinton et al. 1984), but these powerful protective factors are not commonly encountered during the lives of women with learning disability.

ASSESSMENT OF COGNITIVE ABILITY

As in all medical interventions, it is essential to see that the process of assessment does no harm. Denigrating procedures, robbing parents of their dignity and their small stock of confidence, are not in the best interest of the children or of justice. The majority of parents who are aware that their schooling put them outside the mainstream or that their scholastic achievements are under scrutiny are very fearful of losing their children. Giving people psychometric tests under such circumstances leads to gross underestimation of abilities and is clinically unacceptable practice.

Measures used include standardised tests for adults of which the Wechsler Test (WAIS) is still the most commonly used. Often reference is made to other tests made earlier in childhood. The Stanford Binet is slanted towards verbal ability and the Merril–Palmer is a somewhat more useful test of more practical reasoning for use with children. Verbal and performance scores are often disparate, sometimes widely so.

Although by definition, mild learning disability refers to those scores which fall two standard deviations below the mean, that is intelligence quotient scores of 70 or less, it is known that after leaving school, the vast majority of people so labelled during their years of education do not call upon special services and cope without drawing attention to themselves in the general population. Indeed it is only 10 per cent of those in the mild range who do come to the attention of services designed for people with a learning disability.

Intelligence testing alone is no longer acceptable as a measure or as the basis of ascertainment of learning disability. What also requires to be demonstrated is that the person has significant deficits in the region of adaptive behaviour. The scales that measure adaptive behaviour cover such areas as social competence, self-help skills, responsibility, physical handicap and verbal and numerate skills. The tests commonly used are the American Adaptive Behaviour Scales (Nihira *et al.* 1974) or the Vineland Social Behaviour Scales (Doll 1953).

ASSESSMENT OF LANGUAGE AND COMMUNICATION SKILLS

A common mistake is to estimate the degree of verbal comprehension wrongly. Someone may talk fluently, but many of the phrases, although apparently sophisticated, can have been learnt as a whole and their meaning never really understood. The phenomenon of such 'delayed echolalia' is deceptive, leading to the assumption that such a person is understanding what is said. Comprehension may be very concrete. Euphemisms, metaphors or verbal jokes are misunderstood and interpreted as said. An example is the expression 'you're pulling my leg' which got the bewildered denial 'I haven't touched you'. Instructions are interpreted to the letter. Something has been said, such as a task should be done at a particular time, and no allowance is given to factors that might make altering that rule on occasions advisable. In many cases, assessment by a speech and language therapist who specialises in learning disability is invaluable.

ASSOCIATED DISORDERS

Epilepsy is more common in people with learning disability than in the general public. Assessors should ask whether it is well controlled and, if not, is the parent getting adequate, regular monitoring, including that of the blood levels of anticonvulsant drugs? Is there warning of an attack and does the sufferer spend much time in sole charge of young children?

Other chronic problems may include cerebral palsy and sensory impairment. For each, the question to ask is: 'Does this person get the help they need to minimise the handicap they may have from their disability?'

PSYCHIATRIC ASSESSMENT

Dual diagnosis, by which is meant the presence of a psychiatric diagnosis complicating learning disability, is not uncommon, although still unrecognised or denied by some professionals. Depression is particularly common and fits well into the ideas concerning the social origins of depression (Brown and Harris 1978) as this is a group who are highly likely to find themselves trapped in a situation from which they can see no escape. An unrecognised learning disability may be misdiagnosed as a personality disorder, but that term should be reserved for those who have clearly a pattern of aggressive or maladaptive behaviour leading to repeated problems with relationships, society at large and the police, as well as many encounters with a psychiatric service. Such a personal track record is unlikely to be compatible with adequate parenting, but demonstrates the point that it is social functioning rather than performance on standardised tests that makes people in need of specialised services or bars them from enjoying the rights most take for granted.

THE SOCIAL ENVIRONMENT

People with learning disability are very unlikely to have jobs in the present state of the economy, and certainly not one that is well paid. They therefore live very often in conditions of considerable deprivation (Booth and Booth 1993). This was movingly and unforgettably demonstrated by the members of the Elfrida Rathbone Group (Aram et al. 1993), who showed that women known to have problems in cognitive ability were expected to succeed in bringing up children in conditions that many who were supposed to help or to judge them would have found insupportable. A similar conclusion was reached by Quinton and Rutter (1984) in their study of parents with children in care, when they said, 'parenting cannot be seen as an attribute of individuals irrespective of their current circumstances'.

THE PART PLAYED BY THE CHILDREN

The number, ages and spacing of children plays a major role in determining whether a woman or a couple with limited intellectual ability will cope. The case studies in the literature cite many cases where parenting was adequate with one child and just about good enough with two but had fallen apart completely with the arrival of a third. A young relatively still baby may be much easier, particularly in bed and breakfast accommodation, than an active toddler. Illness, temperamental variants and sleep problems will stretch parenting capacity and require help that is both effective and realistic in its expectations of what the parents can do.

There is evidence that parents identified as having learning disability and seen as having problems in parenting are prejudged before any fault is established (Tymchuk 1992). As to whether they reach the theoretical standards of psychological maturity and can plan ahead to anticipate the needs of the children, again they should be judged in relation to others within comparable social groups.

OBSERVATION WITH THE CHILDREN

To be knowingly observed puts anyone under considerable strain and can easily inhibit all natural behaviour. Preferably, reports of natural observation by regular visitors should be used in preference to putting parents in a strange room, with video cameras or one-way screens and issuing orders 'to play with the child'. It is in this sort of situation particularly that the assessment of parenting should be allowed to do no harm. More valid information is gleaned from the natural approaches of a child to a parent and the behaviour of parents as relaxed as possible in their own home.

ASSESSMENT OF THE CHILDREN

Background information from health visitors and later from peripatetic visitors, e.g. speech therapists, Portage workers, followed by reports from the staff of play groups and schools must be collected. As always in cases to be considered under Children Act legislation, the pertinent concept is that of 'significant harm' and the notion of risk must be taken into account and balanced up. Developmental histories taken from anxious parents may not be very full or accurate and must be weighed up against contemporaneous documentation from the health visitor. In families who have frequent moves, such information may be lacking. Families should be asked to compare one child's progress with another, a sibling or 'your sister's child'. Family history is important. Speech delay can be inherited and other members of a family, later coping quite well, may have a similar history. Delay in walking also goes in some families.

Speech and language development is particularly susceptible to delay in children of mothers with learning disability (McGaw and Sturmey 1993), but is particularly likely to occur in those families where the children are living in isolated surroundings with a mother who is also depressed.

However, the evidence is overwelming that there is regression to the mean and that the children of the intellectually weak are likely to be brighter than their parents and their children to be brighter again. The experience of having a child brighter than the parent is not confined, however, to those with learning disability and certainly makes life a series of challenges. There is little evidence that this is a major problem severely impeding children's development, provided that there is access to good education and adequate recreational facilities. Indeed the problem appears to be much more one of teachers who fail to recognise the differing abilities in one family (Zigler *et al.* 1992).

The most reliable guide to future behaviour is past behaviour, the track record, of parenting. Details of specific untoward incidents, such as preventable accidents, delays in getting help or seeking advice, failure to put advice into practice, neglect and lack of minimal supervision for active small children, are useful in assessing the risk to subsequent children. Most important is clear evidence of non-accidental injury while in that parent's care, such as near drowning due to leaving a 1 year old child unsupervised in the bath as well as injury due to deliberate attack.

RELATIONSHIPS WITH SIGNIFICANT OTHERS

Husband or partner

Marriages between more able men and women with learning disability are more common than the converse (Koller *et al.* 1988). The relationship is unbalanced but may be stable if both parties are content with the role to which they are assigned and there is no abuse of the power that the more able partner holds. The husband acts as manager, making all important decisions, dealing with all financial matters and often with the encounters with outsiders such as teachers. However, such power over another is often abused, outsiders are discouraged, including the wife's relatives, and there is no encouragement for the women to acquire skills or self-confidence. Certainly, such arrangements are by no means confined to families where one parent has learning disability, but in those cases, there is a very high risk of breakdown in parenting when the more able partner dies or chooses to leave home.

The husband or partner's personal record is of great relevance. Psychopathy in the husband, particularly if involving violence, is particularly dangerous to children when the mother is excessively submissive or inarticulate, features that not uncommonly coexist with learning disability.

Where both have problems of learning and/or personality difficulties, the outlook for the children is poor. The man, who regardless of measured intelligence, feels the world has treated him badly and cheated him out of his share of good things, is more likely to abuse his wife and to resent, and indeed sabotage, any help offered. Immaturity, often manifested as competing for the wife's attention with the children, greatly adds to the burden of a woman who finds parenting a struggle. Families where both parents have a learning disability may have multiple difficulties but are more likely to have a strong alliance against what may be perceived as a hostile world.

The assessment of the relationship starts with the reception given to the assessor by both partners. Women in this situation are often and understandably nervous as they know they stand at high risk of losing their children but have little understanding of why or what they can do about it. Their anxiety is overt, but that of the partner can be experienced as aggression to visitors, social workers, therapists or alleged experts. Fear of the spouse may be apparent, even when he is not present. Together, their relationship can be assessed when discussing informally their children and their past or present difficulties. Expressions of warmth and concern are as important to record as critical comments. Silences or apathy are significant as well as overt hostility. Most parents have differing styles in dealing with their children but countermanding, by which is meant giving a child the opposite instruction to the other parent, and, even more damaging, belittling or mocking the other parent are by no means confined to families where one parent has a learning disability but is related to an imbalance, and misuse, of power within the family.

The maternal grandmother

The quality of the relationship the mother has with her own mother clearly indicates the quality of her own childhood experience and is closely related to her ability to cope as a mother herself. Clear intergenerational links in psychiatric disorder, especially depression and anxiety, and in parenting behaviour have been noted in mothers and daughters (Quinton and Rutter 1984; Andrews *et al.* 1990). Positive relationships can do much to provide the emotional support lacking in a poor marital relationship or where the father is absent. Major difficulties between the two during adolescence related to the autonomy granted to the girl with learning disability can continue over to adult life. The maternal grandmother in such cases remains a constant critic, undermining always the self-esteem and hence the functioning of her daughter. In some cases, a powerful hint of rivalry emerges with the grandmother actually competing with her own daughter for the attention or even the custody of her grandchildren.

In assessment, it is helpful to be able to see the maternal grandmother alone as well as with her daughter, whose parenting behaviour is being assessed. Whether the learning disability of the parent under consideration is due to sociocultural factors rather than to early insult or a medical diagnosis is relevant, as in the former case, the grandmother may not be able to provide much support because of her own limitations or because of the demands of other members of the family. The parenting 'track record' of the grandmother herself can be seen from her relationships with her other children, their achievements and their parenting capacity.

Occasionally, there is another older woman acting as mentor. An elder sister in this role may be further proof of a supporting family of origin and good childhood experiences if the maternal grandmother herself is unable to take on the role. However, the conspicuous presence of a mother-in-law or non-relative may indicate the isolation of the mother from her own relatives. The crucial question remains: 'Does this person enhance or inhibit the parenting behaviour of the subject of the investigation?' (Tucker and Johnson 1989).

AFTER ASSESSMENT

The process of assessment leads into the next stage of providing appropriate help to assist the parents in their task or to help through the process of relinquishing care. The latter need not be an entirely negative process. To have had a fair hearing and to have seen justice done has been felt to be enough by more than one parent, saying, 'she'll know I fought for her'. It does no good for any child to have a parent destroyed in the process and the tragic result of perceived injustice may be the defiant conception of yet another child who will then be very difficult to safeguard.

FOLLOW-UP STUDIES OF INTERVENTION WITH PARENTS WITH LEARNING DISABILITY

The most extensive follow-up studies involving unbiased samples are those that were undertaken under the umbrella of Head Start, the group of intervention programmes designed in the 1960s to prevent mental retardation by targeting those children considered to be at risk. Early stages of the follow-up were encouraging but there was some disappointment that early gains in IQ were not sustained through the school years after cessation of intervention. Thirty years after the launching of Head Start some interesting and important findings have come out. These show clearly that interventions not involving parents but offering instead 'enriched experience' outside the family, usually in a nursery school, did have only temporary gains in performance and limited generalisation. By contrast, interventions aimed at the parents did have longer lasting effects which were likely to extend beyond the period of intervention and to generalise to another child born subsequently into the same family. The mode of approach to the parents was also important as those approaches which were successful had, as the main thrust of the intervention, the increasing of maternal skills, but above all maternal competence and confidence in her own self-worth (Seitz 1990; Zigler *et al.* 1992).

Follow-up studies are not numerous. Positive interventions are often dismissed as too difficult, too time consuming and too expensive. Reception into care appears easier and is regarded as less painful all round. The intervention programmes have had varied success. There is little relationship between IQ and success in child rearing (Whitman and Accardo 1989). Certainly the involvement of multiple agencies with many visitors to the home is highly destructive. Interventions that are too narrowly based, such as those modelled on behavioural methods, have little success. The complex problems of some families who never manage to introduce order into day-to-day living appear almost intractable. The developmental quotient of the children can be related to maternal behaviour in a way that appears contrary to expectation, being higher in the children of the more punitive and more restrictive mothers (Feldman *et al.* 1985).

Sheltered housing and other forms of shared care are used increasingly for assessment rather than for treatment or rehabilitation of families. When such an arrangement is allowed to continue for the early, most vulnerable years, the few cases appear to have a greater chance of success as shown in an intact family with children able to cope in school.

There are major ethical and methodological problems in designing a study to investigate the efficiency of intervention in families where a parent has a significant learning disability. However, such work is needed to provide the courts and social services with guidance for a group now denied less justice and less opportunity of help than many who have already failed as parents.

REFERENCES

Andrews, B., Brown, G.W. and Creasey, L. (1990) 'Intergenerational links between psychiatric disorder in mothers and daughters: the role of parenting experiences', *Journal of Child Psychology and Psychiatry*, **31**, 1115–29.

Aram, K. and members of the Elfrida Rathbone Women as Parents Group (1993) 'Parents with learning disabilities', in A. Craft (ed.) *Parents with Learning Disabilities*, Kidderminster: British Institute for Learning Disability.

Booth, T. and Booth, W. (1993) 'The experience of parenthood – a research approach', in A. Craft (ed.) *Parents with Learning Disabilities*, Kidderminster: British Institute for Learning Disability.

Brown, G.W. and Harris, T. (1978) *Social Origins of Depression*, London: Tavistock.

Doll, E.A. (1953) *The Measure of Social Competence*, a manual for the Vineland Social Maturity Scale, Minneapolis: Educational Publishing.

Feldman, M.A., Case, L., Towns, F. and Betel, J. (1985) 'Parent Education Project I:

Development and nurturance of children of mentally retarded parents', *American Journal of Mental Deficiency*, **90**, 253–8.

Gath, A. (1988) 'Mentally handicapped people as parents. Is mental retardation a bar to adequate parenting?', *Journal of Child Psychology and Psychiatry*, **29**, 739–44.

Gath, A. (1993) 'The children of Kolevka', unpublished report to Oxfam.

Gillberg, C. and Geiger-Karlsson, M. (1983) 'Children born to mentally retarded women: a 1 to 21 year follow-up study of 41 cases', *Psychological Medicine*, **13**, 891–4.

Gunn, M.J. (1990) 'The law and learning disability', *International Review of Psychiatry*, **2**, 13–22.

Koller, H., Richardson, S.A. and Katz, M. (1988) 'Marriage in a young adult mentally retarded population', *Journal of Mental Deficiency Research*, **32**, 93–102.

McGaw, S. and Sturmey, P. (1993) 'Identifying the needs of parents with learning disabilities: a review', *Child Abuse Review*, **2**, 101–17.

Nihira, K., Foster, R., Shellhaus, M. and Leland, H. (1974) *AAMD Adaptive Behavior Scale*, Washington DC: American Association on Mental Deficiency.

Quinton, D. and Rutter, M. (1984) 'Parents with children in care: II. Intergenerational continuities', *Journal of Child Psychology and Psychiatry*, **25**, 231–50.

Quinton, D., Rutter, M. and Liddle, C. (1984) 'Institutional rearing, parenting difficulties and marital support', *Psychological Medicine*, **14**, 107–24.

Rogers, P.T. and Coleman, M. (1992) *Medical Care in Down Syndrome: A Preventative Medicine Approach*, New York: Marcel Dekker.

Seitz, V. (1990) 'Interventional programs for impoverished children: a comparison of educational and family support models', *Annals of Child Development*, **7**, 73–103.

Tucker, M.B. and Johnson, O. (1989) 'Competence promoting vs. competence inhibiting social support for mentally retarded mothers', *Human Organisation*, **48**, 95–107.

Turk, V. and Brown, H. (1993) 'The sexual abuse of adults with learning disabilities', *Mental Handicap Research*, **6**, 193–216.

Tymchuk, A.J. (1992) 'Predicting adequacy of parenting by parents with mental retardation', *Child Abuse and Neglect*, **16**, 165–78.

Tymchuk, A.J. and Andron, L. (1990) 'Mothers with mental retardation who do or do not abuse or neglect their children', *Child Abuse and Neglect*, **14**, 313–23.

Whitman, B.Y. and Accardo, P.J. (1989) *When a Parent is Mentally Retarded*, Baltimore: Paul Brookes.

Zigler, E., Taussig, C. and Black, K. (1992) 'Early childhood intervention', *American Psychologist*, **47**, 997–1006.

Chapter 14

Parents who are gay or lesbian
Michael B. King

The sexual orientation of men and women has long been regarded as an important factor in determining their suitability as parents. Until recently, the view that homosexual fathers or lesbian mothers were unfit to be parents went largely unchallenged. The assumptions underlying this belief and the evidence concerning it are the subject of this chapter.

Homosexual men and women frequently find themselves in a parenting role. They may enter heterosexual partnerships which bear children because they are attempting to hide from the nature of their sexuality, have failed to recognise it, or simply wish to raise children in a heterosexual family setting. Lesbian women may bear children after sexual intercourse with a man friend or by artificial insemination. Gay men may arrange for a surrogate mother to bear their child. Homosexual men or women may foster or adopt children informally or through the usual legal channels, although the hurdles involved in the latter are often insurmountable.

Homosexual men and women who are parents often conceal their sexual orientation from their children or their heterosexual partner. There is frequently a reluctance to inform outsiders. The gay parent may be unaccepting of themselves, fear disapproval or rejection by their children, envisage that their children will be removed from their care or, if they have a heterosexual partner, anticipate vindictiveness or prejudice on their part. This means that the study of families in which one or both parents are homosexual is difficult to conduct; such parents may be reluctant to take part in research because they fear the consequences of their sexuality becoming known to outsiders. Thus the available evidence about children raised in such families originates from studies in which volunteers have taken part, sometimes anonymously. All our knowledge about gay men and lesbians as parents is subject to this limitation.

OPPOSITION TO HOMOSEXUALS AND LESBIANS AS PARENTS

Formal opposition to homosexual men and women as parents usually only arises in the context of court proceedings in which a gay man or lesbian seeks an adoption order or where there is a custody dispute concerning their own children. However, there is also a degree of informal opposition in society to homosexuals raising children.

What are the principal objections to homosexuals as parents and do they hold up to scrutiny? The most common contentions are that gay men and lesbians are mentally ill; are promiscuous and have unstable relationships; and will influence the sexuality of their children, damage their emotional development, turn them against the opposite sex, molest them or indirectly cause them to suffer stigma and shame at the hands of their peers and others.

Homosexuality as a disorder

An increasingly polarised view of sexuality, originating in British culture more than 200 years ago, has influenced our current concepts of sexual orientation (Davenport-Hines 1990). Although historically there has been little concern with or knowledge about lesbian behaviour, throughout the eighteenth century men who had sex with other men were pursued and punished with increasing severity. The belief that men who preferred sexual contact with other men were mentally disordered, however, only emerged towards the end of the nineteenth century with the coining of the term homosexuality (Davenport-Hines 1990). Much of the interest in homo-sexuality in the twentieth century stemmed from a desire to understand it, often in psychoanalytical terms, and thereby to modify it towards the preferred state of heterosexuality.

From their experience with distressed homosexual men who consulted them, psychiatrists came to believe that there were substantial links between mental illness and homosexuality. Homosexuals were regarded as men with unstable personalities who were more vulnerable to a range of psychiatric disorders. Even as late as the 1980s, review articles have appeared in which homosexual men are regarded as unassertive, inclined to neurotic distress and drug use, have 'failed in the pursuit of women', and for whom sexual reconditioning or training in social skills may alleviate an essential weakness of character (Macculloch 1981). If psychiatric illness is any more common among gay men, this may be largely a result of the prejudice that they experience in modern society (Remafedi 1987).

A major difficulty in studying homosexuality concerns the need for a clear distinction between same-sex desire, responsiveness and fantasy on the one hand and actual sexual behaviour on the other. Kinsey *et al.*'s (1948; 1953) controversial work first provided good evidence for the possibility of a continuum of sexual response. In a study of 3,392 women and 3,849 men in North America, 50 per cent of male and 28 per cent of female subjects reported awareness of erotic responses to members of the same sex. Kinsey suggested that there was a gradation between homosexuality and hetero-sexuality and despite the obvious limitations of self-report, much subsequent work has confirmed the concept (McConaghy 1987). This idea, however, has not gone unchallenged. A recent reanalysis of the Kinsey data (Van Wyk and Geist 1984) has led to renewed claims for a clear dichotomy between a majority of the population who are heterosexual and approximately 5 per cent who are exclusively homosexual.

Kinsey *et al.*'s work was a major step in the move away from the conceptualisation of homosexuality as a mental disorder. By the 1960s and 1970s, disillusionment with psychoanalytical theories, reactions against the negative effects of labelling, a failure of the medical model to explain sexuality and a rise in gay political power had further undermined the illness theories (Israelstam and Lambert 1983). In 1973 the classification 'homosexuality' in the Diagnostic and Statistical Manual II (DSM II) of the American Psychiatric Association (APA 1973) was replaced with the category 'sexual orientation disturbance' and was further modified in DSM III (APA 1980) to 'ego-dystonic homosexuality', a category retained to meet the requirements of homosexuals who were conflicted about their sexual identity. The revised third edition of this manual now includes only a small subheading for persistent and marked distress about one's sexual orientation (APA 1987). The tenth edition of the International Classification of Diseases (WHO 1992) contains the diagnostic category 'ego-dystonic sexual orientation' which can be applied to individuals in whom gender identity and sexual orientation are not in doubt but who wish it were different because of associated psychological and behavioural disorders.

The belief that homosexuality is a mental illness which precludes normal parenting is no longer tenable. In any case, mental illness *per se* is insufficient grounds for objecting to a parent having care and control of their child and requires elucidation of the individual case (Gottsfield 1985).

The lifestyles of gay men and lesbians

As for many minority groups, homosexuals and lesbians are frequently conceived of in terms of stereotypes. The effeminate homosexual and masculine lesbian are the clichés by which homosexuality is recognised in Western societies. In reality, there is at least as great a variation in degrees of masculinity and femininity, choice of sexual techniques, patterns of behaviour and domestic roles in homosexual as in heterosexual people (Bancroft 1989). There is evidence, however, that homosexual men report higher levels of sexual activity and more sexual partners than heterosexual men and women, or lesbian women. Bancroft (1989) has speculated that promiscuity has more to do with maleness than homosexuality.

In a large American study, Bell and Weinberg (1978) derived five principal patterns of living. Although not all gay men and lesbians can be classified on the basis of their lifestyle, these models may serve a general descriptive purpose. People in the first 'close coupled' category are comparable to the stereotype of the happily married heterosexual couple. Lesbians are more likely to be close coupled than gay men. In the second, 'open coupled' arrangement, there is a stable relationship but one or both members seek sexual partners outside it. 'Functionals' are individuals who are not coupled but who enjoy a variety of sexual partners. 'Dysfunctionals' are people who have recurring sexual problems and find it difficult to find satisfactory casual or long-term sexual partners. Finally, 'asexuals' are those people who appear to have a very low interest in sex and rarely seek out partners. People in the latter two categories tend to have the lowest rates of psychological health. These categories are unlikely to be static and probably change depending on the life stage of the individual. For example, functionals are more likely to be younger and describe themselves as highly sexed.

Gay men are more likely to report that they expect a change in their relationship and are less likely to be monogamous within that relationship (Blumstein and Schwartz 1983). Certainly the lack of any legal recognition of homosexual relationships is likely to lead to greater instability. Longitudinal studies, however, over at least the short term, show little differences in the stability of homosexual, heterosexual or lesbian couples (Blumstein and Schwartz 1983).

The sexual development of children

We know very little about the development of sexual behaviour in boys and girls. The concepts of sexuality held in Western society have been strongly influenced by the untestable theories of classical psychoanalysis. Such theories have had considerable influence on the assessments made by mental health professionals and the courts. Until recently it was assumed that the sexual and emotional development of children ideally took place in a home containing a mother and father, both of whom were in good physical and mental health. A recent, widely publicised example of adoption being denied to a mother who was grossly obese makes it clear that such precepts continue to influence judgements made about parenting in Britain.

The belief that a child's psychological development occurs on a background heavily influenced by the potent, yet complementary, sexual forces of mother and father derives directly from Freudian theory and devalues the role of the extended family and matriarchal child rearing practices which are commonplace in the majority of the world's population.

Even empirical observation of children's gender and sexual development has been influenced by psychoanalytical thought. Gender identity is an awareness of being male or female in its broadest sense. In the condition transsexualism there is a serious and long-standing disparity between gender identity and biological gender. Gender identity is usually completely established between the ages of 2 and 4 years (Riddle 1978; Bancroft 1989) and may be a function of both prenatal and postnatal influences (Money and

Ehrhardt 1972). Gender role refers to the blend of traits and behaviours which indicates to self and others that one is male or female. It is the public demonstration of gender identity and varies with the cultural setting (Money and Ehrhardt 1972). Gender-role socialisation begins early and usually enters conscious awareness once gender identity is established. In its most restricted sense, sexual orientation indicates the gender of the preferred sexual partner. Sexual orientation, however, also involves emotional as well as sexual responsiveness.

The determinants of sexual orientation and the timing of its development remain poorly understood. Nor are they necessarily the same in each sex. Unfortunately, much of the research into the biological origins of homosexuality has been related to whether it is a 'sickness or a sin' and therefore whether it should be tolerated (Bancroft 1994). Nevertheless, there is now considerable evidence for a genetic or constitutional foundation upon which social and family factors may have an influence. Evidence has accumulated over recent years that male sexuality (and to a lesser extent lesbianism) may be genetically determined, at least in part. High concordance rates for studies of monozygotic siblings raised together have been reported (Bailey and Pillard 1991), although not all data concur (King and McDonald 1992). Debate about the biological origins of homosexuality has also accelerated with recent evidence for a variation in the size of specific hypothalamic nuclei in women, homosexual men and heterosexual men (LeVay 1991). Almost all these data, regardless of which functional or anatomical area of the brain is implicated, suggest that homosexual men occupy some middle point between heterosexual men and women. Such 'central nervous system hermaphroditism' may merely reflect, however, a frequent assumption in the literature whereby homosexuality is equated with effeminacy (Byne and Parsons 1993).

Although none of the evidence is unequivocal, it indicates that sexuality is constitutionally derived, possibly at a very early stage in development. Unfortunately, the research has focused on male homosexuality instead of sexuality as a whole and has alienated many gay and lesbian groups. Although we have moved on from regarding homosexuality as a disorder, much of the research continues to focus on it in this way. After the recent report that a gene for male homosexuality may be transmitted on the X chromosome (Hamer et al. 1993), there was a great deal of ethical and moral debate about whether prenatal testing to prevent the birth of gay men could be justified.

Quite apart from our increasing knowledge about the biological origins of sexual orientation, the assumption that one parent of each sex is required to provide adequate role models is no longer defensible in modern Western society. Up to one-third of children are now raised in households which vary from this so-called nuclear ideal. Despite recent, unfocused claims by the British government that children raised in single-parent families are more likely to become delinquent, there is little empirical evidence from studies, which control for important confounding influences such as economic status and marital break-up, that the emotional and sexual development of children is seriously affected (Amato and Keith 1991). Although parental divorce appears to lower the well-being of children, the estimated effects are generally weak. This literature on parental absence is relevant to the subject of homosexual parenting. In a careful meta-analysis of ninety-two studies comparing children living in divorced single-parent families with those living in continuously intact families, Amato and Keith (1991) reported that parental remarriage does little to alter the well-being of the child. It even appears that daughters living with stepfathers may be worse off than those who remain only with their mother. Furthermore, the effect on children of the gender of the parent who remains after divorce appears to be mediated mainly through economic factors. Children remaining with mothers tend to receive fewer opportunities than those who stay with fathers who, on the whole, are higher income earners (Amato and Keith 1991).

What can be concluded from all this? Regardless of the logic or ethics of this debate, it is clear that the development of sexuality is unlikely to depend simply on the attitude and behaviour of parents towards their offspring. Although it is often suggested that sexuality develops on a constitutional bed which requires specific environmental cues, contained within this argument is the implicit assumption that homosexuality is a negative thing to be avoided wherever possible. It is beyond the scope of this chapter to enter the metaphysical debate about the value or otherwise of homosexuality. It should be emphasised, however, that this assumption is often present in legal decisions regarding parenting and must be identified for what it is.

Evidence from studies of gay and lesbian parents

Do homosexual or lesbian parents have a specific effect on the emotional and sexual development of their children? The soundest evidence comes from controlled studies of the families of lesbian mothers where possible confounding factors such as marital breakdown, single parenting and financial status have been taken into account.

There have been at least three studies in which standardised measures have been used. In the first, 20 lesbian and 20 heterosexual single mothers living in California were matched for educational background and occupational category (Hoeffer 1981a; 1981b). The children did not differ significantly in the amount of time they spent with their fathers. There were no differences in standardised measures of gender identity or sex-role behaviour between the children in the two groups. Lesbian mothers preferred a more equal mixture of sex-typed masculine and feminine toys for their children than did heterosexual mothers. The majority of mothers in both groups believed that peers had the most influence on their children's acquisition of sex-role behaviour. An unexpectedly high rate of psychological disturbance was found in the children of both groups. This finding may have been due to the method of ascertainment of the mothers who were offered a free psychological evaluation for their children as a part of the study. In the second study, 27 lesbian households containing 37 children were compared with 27 households in which heterosexual women were solo-parents to 38 children (Golombok *et al*. 1983). Over half of the lesbian mothers were cohabiting in a stable relationship with another woman. Ratings of the children were made by assessors blind to the nature of the family. The two groups did not differ in terms of gender identity, sex-role behaviour, sexual orientation (in the older children), emotions, behaviour and relationships, although there were indications of more frequent psychological problems in the children of the single, heterosexual mothers. In the third study, 50 lesbian mothers and their 56 children were compared to 40 heterosexual single mothers and their 48 children (Green *et al*. 1986). No significant differences were found in intelligence, sexual identity, gender-role preferences, family and peer group relationships or adjustment to a single-parent family between the two groups of children. Although the girls of lesbian mothers showed more variety in gender-role behaviours than the boys, these remained within the normal range. Evidence from uncontrolled studies of lesbian mothers supports the findings of these three studies (Green 1978; Harris 1985; Huggins 1989).

Homosexual fathers in sole custody of their children are uncommon because gay men less often apply for, and are frequently denied, custody by the courts. To my knowledge there are no published, controlled studies of the type described above for lesbian mothers. Most evidence is descriptive, based on small samples and weakened by the usual difficulty of establishing a representative sample. Some evidence is based on homosexual men remaining within a heterosexual marriage. Bearing in mind their methodological weaknesses, these reports have failed to raise concern about the psychosexual and emotional development of children raised in such households (Harris and Turner 1985/86; Miller 1979; Bigner and Jacobsen 1989; Bozett 1989). Nevertheless, occasional studies appear to be based upon extremely stereotyped concepts of the lives of gay men (Bozett 1981) and exemplify the dangers of open descriptive studies of volunteers. One recent, controlled study compared attitudes to parenting of 24 gay and 29 heterosexual fathers and reported that there were no discernible differences in parenting style between them. The children of these fathers, however, were not studied (Bigner and Jacobson 1992).

To my knowledge only one controlled study of adults raised in homosexual households has been published. Gottman (1990) found no differences in gender-role preferences or personality factors between 35 adult daughters of lesbian mothers, 35 adult daughters of heterosexual mothers who had divorced and remarried and 35 adult daughters of heterosexual mothers who had divorced and not remarried. Although there was a surprisingly high rate of lesbianism (16 per cent) in this group of 105 women, sexual orientation did not vary as function of family setting.

No specific comparison has been made between children raised exclusively by homosexual and heterosexual parents in which each type of couple has suffered a break-up and repartnering. Finally, although lesbian women are increasingly seeking to have children through sexual intercourse or by artificial insemination (Brewaeys *et al.* 1989), to my knowledge, no study of the development of these children has appeared in a peer-reviewed publication.

Molestation of children

Homosexuality is frequently confused in the legal and public minds with paedophilia in which the prime object of sexual attraction is the immature (usually prepubertal) male or female form. This misconception leads to a concern that homosexual parents might interact sexually with their children and particularly influences decisions about gay men as parents. It less commonly constitutes an opposition to lesbian parenting because paedophilia is largely regarded as a male propensity. Although same-sex paedophilia predominates in sex offenders who have been apprehended for their behaviour, this bears little relationship to same-sex attraction in adult males. In early work it was reported that same-sex paedophiliac men demonstrated an aversion to the adult physique, preferring immature boys with feminine features who lacked secondary sexual characteristics such as body hair and a developed musculature. In a study of 175 male sex offenders against children, Groth and Birnbaum (1978) reported that those offenders who were also involved in adult sexual relationships were in all cases heterosexual. The authors concluded that the heterosexual man constituted a greater sexual risk to under-age children than his homosexual counterpart.

More recent studies have challenged the classification of male offenders into those who are fixated on children as a primary sexual orientation and those who regress from an adult sexual orientation to children under periods of stress (Conte 1991). It would appear that children of both sexes and adult women are often assaulted by the same man (Abel *et al.* 1988). The traditional distinction between paedophilia and incest (Langevin 1983) has also been contested (Conte 1991). Despite these conflicting claims, there is no evidence to suggest that children are at greater risk of sexual molestation at the hands of their homosexual parent or his or her partner than in analogous heterosexual circumstances.

Aversion to the opposite sex

The notion that a homosexual parent will reject a child of the opposite sex, will influence his or her children against the opposite sex or will be unlikely to introduce adults of the opposite sex into the home is a consequence of the stereotyping of homosexuality as a form of rejection of heterosexuality.

Lesbians, in particular, may be disparagingly referred to as 'man haters'. In part this fear also stems from the confusion between homosexuality and paedophilia. In the studies described earlier, comparing lesbian with heterosexual mothers, it was clear that the lesbian women loved their children of either gender and involved them with people of the opposite sex. The majority of the lesbian women in the study by Golombok *et al.* (1983) introduced both homosexual and heterosexual friends into the household and there was no evidence that the children of the homosexual mothers were influenced to avoid contact with peers or adults of the opposite sex. In fact, 12 of the 37 children of lesbian mothers were reported to have contact with their fathers at least once a week compared to 2 of the 38 children of heterosexual mothers.

In a comparison of 26 children raised by 13 lesbian mothers with 28 children raised by single heterosexual mothers in New York City, Javaid (1993) reported that although the lesbian mothers were more liberal about their children's eventual sexual orientation, none favoured homosexuality for their children. Nine of the 13 lesbian mothers had a desire for grandchildren. The majority of the children in the lesbian households had access to the father or other male relations as well as to other heterosexual families.

Stigmatisation by others

It is often feared that children living in lesbian or gay households will become the target of discrimination by peers and others in their community. This may occur for a proportion of children living in such households, as it does for children living in any relatively unusual family situation. Children who have one parent who belongs to an ethnic or religious minority, or a mentally handicapped sibling, may also be subject to prejudice. The children may be scorned at school or may isolate themselves from peers to avoid having to discuss the nature of their home life. Only two of the children of the lesbian mothers studied by Golombok *et al.* (1983) were said to have disturbed peer relationships. In the study by Green *et al.* (1986) children's self-ratings of their own popularity with same- and opposite-sex peers did not differ between lesbian and heterosexual households. Other evidence, however, would suggest that some children may have a conflict between loyalty to their mother and a desire to conform to the heterosexual norms of their peers (Lewis 1980). In an uncontrolled, descriptive study of gay fathers living in San Francisco, Bozett (1980) reported that most fathers took precautions to protect their children from hostility by advising them to refer to the male partner as an uncle or roommate. Most of the fathers recognised the need for discretion in their public identification with homosexual issues, in order to spare their children embarrassment. Some went so far as to send their children to a school outside the neighbourhood in which they lived. The controlled study of lesbian and heterosexual mothers by Javaid (1993) was unusual in that the children in both types of household were asked about their attitudes to marriage, having children and sexual preferences. The girls were generally more open about homosexuality than the boys, but the majority of children of both sexes said that they would not tell their peers about their mother's lesbianism; most feared peer rejection when the mother was actually or hypothetically homosexual. They also felt more uncomfortable with the concept of a gay father than that of gay mother.

Child custody disputes between a heterosexual and homosexual parent often become public, at least in the family's locality. In these cases children may be subjected to discrimination, regardless of which parent they live with.

ASSESSMENT OF PARENTING WHERE HOMOSEXUALITY IS AN ISSUE

Mental health professionals are not automatically asked to make assessments in custody or adoption cases where one or both parents seeking care and control are homosexual or lesbian. There is quite an extensive medical and legal literature to guide barristers and the courts in these matters. However, where there are misunderstandings about the influence of sexuality on an individual case, clear evidence from an expert witness can help to resolve these. In cases where the sexuality of one or both parents is regarded as an important obstacle to parenting, where there is a history of other psychological or social pathology in the gay parent, or in cases where fostering or adoption is an issue, an assessment may be requested. Such a request is made by the court, counsel for one or other parent, or by the Official Solicitor, who in England and Wales acts in the interest of children in the case.

It is important for the professional compiling the report to shift the emphasis from what gay men and lesbians are 'supposed' to be like to an assessment of the individual parent's ability to love and raise the child. In so doing it is useful to cover the following issues.

Personal and emotional development

As in all psychiatric reports prepared for the court, at least a brief assessment of the individual's family and personal history must be given. As developmental issues are so often considered as vital by the courts, they must be carefully documented.

Psychiatric history

It is crucial to explore any history of emotional troubles or substance abuse and to assess its relationship to the person's sexual orientation. Periods of extreme social or emotional instability in a parent are usually regarded negatively by the court, but when this occurs in the context of a homosexual parent, implicit connections are frequently made between the sexual orientation and the apparent instability.

Sexual development

Whether or not it is openly stated, the sexuality of the parent usually takes precedence over all other factors in these cases. The professional must therefore take a detailed history of sexual development, first awareness of sexual orientation, past and present sexual behaviour, the nature and stability of long-term relationships and any difficulties encountered by the subject in coming to terms with his or her sexual orientation. Although it is a sensitive issue, it is wise to explore the age profile of people to whom the client is sexually attracted. Although the evidence, as already described, demonstrates that there is no link between homosexuality and paedophilia, it is advisable to have asked such questions in advance in order to dispel any possible anxieties about the likelihood of sexual abuse of children. In my experience, gay and lesbian parents are rarely offended by such questions.

Counsel opposing custody by a homosexual parent may raise anxieties over this issue, even in the case of lesbian women. Merely raising suspicion about this issue in the court's mind may be damaging for homosexual parents and thus the expert witness must be prepared in advance with a full knowledge of these issues.

Candour about homosexuality

When and how children are told about their parent's homosexuality is also of concern to the court. Unfortunately, there is little guidance for professionals from the literature on this matter. Although it appears that children's responses are mixed when they first hear the news, their reactions are not particularly determined by their age (Harris and Turner 1985/86). The circumstances in which they learn about the sexuality of their parent(s), however, is crucial. If the facts are revealed in the context of a stormy marriage from which the homosexual parent has been forced to leave, or if it is portrayed as a failing or otherwise undesirable characteristic, the reaction of the child is more likely to be one of fear or rejection. The attitude of the heterosexual parent is crucial here and unfortunately, particularly in the context of broken marriages, this is more often negative than positive (Harris and Turner 1985/86).

It is important to point out here that many children may be aware of the sexuality of their parent before it is actually discussed with them. In a comparison of children raised by lesbian and heterosexual mothers Javaid (1993) reported that almost half the 26 children reared by lesbian mothers knew about their mother's sexual orientation without her having discussed it with them. The author speculated that even those who had been told may have known the secret well beforehand.

Gay or lesbian parents disclose their sexual orientation to their children in order to explain the nature of their personal world. Disclosure should not be regarded simply as an admission of sexual facts. In addressing this issue with a parent it is vital to explore how they plan to deal with this matter if their child remains unaware of the reality of the family situation. It is also important to prepare the parent for questions on this subject in court. The court is often grateful for advice from the professional on how the gay or lesbian parent might go about informing his or her children. Usually, children respond best to simple disclosure, without undue emphasis on the specifically sexual side of the matter. I have often recommended in court that the gay parent receives counselling on the most appropriate way to tell the child and how to conduct subsequent discussions. Counselling can be provided for the parent individually or together with their children.

Quality of the parent–child relationship

Assessing the dynamics of the parent–child relationship is complex and is best undertaken by a specialist in child mental health. This opinion should be sought separately from that regarding the sexual orientation of the client. It is important to have some direct evidence of the manner in which the homosexual parent interacts with his or her children and the opinions of the children in the matter. Nevertheless, the professional assessing the parent can gain a considerable amount of information about parenting by dwelling on the following issues. Have there been times when the client has left the family for extended periods and, if so, for what reason? Absences are not usually regarded favourably by the courts. However, even absences by the heterosexual parent may not be regarded as seriously as homosexuality in the other parent.

How will the homosexual parent, given a residence order or formalised contact with the child, conduct his or her sex life? Will measures be taken to ensure privacy of their sexual behaviour? This question is a thorny one for the courts which usually advocate strict privacy. In my experience, however, parents can go too far in trying to ensure privacy, for example by claiming that they lock the bedroom door. Paradoxically, the court may view this as too extreme in that the parents would be unavailable to the children in an emergency.

There may be debate about whether kissing in front of the children (which is perfectly acceptable in heterosexual households) is considered a lapse of privacy. The professional may need to point out in the report, or at the hearing, that there is very little evidence regarding the effects on children of witnessing sexual activity between their parents. To my knowledge there has been little empirical research on this subject, although given the overcrowded conditions in which over half of the world's population lives, it would seem inherently likely that most children witness sexual activity at some time between adult members of extended families.

A further issue that might best be regarded as a part of the quality of parenting involves the extent of disclosure that children should make to others in their community (particularly peers) about the nature of their family. Thoughtful parents will have considered this issue and be able to give an adequate account of themselves. Although the evidence available suggests that stigmatisation of children at the hands of their peers is not a major issue, undoubtedly it may occur, especially if there has been publicity about the custody dispute. The lesbian or gay parent may have particular ideas about how to deal with this issue, including advising her or his children on ordinary discretion as concerns any other private family matter or sending them to schools outside the neighbourhood.

The heterosexual parent

Where possible the mental health professional who is making the assessment should interview both parties in the case. Frequently the court hearing will be generated by the opposition of a heterosexual parent (and often their new partner) to contact by or residence with the homosexual parent. In these circumstances it is important to assess the heterosexual parent's knowledge of and attitude towards homosexuality. It is crucial to make a judgement as to whether a revenge motive is generating the opposition of the heterosexual parent, as such motives may be very damaging to the children's relationship with either parent.

CONCLUSIONS

In decisions regarding the care and control of children, the sexual orientation of parents is a complex issue which raises considerable emotion in families and the courts. Homosexuality is no longer regarded as a mental disorder. Despite cultural stereotyping, most homosexual men and lesbian women live stable, ordinary lives and have similar social and emotional needs as their heterosexual counterparts. We have no evidence that the social, emotional or sexual development of children raised by lesbian women or gay men is affected in any major way by the sexual orientation of the parent with whom they live. Considerable prejudice persists in society against gay men and lesbians and is sometimes reflected in the decisions arrived at by the courts. The professional who makes an assessment of a gay or lesbian parent for the purposes of advising on custody of their children must be familiar with past and current theories about the development of sexual orientation as well as taking account of the particular attributes of the individual parents in each case. Homosexuality *per se* should not be regarded as an obstacle to loving and effective parenting of children.

REFERENCES

Abel, G., Becker, J., Cunningham-Rather, J., Mittleman, M. and Rouleau, J. L. (1988) 'Multiple paraphiliac diagnoses among sex offenders', *Bulletin of the American Academy of Psychiatry and the Law*, **16**,153–68.

Amato, P. R. and Keith, B. (1991) 'Parental divorce and the well-being of children: a meta-analysis', *Psychological Bulletin*, **110**, 26–46.

American Psychiatric Association (1973) *Diagnostic and Statistical Manual*, 2nd edn, Washington DC: APA.

American Psychiatric Association (1980) *Diagnostic and Statistical Manual*, 3rd edn, Washington DC: APA.

American Psychiatric Association (1987) *Diagnostic and Statistical Manual*, 3rd edn, revised, Washington DC: APA.

Bailey, J. M. and Pillard, R.C. (1991) 'A genetic study of male sexual orientation', *Archives of General Psychiatry*, **48**, 1089–96.

Bancroft, J. (1989) *Human Sexuality and its Problems*, London: Churchill Livingstone.

Bancroft, J. (1994) 'Homosexual orientation. The search for a biological basis', *British Journal of Psychiatry*, **164**, 437–40.

Bell, A.P. and Weinberg, M.S. (1978) *Homosexualities: A Study of Diversity among Men and Women*, London: Mitchell Beazley.

Bigner, J.J. and Jacobsen, R.B. (1989) 'Parenting behaviours of homosexual and heterosexual fathers', *Journal of Homosexuality*, **18**, 173–86.

Bigner, J.J. and Jacobson, R.B. (1992) 'Adult responses to child behaviour and attitudes towards fathering: gay and nongay fathers', *Journal of Homosexuality*, **23**, 99–112.

Blumstein, P. and Schwartz, P. (1983) *American Couples: Money, Work, Sex*, New York: William Morrow.

Bozett, F.W. (1980) 'Gay fathers: how and why they disclose their homosexuality to their children', *Family Relations*, **29**, 173–9.

Bozett, F.W. (1981) 'Gay fathers: evolution of the gay-father identity', *American Journal of Orthopsychiatry*, **51**, 552–9.

Bozett, F.W. (1989) 'Gay fathers: a review of the literature', *Journal of Homosexuality*, **18**, 137–62.

Brewaeys, A., Olbrechts, H., Devroey, P. and Van Steirteghem, A.C. (1989) 'Counselling and selection of homosexual couples in fertility treatment', *Human Reproduction*, **4**, 850–3.

Byne, W. and Parsons, B. (1993) 'Human sexual orientation. The biologic theories reappraised', *Archives of General Psychiatry*, **50**, 228–9.

Conte, J.R. (1991) 'The nature of sexual offenses against children', in C.R. Hollen and K. Howells (eds) *Clinical Approaches to Sex Offenders and Their Victims*, Chichester: Wiley.

Davenport-Hines, R. (1990) *Sex, Death and Punishment*, London: Collins.

Golombok, S., Spencer, A. and Rutter, M. (1983) 'Children in lesbian and single-parent households: psychosexual and psychiatric appraisal', *Journal of Child Psychology and Psychiatry*, **24**, 551–72.

Gottman, J.S. (1990) 'Children of gay and lesbian parents', in F.W. Bozett and M. B. Sussman (eds) *Homosexuality and Family Relations*, New York: Harrington Park.

Gottsfield, R.L. (1985) 'Child custody and sexual lifestyle', *Conciliation Courts Review*, **23**, 46.

Green, R. (1978) 'Sexual identity of 37 children raised by homosexual or transsexual parents', *American Journal of Psychiatry*, **135**, 692–7.

Green, R., Mandel, J.B., Hotvedt, M.E., Gray, J. and Smith, L. (1986) 'Lesbian mothers and their children: a comparison with solo parent heterosexual mothers and their children', *Archives of Sexual Behaviour*, **15**, 167–84.

Groth, A.N. and Birnbaum, H.J. (1978) 'Adult sexual orientation and attraction to underage persons', *Archives of Sexual Behaviour*, **7**, 175–81.

Hamer, D.H., Hu, S., Magnuson, V.L., Hu, N. and Pattatucci, A.M.L. (1993) 'A linkage between DNA markers on the X chromosome and male sexual orientation', *Science*, **261**, 321–7.

Harris, M.B. (1985) 'Gay and lesbian parents', *Journal of Homosexuality*, **12**, 101–13.

Harris, M.B. and Turner, P.H. (1985/86) 'Gay and lesbian parents', *Journal of Homosexuality*, **12**, 101–13.

Hoeffer, B. (1981a) 'Children's acquisition of sex-role behaviour in lesbian-mother families', *American Journal of Orthopsychiatry*, **51**, 536–44.

Hoeffer, B. (1981b) 'Lesbian mothers and their children: a comparative survey', *American Journal of Orthopsychiatry*, **51**, 545–51.

Huggins, S.L. (1989) 'A comparative study of self-esteem of adolescent children of divorced lesbian mothers and divorced heterosexual mothers', *Journal of Homosexuality*, **18**, 123–35.

Israelstam, S. and Lambert, S. (1983) 'Homosexuality as a cause of alcoholism: a historical review', *The International Journal of the Addictions*, **18**, 1085–107.

Javaid, G.A. (1993) 'The children of homosexual and heterosexual single mothers', *Child Psychiatry and Human Development*, **23**, 235–48.

King, M. and McDonald, E. (1992) 'Homosexuals who are twins: a study of 46 probands', *British Journal of Psychiatry*, **160**, 407–9.

Kinsey, A.C., Pomeroy, W.B. and Martin, C.E. (1948) *Sexual Behaviour in the Human Male*, Philadelphia: Saunders.

Kinsey, A.C., Pomeroy, W.B., Martin, C.E. and Gebhard, P.H. (1953) *Sexual Behaviour in the Human Female*, Philadelphia: Saunders.

Langevin, R. (1983) *Sexual Strands. Understanding and Treating Sexual Anomalies in Men*, London: Erlbaum.

LeVay, S. (1991) 'A difference in hypothalamic structure between heterosexual and homosexual men', *Science*, **253**, 1034–7.

Lewis, K.G. (1980) 'Children of lesbians, their point of view', *Social Work*, **25**, 198–203.

Macculloch, M.J. (1981) 'Male homosexual behaviour', *The Practitioner*, **225**, 1635–41.

McConaghy, N. (1987) 'Heterosexuality/homosexuality: dichotomy or continuum', *Archives of Sexual Behaviour*, **16**, 411–24.

Miller, B. (1979) 'Gay fathers and their children', *The Family Coordinator*, October, 544–52.

Money, J. and Ehrhardt, A.A. (1972) *Man and Woman Boy and Girl*, Baltimore: Johns Hopkins University Press.

Remafedi, G. (1987) 'Homosexual youth. A challenge to contemporary society', *Journal of the American Medical Association*, **258**, 222–5.

Riddle, D. I. (1978) 'Relating to children: gays as role models', *Journal of Social Issues*, **34**, 38–57.

Van Wyk, P. H. and Geist, C. S. (1984) 'Psychosocial development of heterosexual, bisexual and homosexual behaviour', *Archives of Sexual Behaviour*, **13**, 505–44.

World Health Organisation (1992) *International Classification of Diseases*, 10th edn, Geneva: World Health Organisation.

Chapter 15

Parents who have killed their partner
Dora Black

INTRODUCTION

Every year in England and Wales 100,000 children lose their fathers to prison (Shaw 1987) and an unknown number – in excess of 3,000 – suffer their mother's imprisonment (Woodrow 1992). In addition, about seventy babies a year are born to women serving prison sentences, the birth itself usually taking place in an NHS hospital with an accompanying prison officer. One-third of the imprisoned mothers have children under 4 years of age.

A much smaller number of children are affected by the crime of uxoricide. About fifty families (100+ children) a year are affected by the death of one parent at the hands of the other; overwhelmingly (9:1) it is the mother who is killed (Harris Hendriks *et al*. 1993). In nearly all cases the other parent is imprisoned, although a small number are released on bail and may resume the care of their children unless the children are protected by an order of the court. Most of the spouse killers receive manslaughter verdicts and serve relatively short sentences, after which they may again resume care of their children if there has been no consideration of their welfare by social services or court. This situation happens especially when the children are being cared for by relatives of the perpetrator, who often see their role as caretaker of the children only during the parent's incarceration.

Children of imprisoned parents – orphans of justice (Shaw 1992) – are badly served by the lack of consideration of their welfare. Few children can accompany a parent to prison and, in any case, such provisions do not necessarily meet the children's parenting and developmental needs (Black 1992).

In this chapter I consider the parenting needs of children who are orphaned because one parent kills the other and in particular the issues raised for this group of children in relation to who cares for them, what contact they should have with the parent who has killed, whether the children should return to the perpetrator parent and what criteria should guide the practitioner asked to advise in these matters. I draw on the experience of having assessed, with colleagues, over 250 such children at the Royal Free Hospital. This work has been reported on in detail elsewhere (Harris Hendriks *et al*. 1993).

The issues for children of an imprisoned parent who has killed their other parent are different from those for children whose parent(s) have committed other crimes. For children whose parents have committed other crimes, few would question the need and importance of maintaining contact and of restoring the family unit as soon as possible. Is it different for the children of uxoricide? I believe it is.

WHAT HAPPENS TO THE CHILDREN?

Where one parent kills the other, the children are faced with many problems. Not only are they, in effect, suddenly doubly bereaved, about half of them witness the killing. Of those that do, a majority develop psychiatric problems, notably post-traumatic stress disorder and conduct disorder (Black and Kaplan 1988; Harris Hendriks *et al*. 1993). In addition to the psychological effects of sudden bereavement (Black 1978; 1994) and trauma (Terr 1991; Pynoos and Eth 1985), the change of home and school, the loss of friends and possessions, the need to adjust to new carers, themselves possibly bereaved or else ashamed and distressed by their relative's actions, they may have had many years of living in a violent home which has affected their well-being.

How the children are affected by their experience of the father's violence to their mother has been studied most extensively in groups of children brought by their mothers to women's refuges (Jaffe *et al*. 1990). Compared to children in non-violent homes they have more behavioural problems, especially overactivity, aggression, rebelliousness and delinquency, and more emotional problems, such as depression, phobias and obsessionality. They suffer from academic underachievement, with poor concentration and poor school attendance, and from social problems, such as reduced capacity to empathise, to communicate effectively or to assert themselves, resorting to aggression or passive withdrawal when thwarted.

Post-traumatic stress symptoms were recorded in 80 per cent of uninjured child witnesses of violence (Pynoos and Eth 1985). Post-traumatic stress disorder is usually more severe and longer lasting if the stress is related to the actions of one person or group of people against another and is more likely in uninjured witnesses than in injured abused children, whose perception and memories may focus more on their own pain and injury.

Children react differently to stress and the age and sex of the child contribute to these differences. Pre-schoolers show a high degree of minor health problems and somatic complaints, sleep problems and negative mood. They are fearful and act younger than their age (Alessi and Hearn 1984) and respond poorly to children and adults (Layzer *et al*. 1985). Between 6 and 11 years, children are particularly likely to feel guilty, especially where they feel a conflict of loyalty. Two-thirds of our sample came from homes where there had been long-standing conflict and at least half the children had witnessed repeated violence between their parents and in some cases had experienced physical abuse directly (Harris Hendriks *et al.* 1993).

Many of these children fear their father and hate him for depriving them of their mother. As they are effectively parentless they suffer more trauma as attempts are made to find them a home and the families of the mother and father battle over their custody or give inadequate care because of their own grief, shame or anger. These children may suffer from multiple changes of carer, home, school and friends. Their burdens may be increased if they live with paternal relatives who see it as their duty to maintain the children's contact with the father and may discourage attachment to them in order to 'keep' the children for their father (Harris Hendriks *et al.* 1993).

Children who live with relatives of the victim may have limited or no access to their imprisoned parent, as there may be no one willing or able to take on the job of accompanying them to prison or their carers may refuse to allow it. Although it is the right of the *child* to be accorded contact with the father should they wish, in practice, this right, like many others, may be denied them. They may of course be too frightened or angry to express a desire to see their father, particularly if they witnessed the killing and, indeed, they may express forcefully their wish not to see him. It may need expert evaluation of the risks and benefits of such contact and the first contact visit may need to be conducted by someone with therapeutic skills and a clear vision of what needs to be accomplished, as well as authority to terminate the visit if it is non-therapeutic, in order for the visit to be of benefit to the children.

The children who do not witness the killing may be too young to be told the truth of what happened to their parents or may have the truth withheld from them to protect them. They may be told for the first time at school or from overheard conversations, or not knowing, feel abandoned by their parents or feel that by their actions, they have caused the disappearance of their parents (Shaw 1987). The children too often find themselves stigmatised at school by their parent's crime and whichever family they live with, they may get little help in perceiving the other parent in a balanced way. Academic performance deteriorated markedly in over half our cases and in only 15 per cent was there no effect on learning.

It is too early for us to report on the long-term outcome for children of uxoricide. Few of them receive any immediate or long-term psychothera-peutic help and of the children we know who have reached adulthood, there is a clear association between psychological dysfunction and a return to the care of the perpetrator parent. This appears to be related to the psychological difficulties of accepting the moral authority of a parent who has killed someone you loved and were attached to (Harris Hendriks *et al.* 1993).

Given the difficulties which the children experience, and of which it has only been possible to give a brief summary here, it is not surprising that they pose problems for their carers which are sometimes insoluble.

Case example

Gerty and her brother, both under 3 years old when their father strangled their mother, went to live with a maternal cousin who had older children. Gerty suffered nightly sleep disturbances consisting of screaming for hours, and the family found it difficult to cope with the disruption of their sleep. The final straw came when it got out at the school attended by the older children that Gerty's mother had contracted AIDS when the family lived abroad. The children of the carer's family were ostracised and taunted and the family became scapegoated. They rejected the children. Social services became involved for the first time and the children were placed with foster parents who recognised that Gerty was suffering from nightmares and sought psychiatric help for her. The father, in prison, was certain that the children had been asleep at the time of the killing. In therapy, Gerty was able to show, through play that she had witnessed her mother's death. The content of her nightmares indicated that she was severely traumatised by the experience but she was able to gain some relief from talking and playing out her fears and experiences.

IMMEDIATE PLACEMENT OF CHILDREN OF UXORICIDES

Uxoricide is overwhelmingly a crime of young parents, and young parents tend to have young children. In our sample 40 per cent were under 6 years old at the time of the killing, and a further 41 per cent were aged between 6 and 11 years.

At the time of the killing about 40 per cent of the children we have seen were present in the house and in many cases saw or heard the killing or came into the room where the dead parent was lying. Some of the children tried to revive their dead parent and called for help, either by phoning the emergency services or running to a neighbour. In some cases the children were alone with the dead parent overnight, the perpetrator having run off to hide or to kill himself.

Many perpetrators phone their relatives to come to collect the children who are then not alone for long, and many give themselves up to the police and ask the police to alert relatives to care for the children, or take the children with them to the police station. In the latter case, if there are no immediately available relatives, the duty social worker arranges emergency foster care or placement in a children's home. In cases where the father is missing or dead by his own hand, the only immediate source of information about relatives may be the children, who because of their young age may be able to give very little help. The police are unlikely to evaluate the suitability of relatives or of competing claims, and once the children are placed short term it is more likely that they will stay there and that it will not be considered advisable to disrupt their placement, even if the placement is not optimal.

In our sample, 35 per cent of the children were immediately placed with a relative of the victim, 17 per cent with a relative of the perpetrator, 9 per cent with a family friend and 39 per cent in a foster or children's home. By the time of our assessment, which took place at varying times after the death, 40 per cent of the children had had two moves and 15 per cent had had three or more moves; only 26 per cent were now staying with the victim's family, 14 per cent with the perpetrator's family and 60 per cent were accommodated by the local authority.

A small number of imprisoned women will be allowed to have their infants with them in prison. There are three women's prisons in England and Wales (none in Scotland or Northern Ireland) which accept a total of thirty-six babies in all – at Holloway (London) and Styal (Cheshire) they can stay till 9 months of age and in Askham Grange (an open prison in Yorkshire) until 18 months. There are no prisons for men in the UK which accept accompanying infants or children.

Those few children who accompany their mothers into prison have problems brought about by their incarceration, including developmental delays brought about by lack of opportunities for crawling and interaction with others (Catan 1988). Such imprisoned children have virtually no contact with other members of their family and their separation, if it is necessary after 9 months, can rarely be managed slowly. Separated children cannot be brought to prison frequently enough to mitigate their pangs of grief at the separation (Black 1988; 1992).

Our experience has been that mothers in custody awaiting trial on charges of murder or manslaughter are rarely accompanied by their babies. When a mother has a small child, there is a possibility that she could be remanded to a bail hostel (there is only one in the country which accepts children). If there is more than one child, she may be remanded on bail and may return to care for the children, unless there has been a preventive intervention by social services or through wardship proceedings.

It is more rare for father, even if remanded on bail, to have the children returned to his care. In one of our cases the father was remanded on bail because the magistrates felt that the children (ranging in age from 6 months to 6 years), having been deprived of their mother's care (by their father having killed her), should not be further traumatised by being deprived of their father's care! It was not a good decision. The 6 year old when interviewed, said 'You see, we try to be very good'. This child had witnessed her father kicking her mother's head repeatedly as she lay unconscious, and I believe she was telling me about her fear that if they were not successful in their attempt to be good, the same fate might befall them.

In any case, the father faced a prison sentence if convicted, since he was not denying the charge, and the children would have to lose his care eventually. It made more sense to them to lose him for what at least the older ones could recognise as a just cause immediately following the killing.

LONGER TERM PLACEMENT

It is rare for the parent charged with murder or manslaughter to come to trial in under 1 year. The charge itself may not be decided finally until a few weeks before the trial. Long-term planning for the children is therefore very difficult, especially if the accused is denying the charges. In law, a man is assumed to be innocent unless or until convicted and, understandably, many social services departments are reluctant to enter into long-term permanent planning in advance of the verdict, or indeed to intervene actively at all. In our experience, this delay and uncertainty is not in the interests of the children and, since the children's welfare is paramount under the law, our view is that local authorities should be encouraged to take the best decisions possible, without waiting for the outcome of the criminal trial.

Another problem has arisen following the implementation of the 1989 Children Act. When one parent kills the other, the child could be said to satisfy the criteria for having suffered 'significant harm' and can be placed in a children's home or with foster carers by the local authority. Children do not have to be received into care in order to be placed in foster care by local authorities – they can be 'accommodated'. Once a child is accommodated with, say, a foster carer, they may well be considered to be no longer suffering from significant harm nor in danger of so suffering. That being the case, the local authority may not see a need for the further protection of a care order or for any other order and no court proceedings may be initiated. The children do not therefore have appointed a guardian *ad litem* whose specific role is to consider the welfare checklist and make enquiries of the parties and others, including the children, and to arrange legal representation for them.

Even if the need is perceived and court proceedings initiated, the civil court, if not guided by expert witness, may not appreciate the dangers of disruption of bonds or have evidence put before them of the outcome of returning children to the surviving parent when he is released from prison.

When the parents come to trial, it is possible that even if they are found guilty of manslaughter, they will not receive a custodial sentence. In our experience, this not uncommon with mothers who kill their partners, as there has often been years of abuse from their partner culminating in the killing, and this leads the criminal court to deal with them leniently. It can also happen with fathers who, for example, may receive a hospital order because of mental illness such as depression, only to make a swift recovery and therefore be immediately released. Alternatively, they may receive a short sentence on grounds of severe provocation, and be eligible for almost immediate parole because of the length of time they have already served in prison pre-trial.

If there is no framework of protection, the child is likely to return to the released parent immediately. This may happen to a very young child or baby who may not have had any contact with the imprisoned parent and who may have come to regard their present carers as their sole attachment figures. Although this is clearly not in the best interests of the child, there may be no one knowledgeable about child development or attachment needs advising the released parent or the carers, or the advice may not be heeded.

Case example

Jimmy, aged 4, lived with his maternal grandparents after his mother was arrested for having killed his father. Jimmy was present during the attack, after which his mother collapsed and he was not rescued until the next day, when his mother recovered and called her parents. Mother was arrested and remanded in custody and Jimmy saw her regularly in prison. It was ant-icipated that she would receive a custodial sentence, but at her trial 1 year later, she was released on probation and immediately removed Jimmy from her parents against their wishes. Jimmy, in therapy, which was continued by his mother, showed in his play that he was terrified that his mother would kill him if he misbehaved.

In our opinion, Jimmy should have had a framework of legal protection so that his placement needs could have been properly considered and there would have been the authority to implement a care plan which would have better met his needs for contact with his mother *and* protection from fear.

Just over a quarter of our sample were living with relatives of the victim when we first saw them some months or even years later, compared with over a third just after the killing. In many cases this was because the grandparents found they could not cope with the children, often because they themselves were grieving the death of their daughter and were not functioning well. In a few cases it was because they were too infirm or elderly, or because the children were so disturbed in their behaviour that the combination of their grief and the children's behaviour caused a breakdown in relationships. Sometimes the father insisted from prison that, as the sole parent with parental responsibility, he should be the arbiter of where the children live and moved the children to his relatives or requested accommodation from the local authority. Grieving relatives may find it difficult to consult solicitors or to take firm action to secure the children's placement. Sometimes, it is difficult for both sides of the familiy *and* any social workers called in to take decisions in the best interests of the children, overwhelmed as they often are by the horrific circumstances of the killing.

We have known children's carers who have been intimidated by relatives of the perpetrator, even to the extent of having their life threatened, and, if there are no court proceedings, the children sometimes have been handed over to them in response to these threats to avoid danger. In at least two cases, fear of what would happen on the release of the father led the maternal grandparents and children to disappear and keep their whereabouts secret.

CONTACT ISSUES

If the child goes to live with relatives of the victim they might not see the live parent unless he or she makes an application under the Children Act for contact. If that happens, a guardian *ad litem* will be appointed by the court who will assess the wishes and feelings of the child, as well as what he or she considers to be in the child's best interests. They may request help in the assessment from an expert in child psychology or psychiatry. When I am asked to advise about a child whose father has killed their mother (or vice versa), I try to interview the child on their own, meet their carers, significant relatives from both sides of the family and visit the father in prison.

I start from an assumption that it is likely to be helpful to a child to see their father again. The last time they saw him, he might have been highly aroused, violently attacking their mother. It must be helpful to the child to see him in a quieter, remorseful, repentent mood, the child perhaps noting that he is incarcerated and could not harm anyone else they love, or, indeed, the child. Ideally, they need to hear from him that their mother is dead because it is difficult for young children who did not witness the killing, and who may not have seen their mother's dead body, to believe what they are told by others. They need to be told that by their father and to be told that, although he did not mean to, in his anger he hurt mummy's body so badly that the doctors could not make her better and she died. They need to hear from him that he is sorry that he killed her, sorry that he has deprived them of the care of their mother and father, sorry for the disruption in their life and that he is being punished for the wrong he did and that he is trying to learn not to be violent any more.

Whether it is possible for a child to have this therapeutic experience depends on the attitude of their present carers, and the state of mind, capability and attitude of the father. These must be carefully assessed before making a recommendation for contact. A child who is told by father that it was the mother's fault that she was killed, that she 'asked for it' because she was unfaithful, or threatened to leave him, or is told that the people with whom the child is living are evil or are to blame for the killing because they encouraged the mother to leave him, or is told that father did not do the killing (even though he has been convicted) is not served well by such a visit and may well be traumatised further.

Case example

Trudy was 13 when her father killed her mother. Trudy had been away on a school trip and went to live with her maternal grandparents. Her mother had been unhappy in her marriage for many years and had confided her unhappiness to Trudy who felt that had she been at home that day, her father would not have killed her mother. She felt very guilty that she had been having such a good time on holiday that she had not rung her mother that day. At first she refused to see her father, and her grandparents felt relieved about this although they let her know that they would respect her decision, whatever it was. Her father wrote long letters from prison trying to excuse his action on the grounds that mother had threatened on the day of the killing that she would leave him and never let him see his children again. In any case, he wrote, it was really grandmother's fault that she died. She should have been working to support the marriage, not undermine it by encouraging her daughter to see a lover clandestinely. His letters were full of hatred and blame for others. The grandparents felt they had no right to withhold the letters from Trudy who became more and more confused. She confided in a teacher who offered to accompany her to see father. Trudy began to feel sorry for him, and he played on her feelings causing a conflict of loyalties so that she could no longer accept her grandparents' care. A series of overdoses, followed by running away, led to her admission to an adolescent psychiatric unit where the psychiatrist recommended that father's letters be monitored and not given to Trudy if they continued to excoriate her carers, that father be helped to recognise the damage he was doing to the child he professed to love, and that there be contact only at Trudy's pace and in the presence of a therapist.

ISSUES IN THE ASSESSMENT OF SURVIVING PARENT

Contact

The principles to be borne in mind are that contact is the right of the child, rather than the parent, and that the child's welfare is paramount and contact may not be in their best interests at present although the situation may change in future.

In assessing the desirability of contact, one needs to consider the following factors.

Factors in the child

These include age, prior relationship with parent, whether they witnessed the killing, their wishes about contact and how fearful they are of the perpetrator. If a child feels strongly that they do not wish to see their father, I explore using indirect methods such as play and drawing, whether this is based on fear that he will injure or kill them, or a wish to punish him, or a wish to protect their present carers whom they may know are antagonistic to him. Similarly, if they wish to go, is it solely because they want to please their relatives (usually the paternal ones) or because they want to find out the truth, which has possibly been withheld from them, or for other reasons? Can they be helped to recognise the advantage to them of at least one visit to tell him how angry they are, to ask him why he killed their mother, to find out if he is sorry? If they are adamant that they do not wish to go, when might they feel differently?

If the child is very young, the disadvantages of contact may outweigh the advantages. So many of the very young children in our series were so seriously underattached to their new carers that we would be very cautious about disturbing that tenuous bonding.

Factors in the carers

Could they cope with contact or be helped to cope? Would they be able to accompany the child and cope with her/his distress or curiosity or excitement and pleasure? Would they tend to vilify or exonerate the perpetrator, causing confusion to the child? Would the child's placement be in peril if contact were enforced?

Factors in the perpetrator

These include whether they have taken responsibility for the killing, or blame it on others; whether they are able to consider the effect on the child of losing their parents, or are self-absorbed and unable to take a non-egocentric view; whether they take responsibility for maintaining the child as far as is possible; whether the parent is able to apologise; and how they would be likely to refer to the carers when talking to the child. It is essential that the perpetrator is first interviewed without the child to assess their attitudes and personality as well as whether there are possible psychiatric disorders, such as psychosis, which might make a visit undesirable.

Other factors

It is also necessary to consider the timing, duration and frequency of the visit and specify them in any recommendations made to the court. I usually suggest one visit which is supervised by me or a social work colleague and say that further visits will depend on how the first one went. Assessment of the child's psychological reactions after the visit is essential. The first visit should be a maximum of 1 hour. The frequency of further visits will depend on factors such as whether it is planned that the child will return to the parent after his or her release. If there is no likelihood of return, visits should be less frequent. The distance of the prison, the facilities there, the disruption to the child's life have all to be considered.

Residence

Should children return to the care of perpetrator parents after their release, or if they get non-custodial sentences? And is it different if the mother (only 10 per cent of our series) is the perpetrator? In our study, all the children of the women who were killers were living with their mothers at the time of the killing, but nearly half of the fathers who killed were living separately from their wives and families at the time of the killing. In these cases, and especially where young children are concerned, the loss of a mother is much more significant and may be more immediately traumatic than the loss of a father. Studies of women killers have shown that, unlike men, very few of them are in general violent or dangerous (Black 1992). Yet, relatively few of the fathers who killed their wives had also been violent to their children (14 per cent). In studies of battered wives (e.g. Jaffe *et al.* 1990), it is more common for men to be violent to the children too. It may be that the children of uxoricides, out of shame or because they blame themselves, will hide the fact that they have been beaten by a parent.

In nearly all the cases of mothers who kill, they themselves have been battered and brutalised by their partners for years. There appears to be, at first glance, a case for children returning to the care of their mothers after release. Some would argue the same for fathers. After all, they say, they did not hurt the children, they have paid their debt to society, they are not considered a danger to society, why should they not have their children back?

However, in dealing with domestic crime, society fails to distinguish between the paying of a debt, assessment of the risk of further violence and that of future parenting capacity, and these issues should be considered in relation to both men and women.

We have argued as a result of our experience with those children who did return to the perpetrator, that the child's overriding need for competent, trustworthy parenting for the rest of their childhood makes it unlikely that a return to the parent will be the least detrimental solution. This is despite the parent having paid their debt to society, and being considered at low risk of offending again and even though there were mitigating circumstances of the kind referred to above. Our observations are that younger children who return to the killer parent are wary, anxious, overcompliant and placatory. In adolescence, they disconcert their parent by defiantly repudiating the parent's right to have authority over them. 'You killed my mother/father – why should I do what you tell me?' This opens the way to homelessness, delinquency and the danger of sexual exploitation (Harris Hendriks *et al.* 1993).

In assessing the pros and cons of a return to the perpetrator, other factors require consideration. These include an evaluation of the family history of mental illness to assess the risk of mental illness facing the child and parent. Also to be considered are the availability of family supports, whether there is a home, income, etc. and not least, the child's perception of risk which may be very different from the actual risk.

Case study

Peter was 4 when he witnessed his mother kill his father, when both were drunk. He had witnessed many such fights before, and usually his mother came off worst. At her trial she was convicted of manslaughter on grounds of provocation and given a non-custodial sentence. Peter, who had been cared for by mother's family while she was awaiting trial, returned to her care. She soon started drinking again, unable to cope with the stresses of life outside prison on her own. She and Peter came into family therapy and were given a place in a hostel which helped rehabilitate families. During 2 years of family and individual therapy, Peter apparently worked through his fears of his mother attacking him, but when the couple moved to independent living, his drawings reverted to the pattern of his earlier days in therapy – with equally graphic, but more mature images of the killing. Our hopes that we had helped successfully to restore the mother–child relationship were disappointed.

Interviewing the imprisoned parent

When I visit a parent in prison I take a full personal history of the child or children from them. This is often the only time that these facts will have been properly recorded and in telling the history, the parent will reveal much about their knowledge of, and interest in, the children. One father, when asked what he felt would be best for the children, replied 'I want to see them', thus revealing what he thought was best for him and finding it impossible to think of the children as separate from him. These parents often find it difficult to envisage that their children have suffered as a result of their action. 'I've never done anything to hurt them. Why shouldn't I look after them when I'm out?'

It is important to evaluate the parent's understanding of child development, how they imagine the child is going to feel if uprooted from the present carers, especially if the child is young and if the prison sentence long, as with murder sentences. Asking the parent in detail how they visualise the child actually being brought to see them will often reveal their lack of grasp of the realities of the child's life. They might demand that a young child be brought on a long journey by a person the child does not know, or insist that the child be moved from people to whom he or she has become attached, solely to facilitate contact, or suggest that the child's schooling be regularly disrupted so they can visit during the week when a social worker could bring them.

Assessing the genuineness of remorse, whether the father takes responsibility for the killing, or else blames the mother for her own death, whether he has made provision for supporting the child, independently of whether he has contact, and whether he is ready to apologise to the child for depriving them of their mother, are all important in building up a picture of the value to the child of contact or residence. The father may be able to help a child who is full of guilt to understand that they could not have done anything to stop him from killing mother and his ability to take on this task of relieving his child from guilt needs to be assessed.

Taking a family history is also of value. Father may be the only source of information about mental illness in the family and, of course, about his own upbringing and childhood experiences and their effect on the formation of his character.

Finally, one may be bringing the first news of the children to the parent in prison and it may be helpful in influencing them to consider their children's needs, as opposed to their own, if they hear from someone who is an expert on children and is not 'for' one side or the other, something about the children's state of mind, their dilemmas and their progress. I usually time my visit to occur after I have seen the children so that I can do this.

ISSUES IN THE ASSESSMENT OF FAMILY MEMBERS AS CARERS

Many of the issues discussed above are relevant when considering which members of the family who are applying for the care of the children are the most suitable, if any. Our findings as set out above indicate that, sometimes, neither side of the family is suitable, as they may continue to fight the marital battle by proxy. The effect of the criminal trial in particular can be devastating to cooperation between the maternal and paternal relatives and it is the children who suffer once again (Harris Hendriks et al. 1993; Cooper et al. 1988).

It is difficult for either side of the family to give a rounded picture to the child of both parents, and, in addition, our findings are that the relatives of the perpetrator see their function as one of 'holding' the children for their imprisoned relative and attachment is discouraged. The child is likely to be told that father did not kill mother or that it was her fault. Conversely relatives of the victim are themselves bereaved and may not be able to meet the children's needs for information, protection, affection, security and comfort. They find it difficult to have anything good to say about the perpetrator and the child is left feeling that someone they loved and from whom they derive some of their characteristics is wholly bad, a recipe for the development of low self-esteem.

Social services or the police may have placed the children as an emergency after the killing with the first relatives to come forward as carers. They may not necessarily be suitable and it is important to act swiftly and make a decision based on general principles. Our findings are clear that the children generally do better with the families of the victims than the perpetrators, but that an unrelated carer should be considered more often than in practice they are. Unfortunately, financial considerations will often preclude social services from intervening or they may feel that they do not have grounds under the Children Act (1989) as the children may be flourishing in the short term with relatives and are not currently suffering significant harm. I believe we usually have enough information to say that the children have suffered significant harm by the death of one parent at the hands of the other and are liable to suffer significant harm in future if they are returned to the perpetrator parent.

Sometimes a less than ideal placement can be rendered more suitable and more secure by the use of wardship proceedings. There is precedent for the Official Solicitor as guardian *ad litem* instituting wardship proceedings in a case where the paternal aunt had a residence order and was caring for her brother's, the perpetrator's, children, but requested an outside authority to lay down parameters for contact because without it she felt that, once the father was released, she would not be able to deny him the frequent contact he wanted.

In assessing the relatives, one can also do some good therapeutic work, akin to conciliation or mediation in divorce cases in helping the two sides of the family to cooperate in the service of the children.

ISSUES IN THE ASSESSMENT OF FOSTER/ADOPTIVE CARERS

In the case of very young children, especially where the only people available to care for them are quite elderly and where the parent receives a long custodial sentence, adoption may clearly be the least detrimental option. Adoptive parents may not be happy about open adoption and may feel they want nothing to do with a murderer. They will need careful assessment and counselling to be helped to have less negative attitudes to the children's father (or mother) if they are to be considered as adoptive or foster parents. They need to be able to maintain contact with the father – not necessarily on a frequent or even direct basis, if this would help the child. Foster parents may be able to accompany a child to a contact visit and help them to deal with their anxieties and their sadness afterwards.

Horrific killings ('he stabbed her in a frenzy, inflicting forty stab wounds', is not an uncommon media report) are traumatic to the adults involved or likely to become involved, as well as to the victim and the children of the victim. Foster parents in such cases will need support from social workers or mental health professionals to deal with their own feelings.

Another area to be explored is their willingness to seek psychiatric help for the children if they become symptomatic, especially if they show signs of post-traumatic stress disorder.

WHEN AND HOW SHOULD CHILDREN BE TOLD ABOUT THE KILLING?

Our experience is that children often know more than their carers believe they know. This is because they have witnessed the killing but have not told anyone, or because they overhear adult conversation unknown to their carers. Some older children have seen the newspaper headlines on hoardings or seen local television news. Children may not tell their carers what they know in order to protect them. After all, they have already lost one set and wish to ensure that they keep the next ones. Even if they witnessed the killing, they may not have been able to process their percepts without help. I usually advise carers to tell the truth even to very young children, in a way that is minimally blaming and using simple language. 'Mummy and daddy had a fight, daddy was stronger than mummy. He may not have meant to do it, but he hurt mummy's body so much that it didn't work any more and so she died. She couldn't walk, or talk or see or hear or eat or drink. She couldn't cuddle you any more. It was wrong of daddy to do this and so he is being punished by going to prison.'

CONCLUSION

Many of the considerations which inform assessment of parents in other situations described in this book, pertain in cases where children lose their parents through uxoricide. In addition there are considerations which are special to this unusual situation. Those consulted about the child's welfare have a serious responsibility to ensure that the child is not further harmed by being placed unsuitably or involved in contact and residence which is likely to cause significant harm in the long term.

REFERENCES

Alessi, J.J. and Hearn, K. (1984) 'Group treatment for battered women', in A.R. Roberts (ed.) *Battered Women and their Families*, New York: Springer.

Black, D. (1978) Annotation: 'The bereaved child', *Journal of Child Psychology and Psychiatry*, **19**, 287–92.

Black, D. (1988) 'Imprisoned children', *The Medico-Legal Journal*, **56**, 139–49.

Black, D. (1992) 'Children of parents in prison', *Archives of Disease in Childhood*, **67**, 967–70.

Black, D. (1994) 'Psychological reactions to life-threatening and terminal illnesses and bereavement', in M. Rutter, E. Taylor and L. Hersov (eds) *Child and Adolescent Psychiatry: Modern Approaches*, 3rd edn, Oxford: Blackwell.

Black, D. and Kaplan, T. (1988) 'Father kills mother. Issues and problems encountered by a child psychiatric team', *British Journal of Psychiatry*, **153**, 624–30.

Catan, L. (1988) *The Development of Young Children in HMP Mother and Baby Units*, Brighton: University of Sussex.

Cooper, J., Brown, L. and Christie, R. (1988) *Victim Support: Families of Murder Victims Project*, London: Victim Support.

Harris Hendriks, J., Black, D. and Kaplan, T. (1993) *When Father Kills Mother: Guiding Children Through Trauma and Grief*, London: Routledge.

Jaffe, P.G., Wolfe, D.A. and Wilson, S.K. (1990) *Children of Battered Women*, Newbury Park CA: Sage.

Layzer, J.I., Goodson, B.D. and deLange, C. (1985) 'Children in shelters', *Response*, **9**, 2–5.

Pynoos, R.S. and Eth, S. (1985) 'Children traumatized by witnessing acts of personal violence; homicide, rape or suicide behavior', in S. Eth and R.S. Pynoos (eds) *Post-Traumatic Stress Disorder in Children*, Washington DC: American Psychiatric Association.

Shaw, R. (1987) *Children of Imprisoned Fathers*, London: Hodder and Stoughton.

Shaw, R. (1992) 'Imprisoned fathers and the orphans of justice', in R. Shaw (ed.) *Prisoners' Children: What Are The Issues?*, London: Routledge.

Terr, L.C. (1991) 'Childhood traumas – an outline and overview', *American Journal of Psychiatry*, **148**, 10–20.

Woodrow, J. (1992) 'Mothers inside, children outside: what happens to the dependent children of female inmates?', in R. Shaw (ed.) *Prisoners' Children: What Are The Issues?*, London: Routledge.

Chapter 16

Alternative caretakers
Caroline Lindsey

THE CHANGING CONTEXT OF ALTERNATIVE CARE

Over the last 20 years, there has been a series of fundamental changes in child care practice following family breakdown. The first was the change from the institutional care of children to their placement whenever possible in substitute families. This included the more flexible use of adoption, supported by the use of adoption allowances, for the care of physically and mentally handicapped, older and emotionally disturbed, and other 'hard to place', children.

The second change was the emphasis on rehabilitation with the family and the development of effective methods of working with families to achieve this. This, in turn, has altered the population of children and young people being received permanently into care. They have usually experienced severe deprivation, neglect and rejection and are frequently the victims of emotional, physical or sexual abuse. The decision finally to place a child in permanent substitute care may come after a series of failed attempts to rehabilitate.

Thirdly, the nature of adoption has changed as a result of changes in societal attitudes to single parenthood and the availability of effective contraception. This has meant that there are far fewer babies available for the childless couples, who previously were able, by adoption, to create families that seemed like their own.

Fourthly, recognition of the importance of family attachments for the development of the children's identity and increased emphasis on family rights, has resulted in placements of choice being in the extended family. Where this is not possible, attempts are frequently made to maintain links with the family of origin by arrangements for contact. This applies to permanent fostering placements, but also to adoptive placements. The trend towards 'open adoption', in which contact is established and maintained between the birth family and the adoptive family, has been accelerated by the 1989 Children Act.

These changes in social work practice are underpinned by research findings and have both initiated and been influenced by important new legislation. The

research demonstrated the adverse effects of institutional care on development and capacity for interpersonal relationships and that children unable to
be brought up by their own parents did best in adoptive homes (Tizard 1977;
Hodges and Tizard 1989). Recent and proposed changes in legislation by
means of the Children Act, the *Review of Adoption Law* (Department of
Health 1992) and the White Paper *Adoption: The Future* (Department of
Health *et al.* 1993) have emphasised the life-long significance of the
biological parents, challenging the nature and future of adoption.

THEORETICAL CONSIDERATIONS

In working in the field of fostering and adoption, I have found the frameworks
provided by Attachment Theory and Systems Theory helpful in a complementary way. In addition, I have derived a concept of the 'family of
families' from systems thinking. This is to facilitate an understanding of the
many different forms of families encountered; for example, biological, two-
parent and single-parent families, families of divorce, step- and reconstituted
families and foster and adoptive families. Recognising that there is a 'family
of families' rather than a normative family, from which all other family
systems deviate, is a helpful reconstruction. It allows for the acknowledgement of differences in the life cycle pathways followed by families, particularly in relation to how they come into being, how family life is sustained,
how they separate and the meaning that family life has for them (Lindsey
1993). At the same time as acknowledging the particular characteristics of
the different groups of families, it is, of course, important not to lose sight
of each family's uniqueness.

Systems Theory (von Bertalanffy 1950) provides a theoretical framework
to understand the complex interrelationships between social services, legal
systems and substitute and birth families involving the child, which form one
large system. In particular, it is recognised that all these systems of which
the child is a part affect and are affected by each other in a recursive rather
than a linear fashion. Any intervention with part of the larger system will
have an impact on the other parts, so that a consultation, for example, which
helps to resolve conflict between social workers and carers or birth parents
and foster carers, may result in an improvement of the child's behaviour,
without the child being seen.

In the field of substitute care, the idea that meaning is dependent on context
is crucial in understanding the ways in which family relationships acquire
significance (Bateson 1973). The use of the words 'mother', 'father', 'son'
and 'daughter', for example, have very different meanings in substitute
families than in biological families, whilst at the same time having important
similarities. Social constructionists (Gergen 1985; Pearce and Cronen 1980)
have taken this idea further in suggesting that the way that people give
meaning to their experiences is through social interaction, mediated by

language. In birth families, family relationships are brought into being biologically and subsequently maintained by the ongoing interactions and conversations which give the relationships meaning. In fostering and adoption, family relationships are not created biologically, but are brought into being through a series of different conversations and interactions, which provide the context for their existence. Such conversations include the home study (i.e. home-based assessment), the fostering and adoption panels and the introductory visits, as well as reviews and court hearings.

Attachment Theory provides a framework for understanding the patterns of relationship which are commonly found in children in substitute care. Their early experiences of adverse parenting frequently seem to be reflected in insecure, anxious, avoidant, ambivalent or disorganised attachment to the new caregivers (Ainsworth *et al.* 1978; Main 1994). However, carers and social workers do not always recognise the patterns as deriving from the child's earlier experience and find it helpful to learn that the pattern does not reflect on their current efforts to offer a loving relationship but is based on prior learning – the effect of relationships on relationships (Stevenson-Hinde 1990). This may then allow the creation of a different story about the child's behaviour, which, in turn, provides opportunities for change.

SHORT-TERM CARE

Short-term fostering is the most common placement for children entering care. It is the placement of preference for younger children and groups of siblings, especially when there is an expectation that they will shortly return home. Families are specifically assessed for their capacity to be short-term, as opposed to permanent, carers. In the first place, this must depend on the task envisaged by the family. Are they looking for the job of temporarily caring for a succession of other people's children, offering a service to support parents at times of crisis? Do they see their own family as complete? Do they ultimately believe that a child's place is in their own family of origin, despite all its drawbacks, and would they have concerns about 'stealing' someone else's child if the placement were to be anything other than short term? Do they see themselves as working with social workers and birth families? These factors would make it more likely that a family is suited to the role of short-term foster parents.

Families who are assessed as suitable to be short-term carers sometimes find themselves in the position of having a child left with them for so long that the placement feels permanent. Attachments that seem secure begin to form and serious dilemmas about moving the child are created for the foster carers, the child and the social worker. When, as a consequence, the question is asked of them 'Will you look after this child permanently and consider adoption?', there is a serious risk that the psychological commitment needed to parent a child on a permanent basis is not there. In one case, a couple fostered a child of a similar age to their own. His mother was also well known to them. Once he had settled with them, he made great progress, particularly noticeable in his academic performance. When they were asked to take on the permanent care of this child, the placement rapidly broke down. On consultation with the foster parents and their social worker, it emerged that their conflict of loyalties to the boy and his mother, as well as their distress that the fostered child had overtaken their own child at school, had contributed to the disruption.

A decision to accept the change in task from short term to permanent may be based on a moral imperative to do so and this ultimately may be a contributing factor to disruption of the placement.

PERMANENT CARE

Following the implementation of the Children Act, it is possible for families to care for children and young people permanently in three ways:

- as an adoptive parent, when the parental responsibility passes to the adoptive parents, with or without the birth parents' agreement and with or without an order for face-to-face or indirect contact with them;
- as a foster parent, whilst the child remains in care and the parental responsibility remains with the local authority (and with the child's birth parents, to the extent that the local authority permits);
- or with a residence order made in favour of the substitute parents, giving parental responsibility to them, discharging the care order to the local authority and, in all probability, an order for contact with the birth parents, who also retain their parental responsibilty, but with limited power to act.

Adoption

It still remains the case that adoption potentially provides the child who cannot go home with the best chance of a secure family life because of the commitment given by the adopters to become the child's parents for life. They will, ideally, have created a psychological and physical space in their lives for a child of their choosing and have had some time for preparation. The child, too, should have been prepared for the idea of having new parents and will have been given an opportunity to get to know the family.

There is general agreement amongst researchers that adoption, even of the older child or the child with special needs, produces better outcomes than either foster care or residential care (Tizard 1977; Hodges and Tizard 1989; Triseliotis and Russell 1984).

Given the prior experiences of children being placed for adoption today, adoption requires a capacity in adoptive parents to tolerate extreme disturbances of behaviour, which may persist over several years. It needs the ability to bear the emotional distress that arises from the child's incapacity to give or receive affection. The persisting conflict and loss that the child may feel about the separation from the birth parents, is often experienced as painfully rejecting by the adoptive parents. The increasing expectation that maintaining contact with the family of origin is considered, makes it abundantly clear that adoption is not about creating a family that looks like a biological family. To adopt requires the psychological ability to become part of a triangle – a family system that includes the adoptive family, the adopted child and the birth family. It requires the capacity to help the child to integrate his or her life story with the story that evolves in the newly formed family. This, in turn, means the acceptance of the child's previous experience in an ongoing way, not simply as information in a life story book. These earlier experiences have to be discussed and worked through over and over again, at times of family crises and at different life stages, particularly in adolescence.

Young people are often able to express the longing to be part of a family in a way that only adoption would bring. By contrast, others who have been adopted and know that they would not be happier elsewhere, continue to be unable to make a final commitment to the adoptive family, constantly testing them out and looking over their shoulders metaphorically, and sometimes in reality, at their birth family.

The additional need for psychological and educational help may place another burden on the adopting couple, although it is gradually being accepted that post-adoption support is very important if the adoption of older children and young people with special needs is to succeed.

Foster care

The children who are being considered for permanent foster care often do not differ greatly from those described for adoption. However, they are more likely to see themselves as committed members of their family of origin and wish to maintain their relationships with members of the family. This may make it inappropriate to sever the connection through the legal process of adoption. Their birth parents may be opposed to adoption. As a result, a professional decision may be made not to apply for freeing for adoption, because it is unlikely to succeed or is not in the child's interests because of the conflict this would create.

These children will frequently be less likely to make a close relationship with the foster family and so it will be important that the foster carers are not looking for a reciprocal parent–child relationship, having usually satisfied that need by having their own children. This does not, of course, mean that it will not develop, simply that they find it particularly difficult to make the kind of emotional commitment which might be expected to evolve over time, in an adoptive family.

They may also be seen as so troubled and troubling to their carers that few families would consider taking on their care without the regular support of social workers. Remaining in care means that the placement continues to be supported and also to be scrutinised. The placement is always subject to review and this inevitably creates a sense of impermanence, however transient, and a lack of autonomy for the family. Once the assessment is completed and the placement has been confirmed as an adoption, a process which may take several years, adoptive families can expect to regain their autonomy. Permanent foster carers, however, are taking on an essentially collaborative task with social services and the family of origin, which requires an open family system. By this is meant a family whose boundaries are not rigid and who are able to tolerate the involvement of non-related people in the intimate affairs of family life, without feeling intruded upon.

Many permanent foster carers acquire a professional role, often having a background in social work, developing expertise in caring for very disturbed children. Once the young people have left care, the foster carers no longer have any legal obligation to be involved with them, although some continue to do so, treating them as their own children.

Residence order

There has not yet been sufficient opportunity to evaluate the role of residence orders in substitute care. It provides a compromise between foster care and adoption, which may allow autonomy to a substitute family whilst not going as far as adoption in finally displacing the family of origin. It may prove to have the drawback of leaving families with all the responsibility, but without the ultimate authority which comes with adoption.

However in a recent case, a residence order proved to be a useful compromise when the substitute family did not wish to go against the birth parents' opposition to adoption, whilst the local authority was keen to make a permanent placement. The child and foster family were convinced that her home was with them. In this case, in addition, an allowance and a promise of support was granted by the local authority.

THE FAMILY SYSTEM CREATED BY ADOPTION AND FOSTERING

One consideration which is common to all forms of care by alternative caretakers is the effect on the family system created by the presence of children of different status. For example, in any one family, there may be biological children and grandchildren, as well as adopted and fostered children. It is important to assess how families will take into account the sometimes conflicting needs of their own children and the intense demands of the children placed with them. It raises the question of how to manage the relative sense of belonging experienced by the foster child, the adopted child and the biological child. The effect on the family's own children of the foster and adopted children's birth families also has to be considered. In substitute families with too many children, there is a revolving door effect with disruption to one child consequent on the placement of another.

Research has shown that it is unwise to place same-aged children in one family, supporting the hypothesis that managing biological and foster 'twins' creates too much conflict for the parents (Parker 1966; Trasler 1960). Similarly, there is a danger in placing foster children in families with very young children of their own, supporting the hypothesis that the parents will experience conflict if their drive to meet the attachment needs of their own children is interfered with (Parker 1966; George 1970). It has also been shown that, if more than one foster child is placed in a family, the likelihood of a successful outcome is greater (Trasler 1960). This may be explained as providing protection to the foster childen from the sense of not belonging, by creating a 'foster subsystem'. It is also imperative to consider the possibility of keeping siblings together, because of the protection this offers them. In doing so, a significant subsystem is created in the family, potentially maintaining the old life in the new home. For example, the older of two siblings who has had a parental role throughout life will find it difficult to give this up. Such dynamics need to be addressed by the social worker at the point of placement. However, where the needs of each child are very great and their relationships with each other rivalrous and conflictual, a case may be made for separation, on the grounds that it will not be possible to parent them successfully together.

CHILDREN FOR PARENTS AND PARENTS FOR CHILDREN

Another crucial aspect of assessment for alternative parenting relates to the choice of the child. The extent to which there is, in reality, much of a choice is limited because of the pressure on social workers to place and the lack of relatively undamaged, young children with whom families might have the best chance of success. Nevertheless, failure to take seriously the family's wish for the kind of child they feel able to care for is a recipe for disruption. Families have a sense of the child who will fit in with them and often recognise that child on sight – in a sense, they fall in love. Together with the assessing social worker, they build up a picture of the child, the age, sex, temperament, race and religion, social background and educational potential and the type of problems which they will be able to manage. In consulting over cases where there has been disruption, it is very frequently the case that the factors which had been identified as important for the family had been disregarded because of expedience.

The social worker, too, has to make a judgement about a variety of factors: the families' capacity to care for young children as opposed to adolescents; the role that infertility or the loss of a child will play in the way they parent;

the parents' own experiences of parenting, including the impact of being in care themselves, death of their own parents and boarding school experience; and their mental health. In the case of a couple, the stability of the marriage needs to be assessed, including their likely resilience in the face of an abused child who acts out sexually or attempts to split them, as well as the support in the couple's own and extended family for the idea of adoption or fostering. There needs to be a detailed consideration of the meaning to the family of adoption or fostering.

The children's wishes also need to be taken into account; most importantly their ability to see themselves in a new family. It is essential to take seriously the reluctance or refusal of a young person to give up the wish to return to the original family. This requires skilled work over time to enable a successful placement to take place, if it is possible at all.

It is now fairly well established in practice, and confirmed by the Children Act, that children should be placed in families of the same cultural and racial background, where possible. In my view, this needs to be taken very seriously. Even though there is some evidence that transracial placements are successful (Gill and Jackson 1983; Tizard and Phoenix 1989), there is also other experience which suggests significant adjustment problems for transracially placed children later on (Maxime 1986; 1987). However, whilst fostering or taking care of the children of kith and kin appears to be a culturally widespread practice, adoption, particularly where it is organised by the state, is not acceptable in many cultures. This factor as well as the discrimination and disadvantage experienced by many black families, may continue to prevent them from coming forward as potential adopters. The imperative to make same-race placements becomes problematic when a child is kept waiting for an unacceptable length of time because of an unsuccessful search for the right family. If a young child has been placed, usually on a short-term basis, with a family who are from a different ethnic background, a dilemma is created. On the one hand, there is a danger to the child's future mental health caused by the needless disruption of established attachments and, on the other hand, there is the potential effect on the child's sense of racial identity, being brought up in a family of a different race and colour. Each case needs to be assessed on its merits, but where a non same-race placement is being considered for a child, it is obviously essential to discuss how the family will support the development of the child's racial identity.

THE ROLE OF BIRTH PARENTS IN SUBSTITUTE CARE

The title of this chapter 'Alternative Caretakers' as opposed to 'Alternative Parents' raises a fundamental question in the field of child care. What is the difference between a parent and a caretaker or carer, as they are now frequently known? (It seems to be right to use the term caretaker, an active role, as opposed to caregiver.) This important distinction is not simply one of semantics, but has to do with whether it is possible to replace the birth parent and become the child's psychological parent. If the caretaker is seen as someone who is parenting the child on behalf of the original parent, this is an acknowledgement that there are biological parents whose very existence has significance for the child and for the substitute parents. This is despite the fact that the child clearly regards the adopters as his or her mother and father. Those children who are received into care after living with their own families, and for whom rehabilitation is not possible, may continue to love their parents and to long for, or idealise, the life in their original homes. Hence, their birth parents may retain a role in their lives, both in fantasy and in reality. Clinical experience also suggests that children continue to wish for the original parental couple and this may conflict with their crucial need for an experience of secure attachment figures in childhood.

Ideally, the birth parents should become 'non-parental parents' for the child in permanent substitute care. I mean by this, that the parents accept that they no longer have responsibility for parental tasks, either on a daily basis or in the long term, but have a capacity for concern and interest in the welfare of the child and an ability to support the role of the substitute parents. The process begins with the birth and adoptive parents meeting each other and may continue with indirect contact with the child through exchange of information through a third party, or by letters, telephone calls or face-to-face contact.

Unfortunately, birth parents are frequently unable to become non-parental parents, which results either in them disappearing from the life of the child or continuing to behave as if the child were their responsibility, creating conflict of loyalty in the child and potential disruption of the placement. Substitute parents need to be supported in protecting children from that conflict, so that they are able to develop trusting, secure relationships with them. Professionals need to be able to recognise that although the birth parents will always continue to have a significance for the child, contact may be harmful, particularly when the child has experienced abuse. Children who have been abused may, however, wish to have ongoing contact with those members of the extended family who were not directly involved in their abuse. The success of this will depend on the relatives' capacity to put the child's needs before their own loyalty to the birth parents. When there is to be contact, arrangements need to be made carefully, so that it supports the development of the child in the placement, with the recognition that the needs for contact will change over time.

Courts frequently ask for help in making decisions about whether there should be contact and it is essential to take a child-centred position. It is important to pay careful attention to the child's wishes for contact, expressed both verbally and non-verbally through play and, at the same time, to take into account the effect of loyalty to the new and old parents. It is necessary to assess the nature of the relationship with the birth parent and to evaluate the contribution that the birth parent can make to the ongoing life of the child. Consideration should also be given to the effect of severing the contact, weighing up the impact on the child of the loss against the relief of no longer having to confront the parent who is unable or unwilling to provide care.

CHILDREN WHO NEED INSTITUTIONAL CARE

There are some seriously traumatised children and young people for whom family life does not seem possible because of their inability to make intimate relationships. These are usually children who have had numerous and early disruptions in family placements and who have had experiences of severe rejection and abuse. Their capacity to trust adults and to behave in a trustworthy way is seriously impaired. They constantly act in ways to provoke rejection and test the limits of the adults' capacity to endure their behaviour. Often, they are children who have been unable to overcome the loss of the original parents. Sometimes, they are the victims of marital breakdown and abuse in the families in which they have been placed. For them, a residential setting provides a much needed respite. There is a chance to recover from the effects of their experiences, without the expectation of a reciprocal relationship by the carers. When the residential setting provides a therapeutic environment, including an educational provision, the child is sometimes enabled to move on subsequently to a family placement. This is especially so for those children who retain some hope of being loved and taken care of in a family. Detailed preparatory work, including a working-through of the previous experiences and acknowledgement of the losses and fear of future rejection, is essential as part of this process (Fitzgerald 1990).

CONSULTATION AND TREATMENT IN A CHILD MENTAL HEALTH SETTING

Apart from the post-placement help and support which is provided by social services departments, specialist help is provided in child mental health services including the Child and Family Department of the Tavistock Clinic, where the author works. This provision is used by social workers and families when there is a need to reassess the fostering or adoptive placement. This may be because of concerns expressed by the social worker, the parents or the child, about the quality of the parenting, or the child's behaviour and progress.

There are frequently conflicts of opinion within the social work agency about the success of a placement. These arise from differences in perspective because of the workers' roles, and personal and professional life experiences or as a result of the agency's policies and resources. The chance to discuss these issues in a neutral setting and to recognise the origin of the conflicts is often valued.

It is also helpful to see the foster, adoptive and the birth families, with and without the children, together with the social workers who hold the care orders, in a variety of combinations. These consultations are offered when there is a threat to the continuity of the placement. The difficulties which most commonly arise are those of relationship and attachment and a range of behavioural problems, including stealing, lying, aggression, educational and learning difficulties. The assessment may be that the family is no longer able or willing to parent the child and the task of the consultations may be to enable the family and child to separate. Where the commitment to the placement remains and there is not considered to be a risk to the child, a series of family sessions may be helpful (Byng-Hall *et al.* 1988). In other cases, individual therapy may enable the motivated child to overcome the traumas of previous experiences and build new relationships in the foster or adoptive family (Boston and Szur 1983; Rustin 1992).

CONCLUSIONS

This chapter has attempted to provide a picture of the clinical issues involved in the assessment of alternative carers for children who are unable to be brought up in their families of origin. In these circumstances, when there is much loss and grief, decision-making inevitably involves compromise and the acceptance of second best by families and children. However, the desire that children have for a family life and the wish of adults to provide 'good-enough' parenting for them, helps them to overcome the problems.

REFERENCES

Ainsworth, M.D.S., Blehar, M.C., Waters, E. and Wall, S. (1978) *Patterns of Attachment: A Psychological Study of the Strange Situation*, Hillsdale, NJ: Erlbaum.

Bateson, G. (1973) *Steps to an Ecology of Mind*, St Albans: Paladin.

Boston, M. and Szur, R. (eds) (1983) *Psychotherapy with Severely-Deprived Children*, London: Routledge and Kegan Paul.

Byng-Hall, J., Gorell Barnes, G., Lindsey, C. and Heath, C. (1988) 'Family therapy: work with families in late adoption', in H. Argent (ed.) *Keeping the Doors Open: A Review of Post-Adoption Services*, London: British Agencies for Adoption and Fostering.

Department of Health (1992) *Review of Adoption Law: Report to Ministers of an Inter-Departmental Working Group*, London: HMSO.

Department of Health, Welsh Office, Home Office and Lord Chancellor's Department (1993) *Adoption: The Future*, London: HMSO.

Fitzgerald, J. (1990) *The Hurt and the Healing. A Study of the Therapeutic Communities for Children and Young People Comprising the Charterhouse Group*, Croydon: The Charterhouse Group.

George, V. (1970) *Foster Care: Theory and Practice*, London: Routledge and Kegan Paul.

Gergen, K. (1985) 'The social constructionist movement in modern psychology', *American Psychologist*, **40**, 266–75.

Gill, O. and Jackson, B. (1983) *Adoption and Race: Black, Asian and Mixed Race Children in White Families*, London: Batsford/British Agencies for Adoption and Fostering.

Hodges, J. and Tizard, B. (1989) 'IQ and behavioural adjustment of ex-institutional adolescents: social and family relationships of ex-institutional adolescents', *Journal of Child Psychology and Psychiatry*, **30**, 53–75 and 77–97.

Lindsey, C. (1993) 'Family systems reconstructed in the mind of the therapist', *Human Systems*, **4**, 299–310.

Main, M. (1994) 'Discourse, prediction, and studies in attachment; implications for psychoanalysis', unpublished paper given at the Institute of Psychoanalysis, London.

Maxime, J. (1986) 'Some psychological models of black self-concept', in S. Ahmed, J. Cheetham and J. Small (eds) *Social Work with Black Children and their Families*, London: Batsford/British Agencies for Adoption and Fostering.

Maxime, J. (1987) 'Racial identity – and its value to black children', *Social Work Today*, 15 June, 6.

Parker, R.A. (1966) *Decision in Child Care*, London: George Allen and Unwin.

Pearce, W.B. and Cronen, V.E. (1980) *Communication, Action and Meaning: The Creation of Social Realities*, New York: Praeger.

Rustin, M. (1992) 'The emotional needs of children in care', *Midland Journal of Psychotherapy*, **13**, 2–28.

Stevenson-Hinde, J. (1990) 'Attachment within family systems: an overview', *Infant Mental Health Journal*, **11**, 218–27.

Tizard, B. (1977) *Adoption: A Second Chance*, London: Open Books.

Tizard, B. and Phoenix, A. (1989) 'Black identity and transracial adoption', *New Community*, **15**, 427–37.

Trasler, G. (1960) *In Place of Parents*, London: Routledge and Kegan Paul.

Triseliotis, J.P. and Russell, J. (1984) *Hard to Place – The Outcome of Adoption and Residential Care*, Aldershot: Gower.

von Bertalanffy, L. (1950) 'The theory of open systems in physics and biology', *Science*, **3**, 25–9.

Chapter 17

What constitutes reasonable contact?
Tony Baker

INTRODUCTION

The Children Act 1989 has given us the concept of *reasonable* contact for children who live separately from their parents and whose status is in some way to be decided by a court. This chapter is written as a guide to those who assess and advise, from a position of independence, on the issue of contact for children with parents or other significant people with whom the question of contact has become controversial for some reason.

The determination of what is reasonable in any particular circumstance will be made through considering a number of variables. Factors like the age of the child and their current well-being, the history of their relationships, the permanence of the current care situation and any future plans for change will have a bearing, as will the attitudes and wishes of the child.

The assessment of what is reasonable for a particular child needs to include not only contextual details (like where, when, with whom) but also the frequency and duration of contact. After a long gap, expert advice may include the means by which reintroductions can be made in a way which meets the child's needs. If there is disharmony between the adults who have the care of the child and those seeking contact, the assessment needs to take into account the potential impact of that disharmony on the child.

Special consideration needs to be given to interim contact arrangements while definitive court decisions are awaited. Termination of contact may need to be considered where it is thought likely to be detrimental for the child to sustain contact.

THE CHILDREN ACT 1989

Since the implementation of the Children Act in 1991, the courts are empowered to make contact orders without a specific application in proceedings concerning children. Further, the courts can set conditions about contact which are to ensure that children's needs can be met. The major change of emphasis in this new legislation is that the contact is for the child's benefit rather than a parent's right. If the contact arrangements are not to be specifically defined in court proceedings then the legislation allows for a position of *no order*, which assumes that the various parties to the proceedings are able to make voluntary arrangements for reasonable contact to occur. Courts may still be reluctant to make an order for contact in adoption because the need for an order suggests that contact might be contentious.

The definition of contact is not restricted by direct or face-to-face contact and orders may specifically refer to telephone and letter contact. for instance. Experts who have given an opinion about the future care and therapeutic options for a child will often be asked to give a view about the contact options even if this has not been specifically addressed in their statement to the court.

INDEPENDENT ASSESSMENT

The Children Act gives the court wide powers and discretion in relation to contact in the three situations of divorce, adoption and care proceedings. The role of the expert assessor in advising the legal process is to draw together information based upon a general knowledge of child development, theoretical frameworks that are informed by research and academic understanding and the particular circumstances of the child in question so that an opinion is available which is a synthesis of these components.

It is implicit in this process that the circumstances are not ideal and the court has to find the best compromise option that will meet the child's needs. The management of the aftermath of divorce, adoption and care proceedings is a damage limitation exercise from a child's viewpoint.

When undertaking the assessment it is important to keep in mind the future view of the child as a young adult who will be asking questions retrospectively about the decisions that were made during their childhood. Those questions will be shaped by the young person's knowledge and understanding of their personal history.

It is useful to consider the situation which leads to decisions being made about contact as a disruption in the child's developmental course. The history of that disruption needs to be summarised in conjunction with a description of the quality of relationship that currently exists between the child and the separated parent or other relative, what risks (if any) to the child are inherent in that relationship and a view needs to be formed about those risks and how they can be minimised. The disruption history may also influence the quality of the relationship between the proposed carer for the child and the relative who is seeking contact.

There also needs to be an assessment of the priority that should be given to the contact issue in relation to a child's other needs. The court will be open to a range of options about timing, venue and context, and assessors need to be aware that contact can be reviewed in the light of change and developments and that the expert advice need not be regarded as a final prescription which binds the child and care system in a fixed mode.

GENERAL CONSIDERATIONS

Children thrive when there is a family context which offers them secure attachment, safety and containment (in both physical and emotional terms). Disruption and discontinuity of care jeopardise all three of these elements.

Attachment

Secure attachment is the key to social development. The capacity to form attachments is established and rehearsed in the primary family context and gives children a sense of belonging, connection and relationship which will provide them, ideally, with care, nurture, interest, appropriate stimulation, protection, affection and resources.

Bowlby (1969; 1977) showed that social and emotional development are seriously impaired by repeated disruptions in the attempts of the child to form early attachments. Infants establish a set of attachments to people, to routines and to settings in which attached people are regularly seen by the child. Thus an infant can cope with a pattern of care which is centred in one place but which includes regular care by another person in another setting. The biological parent may not always be synonymous with the psychological parent whom the child regards as the primary conduit of care. As the child grows they increase their knowledge and capacity to understand their situation. They develop a set of expectations and the ways in which these are met will shape their confidence in the world in general and their care system in particular. This forms the basis for the capacity to cope with change and for all children the anxiety that is generated by sudden change may be ameliorated by the pre-existence of secure attachments. Kelly (1984) summarises the work of Bowlby and Robertson and Robertson (1977) and proposes that children grow into secure and functioning adults through bonds of affection or loving relationships which can only be developed and maintained when parent and child have frequent and regular interaction with each other, while the severing and inadequate replacement of these bonds will lead to short-term distress and may lead to long-term psychological damage in the child. Tizard (1979) demonstrated in her study of the later adoption of heavily institutionalised children, that it was possible for children to establish attachment to maternal substitutes outside the 'critical period' described by Bowlby.

Disruption

Bowlby's work on attachment, separation and maternal deprivation can be applied to any situation where a child's continuous relationships are disrupted. Rutter (1981) reviewed the understanding of attachment theory and its implications for children who suffer separations and detachment from primary attachment figures. It is possible to observe that the emotional responses to such separations are rooted in anxiety, guilt, anger and grief. These emotional responses to disruption need managing in the short and long term. They will be modified by the child's capacity to find meaning about their situation and express the feelings that are inevitably generated. Ideally their parents will be available to help in this process but they may be inaccessible to the child because of necessarily protective interventions.

In general terms a child needs information to let them know that, in spite of the disruption, their world can still be safe, they have a place to belong in, even if it is 'just for now'. The information they need includes an idea about who is in charge of them, where they will sleep, what may happen next, why the change has come about and who is responsible. This latter is very important as children will often assume that they have done something to create the disturbance in the first place and that they are to blame. They also need an opportunity to express their own ideas about the disruption.

Older children will be able to develop some appreciation of the losses that arise for them out of this disruption and they will need space to be able to express their own sadness, disappointment or relief.

Safety and containment

Safety and containment are offered to children through the boundaries that are set for them by parent figures. If those parents are themselves out of control or if there are no boundaries set, then the child's world becomes a very unsafe place both physically and emotionally. In these circumstances children have to devote their energy to their survival in an unpredictable and chaotic world because they do not enjoy proper protection. They need their own distress and exuberance to be managed by a parental system that is not overreactive, but rather containing and able to anticipate and effectively prioritise their needs. If the situation is unsafe through external intrusions children will look to their parental system to help them overcome the dangers that truly exist or which they perceive (e.g. dogs that bite, monsters in the dark).

THE ROLE OF CONTACT

Contact can offer children a means of resolving some of the issues highlighted above. It can provide a means of understanding what has and is going to happen, reassuring the child that their belonging is intact, that they have not lost one parent in the divorce process, for instance, that they are not blamed for the disruption, that they are not expected to act as a spy, a messenger, an agent provocateur and above all else that their feelings in the situation can be given some importance.

When disruption leads to permanent change and separation, contact can serve different levels of need. At its most minimal, contact can keep children in touch with their roots in a way that overcomes the feelings of total abandonment by a whole extended family network. For older children, infrequent contact may prove sufficient and even indirect contact through letters and cards may maintain a foundation for renewed contact later when the child develops more autonomy.

Contact can be a way of sustaining a relationship in a context of separate living but it is unlikely to be successful unless it has the support of the current caregivers *and* the separated relative is able to support the existing care arrangements. It will be hampered if there is not some common understanding of the reason for the separation.

Contact may be useful to resolve an emotional issue for a child or young person and such contact could take place as a letter, a telephone call or a visit. Planning and support on both sides is required if the potential benefit is to be maximised. The purpose of such contact is primarily therapeutic and all should be aware that the consequences of such contact can lead to a substantial positive change but they can also be profoundly disappointing.

LITERATURE REVIEW

Research suggests that in situations of divorce and permanent substitute care, children may benefit from contact in some form, especially if it helps their adjustment to the new care arrangements. A key factor in this is the child's understanding of their situation.

In a study of 121 children in foster care for at least a year, Thorpe (1974) compared the well-being and adjustment ratings of the children with their understanding of their placement situation. One of the contributory factors to good understanding was contact with parents. A trend association between good adjustment in foster care and good understanding of the placement situation led to a conclusion that without the opportunity to identify positively with natural parents, some of the children seemed more alone, unsupported and unsure of themselves. Children in her study were less secure when they thought that parental visiting threatened their foster placement and they wished for more security in the placement while maintaining links with their parents.

In a longitudinal study in New York, Fanshel and Shinn (1978) followed the adjustment and development of 624 children who came into public care in 1966. Children who were frequently visited by parents did well on a range of psychological test scores and children in care as long as 5 years were perceived as having greater difficulty coping with foster care. They comment that having two sets of parents in their lives requires considerable adaptation and can be a source of confusion but they thought this may be preferable to total abandonment.

In a study of 200 children Rowe *et al*. (1984) found that a best adjusted group of children were those who were no longer visited by their parents but who were over 5 years old when parental contact ceased. They concluded that conscious memory of natural parents combined with contact opportunities early in the placement gives parents and children the best chance to adapt to a permanent separation, giving a sense of identity and understanding of placement without the confusion of needing to manage two sets of parents.

The parents of children in care are probably the least able and least resourced group and, where they are not given emotional and practical support to maintain visiting, there is a tendency for the contact to end by default. Looking at visiting patterns, Holman (1980) found that when parental contact was maintained, infrequent visiting was more associated with children's emotional and physical difficulties, regular visiting was most beneficial and no contact at all was less problematic than infrequent contact.

Wallerstein and Kelly (1980) considered the question of contact after divorce between children and their non-custodial parent. They describe a need in the children for information about the absent parent and a wish for contact. The intense longing for greater contact persisted over many years, long after the divorce was accepted as a fact of life.

Hetherington (1988) has shown that, even 6 years after divorce, continued involvement with the child by a non-custodial father leads to a better outcome for the child, while Isaacs (1988) concludes that the stability and continuity of contact arrangements are more relevant than their frequency.

Fratter (1991) studied children who were placed in permanent substitute care with continued contact with a birth parent. In this comprehensive study many interdependent issues that might disrupt placement were examined. Age of child at placement, ethnicity and transracial placement, disability or other special needs of the child and attitudes of all key people were compared with success or failure of placements. Being assessed as needing continued contact was not associated with subsequent disruption of the substitute placement and having contact with parents was associated with success of the placement. Being over 9 years of age at placement was more of a contributory factor to disruption of the placement than was maintaining contact with the birth parent. Agencies who recruited adopting parents with a view to open contact did not report greater difficulty in recruitment. Contact appeared to fail because the birth parents found it too difficult to sustain. Preparation and selection of adoptive parents was seen to be especially important, and adoptive parents welcomed the opportunity to meet with birth parents, especially when this took place before placement but after counselling and preparation. Fratter concludes that a child's need for contact does not necessarily conflict with the achievement of permanence and contact can enrich the lives of the children, their adoptive parents and their birth relatives.

This contrasts with the arguments of Goldstein *et al*. (1980) that an individual child's needs for consistency and continuity should be placed above a parent's wishes. They describe a 'psychological parent', as opposed to a 'biological parent'. They argue for continuity so that the child's sense of belonging, attachment and security can be met as fully as possible, without interference or threats of disruption from anyone who is not providing for the child's day-to-day needs.

Solnit (1978) stressed that if parental care is inadequate, agencies must ensure that the *least detrimental* alternative form of care is provided for a child, depending on the child's development.

Bentovim (1980) addressed psychiatric issues for children where consideration was to be given to terminating parental contact. He highlights the potential conflict between the need to identify which form of care offers the 'least detrimental alternative' for the child and the need to ensure that children have access to their biological family. Bentovim suggested that the purpose of contact is to keep alive the idea that the parents are real and could resume the care of the child at a later stage. If contact causes strain or difficulty it should be terminated, especially if ending it is necessary to confirm a new parent figure or to find one. Even when contact is terminated, arrangements should be made to provide children with links to their birth family and their personal history by giving information when younger and even contact when older, so long as this does not compromise the quality of care.

TEMPORARY SEPARATIONS

The implication of temporary separations is that there is a potential for reuniting children with their parents. With young children, under 5 years old, there is a need to sustain some connection that allows the child to experience continued attachment. Goldstein *et al.* (1973) described a child's sense of time in some detail and proposed that emotionally and intellectually an infant or a toddler cannot stretch their waiting more than a few days without feeling overwhelmed by the absence of parents. They considered that for an under five the absence of parents for longer than 2 months is beyond comprehension.

Ideally, such a young child would have a contact routine established so that there would be some sense of order to the contact arrangements. Even young children will benefit from an explanation about the separation and the reason for it. The temporary carers will need to hold for young children the idea that the missing parent still exists and will be available again.

As children mature through latency they can cope with quite long separations from parents so long as they have good information about the current situation and future plans. Children in boarding schools face this situation every term. The Children Act has ensured that children in residential settings can have access to a telephone to maintain links with loved ones.

Children in distress need more reassurance that their attachments are still intact. In enforced separation we can observe children regressing so that their needs in contact become more like those of a much younger child. Information to explain and prepare children is more easily offered to older children and teenagers.

When the separation is traumatic, as may happen in situations of suddenly acrimonious divorce, in abduction, or through sudden physical or mental illness of either the child or a close relative, the child's needs of contact may be desperate, to obtain the information they need which will reassure them about their belonging and the integrity of the family.

INTERIM ORDERS

If there is a prospect of returning infants to parental care, under ideal conditions such young children would have *daily* contact with their parents in which the parents would be involved in the basic care routines of the child. Meetings between parents and temporary carers to discuss the child's needs and ways to meet them within the new care arrangements are a prerequisite for contact at this level. When this contact is to be supervised, or observed for the purpose of writing reports or statements for court proceedings, the contact will need to be discussed carefully so that everyone's expectations are clearly established and the period of the contact does not become a time of dispute between the adults.

When children are over 5 years of age, they may be better able to manage longer periods between contact visits because they are able to hold on to the image of the missing parent(s) for longer. Thus although absent or removed, the parent still retains the operational role of 'psychological parent' and the child can grasp the transitional nature of the interim arrangements. Older children will cope with less frequent contact but under eight years of age this would need to be *direct* contact at least once a week. It needs to be recognised that such children will still need concrete evidence of the absent parent's existence and some manifestation of their continued interest in and love for the child. Children over 8 who may be returning home from care will need contact (if only indirect) at least once a week.

Children will also benefit, in days of uncertainty, by having contact in some form with other relatives, like grandparents, aunts and uncles or even significant family friends. When the removal of older children necessitates placement out of their school and friendship group, the issue of contact with key teaching staff and friends may be crucial because they may have formed their strongest attachments within those relationships if the situation at home was bleak or abusive.

Parents and relatives who are to have contact with children before child protection investigations are complete may need to have preparation before and even supervision during contact, if a judgement is made that there is a risk of contact being abused for their own needs, like protecting secrets. In these circumstances, supervised face-to-face contact is more manageable than telephone contact where there are greater opportunities for unscrupulous relatives to influence children detrimentally.

Parents need to be advised that it is unlikely to be in the interests of a child to undermine the temporary care arrangements, to make promises that cannot be guaranteed, to speak of fighting the authorities even when they, the parents, *know* that the removal has been a terrible error. Whether they like it or not, the child *has* to be where they are placed and it will not help the child if they experience the adults in their world acting or speaking with undue acrimony. Children do not benefit in any way from knowing that they are at the centre of conflict.

PERMANENT SEPARATION

Children who are not to return to the care of either one or both parents will need to establish their belonging and attachments in their new home setting. Younger children may have great difficulty in coping with complex arrangements and in defining their relationships. All children have difficulty in living with uncertainty but all too often they are in limbo awaiting a decision for months.

Children who can hold a memory of the absent parent will probably sustain an attachment to the birth parent if they have had a significant relationship with them. Where there has been a history of physical pain or distress and confusion, the absent parent may be remembered with fear and aversion. The anticipation of contact may present all kinds of dilemmas for a child, and the experience of it can give rise to mixed emotional responses.

Contact for information

The purpose of contact can be simply to keep alive for the child a sense of their roots, a connection to their history. It can serve as confirmation that the birth parent thought about them over the years and keeps open the possibility of re-establishing a relationship of some sort in the future. Contact can keep a child up to date with news of their family of origin. Information about siblings may be as important to update as news of birth parents. Sharing of information need not involve face-to-face contact, and some people find it less distressing to keep contact by means of letters, cards, photographs, school reports, or using an intermediary like a social worker.

Contact to maintain a relationship

This process applies as much to the situation of the child in substitute care as to the child of divorced parents. It is when the separation from a parent makes sense for a child, and when the separated parent can support the child's primary care needs being met in another home than theirs, and when there can be a respectful if not harmonious relationship between resident parents and non-custodial parents, that a child may be enabled to sustain a relationship with a non-custodial parent.

The pattern of contact could include a frequency of monthly visits, or, especially if there are still unresolved allegations about abusive experiences, as little as twice a year. Clearly young children, under 5 years would not be able to manage long gaps between contact visits and maintain a relationship with birth parents as 'mummy' or 'daddy'. Such a situation would be meaningless or confusing for the child. The relationship with the absent birth parent needs to become one of more distant kinship like that of an aunt or uncle while the new parents take on the role of psychological parents.

When the reason for the separation is related to uncontroversial factors, and no fault can be attributed to the natural parents, as might be the case if the birth parents suffer from a disabling condition which severely limits their capacity to act as a primary caregiver, everyone may be better able to accept the placement and contact situation. Children in such a situation would be enabled to understand the care arrangements, would be supported by the birth parents to live with the alternative family and helped to maintain best possible contact with the ailing parents.

This is much less possible when the care order has been vigorously contested, there is hostility to the care plan, there has been discontinuous contact and there is a poor prospect of respectful rapport between the new carers and the birth parents.

Contact may be stressful for children and their needs will be best served by being able to enjoy contact in close proximity to their current carers. If possible, children should be visited in or near their new home and their carers should take an active role in the management of the contact.

The worst scenario is for a young child to be taken on a long journey, by someone who is peripheral to their care routines, to spend exclusive time with a parent they rarely see who is in grief about the loss of this child to the care system. This may be compounded by the parent inviting the child to make expressions of sorrow about the situation, making promises that cannot be kept, asking questions about new carers that the birth parent has not met and finding it possible to be critical about them whatever the child says. Such contact is unlikely to benefit any child.

Contact in adoption

Although the literature reviewed above suggests that openness in adoption may be potentially beneficial for children in permanent substitute care, there are obvious hazards for placement which need to be explored and tested with the adults before involving the children.

It would be a mistake to set rigid expectations of the adoptive family in respect of contact and it needs to be recognised that the child's needs in relation to contact with their birth family may change substantially during childhood. Some children may benefit from the support of their natural parents in making the transition into adoptive care while others may need to concentrate on establishing their attachment in the new family without distraction. An assessment needs to be made of the quality of the child's attachment to the birth parent as well as that parent's capacity to offer the child containment during the changes that are part of the placement process.

Prerequisites for contact in adoption include the following:

1 the birth relative supports the care plan of permanent substitute care (adoption);
2 the birth relative accepts the child will have a new place to call 'home' and new people to call 'mummy' and 'daddy';
3 the birth relative and new parents can establish a respectful and harmonious relationship around the contact issue;
4 there is a common understanding about the reasons for the child not living with the birth family;
5 all parties accept that any contact will take place between the child and birth relatives in the context of the child's new family rather than exclusively with his or her birth relatives.

It may not be possible to establish all the above until some time after placement, especially if the adoption was contested in court. Once an adoption order is made the birth parents lose their parental rights and the adopters are given responsibility for decisions about the welfare of the child. The effect of an adoption order is to extinguish any previous orders affecting the child, but a contact order can still be made after an adoption order.

Contact in divorce

The children of divorced parents do not want to be divorced children unless they have come to regard one or both parents very negatively. Even then, there is often a hope that the parents' situation will change and the children will be able to enjoy their parents again. Parents in divorce may make high demands on their children to meet their own needs because the detachment process invokes its own tensions and anxieties about belonging.

Ideally, children need to be able to sustain good and appropriate relationships with separated parents and they need their custodial parent to support them in maintaining contact. They need the non-custodial parent to accept the primary care arrangements that have been made since the separation.

Where there is a history of conflict, Rutter (1971) and Wallerstein (1991) both concluded that it is the level of conflict between the two parents, both before and after the divorce, that determines the outcome for the child. Young children may show high levels of anxiety around contact (e.g. regression, clinginess, hyperarousal, sleep disturbance, phobic avoidance), while older children may show feelings of undue guilt and responsibility or even anger that is rooted in their feelings of unfairness. Exhibitions of violence may be re-enacted by children. Children may exploit the split between the parents and thereby take power and control in the situation that the parents are failing to manage effectively. The child that is in grief at the loss of a parent may run away to find them or may even act parasuicidally as a way of ensuring that their distress achieves proper attention.

If there are step-parents in either home, the birth parents need to recognise the children's needs to establish respectful and harmonious relationships with step-relatives. This is often a source of major difficulty and Hetherington (1988) describes particular problems of rejection by girls towards their new step-fathers.

Contact arrangements should be made jointly by the adults, or at least after consultation between the adults, before the separated parent makes contact plans with a child. The child may agree to contact with one parent that is later vetoed by the other parent, leaving the child with disappointment and feelings of unfairness. Similarly, when arrangements for contact are not kept, children feel let down. When the experience is repeated a child may feel devalued and betrayed. Trust is eroded by failed promises.

Parents sometimes use contact to obtain information about the separated or divorced ex-partner. They may also give a child a false account of the separation and blame the other parent. Sometimes the vitriol continues to be a dynamic in the contact for years.

In divorce the purpose of the contact is mostly to sustain a relationship between the children and their non-custodial parent. The frequency of the contact needs to reflect this and the child's age and development. Young children (under 5 years) would need to have direct contact at least once a week, with indirect contact by telephone or cards in between visits. In ideal circumstances the other parent will be keeping the separated parent real, through talking, access to photographs and through reference to planned contact. Children need contact routines to be established and if the parents' situation is very volatile the handover arrangements require especial care. With very young children, the direct contact may need to involve close cooperation and if the child is fretful about contact for whatever reason, both parents will need to be present until the routine is established and difficulties overcome. If it seems the parents would be incapable of such a show of goodwill for the sake of their child then it may be that contact has to be suspended until the parents have sorted out their differences.

With older children the contact may well be quite manageable at a weekly frequency or with longer gaps, if necessary. Whatever the circumstances, children will adjust best to arrangements they can understand as offering them continuity of affection and interest.

TERMINATING CONTACT

The Children Act gives statutory primacy to the needs of children. Where contact can be expected to create severe problems for children that may jeopardise their development or cause them to suffer significant harm (physically or emotionally), then the children may need to be protected by an order which terminates their contact with a named person. This would include parents with severe personality disorder who may endanger a child or their carers, parents who are suffering from psychotic illness with dangerous or destabilising delusions, parents who are threatening to a child or who interfere with the child's emotional health and development through falsehood, reckless behaviour or severe abuse of any type.

It may be necessary to suspend contact for a specified period, for instance, during a criminal investigation, where a child is a potential witness in a prospective prosecution, or, where the child is engaged in a developmental or therapeutic process which may be negated by premature or inappropriate contact.

Contact issues are secondary to the principal issue of placement and if contact threatens the viability of the child's placement then, so long as the placement offers the least detrimental alternative, the contact should be terminated notwithstanding the child's expressed wishes. It is to be hoped that the child will be able to accept the reasons for such an order and may need help to do so.

In the divorce context, contact will most commonly be terminated when the child is likely to be exposed to conflict of loyalty and extreme hostility between parents. If there is a history of violence or instability to an extent that the custodial parent lives in fear of the other then the prospect of contact may create such high levels of anxiety and aversion that the child's interests may be served by an order which severs contact.

Where there is a history of abuse and neglect and the child is still suffering the effects of that trauma, it may be that the child's recovery would be compromised by restoring contact prematurely, if at all. An example of this would arise if a child identifies so strongly with the sexual abuse scenario that they are keen to sexualise all their relationships and physical contacts. Until such drives in the child are minimised, suspension or termination of contact for the foreseeable future may be the most appropriate step.

Children may apply in their own right for an order to restrict or terminate contact with a named person.

CONCLUSIONS

There is a body of evidence to suggest that separated children may benefit from contact with members of their family of origin. To maximise that benefit, children need a good understanding of the reason for the separation and the current care arrangements. The notion of a clean break for children who are placed for adoption is being superseded by the possibility of open adoption. Even where this seems to be a viable option within the care plan, the priority needs to be focused on ensuring that the placement is secure and the child can enjoy all the benefits of continuous attachments.

The Children Act emphasises that contact is to meet the child's needs rather than fulfil any other person's rights. Contact orders can be made by a court which is making provision for children in situations of divorce, adoption and care proceedings. The courts have wide and flexible powers in all those situations and expert witnesses will have a most important part to play in advising the courts and any other statutory authority about the ways in which children's needs for stability and attachment can be met either through specific contact arrangements or through restrictions. The use of the notion of *reasonable* contact leads to the need for interpretation of that reasonableness in the light of all the circumstances. Some of the greatest difficulties arise when siblings who live apart have conflicting needs and opposite wishes about contact with each other.

Contact can serve a variety of functions for a child (to provide information, to sustain contact with roots, to resolve an emotional difficulty, to maintain a sense of relationship or family, etc.) and arrangements may need to be both flexible and creative if those various needs are to be met through contact, whether direct or indirect. An example of this would be the use of a proxy to undertake the contact on behalf of the child when there are tensions that the child needs to be resolved through the mediation of a go-between. The use of audio- and video-recording can also assist greatly in overcoming problems especially as part of a process of reintroduction to contact after a long gap or for other therapeutic purposes.

Experts will be aware of the need to review contact arrangements. A recommendation can only be linked to the foreseeable future unless there are clear and compelling reasons to advise termination for all time.

REFERENCES

Bentovim, A. (1980) 'Psychiatric issues', in M. Adcock and R. White (eds) *Terminating Parental Contact*, London: Association of British Adoption and Fostering Agencies.

Bowlby, J. (1969) *Attachment and Loss. Vol. 1: Attachment*, London: Hogarth.

Bowlby, J. (1977) 'The making and breaking of affectional bonds' *British Journal of Psychiatry*, **130**, 201–10 and 421–31.

Fanshel, D. and Shinn, E.B. (1978) *Children in Foster Care*, New York: Columbia University Press.

Fratter, J. (1991) 'Towards more openness in adoption: the perspective of 22 voluntary agencies', in J. Fratter, J. Rowe, D. Sapsford and J. Thoburn (eds) *Permanent Family Placement*, London: British Agencies for Adoption and Fostering.

Goldstein, J., Freud, A. and Solnit, A.J. (1973) *Beyond the Best Interests of the Child*, London: Collier Macmillan.

Goldstein, J., Freud, A. and Solnit, A.J. (1980) *Before the Best Interests of the Child*, London: Burnett Deutsch.

Hetherington, E.M. (1988) 'Parents, children and siblings: six years after divorce', in R.A. Hinde and J. Stevenson-Hinde (eds) *Relationships within Families: Mutual Influences*, Oxford: Clarendon Press.

Holman, R. (1980) 'Exclusive and inclusive concepts of fostering', in J Triseliotis (ed.) *New Developments in Foster Care and Adoption*, London: Routledge and Kegan Paul.

Isaacs, M. (1988) 'The visitation schedule and child adjustment: a three year study', *Family Process*, **27**, 251–6.

Kelly, G. (1984) 'Natural parent contact – a theory in search of practice', in *Permanent Substitute Families, Security or Severance?*, London: Family Rights Group.

Robertson, J. and Robertson, J. (1977) 'The psychological parent', *Adoption and Fostering*, **87**, 19–22.

Rowe, J., Cain, H., Hundleby, M. and Keane, A. (1984) *Long Term Foster Care*, London: Batsford/British Agencies for Adoption and Fostering.

Rutter, M. (1971) 'Parent-child separation: psychological effects on the children', *Journal of Child Psychology and Psychiatry*, **12**, 233–60.

Rutter, M. (1981) *Maternal Deprivation Reassessed*, 2nd edn, Harmondsworth: Penguin.

Solnit, A.J. (1978) 'The rights of a child in a changing society', *Child Abuse and Neglect*, **2**, 193–201.

Thorpe, R. (1974) 'The Social and Psychological Situation of the Long Term Foster Child with Regard to his Natural Parents', unpublished PhD Thesis, University of Nottingham.

Tizard, B. (1979) 'Adopting older children from institutions', *Child Abuse and Neglect*, **3**, 535–8.

Wallerstein, J.S. (1991) 'The long term effects of divorce on children: a review', *Journal of the American Academy of Child and Adolescent Psychiatry*, **30**, 349–60.

Wallerstein, J.S. and Kelly, J.B. (1980) *Surviving the Breakup*, New York: Grant McIntyre.

White, R., Carr, P. and Lowe, N. (1990) *A Guide to The Children Act 1989*, London: Butterworths.

Part IV

Conclusions

Chapter 18

Balanced opinions
Clare Lucey and Peter Reder

Presenting an expert opinion in court is the last stage in a pathway from instruction, through assessment, to reporting and it is, in a sense, a distillation of all the work that has gone before. The preceding chapters have considered how the task of assessment can be approached. This final chapter will emphasise the need for a balanced approach, in which positive aspects of care and family life are considered alongside the problems that have been identified. We shall draw together some of the principal issues that our contributors have raised and highlight their main conclusions. We shall then discuss a number of pitfalls in undertaking parenting assessments for courts and suggest practical ways to avoid them. We shall look at the principles behind writing court reports and propose a structure for them. Finally, we shall offer some guidelines on presenting assessments and opinions in court.

The chapters for this book were written during 1994 – 'The International Year of the Family' – a time when issues about family life were placed under the microscope, with considerable social anxiety about the future of the family and political interest in the roles and responsibilities of parents. New legislation, especially the Children Act, the creation of the Child Support Agency and proposed modifications to adoption law, have further focused attention on the parent–child relationship and the place of professional interventions into family functioning. Professional practices, in turn, are being revolutionised by fundamental changes in the organisation of health, education, social and legal services.

The prevailing social attitude towards family life is one of tension between fragmentary processes (with ever greater numbers of divorced or single parents, homeless people and reports of child abuse) and integrative ones (with greater attention paid to marital and parental responsibilities). Of necessity, this book has focused on problems of child maltreatment and parenting breakdown and may have conveyed an unfavourable impression of family life. This needs to be balanced by a recognition that the vast majority of families provide loving and nurturing child care, enabling children to grow up healthily, with a positive attitude to themselves and to other people. Parenting, far from being a demanding and unpleasant responsibility, is usually experienced as a rewarding and worthwhile role. Even for those families who fail to meet their children's needs, the child care problems can be temporary and reversed with help. Therefore, assessments of parenting play a valuable part in identifying problems that have occurred and considering how to help parents and children resolve them and recover from their effects. In circumstances where children and parents can no longer live together, parenting assessments are able to clarify that this transition has been reached and suggest how to help parents and children move on in their lives.

Contributors to this book have reflected a more optimistic approach to parenting problems in a number of ways. They have emphasised addressing the family's potential to change and trying to help parents improve their parenting skills and their relationship with the child. Separation is only considered as a last resort. A sensitive approach to the families is also described, in which their discomfort at being assessed is acknowledged. In addition, particular characteristics and experiences – such as race, class, intellectual abilities, immigration or racism – are respected.

There has been considerable interest recently in attitudes to race and culture, some of which has helped professionals appreciate the variations in roles and attitudes between families from different cultural and social backgrounds. However, other contributions to the debate have been so dogmatic and confrontational that they have harmed, rather than enhanced, interprofessional and family–professional relationships. In parenting assessments, we believe that issues of race and culture need to be placed alongside all other aspects of the family's life and not made the highest order context which overrides every other consideration.

INTEGRATION

In order to be able to assess parenting breakdown and offer an opinion about prognosis, professionals must have a theoretical framework. The framework gives them a structure within which to understand problems and organise the available information. Although a variety of frameworks have been presented and are used to assess specific aspects of the parenting relationship, they have much in common with each other. For instance, all our contributors conceptualise parenting behaviour as the manifestation of a relationship, which is sensitive to processes at intrapsychic, interpersonal and social/cultural levels. Hence, assessors should be able to observe, understand and integrate factors from all three levels. For example, the availability of family and social support for parents with learning disability or psychiatric problems will make a significant difference to their capacity to care for their children. The context of the parent–child relationship is also considered crucial, as is the developmental dimension.

Bowlby's work has clearly been very influential on those undertaking parenting assessments. Attachment Theory points to a crucial dynamic which, if significantly impaired, has serious effects on a child's development and welfare. It also helps guide opinions about children's placements or contact with parents. In addition, Bowlby's conviction that children report actual, as opposed to imagined, experiences has been validated by clinicians and researchers and must be given due importance during assessment.

Winnicott's (1960) often quoted phrase 'the good-enough mother' is a reminder that parenting does not have to be perfect in order to facilitate satisfactory care, protection and development of children. Assessment of whether parenting has been good enough must address both the behaviour of the parents and its impact on the child. The effect of any maltreatment on the child's development is particularly relevant and the concept of developmental pathways allows the child's experiences to be described and any harm identified. The 'significance' of that harm can be weighed up by considering the degree of deviation from the expected norm along one pathway and the cumulative interaction of a number of pathway deviations. In order to do justice to this essential component of the assessment, professionals must see and talk with children, sometimes at length, in order to ascertain their thoughts, feelings and developmental attainments.

The concept of 'significant harm' is a crucial one, even though difficult to define, because it encourages assessors to focus on the child's experiences of the parenting they have received. It suggests that parenting is an issue of quality and quantity and parenting breakdown results from the child encountering traumatic experiences that are too many and too severe. The preceding chapters indicate that every case of significant harm to a child has, lurking in its shadows, a major element of emotional abuse. This is a pervasive and extremely damaging form of maltreatment and is all the more important to try and assess because it leaves fewer visible clues and the child cannot volunteer that they are being emotionally abused. These problems of recognition are accompanied by problems of definition, but it is evident that professionals should strive to convey to courts information about emotional abuse that the child has suffered.

Few quantifiable tests of parenting are available and, for the most part, assessors rely on unstructured or semi-structured interviews that are based upon the techniques they use when conducting therapy. They meet parents and children individually and together over a series of sessions. It is evident that reliance by some agencies on single 'disclosure' interviews with children to assess allegations of maltreatment is quite inadequate. Since the welfare of the child is at stake, assessments need to be detailed and also reflect a pace that is comfortable for the child.

All of the structures presented in the previous chapters include whether the parents could benefit from therapeutic interventions and become good enough. There is an acknowledgement that one-off 'snap-shot' appraisals may not do justice to a parent's potential to change. Therefore, balanced assessments need to include consideration of whether the parent(s) could be helped to improve their parenting. The help might include focus on parenting skills or on personal conflicts and the consensus seems to be that both need to be addressed.

It is not always possible to form a view about the degree of improvement that is likely in time for a first scheduled court hearing and protracted assessments may be necessary, so long as the child's safety continues to be monitored and the delay in deciding about placement does not compromise the child's development. A critical factor in deciding whether parents might benefit from therapy is whether they accept responsibility for their behaviour or show the likelihood of being able to do so as treatment progresses.

A number of the assessment procedures discussed here have been inter- ventive in the sense that assessments are compared from before, during and after a programme of treatment. The Parent–Child Game of Sue Jenner and Gerard McCarthy, Gerrilyn Smith's framework for assessing a non-abusing parent's capacity to protect, Danya Glaser's approach to cases of emotional abuse and the prolonged psychodynamic assessments of Geraldine Fitzpatrick are all interventive assessments. One important aspect of such procedures is that the context of the work needs to be kept in mind by the therapist(s) and made clear to the family and referrer. The special nature of parenting assessments means that the customary clinical discipline of clarifying when work in the domain of assessment has moved on to work in the domain of treatment does not always operate. At times, families will be both receiving treatment and being assessed. Nonetheless, we would strongly endorse the practices described here that the families must be made aware at the outset that the work is taking place within the domain of assessment and that their response to therapy will be evaluated and reported back to the court (or statutory agency). The experience of other treatment programmes where this distinction is not made clear is that the families sometimes feel confused or even misled. Furthermore, treatment in itself is not protective, and it is important that child protection agencies remain vigilant and continue their monitoring during any interventive assessments.

A consistent theme runs through the chapters on special parenting circum- stances. It is that specific diagnoses or attributes of parents – whether of psychiatric disorder, learning disability or homosexuality – are much less relevant than their interpersonal behaviour and observable parenting skills. Concerns that such parents might not be able to care adequately for their children have largely been based on uninformed prejudice. Hence, the psychological and relationship components of parenting need to be evaluated in all cases, whatever the parental characteristics.

Of course, this book has not been able to address every type of parenting circumstance, but the message is essentially the same in other areas. One example is children raised by single parents. Despite recent comments by politicians, there is little evidence that single-parent status in itself is prejudicial to adequate child care. Even though some studies have suggested an increase in physical abuse and neglect in single-parent families (Sack *et al.* 1985; Gelles 1989), it is the nature of the relationships leading to, and surrounding, the particular family structure that is more relevant to outcome for the child than any psychological factors inherent in single parenthood, whether of single fathers or single mothers (Hanson 1986; Burghes 1994). Schaffer (1990) also concludes from the limited research available that the gender of the parent wishing to care for a child is immaterial and their individual circumstances should be the main concern.

Questions are also raised about the capacity of teenagers to care adequately for children. The results of investigations into maternal age have proved inconsistent. Connelly and Straus (1992) found that the younger the mother at the time of the birth of the child, the greater the risk of child abuse. However, Haskett *et al.* (1994) conclude from their literature review and study that teenage parenthood *per se* does not increase the risk of child maltreatment. Teenage mothers do tend to show rigidity in their parenting attitudes, to have limited understanding of children's developmental capabilities and to favour physical forms of punishment, but there is wide individual variability. The authors recommend assessing each case in its own right, taking into account whether support is available within the nuclear family and the degree to which the teenager accepts the pregnancy.

The parenting circumstances of greater concern are misuse of drugs and alcohol, which are associated with increased risk of all forms of abuse and to have a poorer prognosis for rehabilitation. In addition, psychotic parents who withdraw from treatment and include their children in their delusional ideation pose a significant risk to them, as do a number of parents with severe somatising disorders.

Many of the preceding chapters contain guidelines for prognosis in child abuse and parenting breakdown. These can be combined with the conclusions of other authors, such as Server and Janzen (1982), Dale *et al.* (1986), Elton (1988), Faller (1988), Jones (1991) and Bentovim (1992), to provide indicators of poor outcome. There appears to be agreement that rehabilitation of child and parent(s) is contraindicated when:

- the parent(s) deny that abuse has occurred, do not accept responsibility for their behaviour and/or blame others, such as the child or professionals;
- caretaking problems are not acknowledged;
- the child's needs remain unrecognised;
- there is a pervasive lack of empathy for the child;
- the meaning of the child for the parents continues to dominate their relationship;
- there is no willingness to make use of therapeutic input or to cooperate with professionals;
- the abuse was severe and prolonged and especially involved extreme

psychological abuse or neglect, premeditated sadistic physical abuse or penetrative sexual abuse;
• the parents' relationship includes severe disharmony, dependency and/or persistent substance (including alcohol) abuse;
• the parent's psychotic delusions involve the child.

On a lower order of concern, factors that Asen (personal communication) has found to be associated with a doubtful prognosis include: a child who has lasting injuries, developmental delay or disturbance of attachment; parents with a poor prognosis psychiatric disorder, unrealistic expectations of the child, poor impulse control, evidence of rejecting or critical behaviour or denial of past abuse; families with generations of abuse or social isolation; and lack of resources in relevant professional agencies. Elton (1988) would add to this list: inconsistent or dubious acceptance of personal responsibility; non-acceptance by both parents that they share responsibility; limited potential for change; and unreliable or ambivalent relationships with professionals.

Even though these are consistent inferences from research and clinical experience, caution must be exercised in translating from the general to the particular. High-risk checklists can be very misleading. Each case needs to be considered in its own right and assessment made of the unique character-istics of the parenting behaviour and the parent–child relationship. The final opinion can then be informed and guided by the findings of research and experience.

In a few cases, a single recommendation emerges as the assessment proceeds. For example, it may quickly become apparent that a number of very poor prognostic factors are present, or that a prolonged therapeutic assess-ment is necessary. However, in the majority of court cases referred to mental health professionals, the recommendations depend on a fine balancing of positive and negative aspects of the parents' caretaking abilities. Examples include: parents who look after their children adequately between episodes of maltreatment; children who have clearly experienced emotional abuse, but have also developed a positive attachment to that parent; or a separated couple who are in the midst of a contact or residency dispute and bitterly accuse each other of inadequate parenting, which professionals are unable to confirm or refute.

We believe that it is only possible for assessors to form an opinion in such marginal cases after a lengthy and detailed internal debate, weighing up all the available information, the various inferences that can be drawn, the options that are available and the compromises that might be necessary. This process takes time and experience, but can be assisted by discussion with others, such as the guardian *ad litem* or a colleague.

The final recommendation is guided by a number of premises and priorities. First and foremost is the aim to maintain children within their natural families whenever possible and the assessor must weigh up the advantages and disadvantages of the child moving into the care system or remaining with the natural parents. A general principle is that therapeutic interventions should be offered whenever appropriate, to be followed by reassessment, before the court makes a final decision. However, of higher priority in the balancing process is that children's needs outweigh parental needs, even if the recommendation is likely to criticise and upset parents or make them feel like 'losers'. For instance, young children may be at a critical stage in their emotional development and, even though the parents show a long-term potential to change through treatment, the children's time scale must override that of the parents. Other important considerations in giving priority to children's needs are: the possible effects of a number of moves, including separation followed by rehabilitation, especially in the context of their age and attachments; the likely consequences of having contact with parents who maintain their battle with each other through the child; and the children's own opinions, since the older they are, the more they are capable of giving coherent views about their future and acting in ways that will determine that success or failure of any placement.

Despite our belief that 'significant harm' is a legal term and not a mental health one, it does help focus assessors' minds on the effects of parenting *from the child's perspective*, so that their opinions will be influenced by the degree of interference to the child's development that has already occurred, or may do so in the future, and the parent's capacity to meet the child's needs.

Of the factors we have included in our framework for assessment in Chapter 1, we give high priority to: the parent's willingness to acknowledge responsibility for their abusing behaviour; their capacity to put the child's needs first; their ability to protect the child from future maltreatment; and their attitude towards working cooperatively with professionals. If parents deny having physically abused their child, then the mental health professional's opinion depends on the strength of the medical evidence. In contact disputes, the child's general response to being in the presence of the alternative parents and the rapport between each parent and child is an important guide. If parents do not believe that any therapeutic help is needed, the histories of their relationships in general, and of child care in particular, are reasonable predictors of future behaviour.

For ourselves, if these premises still leave us undecided, we rely on the nature of the child's significant attachments. Secure-enough attachments promote considerable emotional resilience in children and enable them to withstand many adverse parenting experiences.

This balancing process can be reflected in the final report by describing the strengths and weaknesses of the various parties and then framing the opinion in terms of: if [this] occurs, then the consequences are more likely to be [that]. Courts usually appreciate reports in which the recommendations include a summary of the alternative decisions available to them and the pros and cons of each one.

There will be some cases in which, despite all attempts to improve the parent–child relationship, the recommendation is that the child should live with alternative caretakers. Even when children are permanently separated from their natural parents, they will probably continue to have some contact with them. As with other aspects of parenting assessments, decisions about the nature and frequency of contact need to be made from the child's perspective and to consider what benefit the child will derive from it. In the event of permanent separation, we were very struck by Ann Gath's comments that implementing the decision need not be punitive to the parents concerned and can even be therapeutic, allowing child and parents to make the transition into new phases of their lives.

PREPARING COURT REPORTS

The mass of background information, clinical observation and theoretical ideas generated by the assessment must next be organised into a balanced opinion that is understandable to family members and their legal representatives. Above all, reports must be able to inform judges and help them reach their decision. From the perspective of the judge, the report should succinctly describe the psychological functioning of the parents and children, clearly elucidate the issues relevant to the hearing, argue the advantages and disadvantages of decisions available to the court and be courageous enough to take a stance and offer a recommendation. The judge must arrive at a conclusion and will particularly value solution-oriented reports. Assessors should therefore attempt to suggest possible solutions to the dilemmas they have been asked to address, however difficult this may be.

AVOIDING PITFALLS

Each phase of the assessment–report–evidence sequence has potential pitfalls and we would like to suggest ways of approaching each stage so as to anticipate and manage the difficulties (see also Carson 1985; Grounds 1985; Gardner 1989; Cooke 1990; King and Trowell 1992; Sturge 1992).

Receiving the referral

Initial enquiries to professionals asking for expert assessments usually come by telephone from solicitors, local authorities, guardians *ad litem*, legal representatives or the Official Solicitor, who follow them up with a formal letter. They often convey a time pressure and urge the professional to complete the report well in advance of a preset court date. It is advisable not to agree to a hurried timetable, but to estimate the likely number of meetings required and state the date by which a properly considered report could be ready. That estimate will be guided by an initial picture of what the case is about, including the nature of the particular dilemmas, who is seeking what response and the stance that each party is adopting. Mental health professionals will need to clarify what has initiated court action now and who is hoping to be supported by the expert opinion. It is also useful to know what other reports have been prepared and ensure there is freedom to read them and speak to other involved professionals. Such questions to the referrer allow the undercurrents operating in the case to be identified, confirm the expert's independence from them and establish the ground rules for participation.

At the referral stage, professionals invited to offer an expert opinion should establish that: they will form an independent opinion, which may not necessarily favour the party requesting it; they will represent the child's interests; and the report will be made available to the court and all other parties, whatever the final opinion. The level of the court, the date of the relevant court hearing, the time scale agreed for the assessment and reporting and who will be responsible for paying the professional's fees should all be made clear.

The initial inquiry should be followed up by a formal letter of instruction which outlines the case details and summarises the legal process so far. The letter should clearly state what issues the professional has been asked to address and confirm the other details discussed over the telephone. Often, the instructing letter comes accompanied by a bundle of paper evidence. It is best to ask the instructing solicitor to label and type an index of the papers supplied, since it avoids a tedious task later on when writing the report and ensures that the documents are identified correctly. The referrer should also enclose a copy of any order from the court requesting the mental health assessment and report.

Conducting the clinical assessment

It is helpful at the outset to draw up a plan of the assessment components in order to guide who is seen, how often, where and when. Clearly, this should only act as a preliminary guide, since the assessment needs to be moulded to the nuances of the case as they emerge. We have already discussed in Chapter 1 the value of meeting the social worker currently involved in the case in order to draw up a genogram of the family and a chronology of relevant events.

Letters of invitation to the various family members should be neutral in tone, since they are liable to be scrutinised for evidence of bias. One of us made the mistake of using headed note paper shared with the local authority and it became a major task convincing the parents, who were in dispute with that authority, of the independence of the psychiatric assessment. It is useful for mental health professionals to introduce the first meeting with each family member by explaining their role, the meaning of their independence, their use of audio or audio-visual equipment, note taking and the limits of confidentiality.

All interviewers should employ similar listening skills, remain just as sensitive to anxieties and exhibit the same respect as in therapeutic activities. However, most professionals take notes during the interviews. This can be especially helpful to record verbatim quotes and to ensure that dates and other details are remembered accurately. These notes should be written in such a way that they could be made available to the parties if requested. The case file should keep together the instructing letter and all other correspondence, documents and assessment notes, including a record of cancelled, failed or rescheduled appointments or late attendances. They should be arranged in the order that most easily enables the professional to turn to them when in the witness box. Tabulating the documents with sticky labels can also help. Experience has also taught us that it is useful to place a sheet listing the chronology of events in the family's history at the top of the pile.

At the end of the assessment phase, effort should be made to discuss the main conclusions with relevant parties. However, the opinion should not be made open to debate, since that is the purpose of the court hearing.

Writing the report

Guiding principles for report writing are that they should clearly communicate their message and be a balanced distillation of clinical observations and hypotheses generated by the assessment. The issues in court cases are rarely unequivocal and extreme views or absolute assertions are unlikely to be helpful to the child or the court. Opinions that go beyond the professional's area of expertise are also liable to be exposed during the court hearing. The language should be understandable by non-mental health professionals and free of jargon. The report should address the issues specified in the instructing letter and conclude with an opinion, together with the reasons for reaching it. Brevity (such as ten to fifteen A4 pages) is preferable to long, undigested, verbatim accounts of each interview.

Bowden (1990), Black *et al.* (1992) and Tufnell (1993) have described somewhat similar structures for court reports with only minor variations between them. There is no correct way to write a report and there are as many different examples as experts. However, most reports will contain the following elements.

1 An *introduction*, including an indication of who is requesting the report and the issues addressed.
2 A statement of the author's *qualifications*, including name, professional address, title, degrees, membership of professional bodies, general and specialist expertise and summary of relevant interests or publications (it is advisable not to be overly bashful since, in court, counsel may well attempt to challenge the professional's authority as an expert).
3 A list of the filed *documentation* that has been read as background to the

assessment, including all titles, authors and dates (either listed early on in the report or as an appendix at the end).

4 Details of the *interviews* arranged, including who was seen, when, where and for how long, as well as unkept appointments.

5 A brief synopsis of the *current situation* and how these proceedings have arisen.

6 The principal *issues* that have been addressed in the assessment.

7 A *summary of the interviews*, in which the key features of the meetings with each person are collated and condensed, using verbatim quotes and observations of behaviour (rather than vague generalisations) to illustrate specific points.

8 The assessor's *impression* of the background information and interviews, based on clinical experience and theoretical principles.

9 An *opinion*, oriented towards each of the questions posed, illustrated by brief reference to the assessment material where relevant and presenting an understanding of how the present dilemmas arose and any predictions that can reasonably be made.

10 *Recommendations*, which address the options available to the court and include a balanced consideration of their advantages and disadvantages.

Most courts appreciate reports that have numbered paragraphs, since this makes it easier to turn to them during the hearing. Once the draft report is prepared, it should be checked for accuracy of information, spelling and grammar, typed, dated and signed.

A useful exercise at this stage is to imagine oneself in the position of each of the parties' legal representatives and argue the case from their perspective. The report can be dissected in order to bring out the aspects that might support one side or the other, in just the same way that barristers do when preparing for the court hearing itself. This 'advanced warning' will enable professionals to prepare responses to likely cross-examination questions and also ensure that they have, indeed, thought through their recommendations impartially.

Then, the original good copy of the report should be sent to the referrer, with copies retained for the case file, and a statement of fees should be submitted at this point. This will include time spent reading the background documents, conducting the interviews, reviewing audio-visual tapes, researching the literature, writing the report and then having it typed.

Sometimes, new information becomes available after the report is completed. If it materially alters the original opinion, a supplementary report can be supplied, justifying any change of mind.

Going to court

Going to court is the final, public presentation of the professional's opinion, where it becomes open to critical scrutiny. For many, it is an experience which provokes high anxiety, since the courtroom appears to have much in common with the gladiatorial arena. It is explicitly adversarial, with each side striving to win the contest. Witnesses can be likened to foot soldiers in the gladiatorial army, who may be subtly encouraged, or aggressively coerced, to declare allegiance to one side or another.

Seemingly small points can help reduce courtroom anxiety. These include knowing the date, time and location of the hearing, discovering how long it will take to find the court, leaving in plenty of time so as to arrive unflustered, arranging where and when to meet the instructing solicitor and knowing how to address the judge (or magistrate). The wearing of sober professional dress is strongly advised.

Only at this last stage does one meet the barrister who will introduce the report to the judge through examination-in-chief. The barrister will initiate a conversation in the corridor, which, on the surface, is a pleasant chat. However, it is not and the barrister is running through the case, checking issues, clarifying points and, importantly, probing those areas of the report which might undermine their chosen strategy or that appear ripe for cross-examination. It is useful to make a note of the topics raised by the barrister, since the slow pace of court hearings gives witnesses time to prepare answers to similar questions in cross-examination.

Preliminary negotiations in the corridor are a regular feature of court hearings in which opposing parties test out whether a compromise can be reached. The late morning start time for formal proceedings is intended to facilitate this last minute attempt to introduce consensus into an otherwise adversarial system. Different ideas, alternative interpretations, modifications to the opinion, compromise solutions and revised plans will be suggested and it may seem best to concede. However, in view of the hours of thought that have gone into the original opinion, it should not be changed lightly and a new one agreed in haste for the sake of appearing helpful. Views should only be altered if the new information is valid and of significance and not because a barrister is persuasive. Hence, witnesses should be cautious about discussing the case with the other side's lawyer and it is preferable to communicate through one's barrister.

Once inside the courtroom, the proceedings may be conducted in a formal manner or in a more informal atmosphere, depending on the level of the court. Irrespective of the degree of formality, mental health professionals will feel in strange and unfamiliar territory, where the rules are rarely made explicit. It is wise to allow one's legal team to take the lead and the witness should sit where indicated, remain silent unless addressed and adopt a serious demeanour throughout the hearing. When called to the witness box, witnesses should (attempt to) walk in an assured manner and stand with their body turned towards the judge, not the row of barristers. This helps avoid becoming embroiled in an emotive exchange with cross-examining counsel and continuously reminds professionals that their task is to inform the judge. It also allows witnesses to watch the speed at which the judge is making notes and modify accordingly the pace of their delivery. The usher will enquire whether the witness wishes to swear an oath on the bible (or other religious text), or else affirm, and will then pass over the card containing the appropriate words. Swearing in or affirming can be treated as a rehearsal for speaking slowly and clearly – to the judge.

Evidence-in-chief begins with their barrister asking the witness to identify themselves and state their professional qualifications and place of work. The barrister then guides the witness through the report and this is the opportunity to present one's considered views to the judge, speaking clearly, concisely and with the minimum of jargon. It is best only to answer what has been asked, unless it becomes apparent that the barrister has not properly understood the main issues that need to be extracted from the report.

Then comes cross-examination by the other side's barrister, who will go through the case again but with different foci. They will attempt to demonstrate flaws in technique, bias in understanding, prejudice in opinion and inappropriateness of recommendation. They will urge the professional to adopt a different view of the case than the one presented to the judge so far.

Reder *et al.* (1993) have identified a number of processes to which witnesses are subjected when being cross-examined. Their central thesis is that professionals draw certain meanings from the information generated during the assessment and they attend hearings intent on conveying this meaning to the court. However, cross-examining barristers are aware that opposite, yet equally valid, meanings can be construed from the same set of information. After all, a bottle can reasonably be described as either half-full or half-empty. Meanings can be changed in a variety of ways and, in order to turn a witness's opinion to the advantage of their client, cross-examining barristers use strategies of *discrediting, controlling the range of information, changing meanings* and *introducing logical fallacies.*

Discrediting

Since the significance attributed to the content of a message depends on the presumed reliability of the messenger, opinions can be challenged by implying that the professional is not such an expert as is claimed, or has used a flawed clinical technique. For example, opinions may be quoted from an alleged greater expert or from publications in the literature, or inappropriately leading questions pointed out in video-taped interviews. All this may be reinforced by a denigrating tone of voice or disparaging body language.

Controlling the range of information

A common ploy is to invite witnesses to alter their opinions because of a hitherto unavailable piece of information. Alternatively, barristers may propose that the hearing should restrict the information considered to a particular issue or period of time in the history of the case. Either way, the coherent sense that the assessor has made of the mass of information is in danger of being disrupted.

Changing meanings

Overall meanings can be transformed by the careful selection of different words to describe events, or by posing alternative, and eminently plausible, explanations for them. Thus, a mother with a severe mental illness was repeatedly referred to by her barrister as 'a troubled woman with ups and downs'. The trademark of cross-examination is when an issue is broken down into its component parts and a series of closed questions posed to which only 'yes' or 'no' answers seem possible. This technique often opens with a seemingly innocuous premise to which witnesses are invited to ally themselves, continues with an apparently acceptable interpretation for each component part of the events and ends with the witness helplessly committed to the opposite point of view.

Logical fallacies

Barristers may decide to ask questions that confuse the general with the particular, or vice versa. A premise may be suggested to the witness, which, once accepted, becomes the context for understanding all that follows – such as, surely all children are aggressive and therefore nothing can be inferred from this particular child's behaviour. Alternatively, barristers may unreasonably suggest that one specific description stands for all attributes of that person: for example, since the child is now asymptomatic, she could not possibly be suffering from any ill-effects of the parenting she has received.

Once witnesses are aware of these various strategies used by barristers, they can rehearse techniques to counter them. Reder *et al.* (1993) propose a number of possible responses, with the general principle being that witnesses should regard cross-examination questions as invitations to restate the meaning that they originally intended. It is similar to a *viva voce* examination technique in which candidates are able to demonstrate their knowledge by elaborating on each issue that they have included in their answer. Thus, in court, suggestions that a new piece of information might transform the witness's opinion can be countered by reaffirming the more pertinent information that has formed the basis of the assessment. Again, witnesses might reply that certain explanations proposed in the question '. . .do not adequately convey what I intend and in my assessment I found that. . ., from which I have concluded that. . . '.

In our view, the witness box is not the place to alter a considered and reasoned opinion. Preparatory work at the report stage should have addressed the possible alternative explanations and weighed up their validity in order to reach a balanced opinion. Nonetheless, if, during cross-examination, the barrister makes a point with which one agrees, it is reasonable to say so. Areas of weakness in the assessment should also be conceded, where appropriate, and acknowledgement made of marginal issues. Witnesses must ensure that their message is available to the court and that it stands up to argument. Judges welcome opinions which accept that a particular explanation may be possible, but state whether it is more or less likely.

At the end of cross-examination, the judge may decide to ask some questions before offering thanks and letting the witness stand down. That is not the end of the matter, however. Occasionally, experts are called back to advise the judge further: but, in all instances, the witness will leave the courtroom in a state of emotional tension and hyper-alertness brought on by the cross-examination. It takes time to wind down and it can be extremely helpful to talk over the experience with a colleague afterwards.

CONCLUSIONS

Parenting assessments require considerable professional skill, knowledge and experience. They are extremely demanding of professional time, requiring bundles of papers to be read, family members to be interviewed, accurate records kept, hours devoted to thinking through and writing the report and blocks of time to be reserved for court attendance. They are also emotionally taxing on the professional, who often hears harrowing case material and meets children (and parents) with traumatic backgrounds. Writing reports and attending court require enormous concentration.

This is balanced by the rewards. Mental health experts find themselves using their clinical skills at 'full stretch' and the discipline of reducing a mass of information into a coherent report and opinion can be intellectually satisfying. It is also rewarding to know one has reached a balanced view and weighed up seriously the strengths and weaknesses of the parents. Above all, psychiatrists and psychologists are able to make a major contribution to the welfare of children and ensure that their voices, conflicts, fears and wishes are heard by courts considering their future.

Finally, a society's attitude to children and the extent to which it is prepared to invest in improving family life are measures of its culture of concern. It is evident from the accounts given in this book that assessments of parenting need to be detailed and interventions into problems of child care are intensive procedures, requiring expert skills and appropriate resources. If society wishes to invest in the future of children and their families, it must adequately finance and support this specialist work. An indication of the value society places on children's well-being will be the extent to which it invests in measures to prevent and treat parenting breakdown. These might include socioeconomic improvements (such as housing, education, employment), professional resources to identify parents at risk and help them at an early stage and therapeutic interventions to break the intergenerational cycle of abuse. In this way, the welfare of children during their formative years will be promoted, enabling them to enjoy their childhoods and become successful parents in the future.

REFERENCES

Bentovim, A. (1992) *Trauma Organised Systems: Physical and Sexual Abuse in Families*, London: Karnac.

Black, D., Wolkind, S. and Harris Hendricks, J. (1992) *Child Psychiatry and the Law*, 2nd edn, London: Gaskell and Royal College of Psychiatrists.

Bowden, P. (1990) 'The written report and sentences', in R. Bluglass and P. Bowden (eds) *Principles and Practice of Forensic Psychiatry*, Edinburgh: Churchill Livingstone.

Burghes, L. (1994) *Lone Parenthood and Family Disruption*, London: Family Policy Studies Centre.

Carson, D. (1985) 'Doctors in the witness box', *British Journal of Hospital Medicine*, **33**, 283–6.

Connelly, C.D. and Straus, M.A. (1992) 'Mother's age and risk for physical abuse', *Child Abuse and Neglect*, **16**, 709–18.

Cooke, D. (1990) 'Being an "expert" in court', *The Psychologist*, May, 216–21.

Dale, P., Davies, M., Morrison, T. and Waters, J. (1986) *Dangerous Families*, London: Tavistock.

Elton, A. (1988) 'Assessment of families for treatment', in A. Bentovim, A. Elton, J. Hildebrand, M. Tranter and E. Vizard (eds) *Child Sexual Abuse within the Family: Assessment and Treatment*, London: Wright.

Faller, K.C. (1988) 'Decision-making in cases of intrafamilial child sexual abuse', *American Journal of Orthopsychiatry*, **58**, 121–8.

Gardner, R.A. (1989) *Family Evaluation in Child Custody Mediation, Arbitration and Litigation*, Cresskill NJ: Creative Therapeutics.

Gelles, R. (1989) 'Child abuse and violence in single parent families: parent absence and economic deprivation', *American Journal of Orthopsychiatry*, **59**, 492–501.

Grounds, A. (1985) 'The psychiatrist in court', *British Journal of Hospital Medicine*, **34**, 55–8.

Hanson, S.M.H. (1986) 'Parent-child relationships in single-father families', in R.A. Lewis and R.E. Salt (eds) *Men in Families*, Beverley Hills CA: Sage.

Haskett, M.E., Johnson, C.A. and Miller, J.W. (1994) 'Individual differences in risk of child abuse by adolescent mothers: assessment in the perinatal period', *Journal of Child Psychology and Psychiatry*, **35**, 461–76.

Jones, D.P.H. (1991) 'The effectiveness of intervention', in M. Adcock, R. White and A. Hollows (eds) *Significant Harm*, Croydon: Significant Publications.

King, M. and Trowell, J. (1992) *Children's Welfare and the Law: The Limits of Legal Intervention*, London: Sage.

Reder, P., Lucey, C. and Fellow-Smith, E. (1993) 'Surviving cross-examination in court', *Journal of Forensic Psychiatry*, **4**, 489–96.

Sack, W., Mason, R. and Higgins, J. (1985) 'The single-parent family and abusive child punishment', *American Journal of Orthopsychiatry*, **55**, 253–9.

Schaffer, H.R. (1990) *Making Decisions about Children: Psychological Questions and Answers*, Oxford: Blackwell.

Server, J.C. and Janzen, C. (1982) 'Contraindications to reconstitution of sexually abusive families', *Child Welfare*, **61**, 279–88.

Sturge, C. (1992) 'Dealing with courts and parenting breakdown', *Archives of Disease in Childhood*, **67**, 745–50.

Tufnell, G. (1993) 'Psychiatric court reports in child care cases: what constitutes "good practice"?', *ACPP Review and Newsletter*, **15**, 219–24.

Winnicott, D. (1960) 'Ego distortion in terms of true and false self', in *The Maturational Processes and the Facilitating Environment: Studies in the Theory of Emotional Development*, London: Hogarth, 1965.

Author index

Subject index